SIEGFRIED SASSOON

I. Siegfried Sassoon in the early 1930's.

Courtesy of the Central Office of Information, London

SIEGFRIED SASSOON

A critical study

BY

MICHAEL THORPE

UNIVERSITAIRE PERS LEIDEN

LONDON - OXFORD UNIVERSITY PRESS

1966

Distributed outside the Netherlands by the
Oxford University Press

© UNIVERSITAIRE PERS LEIDEN 1966

Printed in the Netherlands

To
S.S.
with respect

CONTENTS

APPENDICES

ILLUSTRATIONS

ABBREVIATED TITLES USED IN REFERENCES

C.P.	=	*Collected Poems, 1908-1956*
M.	=	*Meredith*
M.F.H.	=	*Memoirs of a Fox-Hunting Man*
M.I.O.	=	*Memoirs of an Infantry Officer*
O.C.	=	*The Old Century* (and Seven More Years)
S.J.	=	*Siegfried's Journey*
S.P.	=	*Sherston's Progress*
W.Y.	=	*The Weald of Youth*

PREFACE

"I do find it remarkable," said Robert Graves in one of his Clark Lectures at Cambridge in 1954-1955, "that the extraordinary five years of Siegfried Sassoon's efflorescence (1917-1921) should be utterly forgotten now." The recent spate of writing on the literature of the Great War has ensured that this is so no longer, but the "efflorescence" Graves defines has been remembered to the almost total exclusion of all else that Sassoon has written in over half a century. One should not complain: criticism of contemporary writing has never observed proportion, and this century is no exception to the rule. This book has been written, not to puff Sassoon to the heights of his heavily appreciated contemporaries, but to try to give due praise and to attune the reader's ear to a theme that deserves to be heard.

The subtitle—'A Critical Study'—points to a limitation that no careful reader of Sassoon will miss: for the fact that he has been, during the past forty years, "a reticent revealer of himself" (to use his own phrase about Galsworthy) would have made the literary-biographical approach unusually hazardous. I have, therefore, tried to follow Sassoon's own good example in *Meredith* and to state what seems certain, to infer what seems reasonable, and to be wary of undue speculation. Whilst feeling that no writer who publishes in his time can expect to enjoy the prerogatives of the utterly private man, I respect the sentiments which Sassoon expressed in his little poem 'The Deceiver', which was prompted by the prospective publication of Sir Geoffrey Keynes' *Bibliography*:

> I saw that smiling conjuror Success -
> An impresario in full evening dress -
> Advancing toward me from some floodlit place
> Where Fame resides. I did not like his face.
>
> I did not like this too forthcoming chap
> Whose programme was 'to put me on the map'.
> Therefore I left his blandishments unheeded,
> And told him I was not the man he needed.

As this is the first comprehensive work on a writer valued too exclusively for a fraction of his output — the war poetry of the years 1915 to 1919 — particular attention has been paid to his later work, with an emphasis on the *Memoirs* and autobiographies. Quotations are more numerous than is usual in a book of this kind, my purpose being, not only to criticise Sassoon's writing, but also to keep the writing itself well in the reader's view. A similar point should be made with regard to the exhaustive discussion of Sassoon's 'Views on Poetry' (Chapter X). The aims of that chapter are twofold: firstly, to make clear the framework of ideas underlying the poetry, which is the essential basis for a full understanding of any poet's work; and secondly, my consideration of Sassoon's role as "appreciator" in *Meredith* inevitably involved an appraisal of certain theories and values that have become attached to the ideal of 'simplicity' in poetry.

To facilitate reading, notes containing lengthy factual information or expansive illustration and example are included in Appendix A. Where quotations from Sassoon's works are frequent, page references have not invariably been given in footnotes in order to avoid cluttering the text: the interested reader can find these references—to Chapters V-IX—given under the heading 'Page References', according to the number of the page on which they appear; references to *Collected Poems* can be found after the title of each poem in the Index.

I have not included a detailed bibliography of Sassoon's works. The notes supply full references and it seemed, in any case, superfluous to add another to the lists already available in Sir Geoffrey Keynes' *A Bibliography of Siegfried Sassoon.*

* * *

I am especially indebted to Professor A. G. H. Bachrach, the Leiden Professor of English Literature and Director of the Sir Thomas Browne Institute, whose idea it was that the book should be published at Leiden and who gave much useful advice during its preparation for press. I am indebted to the Institute for material assistance in launching it.

I should also like to recall Professor D. J. Enright's good-humoured help and moral support during the initial stages at Singapore University. For many kind and critical comments, particularly upon my conclusions, I am thankful to Professor Edmund Blunden, whose affinity with Sassoon is closer than any other living writer's and whose understanding of his work is doubtless greater than mine: as a small tribute to this I have headed part of Chapter VII (beginning on p. 131) with a line from Professor Blunden's poem 'A Country God'.

I owe a considerable general debt to Sir Geoffrey Keynes, for the information contained in his *Bibliography of Siegfried Sassoon*. For painstaking help with the illustrations I am grateful to Mrs Claire Blunden and Mr D. R. W. Silk, also to Mr Douglas Cleverdon for the hint that led to the inclusion of the Max Beerbohm cartoon, which was kindly allowed by *The Spectator*. Another encouraging voice was that of Mr G. S. Fraser. To Mr. Sassoon himself I am thankful for allowing the reprinting of his early poem 'The Daffodil Murderer' and for permitting the reproduction of the photographs and MS.

Mr F. Snater and Mr Jon Stallworthy, of Leiden and Oxford University Presses, have both been extremely helpful throughout the somewhat protracted preliminaries to publication.

My wife, an untiring typist and a pitiless critic, has stayed the course courageously.

M.T.

Sir Thomas Browne Institute
The University of Leiden.
March 1966.

PART I

LYRICIST AND SATIRIST

1

POETIC BEGINNINGS

§ 1 *Lyrical Poems: 1908-1916*[1]

Almost from the first, Siegfried Sassoon was intended for a poet. His mother was an artist and a lover of the arts who devoted herself to nurturing a love for the beautiful in her son. The first two volumes of Sassoon's autobiography relate how she created a little world at their Weirleigh home in which her son might grow happily towards poetry. The process, if pleasant, was not—and could hardly be—a rapidly maturing one. Though the wider Sassoon family played their part in the cultural life of the 'nineties—his aunt Rachel edited simultaneously *The Observer* and *The Sunday Times* and still found time to compose music, his uncle Hamo Thornycroft was a celebrated sculptor, while Sir Edmund Gosse was an old family friend—this did little to bring out in the young Siegfried what was new in the Sassoon artistry: a capacity for verbal creativeness. Verbal facility came early, but his reading in the Pre-Raphaelites, Swinburne and the dim magazines of his youth, coupled with his provincial, relatively cosseted life, served only to prolong into his late twenties a callow youthful romanticism. He had passed twenty-one before he took advantage of his family's literary connections to bring his verse to the notice of some who might have given him timely guidance long before. Even so, though Edmund Gosse and Edward Marsh, two of the most influential pundits of the time, read his work and advised him sensibly they did not—and could not—bring out his individuality as a poet. Wider experience of life could alone have done that. Only Rupert Brooke of those he met in pre-Great War London might have led him further, but their solitary meeting was, as Sassoon narrates in *The Weald of Youth*, an abortive encounter between minds at very different stages of development. A studied genteel upbringing, whilst cultivating his sensibility, very nearly stifled his imagination: this was to be forced into life at last by

1. See Appendix A, (1).

the impact upon him of the Great War, declared when Sassoon was in his still immature twenty-eighth year.[2]

The young Sassoon's most enthusiastic reading was in the Pre-Raphaelites, Swinburne and the Rhymers, Lionel Johnson and Ernest Dowson (he does not mention Yeats) and Edward Fitzgerald. In his early efforts, the stylistic influence of these poets is clear, but there is little trace of their purposes or their feelings. From Swinburne he seems to have caught an intoxication with sound, but there are none of Swinburne's themes. Love poems are conspicuously absent, on themes real or imagined—the most striking respect in which he differs from all the poets he admired. Neither is there any 'decadent' emotion: none of the radical sense of the futility of the world in which one is living which gives Dowson's poems their sickly tone, nor is there any trace of spiritual struggle, such as is present in Johnson's best work. A mild escapism is the chief characteristic he shares with the Pre-Raphaelites, though not, unlike them, as a protest against existing conditions: it is rather a desire to escape into something more exciting than his own comfortable world. This escape takes the form, not of Rossetti's ideal love, or William Morris's ideal Socialism, or of Swinburne's twin passions for improbable Love and impossible Liberty, but of a pagan desire for identification with nature.

Two-thirds of these early poems are expressions of what Sassoon calls "vaguely instinctive nature-worship"[3], a feeling which, he adds, drew him strongly to Meredith. Despite this, Meredith was not his model: as his friend Helen Wirgman told him, he might have written much better poems if he had followed Meredith's example. As it is, feeling is clouded and dissipated by the proliferation of a Pre-Raphaelite-Swinburnian diction which had already reached its ultimate dilution in Dowson and Johnson. All the *fin de siècle* epithets are there: dim, glimmering, strange, lovely, darkling, sweet, secret, ecstatic, beautiful, ethereal, celestial. To these are added medieval affectations and archaisms which show the influence of D. G. Rossetti: ye and thee, arrayment, whist, roundelay, bosky, ere, vagrom-hearted, and phrases such as "fair-glimpsed vale" and "piping the daffodilly".

No-one is more aware than Sassoon himself that these influences had a retarding effect: little adverse criticism can, or should, be added to that which he has made in *The Weald of Youth*. What remains puzzling

2. See Appendix A, (2).
3. *W. Y.* p. 31.

is why Sassoon has retained so many (not so few) of his early poems in his collected edition. His principles of selection seem arbitrary: in *The Weald* he can be severely critical of the "banality" of the line, "Old days that are filled with the fragrance of dream", wondering why he allowed it to pass for printing in *Sonnets and Verses*, yet in the *Collected Poems* he has been prepared to perpetuate, not only numerous weak lines, but entire poems—such as 'Night-Piece', 'October', 'Dryads', 'Companions'—which have as little claim to survival. This is not to suggest that he should, like Robert Graves, have revised his early poems or dropped them altogether—most need, in the strictest sense, considerable revision: one prefers to suppose that he wished to offer an honest pattern of his development. If so, these poems reveal the poverty of choice with which he was faced: from a critical viewpoint they are chiefly valuable as a measure of the extraordinary change wrought in Sassoon's writing by his War experience.

Their chief value to the poet Sassoon was to become is that they gave him prolonged practice which, however banal the subject-matter or derivative the diction, enabled him gradually to refine his capacity for rhyming verse. The poems he has allowed to survive have more of the flow of Swinburne than of the neat stanzaic patterns of the Rossettis: 'Villon', 'Storm and Sunlight', 'Wind in the Beechwood' and 'Before Day' are good examples of this. They suffer remarkably little from the Pre-Raphaelite vice of pairing unstressed endings—only/lonely, pity/city are exceptions. The sing-song regularity of 'Nimrod in September', 'A Wanderer' and 'Arcady Unheeding' is also not the rule. This seems to be chiefly because he has caught from Swinburne a pleasure in sheer *sound*. He has the poet's delight in words for their own sake and creates from them attractive patterns of sound—the sensuous dream-picture of 'Ancestors', the brisk movement of 'Goblin Revel', the resounding vowels of the first part of 'Storm and Sunlight' are clearly deliberately contrived. The words mean very little—and there is not, at their centre, any feeling so strong even as those for which Swinburne builds up verbal equivalents, nor is there any compensating imagery. 'Ancestors', for example, reflects his liking for *Omar Khayyam*, but there is no delicately evocative picture, only "dimly-gesturing gardens", "glimmering halls," and "sweet influences." Similarly, though 'The Heritage' seems to owe its formal melancholy and its conclusion to 'Ode to a Nightingale', both language and feeling are artificially invoked.

The faults of most of the poems are clearly related to the vagueness of the emotion they express, a dreamy paganism that is a mere shadow of the 'Nightingale' feeling, best shown in these lines from 'Wind in the Beechwood':

> let me fade
> In the warm, rustling music of the hours
> That guard your ancient wisdom, till my dream
> Moves with the chant and whisper of the glade.

There is never any tension, not even imagined despair: in 'October' and 'Before Day' there is a slight adolescent melancholy, and Death appears occasionally, in 'An Old French Poet', 'Today' and 'Wisdom', only to be defied and rejected in an exalted seizing of the present,

> The world's my field, and I'm the lark,
> Alone with upward song, alone with light!   ('Wisdom')

It would have been impossible, as his autobiographies show, for Sassoon to give the impression that this was not his dominant feeling at this period, that he was anything but 'well-adjusted' to his surroundings. His most disquieting feeling seems to have been a vague urge for definition, a desire to have tragic emotion, which is reflected in the hollow disillusionment of 'Alone' and the more genuine loneliness of 'Before Day'.

Significantly, most of the better poems date from the period subsequent to Sassoon's first contact with Edward Marsh, who supplied him with the most objective criticism he had yet received. Marsh's most valuable piece of advice[4] was: "It seems a necessity now to write either with one's eye on an object or with one's mind at grips with a more or less definite idea. Quite a slight one will suffice." The tone of this suggests that Marsh did not wholly comprehend the force of his own words—an impression borne out by his praise of 'Morning-Land' and 'Dryads' for following these precepts unconsciously, but perhaps he was only letting the young poet down lightly. Sassoon had only come to Marsh's notice in early 1913, chiefly because of *The Daffodil Murderer*, in which, under the impulse of genuine feeling, he had done

4. Among much quoted in *W. Y.*, pp. 138-139.

far more than previously to fulfil Marsh's requirements, even if the 'idea' was not entirely his own. From then onwards, Sassoon seems to have written more critically, gradually refining his style and expressing his feelings more clearly. It is, however, only in a few poems either revised for *The Old Huntsman* or published there for the first time that we have satisfactory wholes, almost entirely free from the earlier weaknesses of style.[5]

'Before Day' is the best example of this growing capacity for self-criticism, since it is the only poem we have in two versions—thanks, by a lucky chance, to Edmund Blunden. In his essay, "Siegfried Sassoon's Poetry", Blunden singles out 'Before Day' for special praise as "a beautiful, natural song of personality and England's meaning."[6] In doing so, he quotes the whole of the original version from *Twelve Sonnets* (1911), which differs in several ways from that included in *Collected Poems*. The final version first appeared in *The Old Huntsman* (1917), having been revised probably no later than 1916; revision at a later date might have involved more extensive changes. In the 1911 version lines 5-8 are as follows:

> When fieldward boys far off with clack and shout
> Still scare the birds away in sudden rout
> Come ere my heart grows old, and filled with doubt.
> In passional summer dawns I call for thee.

The later version retains line 5 unchanged and continues:

> From orchards scare the birds in sudden rout,
> Come, ere my heart grows cold and full of doubt,
> In the still summer dawns that waken me.

Here, line 6 continues the concrete pictures and maintains the sharp effect of line 5: "cold" in line 7 has a more physical effect and avoids the trite "old": "still summer dawns" is simpler and again more concrete, a great improvement on the affected "passional." There is

---

5. Sassoon's revisions for *The Old Huntsman* were by no means thoroughgoing: poems so weak as 'Nimrod in September' and 'Storm and Sunlight', first published in *Discoveries* (1915), were emended for this volume, according to Keynes (p. 34), only to produce the versions we now have. Whilst refining his latest work in 1916-1917, Sassoon seems to have been reluctant to tamper with the earlier very much; perhaps sentiment forbade, or he simply had insufficient time.
6. *Edmund Blunden, A Selection of His Poetry and Prose*, 1950, p. 314. (The date of the version Blunden quotes is clear from his identification of it as "The first sonnet in a quarto volume privately printed ... twenty years ago".)

another revision, which further sharpens the picture, where in line 11 "Out of the songless valleys" is substituted for "A shadow amid shadows." Blunden might, with more accuracy, have praised the later version as a "natural song"; even so, more than enough affectations are retained—"dim Arcady" and the "poet-outcast" sentiment of the closing lines. Nevertheless, the revisions show an increased care for the visual impact and the unity of sound and meaning.

'Before Day' is Sassoon's most successful early poem on a theme—the early morning—about which he wrote with "most fullness of feeling"[7]; it was to be a recurrent theme in his writing. Another more purely descriptive poem, 'Daybreak in a Garden', suggests a similar mood; though its effect is spoilt by conventional and affected phrasing ("The lark his lonely field for heaven had forsaken") in the rest of the poem, the first four lines give a clear picture and suggest by sound the slight beginnings of day:

> I heard the farm cocks crowing, loud, and faint, and thin,
> When hooded night was going and one clear planet winked:
> I heard shrill notes begin down the spired wood distinct,
> When cloudy shoals were chinked and gilt with fires of day.

The other most successful early poems are ones in which Sassoon has turned to a definite theme outside the solitary dream-world—though 'Haunted', the best of them, is an imaginative off-shoot of this. Two, 'David Cleek' and 'Morning-Express', are light but cleanly handled. 'David Cleek' is an amusing blasphemy on a benign Sportsman's Heaven in skilfully varied couplets. Sassoon is now prepared to admit such expressions as "snuff you out" and puns like "royal and ancient hills of light" as the legitimate stuff of poetry. 'Morning-Express', though not brilliantly observed, moves well and has a sustained mock-heroic tone, making the small seem great; it would make an excellent children's anthology piece.[8] In 'Blind' there is a welcome concern with a more serious human subject. Though the effect is not moving—the blind man is too idealized for that—language and image show a striving for naturalness and precision. The smooth "weaving unconscious tapestries of life" contrasts well with the deadness of "thrust in-

7. *W. Y.*, p. 35.
8. Though Virginia Woolf, conscious perhaps of how little Edwardian poetry reflected an eye even remotely on the object, singled out this poem in her *Old Huntsman* review (*Times Lit. Supp.* May 31, 1917) as "a solid and in its way beautiful catalogue of facts", indicating a "vein of realism" the war was to open up.

ward, dungeoned from the sky"; "starless" suggests "stareless", and "rumbling city" sets off the groping, feeble movements of the blind man, putting the reader inside his head and bringing out the uncertainty of his response to the unseen and hostile movement without.

The most ambitious of these poems, 'Haunted', is the only one —apart from the War poems—that Edward Marsh honoured by inclusion in *Georgian Poetry* (the 1916-1917 volume). It must be said that it fails in its primary purpose, since Sassoon has been unable to invent a sufficiently tangible and outlandish horror: "The evil creature in the twilight looping" and the "Something" that

> clambered
> Heavily from an oak, and dropped, bent double,
> To shamble at him zigzag, squat and bestial

are stereotypes. The ending is anti-climatic, though "slow fingers" has the right kind of suggestion; the repetition of "peer" in the crucial line 33 is deflating—and remarkably careless. The virtues of 'Haunted' are stylistic: Sassoon is now able to write over forty varied blank verse lines in a language almost completely free of archaisms and redundancies. The scene is well constructed by means of concrete natural description, which provides a sinister setting for the dramatic situation.[9] The smothering diction has gone: where once there would have been 'strange bird' or 'faint music' we have "the long churring nightjar's note", "willow-music blown across the water/Leisurely sliding on by weir and mill" and—there has been nothing so deadly in nature before—a sunset that "Died in a smear of red."

§ 2 *The Daffodil Murderer*

Sassoon's most promising pre-War poem, *The Daffodil Murderer*, is not included in the *Collected Poems* at all. Presumably, this is because it is not totally original, being intended—though the title points to Masefield's *Daffodil Fields*—as a parody of that poet's *The Everlasting Mercy*, which was one of the most popular poems of the time.[10] At the least, it

9. See especially 11. 1-6, 10-12, 20-23.
10. *The Everlasting Mercy* was first published in November, 1911; the 11th Impression appeared in March 1913. *The Daffodil Murderer* was published in an edition of 1000 copies in February, 1913. For the text of 'The Daffodil Murderer', see Appendix B, p. 273.

is a pastiche, not a parody, and in some ways superior to Masefield's poem. Sir Edmund Gosse and Edward Marsh praised it, and so different a critic as V. de Sola Pinto has followed suit; while Robert Nichols thought the first half was parody but that Sassoon ended, he clumsily puts it, by "successfully endeavouring to rival his master."[11] Thomas Hardy, oddly turning its merit inside out, wrote "Its fault is that it is not quite sufficiently burlesque to be understood."[12] Sassoon stresses its value to him: "While continuing to burlesque Masefield ... I was really feeling what I wrote—and doing it not only with abundant delight but a descriptive energy quite unlike anything I had experienced before."[13]

In writing *The Daffodil Murderer*, Sassoon set himself a more difficult theme than Masefield's. Masefield had spoken in the voice of Saul Kane, a brutish poacher turned revivalist, recounting his past wickedness and how he was converted one evening in a pub by a Quaker 'visitor', "A tall pale woman, grey and bent." The ending is, one might say, 'satisfactory': Saul piously wishes, after an exalted passage in praise of God's Good Earth seen anew, "That I may flower to men." Sassoon's Saul, on the other hand, is a Sussex farm-labourer, less 'evil' though given to drink, condemned to death for unintentionally killing the 'chucker-out' from the village pub. Whilst awaiting his hanging, he dictates his story to the prison chaplain. He is prepared, pathetically, to reject the world of men: life has been a struggle, death will be release—"fate had bested me"; he hopes only for peace and God's mercy, "When I'm away and out beyond."

Technically, Sassoon's poem is much less accomplished than Masefield's. He departs frequently from Masefield's easy Chaucerian octosyllabics and his range of language and invention is much narrower: he has nothing comparable to the melodrama of the fight or the drunken Saul's scourging of the town, and there is no subsidiary character interest such as the parson and Mrs. Blaggard give in Mase-

---

11. Introduction to *Counter-Attack* (New York, 1919).
12. *Friends of a Lifetime: Letters to Sydney Carlyle Cockerell*, ed. V. Meynell, 1940: Hardy's is dated September 17th 1915.
    The only review of the poem was in *The Athenaeum* (February 22, 1913) and this is the whole of it: "This is a pointless and weak-kneed imitation of 'The Everlasting Mercy'. The only conclusion we obtain from its perusal is that it is easy to write worse than Mr. Masefield." Keynes (*Bibliography* p. 33) suggests that the hostility of this notice was inspired by the enmity between Crosland and *The Athenaeum*, a view strengthened by the fact that the journal did not seize this opportunity further to belittle Masefield, for whom its reviews had shown scant sympathy.
13. *W. Y.*, p. 124.

field's poem. *The Daffodil Murderer* has the additional disadvantage of sharing the faults of its model. The popularity of *The Everlasting Mercy* was chiefly due to the 'boldness' of its manner. Here was a poet bringing the common people to life in their own language—their dialect and their swear-words. Masefield's phrase "closhy put" has often been quoted in illustration of this, yet examination of the poem reveals that this is the only memorable expletive; 'bloody' is *under*-worked, considering the subject, and a concern for good taste has completed the work of castrating the common man's language. The taunts in the quarrelling passages of both poems are ludicrous, an unhappy mixture of the common man and the upperclass schoolboy: Sassoon follows "blasted skug" with "ugly mug", "Leggo my ear", and "knock-kneed shrimp." Masefield's more frequent use of 'bloody' gives only superficial reality: he had, we understand, 'knocked about' the world, Sassoon had not and was the more to be forgiven. Certainly, it could not then have been done with utter frankness,[14] but D. H. Lawrence soon showed a better way in 1913 with poems like 'Whether or Not', 'The Collier's Wife' and 'Violets'.[15] It is strange that Pinto should praise, not these, but *The Everlasting Mercy* for "putting into verse the language that Englishmen were actually using in the pubs, the cottages and the streets."[16] Certainly Masefield's and Sassoon's poems come far closer to common life than such things as Drinkwater's 'The Fires of God', which had appeared in *Georgian Poetry: 1911-12*, but they could only have been taken as truly representative of it by the ignorant reader.

Whatever the poem's limitations, the important thing is that in writing *The Daffodil Murderer* Sassoon liberated springs of feeling for which he owed nothing to Masefield: "Never before had I been able to imbue commonplace details with warmth of poetic emotion. I was at last ... writing physically."[17] At the highest moments of the poem Sassoon responds with an unaffected simplicity: in the scene, for example, when on a pitch-dark night Saul lies in wait with his accom-

14. In the pseudonymous Preface to *The Daffodil Murderer*, written by its publisher T. W. H. Crosland, a facetious excuse is made for the purity of the language: "in order that the severest taste might not be offended the murderer dictates what he has to say to the Prison Chaplain. By this thoughtful expedient a clear flow of unobjectionable language is secured and the reader will doubtless appreciate the comfortable result" (p. 7).
15. First published in *Love Poems and Others* (1913); re-published in *The Collected Poems, Vol. I*, 1957.
16. *Crisis in English Poetry* (1880-1940), 1951, p. 128.
17. *W. Y.*, p. 125.

plice, shrinking from what he is about to do to his victim "Bill" he recalls how

> in the summer weather
> When Bill and me was boys together,
> We'd often come this way when trudgin'
> Out by brooks to fish for gudgeon.
> I thought, "When me and Bill are deaders,
> There'll still be buttercups in medders,
> And boys with penny floats and hooks
> Catchin' fish in Laughton brooks."   (11.418-425)

On his last night, as dusk falls, Saul thinks of those free outside and tries to imagine what they think of him, of his wife and how she will face their parting, and marks the common sounds he will never hear again. His mind runs back over the seasons, feeling "There's summat mortal strange/In storm and shine and change", and fusing ideal pictures of them:

> I see it now so clear,
> The waking of the year,
> When Easter wind is keen
> And woods are growing green;
> O dusty summer days
> When cattle drink and graze
> Till harvest builds the rick,
> And ground's as hard as brick.
> O autumn falling slow,
> When maids and children go
> For blackberries, and fill
> Their baskets on the hill.   (11.534-545)

In sustained simplicity of language these lines are a poignant measure of the condemned Saul's feelings; they have stronger human appeal than Masefield's redeemed Saul's lengthy paean to "All earthly things." For the first time, Sassoon is using to good effect the "plain Wordsworthian language" he advocates in his later lecture On Poetry.

It would be wrong to exaggerate the quality of The Daffodil Murderer —barely fifty lines (a tenth of the whole) reach the standard of those quoted; and it is surely misleading to say, with Pinto, that it shows "a sense of the hollowness of the gentlemanly paradise in which he (Sassoon) spent his youth, and a deep sympathy for the common man who was excluded from that paradise."[18] Few lines could support this construction; chiefly those where Saul fancies the stars looking down compassionately, seeing "some beggar breaking stone/For workhouse task" and also:

> They see the King and Queen at Windsor,
> And hear the story that he spins 'er
> Of how he's been to pheasant-shoots
> With Jew-boy lords that lick his boots;
> And they look down on all the wonder
> And sorrow that do make men ponder.   (11.408-413)

It would require little imagination to conceive of the poor man contemplating the privileged in this fashion—but the privileged here are far from including Sassoon himself. Sassoon's Saul is an individual whom he pities: he was roused to write of him by Masefield's example and there is no evidence that he would have tackled such a subject otherwise. No similar poem follows in the pre-War years, certainly none hinting that Sassoon was looking critically at his own "gentlemanly paradise": that he did not do so is borne out by the evidence of his own autobiographies. What is characteristic of Sassoon, as the War poems were to show more powerfully, is his capacity to feel for the suffering victim; *The Daffodil Murderer* has, in parts, the power to move —and this says much. It does not show the stirrings of a social conscience to complain, in Saul Kane's mouth, that some people are better, and many worse off than they deserve to be.

Had *The Daffodil Murderer* tapped a vein of general sympathy, there was ample subject-matter to hand to exploit it. But before the War Sassoon was (as he admits) never venturesome. His other most accomplished early poem, 'The Old Huntsman', written, Sassoon tells us,[19] in early 1915 shortly before he went out to France shows a transmuted awareness of this limitation.

In a blank-verse 'conversation-piece' of some 200 lines, Sassoon impersonates an old huntsman, now beyond active life, reflecting upon past joys and lost opportunities. The poem is a not entirely successful blend of the poet's imaginative perception with his subject's rambling, colloquial manner: Sassoon is both interpreting the old man's thoughts and, in part, clearly expressing his own inmost feelings. Lines 1-26

18. Op. cit. p. 143.
19. *S. J.*, p. 17.

establish the narrator's tone convincingly, with the colloquialisms trimmed sufficiently to produce poetic speech; then in line 27, with "my bleared old face that stares and wonders", the poet stands back. Lines 28-108 return to almost entirely unimpeded reflection from within—the Huntsman's dream of Hell (73-101) is especially convincing, but the crucial insight comes in the poet's voice: "But where's the use of life and being glad/If God's not in your gladness?" Lines 110-152 provide further natural reflection, till again we come to lines in which the poet's sensitivity obtrudes: "The naked stars make men feel lonely, wheeling/And glinting on the puddles in the road." In lines 159-172—"This world's a funny place to live in"—the poet's perception of the value of the joys now gone, once taken for granted, almost completely supersedes the narrator's. With,

> I never broke
> Out of my blundering self into the world,
> But let it all go past me, like a man
> Half asleep in a land that's full of wars.

Sassoon speaks openly. In this brief respite before going to war, Sassoon realized his dilemma—that he was a man potentially of both worlds who had so far cast himself in only one: as in the old huntsman there is a mixture of coarseness and unsatisfied sensitivity, so in him it seems that only the less significant side has had full scope—and now the other may never do so. Like Wells's Mr. Britling—and many others—"He'd dropped into the good things that suited him." [20]

Both the strengths and the weaknesses of Sassoon's early life are crystallized in 'The Old Huntsman'; when he wrote, Sassoon was highly conscious of the latter. Its greatest strength, his sense of kinship with nature, was to remain, to be rediscovered to the full in his retrospective prose: for the present, as a poet, he was handicapped by a half-awareness, at best, of humanity. [21]

---

20. *Mr Britling Sees It Through* (1916), Odhams Press Uniform Edition (undated), p. 88.
21. The superficiality and the thin moral tone of much reviewing in the first decade of this century are well conveyed in this comment upon *The Old Huntsman* by an anonymous reviewer (*The Athenaeum*, July 1917): "The title piece is a racy monologue by an old huntsman, full of grumbles and regrets, in quite good blank verse, with some unnecessary profanity."

II

EFFECTIVE PROTEST

As if the soldier died without a wound;
As if the fibres of this godlike frame
Were gored without a pang; as if the wretch,
Who fell in battle, doing bloody deeds,
Passed off to Heaven, translated and not killed;
(Coleridge, 'Fears in Solitude' (1.117-121)

... this sudden, stern ecstatic sense of unification, of peace, wrought by
the stress of a great call ... It is like the wakening of a new chivalry.
(*The Athenaeum*, June 19, 1915)

It must be remembered that in 1914 our conception of war was completely
unreal. We had vague childish memories of the Boer War, and from these
and from a general diffusion of Kiplingesque sentiments, we managed to
infuse into war a decided element of adventurous romance. War still
appealed to the imagination.
(Sir Herbert Read, *The Contrary Experience*, 1963)

§ 1 *Happy Warrior*

Of the 35 poems in *The Old Huntsman*,[1] about one third were written
in the spirit of Happy Warriorism to which Read bears witness.[2]
Rupert Brooke gave the lead for such poems as Sassoon's 'Absolution',
with its exultant acclamation of the comradeship of the young—"We

---

1. For bibliographical details see Appendix A, (3).
2. An excellent book for gauging this romantic spirit is an anthology, *Songs and
Sonnets for England in War Time*, containing some fifty martial poems of 1914, many
of them by famous elderly civilians such as Chesterton, Hardy, Kipling, Newbolt,
William Watson — and the Bishop of Lincoln. Introducing this book, John Lane
(of the Bodley Head) writes: "What can so nobly uplift the hearts of a people
facing war with its unspeakable agony as music and poetry? The sound of martial
music steels men's hearts before battle. The sound of martial words inspires human
souls to do and to endure. God, His Poetry, and His Music are the Holy Trinity
of war." And so, in the beginning, it was. (Many other such collections of patriotic
poems were hurriedly put out "at a popular price" in the early months of the War:
bearing such stirring titles as *The Flag of England* and *The Country's Call*, they are
well worth seeking in the unstable columns booksellers keep on the floor.)

are the happy legion"—morally set apart by their sacrifice. With "having claimed this heritage of heart,/What need we more, my comrades and my brothers?" Sassoon echoes the closing lines of Brooke's 'The Dead': "Nobleness walks in our ways again,/And we have come into our heritage."

Sassoon's poems romanticizing war were, like Brooke's and many others', written before the experience of war had really begun and before the spirit with which it was entered upon had been extinguished by the accumulation of unremitting horrors that took all the sense of "cleanness" out of even the most self-deceived. Thus, it was possible in early 1916 for Sassoon to write of even a brother's death (at Gallipoli, in August 1915) with sombre exaltation. In 'To My Brother', the dead man is made a symbol and example of selfless courage; bravery and resolution are sufficient in themselves, the exercise of man's highest qualities. In words which recall both the sentiment and situation of Tennyson's disastrous ending to *Maud*, where the sick hero, the prototype of these modern warriors, finds purpose and release in the outbreak of the Crimean War—"We have proved we have hearts in a cause, we are noble still"—he proclaims, "We have made an end of all things base./We are returning by the road we came."

In this spirit it was possible to obscure the reality with a romantic aura of patriotism and chivalrous sacrifice. In 'The Dragon and the Undying' the slain are etherealised; we are invited to dwell, not upon the manner of their death, but upon the beauty of the corpse prepared for viewing: "Their faces are the fair unshrouded night,/And planets are their eyes, their ageless dreams." The Dragon War "lusts to break the loveliness of spires"—not the limbs of men.[3] 'France' tells us that these warriors are fortunate in having a country fit to die in—whether *for* is not yet a problem:

> they are fortunate, who fight
> For gleaming landscapes swept and shafted
> And crowned by cloud pavilions white.

3. In its brief notice of *The Old Huntsman* (July 1917), *The Athenaeum* showed a corresponding concern for the graces at the expense of the reality: "Why he writes fourteen-line iambic decasyllabics, as in 'The Dragon and the Undying', without investing them with the gracious form of the sonnet, it is hard to discover." Apart from the previously-quoted sentence on the title poem (Chapter 1, note 21), this is the only reference made by that journal to any individual poem in this volume. Clearly, not everyone was impressed.

The last line is reminiscent of medieval fields of war. Also reminiscent of the medieval is the conviction, held by many poets at the outset —as also in Germany—that God is on their side. The English are Christian soldiers, cast in the bright and hallowed role cherished by what Professor Pinto calls the Nation at Home. 'The Redeemer' typifies the crusading spirit of 1915: the modern saviour is the Kiplingesque "English soldier, white and strong,/Who loved his time like any simple chap"; he is "not uncontent to die/That Lancaster on Lune may stand secure." In 'A Subaltern' and 'A Whispered Tale', hints of the reality creep in with lines like "squeaking rats scampered across the slime", but they are not allowed to destroy the picture of a rough-and-ready nobility that rises above adversity. The manly answer to "hell" is to light one's pipe and bear it; the bright image of the "good simple soldier" outshines the monstrosity of his slaughter and the horrors are subdued to cliché.

For Sassoon himself, what chiefly sustains is the vision of ideal beauty that animates his youthful writing. In 'Before the Battle', written on 25th June, 1916, shortly before the terrible Somme offensive and his first experience of trench warfare, he spurns war's destructiveness and invokes the spirit of nature: "O river of stars and shadows, lead me through the night." Faith in an underlying harmony gives him strength to endure, so that the suffering can be embraced and even glorified as if it will burnish, not scorch, this faith: "But in my torment I was crowned,/And music dawned above despair." It is possible for "beauty" to be "garlanded in hell" ('Secret Music').

The most telling of Sassoon's earliest war poems is 'The Kiss'—if we accept the satiric interpretation. Graves tells us that it was "originally inspired by Colonel Campbell, V.C.'s bloodthirsty 'spirit of the bayonet' address at an army school. Later, Siegfried offered it as a satire, and it certainly comes off, whichever way you read it."[4] This ambivalence is characteristic. It could, as Graves points out, be taken to represent either of two sides of Sassoon's poetic character—Happy Warrior or Bitter Pacifist. There seems no doubt that its purpose was originally straightforward: the romantic vocabulary applied to the bayonet—"up the nobly marching days/She glitters naked, cold and fair" and "Sweet Sister, grant your soldier this"—is not the kind of language Sassoon was likely to use ironically in early 1916. Included

4. *Goodbye to All That*, Penguin Edition, 1957, p. 226.

in *Georgian Poetry: 1916-17*, it was doubtless taken at face value: though the phrases "splits a skull" and "sets his heel" have a direct brutality that might have shocked, an intentional irony would have failed, since the *fact* remains vague—there is no face, no clear human victim. A further point in favour of the non-satiric interpretation is that the poem reads like an unconscious echo of the chilling paean to the virtues of " Clear-singing, clean slicing;/Sweet spoken, soft finishing" in 'The Song of the Sword', by W. E. Henley (1892), whose poetry the young Sassoon had read avidly.[5]

With the exceptions of 'The Kiss', 'The Redeemer' and 'Before the Battle', three poems fairly representative of Sassoon's part in the first phase of war poetry, all the poems so far mentioned were excluded from his *War Poems*. No similar poem occurs in the volumes following *The Old Huntsman* and none could have been written by an honest and sensitive poet after the terrible massacres of 1916. While there was hope of an early end, the simple motives of pure patriotism, of joining with one's fellows in a righteous cause, reinforced by the sheer physical exaltation felt by youth in positive action, could sustain in the face of reality, even masking the true face of that reality. But the quick and clean satisfaction that chivalry needed never came.

§ 2 *Bitter Pacifist*

The ferocious destruction in 1916-17 of what had sustained at first —the death and maiming of comrades and friends, the smothering of chivalry and heroism beneath the mud and the bombardments— aroused in Sassoon, as in others, a revulsion against the War of an intensity far exceeding that with which he had held his original untarnished ideals. Bitterness is the keynote of the satires that occupy the central place in *The Old Huntsman* and *Counter-Attack*: bitterness against all who are excluded from the martyrdom and who can be held in some way responsible for its continuance. The counter-attack is directed

---

5. Owen's 'Arms and the Boy' unambiguously expresses a revulsion against "the unnaturalness of weapons" of a kind Sassoon probably never felt; Owen, unlike Sassoon, seems never to have been tempted to take the bayonet, or any other weapon, as a lover. An interesting sidelight on this question is provided by Douglas Jerrold who, expressing surprise at Sassoon's claim that Colonel C's lecture had a good effect on the men, goes on to say: "they [our men] strongly resented being asked to feel full of hatred of their enemies, and were frankly disgusted, and said so, at being asked to take pleasure in the work of killing" (*Georgian Adventure*, 1937, p. 187.)

chiefly against the Nation at Home—the Church, the State, the civilians (whether ignorant or indifferent)—and the 'brass-hats' of the General Staff. Sassoon has suddenly seen 'the truth' and he voices it without concession in a volley of indignant eruptions in which raw emotion, more than any 'art', is the compelling factor.

Almost every poem Sassoon wrote from 'Stand-to'[6] onwards is a form of protest against the War. The sheer force of feeling, undiluted and unobjectified, carries home a poem like 'Stand-to'. As Sassoon says, it is "a jaunty scrap of doggerel," but it has the ring of truth—the truth of a moment of sudden realisation. Ten slangy lines unheroically describing his feelings are capped with the prayer:

> O Jesus, send me a wound today,
> And I'll believe in Your bread and wine,
> And get my bloody old sins washed white.

This is Sassoon's distinctive voice—a seemingly cynical, almost inarticulate tossing off of emotion. It is already a far cry from the polished decasyllabics—a vehicle for polished and correct sentiments —of 'The Redeemer'. In other relatively early poems we see a growing sureness of touch in the use of the colloquial style—for which, in *The Daffodil Murderer*, he had already shown an aptitude—and the feeling of disenchantment that it expresses being turned outwards to voice a fierce sympathy for the now purposelessly suffering soldier. The ignorant "Davies" of 'In the Pink' is also flatly contrasted with his Christ-like forerunner; he does not know what he is fighting for: "Tonight he's in the pink; but soon he'll die/And still the war goes on—*he* don't know why." In 'A Working Party' this commonplace hero dies and is "carried back, a jolting lump/Beyond all need of tenderness and care." Both these poems have the beginnings of the qualities of expression and description—the clipped, colloquial style of the first and the vivid trench scene of the second which seems to overmaster and swallow up the casual death of just another "decent chap"—that Sassoon continually refines from now on.

What must have shocked and affronted the reader who had been uplifted by the emotional chivalry of such books as Robert Nichols' *Ardours and Endurances* (which went through three printings between

---

6. "The only one," he writes of his poems of early 1916, "which anticipated my later successes in condensed satire" (*S. J.*, p. 17).

July and October, 1917) is the stark frankness of the description and
the hardness of tone. Sassoon is under the compulsion to *show* and his
poems burst with the impatience to get the truth out.[7] The truth is
simply this ('Counter-Attack'):

> The place was rotten with dead: green clumsy legs
> High-booted, sprawled and grovelled along the saps
> And trunks, face downward, in the sucking mud,
> Wallowed like trodden sand-bags loosely filled;
> And naked sodden buttocks, mats of hair,
> Bulged, clotted heads slept in the plastering slime.
> And then the rain began,—the jolly old rain!

As if, the last line suggests with grotesque irony, that were not the
last straw! Nothing, it seems, is to be treated with reverence, not even
the weaknesses and misfortunes of one's own comrades. These are
seized and thrust brutally in the reader's face: the dying soldier's
delirium in 'Died of Wounds', "hoarse and low and rapid rose and
fell/His troubled voice: he did the business well;" and in 'The Hero',
"He thought how 'Jack', cold-footed useless swine/Had panicked …"
It is not merely the truth that shocks, but the fact that this truth is
such common fare that it can produce this hard-bitten reaction. Pity,
we think, must be in short supply: then the poem has done its work,
for it is *our* pity that is needed. In poem after poem, Sassoon deliberately shears off the euphemistic trappings that clutter the notion of the
Supreme Sacrifice. There is the hard-bitten joke in 'The Tombstone-
Maker': "I told him with a sympathetic grin,/That Germans boil
dead soldiers down for fat"; the brutal simile of 'The Effect': "When
Dick was killed last week he looked like that,/Flapping along the fire-
step like a fish"; the right words for the actual business of killing:
"Our chaps were sticking 'em like pigs" ('Remorse'); and the business-
like, dismissive line that sets the seal on the earthly careers of "The
many men, so beautiful" of 'Twelve Months After': "That's where

7. "In a sense, as that Great War unmasked its ugliness, the problem of the legion
of soldier-poets was primarily one of reporting" (Edmund Blunden: *War Poets
1914-1918*. 1958, p. 27). It had been a different matter in 1915 and early 1916,
and it is not difficult to sympathise with the then natural spirit of F. W. Harvey's
courageous and sentimental little book, *A Gloucestershire Lad* (September 1916),
as it was summed up in the Preface by his Commanding Officer: "The poems are
written by a soldier and reflect a soldier's outlook. Mud, blood and khaki are rather
conspicuously absent. They are, in fact, the last things a soldier wishes to think or
talk about. What he does think of is his home."

they are today, knocked over to a man." It is not difficult to understand why, as Sassoon tells us in *Siegfried's Journey*, "an old Cambridge man" wrote to *The Cambridge Magazine*, as "'an average Englishman, pained, not to say disgusted, that such a thing as the poem 'The Hero' should appear in a magazine connected with the University of Cambridge'."[8] It was like finding a corpse left on one's doorstep as a practical joke designed to remind one of the meaning of death. Sassoon includes no scrap of relief in his parcels of truth: the ex-warrior who "[thanks] God they had to amputate" ('The One-Legged Man') and the 'ignoble' one in 'Arms and the Man'—"though his wound was healed and mended,/He hoped he'd get his leave extended"—can have provided scant consolation for the armchair patriot. The guilt is left firmly in the reader's hands.

The immediate effect of such a poem as 'Does It Matter?' must often have been to alienate the civilian reader from the poet himself. For Owen, this poem would have been a mere sketch of his primary emotion: whereas, in 'Disabled', Owen focuses attention unwaveringly upon the man, the chill, grey figure alone with his apprehensions of a sadly limited future, Sassoon makes the victim his point of departure and civilian callousness his prime target. Each has its legitimate effect: Sassoon's is a barb that sticks, whilst Owen's shaft goes deeper to a heart that cannot escape involvement with the victim's feelings. Sassoon rarely avoids this alienation: as the Enemy of Cant he does not seek to. He seldom employs elaborate irony, very much of which would have defeated his purpose. The nearest he comes to this is in 'How to Die' and 'Lamentations', where he affects to adopt the romantic viewpoint. In 'How to Die' he parodies the heroic manner so successfully that even the closing lines might mislead the insensitive reader. In both, the irony is betrayed by the application of the cheap phrase to the serious theme, so providing a satiric transformation of

---

8. One can set against this a contemporary insight from an unexpected source: Lord Esher, a member of the Committee of Imperial Defence, wrote to Edward Marsh, "There is a rough splendour about your friend Siegfried. It is good for the character of our people that a picture of War should be presented by a man so close up against it in the crude manner of El Greco" (*Edward Marsh*, by C. Hassall, p. 458).
  For a sounder critical voice one may turn to Virginia Woolf who, reviewing *The Old Huntsman* in *The Times Literary Supplement* (May 31, 1917), chose to quote 'The Hero' entire, prefacing it with these words: "If you chance to read one of [the war poems] by itself you may be inclined to think that it is a very clever poem, chiefly designed with its realism and surface cynicism to shock the prosperous and

the equally cheap euphemisms for death. Thus, the one soldier is praised for dying with "due regard for decent taste," and the other castigated for grieving immoderately "all because his brother had gone west." Surely this grief was excessive—had not his brother died in the service of his country? "In my belief/Such men have lost all patriotic feeling." Is this, the reader might have asked, a fair emphasis? Fair or not, it was a picture of the truth.

The truth, as Sassoon presents it in his more characteristic satires, is hard and clean-cut. He had no doubt that he held a number of incontrovertible truths in his hands. He possessed the kind of certainty about this which is probably the satirist's essential attribute. For this reason, his most telling satires are short poems in which he says *one* thing, with clarity and conciseness. In them a conviction is crystallised once and for all: that the Church is hypocritical, the civilians are callous, that the Staff is cynically incompetent. The outstanding examples are "'Blighters'".'The General','Base Details' and "'They'". These are fierce, contemptuous pieces, moments of hate that carry the reader with them at once.

The broad outline of Sassoon's method is well described in his own words: "I merely chanced on the device of composing two or three harsh, peremptory, and colloquial stanzas with a knock-out blow in the last line."[9] "'Blighters'", inspired by seeing a jingoistic Hippodrome show before he went out to France again in 1917, is the most bitter. The indignation is conveyed in two deft strokes: he first paints the scene in lurid caricature—"they grin and cackle at the show," "prancing ranks of harlots shrill the chorus"—then immediately juxtaposes it with the righteous prophet's vision of the tank lurching down the stalls, bringing the only reality the poet acknowledges into tune with 'Home, sweet Home.' No space is allowed for reflection:

(note 8 contd.)
sentimental. Naturally the critical senses rise in alarm to protect their owner from such insinuations. But read them continuously, read in particular 'The Hero' and 'The Tomb-Stone Maker', and you will drop the idea of being shocked in that sense altogether." She is concerned about the power to move, not merely shock: "As these jaunty matter-of-fact statements succeed each other such loathing, such hatred accumulates behind them that we say to ourselves 'Yes, this is going on; and we are sitting here watching it', with a new shock of surprise, with an uneasy desire to leave our place in the audience, which is a tribute to Mr. Sassoon's power as a realist. It is realism of the right, of the poetic kind." (Virginia Woolf's distinction as a critic in her time is well shown in this quotation: more typical reviewing was of the kind instanced in note 3.)
9. *S. J.*, p. 29.

the bitterness justifies itself with the last line, "To mock the riddled corpses round Bapaume." In 'The General' also the truth is made to stand out starkly as the climax of a poem perfect in the equivalence of feeling and tone:

> "Good-morning; good-morning!" the General said
> When we met him last week on our way to the line.
> Now the soldiers he smiled at are most of 'em dead,
> And we're cursing his staff for incompetent swine.
> "He's a cheery old card," grunted Harry to Jack
> As they slogged up to Arras with rifle and pack.
> . . . . . .
> But he did for them both by his plan of attack.

The sing-song rhythm of the first two lines conveys the brisk and casual manner of the general and also of the soldiers' death. To change in the next two lines to the heavily accented "we're cursing his staff for incompetent swine" is a grim introduction to the easily moving fifth and sixth lines—the unquestioning willingness to serve and die—and the last line completing a neat triplet with the impression of the tidy despatch of lives. The scathing ending is put into the words of one wearily accustomed to such events—and the effect is enhanced if we know that in the Battle of Arras British casualties alone totalled 132,000 killed, wounded and missing, in less than a month. In the face of such facts, the fewer words the better.

As Pinto has pointed out,[10] 'The General', like its companion-piece 'Base Details', "'Blighters'" and many of the other satires, obeys the simplest prescriptions of Georgian rhyming verse in everything but the diction, so that the satiric effect is accentuated by clothing a disreputable body in formal dress. The diction makes all the difference: Sassoon not only hit upon the method of describing the physical reality as it was, he also caught the voice of the reality. Blunden greatly admires 'The General' for this.[11] Owen, too, noticed it; according to

10. *Crisis*, p. 144.
11. "The seven lines, in which so much conversation and experience of the long departed British Expeditionary Force are distilled, may abide with that Greek epigram translated thus:
> Tell the Spartans, passer-by,
> At their bidding here we lie."
> (*War Poets*, 1914-18, p. 30)
(This poem was also singled out for full quotation by Virginia Woolf in her review of *Counter-Attack*, Times Literary Supplement, July 11, 1918.)

Welland,[12] he was especially impressed by the necessity to use 'the very words', as he set out to do in poems like 'The Dead Beat' and 'The Chances'—in the latter poem excelling anything of this kind achieved by Sassoon: it may be supposed, however, that both poets, consciously or unconsciously, owe something to the example set by Kipling's *Barrack-Room Ballads*.

Sassoon's ear for the very words extends beyond the soldier's cheerful and ignorant blasphemies and bonhomie to the dreadful euphemisms by which the non-combatant comfortably deflated the reality's true meaning: the Scarlet Majors lamenting "we've lost heavily in this last scrap," their "gross, goggle-eyed" counterparts at home assuring themselves that "Arthur's getting all the fun/At Arras with his nine-inch gun" ('The Fathers'), the vicariously intrepid journalist of 'Editorial Impressions'. All the false attitudes to the War are dramatised; their hollowness is exposed simply because Sassoon allows them to speak for themselves. An excellent example of this method is "'They'", "the one", Sassoon tells us, "most quoted by the reviewers, both adverse and favourable."[13] Its notoriety was to be expected: like 'Stand-to', it was calculated to affront one of the most dearly cherished convictions at home—that the War was a contest sanctioned by Heaven and that the British were God's favourite team. The method is closely similar to that of "'Blighters'": first an ominously inoffensive stanza rehearsing the Bishop's clichés about the ways in which the War will have altered those who "lead the last attack/On Anti-Christ." The second stanza takes up his "They will not be the same" and applies his words to the lowest, most real, level of meaning, as 'they' will see it: "For George lost both his legs; and Bill's stone blind." But the last word, a characteristically impotent ambiguity, is forced upon the Bishop—"The ways of God are strange!" "They" is Sassoon's shrewdest thrust at, to use Shelley's phrase, "the priest's delight" in war, and the fact that it could be made so easily with the enemy's own weapons illustrates what sitting ducks many of his targets were. In such circumstances, the hunter's aim is liable to tire: though in 'Choral Union' and the later 'Joy-bells' Sassoon tackles the theme from differing angles, he does so almost with good humour and fails to achieve full penetration.[14]

12. See *Wilfred Owen: A Critical Study*, (1960), p. 51.
13. *S. J.*, p. 29.

'Fight to a Finish', a piece of wish-fulfilment in which the Nation Overseas has the chance to deal with its worst enemy, the Nation at Home, epitomises the strengths and limitations of Sassoon's satires. It is the soldier's emotional reaction against jingoism and involves a brutal inversion of standards. There are no rights in this poem, only the hatred of 'us' for 'them'. 'We', the "grim Fusiliers", make 'them', like pigs, "grunt and squeal"; we are "trusty", they "Junkers". Black and white are flatly opposed: just as the "Yellow-Pressmen" falsify the troops' sufferings, so the troops are distorted into idealized, righteous soldiers of wrath. The poet himself ("with my trusty bombers") is dangerously like the leader of a childish gang. But one only realizes this upon reflection. The sheer force of the language, the vividness of the scene, the basic truth—that the hypocrisy and indifference at home deserve rude exposure—are enough for the initial impact. But the tone of this and such poems as 'Their Frailty' and 'Glory of Women' verges upon obsessive hysteria: they inevitably lose force with the passing of time.

The intensity of hatred evinced in Sassoon's satires is, as a revelation of its disintegrating effect upon personality, a salutary indictment of the War and of war itself. It was not his temperament to absorb raw experience, as Owen did, at the time for transmutation into deeper poetry later: "I was a booby-trapped idealist, and 'young men', as Francis Bacon wrote, 'stir more than they can quiet, fly to the end without consideration of the means.'"[15] He passed the hatred on: taking the hands of those spared his direct experience and forcing them to touch the truth—that suffering which Yeats (whose demands of the war poets were far more exacting than those he made upon the work of his friends) thought it "best to forget ... as we do the discomfort of fever". Satire, if not the highest, is a legitimate form of poetry—and it was Sassoon's distinctive achievement to put it to wholly original

14. It is noteworthy that, like Owen in 'At a Calvary', it is institutionalised religion that Sassoon attacks. Elsewhere, the cynical note of 'To Any Dead Officer' or 'Stand-To' is counterbalanced by the deeper feeling underlying the invocations with which he ends 'At Carnoy' and 'Attack'. For both Owen and Sassoon God "*seems not to care*": faith, however loosely it may have been held, is something positively threatened—not least in the degraded jingoism of the Church. The well-meaning chaplain in Roy Fuller's 'Spring 1942', on the other hand, can only represent his personal convictions: he is quiet, ineffectual, knowing the limits of his place; his hearers have never thought him more than one like themselves, fallible and adrift: "We made no reply to that / Obscure, remote communication" (*Collected Poems* 1962, p. 56). When doubts are inbred, there is little room for shock.
15. *S. J.*, p. 193.

ends. In *showing* the dreadfulness of the War, in its surface aspects, he preceded Owen and surpassed him and all English poets who had previously written of war. His satires have, quantitatively, greater 'bite' than those of his fellow war-poets and a sheer brutality of utterance that matches the reality.[16] No English satirist since Byron had had such power of invective—though he lacks even Byron's constructiveness. He relieved the pressure of his emotion by *speaking* the brutality, over and over again.

These poems are the raw stuff of poetry. The reader who would feel their strength should come to them with a mind, not cool and detached, but that can still grow hot with imagining what forced them into being. Such a mind was Virginia Woolf's in 1918, and she acutely justified Sassoon's realistic poems in these words: "There is a stage of suffering, so these poems seem to show us, where any expression save the barest is intolerable; where beauty and art have something too universal about them to meet our particular case."[17] Now, more so after the event, it is natural that some should feel bludgeoned rather than roused, and the effect, as Middleton Murry felt, may be "to [numb], not [terrify], the mind".[18] Yet the response these poems elicit is likely, for many of us, to remain a more active one. It is still possible to say of them, with a reviewer of forty years ago: "Their emotion is still too closely knit into our experience to justify or indeed make desirable a wholly detached criticism."[19] Admittedly, for Owen, who had a more philosophical eye upon cause and effect, mere communi-

16. Significantly, one of the most recent memoirists of the Great War, Sholto Douglas, quotes Sassoon in this respect far more than Owen (*Years of Combat*, 1963).
17. Review of *Counter-Attack* (*Times Literary Supplement*, July 11, 1918.) 'Beauty and art' may reconcile us to the worst—and this was the last effect Sassoon desired at the time. Robert Nichols, in his myth-making Introduction to the American edition of *Counter-Attack* (where 'Sassoon the Man' is described as having "the air of a sullen falcon") reports the positive aspect of Sassoon's attitude convincingly, though in characteristically mannered prose: "I remember him once turning to me and saying suddenly apropos of certain exalté poems in my *Ardours and Endurances*: 'Yes, I see all that and I agree with you, Robert. War has made me. I think I am a man now as well as a poet. You have said the good things well enough. Now let us nevermore say another word of whatever little may be good in war for the individual who has a heart to be steeled ... It is dangerous even to speak of how here and there the individual may gain some hardening of soul by it. For War is hell and those who institute it are criminals. Were there anything to say for it, it should not be said, for its spiritual disasters far outweigh any of its advantages'."
18. *The Evolution of an Intellectual*, 1920, p. 72.
19. Review of *Selected Poems by Siegfried Sassoon*, *The Times Literary Supplement*, June 4, 1925.

cation was rarely enough ('Dulce et Decorum Est' and 'The Dead Beat' are the poems most akin to Sassoon's in manner): he sought to create, not force, a change of heart. Several of his poems are like paintings in depth exploring themes upon which Sassoon had earlier sketched a few bold strokes: we could supplement 'Does It Matter?' with 'Disabled', 'They' with 'The Chances', 'Suicide in the Trenches' with 'S.I.W'. (or Herbert Read's 'The Execution of Cornelius Vane'), 'Base Details' with 'À Terre'.[20] But the effect would be to supplement, not supersede.

§ 3 *Himself Bewildered*

In *Siegfried's Journey*, Sassoon says that, once the War was over and he had some leisure for reflection, "I could now safely admit that army life had persistently interfered with my ruminative and quiet-loving mentality. I may even have been aware that most of my satiric verses were to some extent prompted by internal exasperation."[21] His most subjective poems bear out the truth of this piece of self-analysis. Through them, we can trace the history of his inner self and see how the vacillations of feeling and contradictions of attitude to which, in the *Memoirs*, he freely confesses, are also reflected in the poetry.

A few poems in *The Old Huntsman* show Sassoon striving, during his first months in France, to hold fast the innocent vision that had animated the early nature poems. 'When I'm Among a Blaze of Lights' well conveys the exasperation he mentions. It is a rather prudish piece, a peevish broadside against the tawdry pleasures of his fellow-officers, which repel the sensitive solitary: "Then someone says 'Another drink?' /And turns my living heart to stone." /A Mystic as Soldier',

20. In only one case where their treatment of a theme is closely similar is Sassoon's less one-sided than Owen's. In 'Ancient History' and 'The Parable of the Old Men and the Young', both use Old Testament stories as satirical allegories of the sacrifice of youth by a purblind old generation: Sassoon the triangle of Adam, Cain and Abel, Owen the Abraham and Isaac story. Though Sassoon characterizes his Adam fiercely—"a brown old vulture in the rain, / Shivered below his wind-whipped olive-trees; / Huddling sharp chin on scarred and craggy knees"—he ends by drawing attention to the pitiable condition of the bereft father: "He bowed his head—/The gaunt wild man whose lovely sons were dead." Owen's poem ends as bitterly as it begins. (Whilst the element of pity is probably due to the fact that 'Ancient History' is much later than the other poems treated here—it was first published in September, 1918—it is nevertheless couched in a superior tone which makes it no poem of reconciliation.)
21. p. 74.

continues the theme on a more abstract plane, romanticizing the poet who "lived my days apart,/Dreaming fair songs for God", and is now compelled to "walk the secret way/With anger in my brain," his poetry stifled ,perhaps forever. Yet the last poem in *The Old Huntsman*, the "jingle" 'A Letter Home', which was sent to Robert Graves, ends a collection that contains such poems as "Blighters" and 'The Hero' on a note of facile optimism. The mood is a variant of the initial Happy Warriorism and surmounts even the death of his and Graves's courageous mutual friend, David Thomas, who is made into an elegiac pastoral figure, with the assertion:

> I know
> Dreams will triumph, though the dark
> Scowls above me where I go.

But there is a hectic note in the rapid, irregular couplets—a defiant clinging to sanity and hope which can only be called bravado. It is an indication of how insecurely based was the standpoint from which Sassoon wrote his satires.

With *Counter-Attack*, there is no longer the least sense of surety that "dreams" will triumph or even sustain. 'Break of Day' is a tenuous reverie—"a happy dream to him in hell"—which for a few moments before the attack tranquillises the soldier with peaceful memories of "riding in a dusty Sussex lane/In quiet September." But Sassoon seems unsure whether to intend the dream as a blessing or a mockery sent by "God's blank heart grown blind". Wholly unambiguous is the feverish self-communing of 'Repression of War Experience', where war infects everything associated with peace and tranquillity: the blundering moths that scorch themselves in the candle flame are patently symbolic, the "breathless air" of the garden and the darkness of the trees form an atmosphere of brooding menace. The memory of the guns shatters the stillness; it is this, not "dreams", that lives in the mind:

> Those whispering guns — Christ, I want to go out
> And screech at them to stop — I'm going crazy;
> I'm going stark, staring mad because of the guns.

The poem is not wholly successful: the hysteria is only conveyed forcibly in these last lines; it does not *rise* to them. At a crucial point, in the petulant castigation of the ghosts of "old men with ugly souls/Who

wore their bodies out with nasty sins", Sassoon's language fails him
and he overbalances into the ludicrous. As will be shown more fully
later, when his attack is not limited to a precisely conceived object of
hatred, he is prone to give way to dull imprecations and clichés that
dangerously deflate the feeling.

Other poems in *Counter-Attack* reflect the overwrought mental condition that Sassoon later analyses so dispassionately in *Memoirs of an
Infantry Officer* and *Sherston's Progress*. 'Sick Leave', 'Banishment' and
'Autumn' all arise from the Craiglockhart period, when he was wrestling with the problem of how to reconcile his pacifist convictions with
the feeling that he was betraying his comrades by not returning to the
Front. 'Sick Leave', which Graves identifies as definitely written at
that time,[22] is by far the most impressive of the three, with its restrained
and unaffected opening, "When I'm asleep, dreaming and lulled and
warm,—/They come, the homeless ones, the noiseless dead", and the
simple statement, "They whisper to my heart; their thoughts are
mine". Commonplace creeps in at the end, with the bond of blood—
yet this was doubtless a common feeling and a deep one. It does not,
in Sassoon, indicate anything approaching Owen's obsession with the
significance of blood-letting. Though 'Sick Leave' says all that need
be said on the theme of the betrayal of comradeship, he returns to it
in 'Banishment' and 'Autumn' with a disfiguring rhetoric. In 'Banishment', an apologia for his public protest against the War, he strains
after a consciously poetic dignity: though doubtless the emotion was
genuine, it is falsified by phrases like "smote my heart to pity" and
"ever in my sight/They went arrayed in honour". A reader of the
Memoirs will not doubt that the failure is one, not of sincerity, but of
poetic tact. In 'Autumn', he even harks back to the poetic diction of
his early style, romanticising war's destruction in conventional images.
The melodramatic concluding lines, "O martyred youth and manhood
overthrown,/The burden of your wrongs is on my head" come strangely
from the poet of 'How to Die'. They are, however, consistent with the
highly emotional nature of his response.

They also betray another weakness to which their author confesses
—an inclination for self-dramatisation, which was responsible for an
attitude to the War, when he returned to it from Craiglockhart, emotionally akin to that of his Happy Warrior beginnings. 'Dead Musi-

22. *Goodbye to All That*, p. 225.

cians'—"upon my brow/I wear a wreath of banished lives"—and
'The Dream' are both marred by a high-pitched rhetorical note.
Sincere feeling is shown in 'The Dream', with the sensitive and com-
passionate observation of the soldiers' petty miseries:

> I'm looking at their blistered feet; young Jones
> Stares up at me, mud-splashed and white and jaded;
> Out of his eyes the morning light has faded.

but as soon as the poet introduces himself and "The secret burden that
is always mine" he gropes to express the inexpressible. The wild
phrases, "accursed line", "blundering strife", "the foul beast of war
that bludgeons life" draw attention to the emotional nature of the
poet's sense of helpless responsibility. The poet's emotion is in the
centre, not the tragedy to which he bears—or should bear—witness.
A poem like Owen's 'The Sentry' works in the reverse way, with no
insistence on the feelings the "I" possesses.

§ 4 *A Larger Sympathy*

The weaknesses ou the subjective poems—the rawness of the emotion
and the undisciplined expression of it—mar also most of the poems of
private grief or of compassion for fellow-soldiers, individually or *en
masse*. Seldom is the feeling allowed to work through, or emerge from,
the poem itself. More often, feeling outruns expression. The hated
phenomena of war—the "cursed wood" that must be stormed, to face
death "like a prowling beast"—too readily become stereotypes that
evoke no sharp response. The men themselves—"the kind, common
ones…/What stubborn-hearted virtues they disguised!" ('Conscripts'),
"Young Fusiliers, strong-legged and bold" ('In Barracks')—are
sentimentalised. There is a dangerously high proportion of cliché in
the poems of strong feeling, as if he had not the urge for precision or
the artistic conscience to vary his expression. While in the poems of
protest this roughness serves him well as part of the angry voice almost
inarticulate with the urgency of a message whose audience is assured,
in a poem intended to evoke a deeper response the deadness of the
language dulls the effect. Phrases like "the wild beast of battle"
('Prelude: The Troops'), "dreams that drip with murder" ('Survivors'),
and the almost perfunctory metaphorical use of "hell", blur the impact

of poems in which everything depends on the intensity of description. 'Prelude' and 'Survivors' have similar themes, but little of the force of Owen's 'Exposure' and 'Mental Cases'. Sassoon's pen is too liable to slip over the concrete reality which it is his first duty to communicate and which Owen evokes by both word and rhythm: he rushes instead to press upon the reader his own feelings and his view of what the reader's should be. The "seemingly casual, cliché style" that Blunden justly admires [23] is a two-edged weapon. The clichés that in the satire work by contrast with the overwhelming reality have an artistic justification which their counterparts in the poems of compassion, in vainly seeking to match the reality, cannot share.

However genuine his feeling, in expressing it Sassoon is too inclined to adopt the materials nearest to hand. Thus, for the lengthy elegiac poem, 'The Last Meeting', whose subject was dear to him (it is his friend, David Thomas, who is more buoyantly recalled in 'A Letter Home'), he chooses a lush romantic style that smothers both the subject and some strong atmospheric description beneath a spurious richness of language. A comparison of a few lines from this poem with a similar passage from Owen's 'Asleep' illustrates how in moments of strong feeling sheer words are liable to get the mastery of Sassoon:

> Ah! but there was no need to call his name.
> He was beside me now, as swift as light.
> I knew him crushed to earth in scentless flowers,
> And lifted in the rapture of dark pines.

Owen's feeling, on the other hand, is not inflated; it makes no romantic leap to the unknowable, but through the concrete is more suggestive of the poignant quality of man's unknowing:

> —Or whether yet his thin and sodden head
> Confuses more and more with the low mould,
> His hair being one with the grey grass
> And finished fields of autumn that are old . . .
> Who knows? Who hopes? Who troubles? Let it pass!

With contrasts such as this (and others previously made) in mind, one is forced to admit the broad justice of D. J. Enright's statement that: "Sassoon's most interesting poetry is composed of what have been

23. *War Poets, 1914-1918*, p. 31.

called the 'negative emotions'—horror, anger, disgust—and outside that field he inclines to become sentimental in a conventional
way."[24] It has become a critical commonplace to set Sassoon down, as
B. Ifor Evans does, as "outstandingly the most effective" writer of the
'realist stage' of War poetry,[25] reserving for Owen the prime place of
honour as the poet capable of going deeper than emotional and biassed
outbursts (as "Blighters" and 'The Fathers' are biassed) to a quality
of pity that is 'not strain'd'. Pinto describes Sassoon's war poetry as
"purely destructive"[26], in that it creates nothing with which to rebuild;
Johnston, in *English Poetry of the First World War*, shares this view.
While one would not quarrel with the essential justice of these judgments (though Pinto's has an exaggerated negative emphasis), any
more than Sassoon does in his generous comments on Owen, it can be
shown that his response to the War is not confined to angry satire,
sentimentality or a morbid preoccupation with his own predicament.
A handful (admittedly) of his poems have a moving directness and
simplicity which eschews sentimentality or morbidity; on a humbler
scale than Owen's they plead human sympathy and understanding.

As with the satirical epigrams, this is best expressed within a brief
compass, when he is not consciously striving for the large statement:
the praiseworthy poems are 'Two Hundred Years After', 'The Hawthorn Tree', 'The Dug-Out', and, though it is not a perfect whole,
'Enemies'; with some reservations, the longer descriptive pieces,
'Concert Party' and 'Night on the Convoy', may be added to these.
The range of feeling in these poems is wider than that customarily
associated with Sassoon.

In the early sonnet 'Two Hundred Years After', he achieves the
physical immediacy and simple expression of feeling that are so often
absent from the more sensational Front Line poems. It is cleanly and
economically constructed. We are first given a vivid picture of one
of the most familiar—and least spectacular—sights of the War, a
column drawing the rations up to the Line under cover of darkness.
There is no intrusive comment; the picture is allowed to do its own
work, to serve as a symbol of the futility of the struggle. This done, it is
obliterated from the watcher's gaze by "a rainy scud" and the lights
of the village—of normality, of peace-time continuity—appear. The

24. 'The Literature of the First World War': *The Modern Age*. Penguin, 1961, p. 162.
25. *English Literature Between the Wars*. 1948, p. 103.
26. *Crisis*, p. 145.

few, compassionate words of the old man who has seen this ghostly scene often have a Hardyan simplicity: "Poor silent things, they were the English dead/Who came to fight in France and got their fill." This is indeed all that is likely to be said: it needed distinctive insight to grasp the enduring meaning of the common scene and poetic tact to point its significance without mawkishness.[27]

Another (surprisingly) early poem, 'Enemies', is less finished. It begins poorly with the vague "queer sunless place" and the accustomed reference to "Armageddon", but in the crucial part Sassoon avoids the romantic elaboration of 'The Last Meeting' and allows the one he grieves for to be only suggested. The flat simplicity of statement convinces: "One took his hand/Because his face could make them understand"—wisely, there is no attempt to show why this is so. But what matters most is the idea—the meeting of human beings beyond the hatred and the slaughter—a mere sketch, admittedly, for 'Strange Meeting' or even Sorley's sonnet 'To Germany': the link between enemies is far from being forged. One is inclined to wish Sassoon had attempted something more ample on this theme: though it is implicit in his war poetry as a whole that he has no strong anti-German feelings, his failure to crystallise this into a positive attitude exemplifies his limitations.

'The Hawthorn Tree' shares the Hardyan simplicity of 'Two Hundred Years After'. It is a welcome antidote to the bitterly accusing 'Glory of Women' and 'Their Frailty', with their unqualified scorn for the selfishness of woman's love. In 'The Hawthorn Tree' he allows the woman to speak, to express her love as far as she can. Her perception is limited to this love and partly blinded by it; if she is guilty, it is of ignorance and innocence, not indifference. She knows only that her son has "fearsome things to see", being unable to begin to imagine the extent of his sufferings. In their place she yearns to put a thing of pure and simple beauty which she touchingly believes might cure all —"just one glance/At our white hawthorn tree" (its whiteness is appropriate: he avoids the pitfall of introducing a contrasting red; the voice is strictly the mother's). The rain that cleanses the scene she

27. No doubt, however, Sassoon's poem gives artistic expression to common enough soldiers' fancies. Cf. Frank Richards, *Old Soldiers Never Die*, p. 81: "One man used to say that when the war was over the ghosts of dead soldiers would be marching over these fields every night, cursing and grousing as they were moving along, and that no farmer would ever be able to live around these parts again."

would have her son see suggests tears, but cannot move her to them; her grief is beyond such things:

> But when there's been a shower of rain
> I think I'll never weep again
> Until I've heard he's dead.

Without intruding his own, Sassoon has rendered truthfully the quality of another's deepest feelings.

The success of 'The Dug-Out', on the other hand, derives from the tension between subjective and compassionate feeling and also from judicious under-statement. In the latter respect it contrasts well with the over-explicit 'Dreamers'. This is the whole poem:

> Why do you lie with your legs ungainly huddled,
> And one arm bent across your sullen, cold,
> Exhausted face? It hurts my heart to watch you,
> Deep-shadow'd from the candle's guttering gold;
> And you wonder why I shake you by the shoulder;
> Drowsy, you mumble and sigh and turn your head ...
> *You are too young to fall asleep forever;*
> *And when you sleep you remind me of the dead.*

He avoids the sentimental treatment the subject invites (a lament for the doom of the clean, corn-haired youth in the full flower of manhood, etc.): he focuses attention instead upon the symbolic ugliness of the youth's posture, which is reinforced by the body's alienation from the candle. Sleep is a cruel mockery of death: not just the youth's, or of all those that have died, but of the poet's own that may be imminent. When he shakes the youth by the shoulder, it is the instinctive reaction of one who shares his vulnerable humanity. The poem is not obviously (certainly not consciously) self-regarding: there is a subtle tension between the sense of pity—"You are too young"—and the sense of identification with the youth—"you remind me of the dead".

'The Dug-Out' was one of Sassoon's last poems to arise directly from the War—it is dated July 18th, 1918, but according to *Siegfried's Journey*[28] was probably written two months later; it promises a greater refinement of expression which was to be denied the opportunity to mature. In two other poems of this period, also included in *Picture-Show*, Sassoon is moving towards the more self-subduing attitude which he

28. See p. 71.

had by then come to desire. 'Concert Party' is the more successful. He relies entirely upon description of the scene and the atmosphere, by which he suggests the pathos of the contrast between the expectations of the deprived troops and the commonplace nature of what moves them. The poet is the compassionate observer, but identified with the men, not superior to them—" *We* hear them, drink them"; at the end he does stand apart, but not to moralise: "Silent, I watch the shadowy mass of soldiers stand./Silent, they drift away, over the glimmering sand." The scene is made so clear to us that we know what is left unsaid. This is not so in the similarly descriptive 'Night on the Convoy'. Here, he insists too much upon what could be inferred, risking the commonplace of "lads in sprawling strength" and the obviousness of:

> In the stark
> Danger of life at war, they lie so still,
> All prostrate and defenceless, head by head . . .
> And I remember Arras, and that hill
> Where dumb with pain I stumbled among the dead.

When we turn to the last poems where he is concerned with issues 'above the battle', we find that their most memorable quality is not their expression, but the sentiments they contain. Away from the concrete and visible reality, and dealing with necessary though not moving themes, he relapses disappointingly into dullness and rhetoric. The feeling of 'Reconciliation' is, as we have seen, nascent in 'Enemies' and the pitying thought for the "German mother" in 'Glory of Women'. It is a timely message, expressed directly and unpretentiously, but it is prosaically undistinguished. 'Aftermath' is more culpable. Something of a postscript, since it was written in March 1919, Sassoon calls it "an effective recitation-poem" [29]—that is, a piece of popular emotion. Its long, measured periods lend themselves readily to declamation, but it will not bear cold-blooded examination, being almost entirely dependent upon cliché and emotive phrasing—"Look up, and swear by the green of the spring that you'll never forget." Doubtless it had its purpose and its effect, though one is grateful to Sassoon for informing us that, on one occasion when he rehearsed it in America, a group of charwomen were far from being carried away.

29. *S. J.* p. 141.

§ 5 *Postscripts*

Though Sassoon intended 'Aftermath' to be "my last word on the subject", this word was actually—and more effectively—spoken some years later in two poems included in *The Heart's Journey*: 'To One Who Was With Me in the War' was first published in 1926, and the sonnet 'On Passing the New Menin Gate' in 1928.[30]

These poems have the force of accumulated reflection. In 'To One Who Was With Me', he again employs the heightened conversational tone of such poems as 'To Any Dead Officer' and 'Repression of War Experience' for an imagined return to the war-time past.[31] His purpose is to dispel the treacherous "sense of power/[That] invades us" when we remember war's positive value, the comradeship of "that Company which we served with": treacherous because "Remembering, we forget/Much that was monstrous" and "We forget our fear." He plays the "game of ghosts" with dramatic effect: together they go, stooping and ducking along the trenches—brought concretely to life again, as in 'A Working Party'—till, "Round the next bay you'll meet/A drenched platoon-commander ..." This is the other self—the true self that you were, with a face strained and anxious, "Hoping the War will end next week." Fittingly, the poem ends with the ironic question, "What's that you said?" There need be no answer: to resurrect that previous self nostalgically would be to invoke the worst also. This poem might well complement Blunden's 'The Watchers':

> When will the stern fine "Who goes there?"
> Meet me again in midnight air?
> And the gruff sentry's kindness, when
> Will kindness have such power again. [32]

---

30. Two poems included in *Vigils* (1934) are less to the purpose. 'War Experience' is a more private piece of analysis than 'To One Who Was With Me', in which Sassoon records how time has wrought a change of heart: "Not much remains, twelve years later, of the hater / Of purgatorial pains." 'Ex-Service' is a relatively weak return to the theme of 'Menin Gate'; it lacks the concrete point of reference of the earlier protest and suffers also, though this is not Sassoon's fault, from the debased contemporary usage of "swindled" and "dud"; the effect of the ghosts' reproaches is faintly pathetic.
31. 'To One Who Was With Me' was, as its form suggests, inspired by a reminiscent conversation—with Ralph Greaves ('Ralph Wilmot' of *M.I.O.*, a brother of 'old man Barton') who lost an arm ten days after Sassoon was sniped: this information was supplied by the author.
32. *Undertones of War*, pp. 365-366; another poem, 'Return of the Native', referred to below, is on pp. 364-365.

and compared with Martin Armstrong's grotesque nostalgia it shows
a fine sense of balance:

> O give us one more day of sun and leaves,
> The laughing soldiers and the laughing stream,
> And when at dawn the loud destruction cleaves
> This silence, and, like men that move in dream,
> (Knowing the awaited trial has begun)
> We climb the trench, and cross the wire, and start,
> We'll stumble through the shell-bursts with good heart
> Like boys who race through meadows in the sun.[33]

It is a relief to turn from this mockery of the dead to 'On Passing the
New Menin Gate', Sassoon's last word on the War and a strong
example of the kind of remembrance they would surely have appreciated; again, in comparison with a related poem of Blunden's,
'Return of the Native', resolutely disenchanted. If 'To One Who Was
With Me' warns against forgetfulness of the worst, this poem affirms
that the best has been forgotten also, this forgetfulness symbolised by
the massive memorial at Ypres. It points the sharp contrast between
the plain truth—"The unheroic Dead who fed the guns", "the doomed,
conscripted, unvictorious ones"—and the vulgar memorial whose
sheer size overwhelms and obliterates the memory: "a pile of peace-
complacent stone." By this, the living have paid off their debt. The
poem is both anti-heroic, not idealising the dead, and against the cant
of the wasters of peace; the taut language exactly conveys barely
controlled disgust:

> Was ever an immolation so belied
> As these intolerably nameless names?
> Well might the Dead who struggled in the slime
> Rise and deride this sepulchre of crime.

It is tempting to wish that these forceful and deeply considered poems
had been Sassoon's last that one can call war poems.[34] Unhappily,
in 1940 he felt impelled to give an elder poet's encouragement—but
hardly an old soldier-poet's—to the youth that once more could not
choose but fight. His two short patriotic poems, 'The English Spirit'
and 'Silent Service' do their conventional work (as 'Aftermath' did)

33. *Mercury Book of Verse* (1931).
34. *The Road to Ruin*, though on the subject of war, will be discussed in Chapter *IV*.

in a martial tone reminiscent of Milton and Wordsworth—and, sadly, of his own early First War poems. England opposes "Apollyon", "daemons in dark", and, more concretely, "The cultural crusade of Teuton tanks". She is the defender of earth's freedom and, it is implied, supported by God himself: "In every separate soul let courage shine—/A kneeling angel holding faith's front-line"—though it remains unclear whether the faith is to be in "ourselves" or in divine sanction. Such poems do have their purpose—they appeared in *The Observer* in 1940—but one cannot avoid a sad comparison between these inflated pieces and Hardy's 'Men Who March Away' (if one must have the martial mood), or, in a mood more in tune with a Second Great War, Herbert Read's 'To a Conscript in 1940':

> But you, my brother and my ghost, if you can go
> Knowing that there is no reward, no certain use
> In all your sacrifice, then Honour is reprieved.[35]

But Sassoon, twenty years before, had already played his part in shaping the response of the new war poet:

> Pity, repulsion, love and anger,
> The vivid allegorical
> Reality of gun and hangar,
> Sense of the planet's imminent fall:
>
> Our fathers felt these things before
> In another half-forgotten war.[36]

35. *Collected Poems*, 1946, p. 82. To extenuate the faults of Sassoon's contributions to patriotic feeling, we have what he wrote to Sir Sydney Cockerell on June 6, 1940: "The poem in the *Observer* ['Silent Service'] was written from a sense of duty; it seemed to be the only point of view I had any right to express, and I deliberately made it as simple—even commonplace—as I could. There was merely the obvious fact that all can help by courage and self-control. I am sending you the one which appeared in the same place a week before. I wrote it ['The English Spirit'] to let people know my conviction that 'pacificism is not enough' against the powers of evil—as I'd realised fully before 1938" (*The Best of Friends*, 1956, p. 78). He had long been sickened by the prospect of war and it needed an act of will to write of it again at all.
36. Roy Fuller, *Collected Poems*, 1962. p. 55: 'Another War'.

III

TRANSITION

The *Selected Poems* of 1925 contain no poems of a date later than those included in *Picture-Show* (1919-1920), presumably because Sassoon felt that his selection would form a more integrated whole than would have been the case had he included some of the peace-time satires of the early Twenties. A reviewer of the 1925 volume certainly felt that there was a coherent pattern and expressed the hope that the poems with which that book ends (chosen from *Picture-Show*) "reflect a tranquillity that is not lacking in ardour and an absolution not alien to peace."[1] Now, reading *Picture-Show* within the whole pattern of Sassoon's development, the reader is conscious of an ardent search for tranquillity and absolution rather than of any achieved equilibrium of feeling: it is in every sense a transitional work.

Picture-Show was the first collection of a varied character that Sassoon had published for two years.[2] He returns in it to the peace-time theme of nature and takes up that of love (somewhat belatedly for a young poet), but the echoes of war are strong enough to dominate all other impressions. The most interesting poems express his reactions to psychological problems that were the legacy of war: how to endure bitter and harrowing memories and how to readjust to ordinary life when suddenly deprived of the clearly-defined purpose war had at least provided. In *Siegfried's Journey* he describes 1919 as "a year of rootless re-beginnings": the poems of *Picture-Show* reflect the instability of the formidable poetic personality war had made of him, a personality which had somehow to strike out fresh roots. He was to learn the force of Eliot's later insight in 'A Note on War Poetry', that "a poem might happen/To a very young man: but a poem is not poetry—/That is a life."[3] The poem had happened: the life remained to be lived.

1. *The Times Literary Supplement*, June 4, 1925.
2. Appendix A, (4).
3. From *London Calling*, 1942: quoted in *The Achievement of T. S. Eliot*, by F. O. Matthiessen, 1947.

The title poem epitomises the poet's situation. He is the spectator still of an unreal life, in which the men he had known come and go as in a dream-sequence, in a feverish flux from which he can distil no coherent meaning. Though Sassoon has turned a new art from to imaginative use, he is unable to make it carry more than a platitude: the image, "And life is just the picture dancing on the screen," is the old one of Man the puppet of the Fates. The problem must be to shake off this dazed condition and to turn constructively towards the future. This is acknowledged in "To Leonide Massine in 'Cleopatra'", which is not about Massine at all but about the necessity to break away from War's tyrannous memories. Massine's dancing reminds him of his recent experience of death in earnest: "Leaping along the verge of death and night/You show me dauntless youth that went to fight." The tripping measure is not, it seems, ironic; it accords with the hollow rhetoric of the ending: "O mortal heart/Be still; you have drained your cup; you have played your part." Painful memories are only, as yet, formally mastered; this is also apparent in the stale and conventional phrasing of 'Wraiths':

> They know not the green leaves;
> In whose earth-haunting dream
> Dimly the forest heaves,
> And voiceless goes the stream.
> Strangely they seek a place
> In love's night-memoried hall;

The memory of the dead is to be with him continually and will be evoked more strongly later. At present, he is probably too close to the event to have found an individual voice of painful reminiscence. There is no clear personal imagery: he falls back instead upon the faded romantic vocabulary from whose influence the War had temporarily freed him.

A disconcerting regression in style—from the sharpness and clarity of the best war poems, with their simple and living colloquialism to the vagueness of expression and the preference for sound before sense that characterizes the pre-war poetry—is the great weakness of many of the subjective poems in this volume. For poems on themes he had known so intimately as death and the irreparable loss of friends, it is unfortunate that he should resurrect a style that produces an effect of remoteness and artificial feeling. This weakness is epitomised in 'Memory',

with its conventional evocation of carefree childhood and its yearning
for the old world now shattered forever:

> O starshine on the fields of long-ago,
> Bring me the darkness and the nightingale;
> Dim wealds of vanished summer, peace of home,
> And silence; and the faces of my friends.

These sentiments, like those of 'Wraiths', will be repeated later in a
more individual voice. 'Butterflies' and 'Vision' come strangely from
one who had censured (at Craiglockhart) the "almost embarrassing
sweetness in the sentiment" of some of Owen's early work. In 'Butterflies' there is a thin conventional analogy between the brevity and
unknowing of the butterfly's life and those of the poet. The cliché,
"birds that make/Heaven in the wood" and the inaccurate description
of the butterflies' movement—"deftly flickering over the flowers"—
are irritating. 'Vision' is a pot-pourri of Bridges and Keats. The opening line, "I love all things that pass" recalls Bridges' "I love all
beauteous things" and the lament for transience, "O Beauty, born of
lovely things that die!" is more fully indebted to Keats's, "She dwells
with Beauty—Beauty that must die." The romanticism is rounded off
with the picture of Grecian youth equipped with "rhythmic-flashing
limbs that rove and race", reminiscent of the mystic cleanliness of
youth in Brooke's war sonnets.

However, Sassoon has not quite lost his war-time voice. This comes
through, appropriately, in a few longer poems where he speaks more
plainly of the problems that confront him in his effort to come to terms
with himself and with reality. One of these is how to subdue insistent
thoughts of death. This is presented ironically in 'To A Very Wise
Man', a carefully constructed poem in which he adopts the easy
conversational approach of 'To Any Dead Officer'. He first sketches the
landscape of the wise man's omniscient brain, his soul "full of cities
with dead names,/And blind-faced, earth-bound gods of bronze and
stone." Then he switches abruptly to the reality of human fears,
which one may try to smother by escaping into a delusive beauty, as
the bee shuns the "curtained gloom." The final stanza presents the
poet with ironic self-effacement as one anchored for consolation to the
world's tangible offerings: "I'm but a bird at dawn that cries 'chink,
chink' —/A garden-bird that warbles in the rain." The wise man, on
the other hand, is "the flying-man, the speck that steers/A careful

course far down the verge of day", his knowledge inclusive. He can reconcile reality and purpose—or so one may believe; but in a sceptical ending recalling that of 'To Any Dead Officer" Sassoon is not so sure: "You soar ... Is death so bad? ... I wish you'd say." Philosophy is cold comfort once you have seen the brutal face of the reality. This is neither a very profound conclusion nor a very helpful one to the poet: his role of singing-bird is doubly ironic.

What shall the poet sing now? So far Sassoon is able to do little more than dally with the question. 'Prelude to an Unwritten Masterpiece' was no doubt prompted by a consideration of Gosse's well-meant but conservative advice that he should undertake a long poem drawing on his knowledge of country life, chiefly as an escape from the War, but also no doubt so that he might at least explore his genuine experience: but at the time he felt the urge "to address the age on more startling and momentous themes."[4] However, though he could write penetratingly of the popular escapism of his slight lyrics—

> You like my bird-sung gardens: wings and flowers;
> Calm landscapes for emotion; star-lit lawns;
> And Youth against the sun-rise ... 'Not profound;
> But such a haunting music in the sound:
> Do it once more; it helps us to forget'

—their attraction was by no means dead to him. 'Prelude' is not the poem of one who intends, or thinks himself even likely to be capable of, writing a 'masterpiece'. There are indeed, he frivolously concedes, lurking horrors beneath the sunrise: we may know of these from dreams that signify "Some complex out of childhood; (sex of course!)" and if we care to pursue them we may come face to face with a fearful unknown that in childhood meant "I'd no chance/Of getting home for tea," but now means darkly more. The poem ends with a mocking vision of himself as a prophetic bard: "My beard will be a snow-storm, drifting whiter/On bowed, prophetic shoulders, year by year." A hypothetical friend's reaction to his "dark tremendous song" would be "'Why can't you cut it short, you pompous blighter?'" His own, it seems, would be similar; the irony is defensive: he disclaims all pretensions to the tragic view and contents himself with suggesting that it can be over-subtle. 'Limitations' is the natural corollary to 'Prelude'. Like 'Prelude', it is

4. *S. J.*, p. 101.

a piece of self-communing in a conversational, discursive manner, but one in which his plight is considered more constructively. Its point is that greatness is not all and that to be a poet is to be thoroughly alive, with at least a sense of life's meaning, however far short of expressing it one falls. It is much—enough—to reveal what is within: "You've got your limitations; let them sing,/And all your life will waken with a cry." Adam, "carving eagles on his beechwood cup", epitomises the true (and humble) poet:"Young Adam knew his job; he could condense/Life to an eagle from the unknown immense." The important thing is to go on, whatever limitations you may feel:

> When those forty platitudes are done,
> You'll hear a bird-note calling from the stream
> That wandered through your childhood; and the sun
> Will strike the old flaming wonder from the waters . . .
> And there'll be forty lines not yet begun.

This is a characteristically Meredithian expression of faith, not of clearlydefined purpose; it remains questionable in how many new shapes "the old flaming wonder" can be expressed. But there is a sense, as in childhood, of standing before a life that offers unlimited scope for exploration: "The window stands wide-open, as it stood/When treetops loomed enchanted for a child."

Sharing the directness of these three poems is 'Falling Asleep' which with 'Limitations' was included in the American edition and can thus be taken as representative of Sassoon's feeling towards the end of 1919 (it was first published in October of that year). In it we see that some degree of balance and a sense of peace have been achieved (it is not, therefore, surprising that Sassoon should remark in a letter to J. C. Squire, "Everyone seems to like 'Falling Asleep'."[5]. The setting is that desired in 'Memory', the "home/And silence" of youth, but it is now more clearly evoked, with particularised detail, as in 'Haunted' and 'The Old Huntsman':

>   . . . across the park
> A hollow cry of hounds like lonely bells:
> And I know that the clouds are moving across the moon;
> The low, red, rising moon. Now herons call
> And wrangle by their pool; and hooting owls
> Sail from the wood above pale stooks of oats.

5. Quoted in *A Bibliography*, p. 57.

The recollected "faces of my friends" have become a less bitter memory, one rather of brooding sadness; their "beauty", not their mangled corpses, shapes the dream: "I can watch the marching of my soldiers,/And count their faces; faces; sunlit faces." The "dim wealds" yearned for in 'Memory' have, at least, a new power to soothe:

> Falling asleep . . . the herons, and the hounds . . .
> September in the darkness; and the world
> I've known; all fading past me into peace.

The shadows, especially those cast by the irreparable loss of friends, will remain, but for many years to come it will be this healing influence of nature that, almost alone, sustains.

Of the remaining poems in *Picture-Show*, the principal fresh departure is a group of love lyrics. But the freshness is one of theme, not of expression. Of the six poems, only 'The Dark House', the most objective, is wholly successful (within its limitations), whilst 'The Imperfect Lover' promises with its Donne-ish beginning, only to disappoint. The style is derivative in the same way as that of his early poems: saturated with outmoded romantic diction and the dreamy vagueness of the minor Pre-Raphaelites.

'Idyll', 'Parted', 'Lovers' and 'Slumber-Song' appear to be exercises; it is hard to judge whether they arise from actual experience. They are either wishful pieces of invention (significantly, the loved one is never, even slightly, described), or else their artificiality reflects a conventional reticence that tells against the individual expression of feeling. 'The Imperfect Lover' promises more. The challenging opening—"I never asked you to be perfect—did I?"—has the directness of Donne, and like Donne, too, is the sceptical and sarcastic, "I never prayed that you/Might stand, unsoiled, angelic and inhuman,/Pointing the way toward Sainthood like a signpost." This promises a lively, argumentative poem, and the second stanza, in which the conventional phrases for perfect love are, seemingly, used ironically maintains the tone—though the reader of the other poems has misgivings. These are too well justified in what follows—in a tone of unrelieved solemnity, the humourless passion, one might think, of the conventional Latin lover: "The gloomy, stricken places in my soul"; "... if we loved like beasts, the thing is done,/And I'll not hide it, though our heaven be hell;" and finally, "I'd have you stand/And look me in the eyes, and laugh, and smite me"—the distraught lover bares his breast for the knife. This is the language of melodrama and it is remarkable that Sassoon should have relapsed into it. He had already, in his satire and poems like 'The Hawthorn Tree', discovered the virtues of a plain directness and the speaking voice, the very virtues that distinguish the love poetry of his contemporary, D. H. Lawrence, yet these desert him when love is the theme. This is the greater pity since 'The Imperfect Lover' is about no ordinary lover's quarrel—"you've learned to fear/The gloomy, stricken places in my soul"—there was scope for a rare exploration of a disturbed relationship, especially in the absence of other compelling themes.

One can only suppose that Sassoon's natural reticence causes him (perhaps unconsciously) to falsify the intensely private emotion by expressing it in conventional terms: this reticence limits his range similarly in the autobiographies, from which he excludes all reference to sexual feeling or relationships, despite the fact that *Siegfried's Journey* covers the period in which 'The Imperfect Lover' was written.[6]

The most successful of the love poems—a poem, rather, with love for theme—is also the least personal. In the construction of 'The Dark House' he was probably influenced by Hardy's 'Satires of Circumstance'. Like them, it is a clear-cut "glimpse" of a scene and a common action with reverberations of feeling far beyond what is seen. The scene is sketched with economy of language and detail:

> Dusk in the rain-soaked garden,
> And dark the house within.
> A door creaked: someone was early
> To watch the dawn begin.

The juxtaposition of the false lover's stealthy departure with the sudden call of the "quavering thrush"—nature's suggestive rebuke—is

6. The other intensely personal poem in this volume, the 'Elegy' for Robert Ross, is also strained. It is an elegiac exercise which gives only an abstract idea of Ross's qualities—he is not made to live in any way. The declamatory eulogy is strident: "O heart of hearts! ... O friend of friends!" It is, the uninitiated reader might suppose, a 'duty' piece: yet in *Siegfried's Journey* Sassoon affectionately makes Ross live and shows a sincere appreciation of his qualities. In prose, he rarely fails to sketch a portrait with vitality: in poetry, intimacy is liable to be sacrificed to conventionality. This is not the case, however, with poems like 'To A Childless Woman', which is typical of several in later volumes where he voices his compassion for an individual's misfortunes. This poem has a convincing tone of fumbling sincerity; the less intimate relationship of the subject seems to liberate his natural voice.

characteristically Hardyan in its disciplined evocation of an elemental situation.

If we ascribe 'The Dark House' to Hardy's influence, the love poems cannot be said to promise any significant development. They certainly herald no preoccupation with the theme: Sassoon briefly returns to it in later volumes and then abandons it altogether.[7]

The broadest way forward for his poetry—and that which his war poems might have led the reader to expect—seems indicated by 'Everyone Sang', which is significantly placed at the end of the collection, a signpost, as it were, to the future. "Thus", writes Sassoon, "I saluted the post-war future and my own part in it ... The singing that would 'never be done' was the Social Revolution which I believed to be at hand."[8] It is not, he corrects a common misconception, the singing of soldiers on the march—though the poem also greets the Armistice (but retrospectively: it was written in April, 1919) and expresses the general feeling of liberation. As a 'Socialist poem' it shows a spirit of naive optimism, as writers like Herbert Read and Robert Graves must have thought at the time—"'everybody',", comments Graves sourly, "did not include me."[9] Sassoon overlooks Graves at least when he says, "No-one has ever said a word against it." Liberal allowance must be made for the heady feeling of the moment; the most that can be said is that, like 'Aftermath', it is a poem perfectly attuned to its purpose: to express thought-quenching emotional release following a time of great stress. Read in cold blood, it does not move. What is more important is that its fragile spirit of idealism is significant to an understanding of the tendency of Sassoon's poetry during the next twenty years, in which we find a mounting disillusionment and disgust with the way the world went, accompanied by a gradual withdrawal from that world. Merely to recall the fact that Yeats's 'The Second Coming' was written two months earlier points more forcefully than any criticisms of this poem can the limitations of Sassoon's war-won wisdom.

7. Appendix A, (5).
8. *S. J.*, p. 141.
9. *Goodbye*, p. 228.

IV

RELUCTANT SATIRIST

§ 1

An enthusiastic reader of Sassoon's war poems who followed his progress in the early nineteen-twenties had only tantalizing glimpses of the poet he had known.[1] Gone was the savagery, the crushing onesidedness of "'They'" and "'Blighters'"—or almost: there were still the Dean who,

> For possible preferment sacrificed
> His hedonistic and patrician bias,
> And offered his complacency to Christ.
>
> ('The Blues at Lord's')

—and the blistering last word (boldly accented) on an old enemy,

> But on the Provost's left, in gold and blue,
> Sat ... O my God! ... great Major-General Bluff ...
> Enough enough enough enough enough!
>
> ('Founder's Feast')

—and even, for the sake of historical perspective, a dismissive stanza on a time-honoured 'bluffer',

> On regimental flags his fights persist;
> But I've no zeal to bolster up the story
> Of an imperiwigged stingy strategist
> Who caracoled upon extortionate glory ...
>
> ('Memorandum')

—but these stood out. Gone was the epigrammatic, mnemonic brevity, to be succeeded by a leisurely, nonchalant tone:

1. See Appendix A, (6), for bibliographical details.

So that's your Diary—that's your private mind
Translated into shirt-sleeved History. That
Is what diplomacy has left behind
For after-ages to peruse, and find
What passed beneath your elegant silk-hat.

('On Reading the War Diary of a Defunct Ambassador')

Strolling (to put it plainly) through those bits
Of Londonment adjacent to the Ritz . . .
Something I saw, beyond a boarded barrier,
Which manifested well that Time's no tarrier.

('Monody')

So you have touched ten million! Well, I've noted
The annual increase of your circulation
From big to vast, from corpulent to bloated,
With, I confess, fastidious consternation.

('Lines')

This was the new voice: urbane, ironic, controlled—and this is what
Sassoon was aiming at. of the first of these 'Satirical Poems' to be
written and published, 'Early Chronology' (1919), he writes:"It was
the pattern for a series of descriptive pieces in which I assumed a
laconic, legato tone of voice, and endeavoured to be mellow, sophisticated, and mildly sardonic."[2] He was exercising a conscious discipline
which, he admits, produced some "overwritten" pieces, "little more
than exercises in verbal accuracy and adroitness, but they served me
well in my resolve to acquire a controlled method of expression." How
much forceful satire was sacrificed to this resolve need not be guessed,
but it seems to be largely because of it that few of these poems succeed
as satires, whatever merits of description or shrewd social comment
they often possess.

It is not only the savagery of tone that one misses, but also the suc-
cinctness of phrasing that forged whole poems amongst the war satires
into weapons uniformly sharp. Yet the part can still strike, if rarely the
whole, in alliterative and precisely worded stanzas:

2. *S. J.*, p. 167.

I can imagine you among 'the guns',
Urbanely peppering partridge, grouse, or pheasant—
Guest of those infinitely privileged ones
Whose lives are padded, petrified, and pleasant.

('On Reading the War Diary')

One recalls Byron's, "But all was gentle and aristocratic/In this our party; polish'd, smooth, and cold": in each case, three hammering epithets leave no room for escape. Byronic, too, is this cool appraisal of the technique of the 'Society' hostess:

I have seen her fail, with petulant replies,
To localize him in his social senses:
I have observed her evening-party eyes
Evicted from their savoir-faire defences.

('Breach of Decorum')

And these lines, though lower-toned, almost recapture the crisp movement and the downright, cutting voice of " 'Blighters' ":

If Sargent could have called his soul his own
And had not been the hireling of the Rich,
There'd not be many portraits now re-shown
Of ladies lovelified to ball-room pitch;
Nor would these multiplied admirers crush
To crane their necks at sempiternal hostesses
Whom by the brilliant boredom of his brush
He silenced into fashion-dated ghostesses . . .
    Nor would my soul feel quite so mocked and chilly
    When I rejoin plebeian Piccadilly.

('On Some Portraits by Sargent')

On social affectation Sassoon can be incisive and scathing; these lines have most of the technical merits one desires from satire: speed of movement (by means of alliteration and strong endings), a mixture of downright invective and plain English with an outlandish and inventive vocabulary—"lovelified", "ghostesses", "sempiternal", to produce a ridiculous effect, which is echoed in sound by the triple rhyme (also Byronic) and the weak endings of the last couplet, as the poet washes his hands of the subject.

Especially characteristic is a Pateresque fondness for the out-of-the-way word: throughout these poems rarely-used Latinisms, coinages and double epithets proliferate. They are probably a by-product of Sassoon's search for compressed expression: their positive satirical effect, as here, is to lend a spurious elevation to the commonplace or absurd; this method works most successfully in 'Concert-Interpretation', the most sustained piece of ridicule, and the ironic 'Evensong in Westminster Abbey'. 'Evensong' will receive further comment later' 'Concert Interpretation', like 'Portraits', a broadside against modish intellectualism, is perfectly balanced. Like much good satire, its success rests upon a perception of an incongruity: between the audience's bloodless approval of the very thing they had at first rejected with disgust and the uninhibited suggestion of this thing. Without intrusive comment, Sassoon builds an absurd fancy upon this perception, "not declaiming against vice but only laughing at it." He sees that nothing really moves this audience—by denying their natural feelings (however mistaken) and adjusting their tastes to this "gallantry of goats" they have surrendered what little life they possessed; he tries to goad them into a more fitting response:

> Lynch the conductor! Jugulate the drums!
> Butcher the brass! Ensanguinate the strings!
> Throttle the flutes! . . . Stravinsky's April comes
> With pitiless pomp and pain of sacred springs . . .
> Incendiarize the Hall with resinous fires
> Of sacrificial fiddles scorched and snapping! . . .

The force and movement of this derive both from the alliteration and the outlandish vocabulary which performs the dual function of weighting the sound (vital in this context) and pointing the ludicrous improbability of such corybantics. More often, however, this vocabulary is an incidental diversion, a whimsical mannerism that characterizes Sassoon's intentional lightness of touch: from a negative viewpoint, it tends to inhibit speed of movement and directness of impact, and in such poems as 'Observations in Hyde Park', 'Memorandum' and 'A Stately Exterior' becomes a tiresome obsession.

Speed and directness could only have issued from a decided, urgent mind. From such a mind had come the spontaneous voice of indignation that once could carry by storm; now, when the spontaneous voice is heard, it proclaims no more than that the control has failed, as, for example, throughout 'The Case for the Miners': "I strive to hold my own; but I'm unable/To state the case succinctly." In the weak imprecations of 'A Post-Elizabethan Tragedy' — "They squeeze and smoke; a jabbering, conscious crowd/Of intellectual fogies, fools, and freaks"—we find him, as so often, in the uneasy Tennysonian role of lyricist turned reluctant satirist, "shrilly upbraiding the vices of his contemporaries."[3]

How is one to account for this modification—or, so far as satire goes, weakening—of tone? Not simply by the fact that Sassoon deliberately sought to acquire it; whatever his intentions, surely strong feeling would have burst through them. The explanation lies rather in the altered nature of his subject-matter and in the softening of his attitude toward it. The cut-and-dried issues of the War were no more —and such issues are what the satirist thrives upon. But it had seemed likely, as we have seen, that he would turn to writing in the cause of Socialism—an inclination which seemed confirmed by his acceptance of the Literary Editorship of the Labour *Daily Herald* in 1919. There surely, in the 1920s, the issues were, for the satirist's purposes at least, cleanly enough cut. Yet almost as soon as he turns his famous artillery upon privilege and plutocracy and bourgeois manners, his sights begin to blur. He truly says, "I am not by temperament an arguer."[4] Even when the issues are as clear as those behind 'The Case for the Miners', "Something goes wrong with my synthetic brain." He comes entangled, not only in "superficial details" of the "Standard of Living" question, but also in a superficial response: he and his "port-flushed friends" are wrangling over the fate of strangers. It is not enough for the satirist to demand, "How would you like it?" He must either organise cold facts to bring the point close (as in the realistic war poems, but Sassoon, like Chesterton, is a poorly documented rebel) or be able to preserve an ironic detachment. The end of 'The Case' gives away the point and the poet: "I'd almost like/To see them hawking matches in the gutter."[5] Similarly, he "almost" condemns the line of "half-cultured coxcomb Kings" reflected upon in 'Fantasia', but not quite:

3. These words are Sassoon's, taken from his review of *Tennyson*, by Harold Nicolson, *The Daily Herald*, March 28, 1923: this affinity, on his weaker side, with Tennyson, was even then strong and was to grow—though when he wrote the article he was clearly unaware of any such thing.
4. *S. J.*, p. 78.
5. It is noteworthy that 'The Case for the Miners' is the only one of his reprinted poems inspired by a specific incident of political significance—the flooding of the Tonypandy mine, 1921 (See *The Nation & Athenæum*, 16 April 1921).

> Fountains upheave pale plumes against the sky,
> Murmuring, "Their Majesties came sauntering by—
> Was it but yesterday?" . . . Proud fountains sigh
> Toward the long glades in golden foliage clad,
> "Kurfürsts could do no wrong" . . . And the woods reply,
> "Take them for what they were, they weren't so bad!"

('And there', one is tempted to rhyme on, 'but for the Grace of God go I'). Though he believed satire should be "touched with concession", as Raleigh puts it, Dryden would have made none such as this: it defeats the *whole* purpose.

But then, one asks, what is Sassoon's purpose? Even in attacking the least defensible manifestations of materialism, he is diffident:

> Resolved to satirize Hotels-de-Luxe,
> Shyly I sift the noodles from the crooks
> Beneath whose bristly craniums a cigar
> Juts and transmutes crude affluence to ash.

This is mildly funny, but it does not cut—where, Sassoon seems to ask, shall I begin? The detail is predictable, the diction irritable— "The band concedes them Tosca with their tea./Bored and expensive babble clogs the air—" and the ending half-hearted:

> And in them all my satirist-self discovers
> Prosperity that lives below the law . . .
>   (You ask what law I mean . . . Well, my impression
>   Is that these folk are poisoned by possession.)

('The Grand Hotel')

Press-barons, mob-patriotism, stately homes: each has its turn, but in the same diffident, often laboured voice. In 'Afterthoughts', 'Lines', 'Mammoniac Ode' and 'Memorial Service', sheer length dilutes the effect; there are too many slack lines, and a fatal obviousness of attack—not enough is left unsaid:

> Then a prelate, with prayer
> To the God of Commercial Resources and Arts that are bland,
> Was broadcasted likewise, his crozier of office in hand

('Afterthoughts')

I must congratulate those well-contented
And public-spirited Firms who advertise
Their functions, their ideals, their whole existence,
Across the current acreage of your sheets
With privileged and opulent persistence.

('Lines Written in Anticipation . . .')

Gold plate. Resources. Interest. Incomes. Power of purchase.
Pays Unemployment. Buys champagne, and builds new
        churches . . .
The finest Sport on earth is job-stock Speculation . . .
Deliver us, O Lord, from Currency Inflation.

('Mammoniac Ode')

Sometimes Sassoon does not know where to stop, as in the superfluous ending of 'First Night: Richard III' — 'And the whole proud production paled and passed,/Self-conscious, like its brilliant audience" — or how not to begin, as in the priggishly censorious 'In The National Gallery': "Faces irresolute and unperplexed, —/Unspeculative faces, bored and weak."

Nowhere does Sassoon wholly succeed in cutting down one of the grosser targets the rampant materialism of his time offered. He has set himself a moral task, but his heart is plainly not in it. The one-sided, destructive method of the true satirist no longer comes to him naturally; he tries to goad himself into it, with the result that he often becomes wordy or petulant. He now lacks the satirist's overweening self-confidence.[6] The extreme emotions—hatred, contempt, disgust—that animate satire are rarely evident: in their place there are disapproval, annoyance and irritation.[7] There is no thoroughgoing hatred, however unreasonable, no reforming purpose, no passionate conviction: there is nothing like Dryden's zest for conflict, Pope's for self-defence (and Augustan standards), Byron's for Liberty—or among his contemporaries the cocksureness of Osbert Sitwell, the settled religious standpoint of Humbert Wolfe, or Eliot's acute sensitivity to the "boredom" and the "horror". Whereas Sitwell can irritate without betraying irritation,

6. "Sassoon's is too pensive and withdrawn a spirit for the service of this blunt drill-sergeant's art" (Humbert Wolfe: *Notes on English Verse Satire*, 1929, p. 155): an important, yet partial truth, if one recalls the single-minded war satires.
7. "Unless the satirist's embitterment is more essential than irritation and has its roots in a sort of ecstasy, his artistic victory is incomplete, and many of these verses are only complete in their cleverness" (Review of *Satirical Poems*, *The Times Literary Supplement*, June 3, 1926).

> We are the greatest sheep in the world;
> There are no sheep like us.
> We come of an imperial bleat . . .

('The True-Born Englishman')[8]

and Wolfe can safely taunt his Press Lord in the Devil's voice,

> "Be not afraid, all that you were, and are,
> Is but the putrefaction of a star
> And nothing that you could have done, or can,
> Could change the grovelling destiny of man."

('News of the Devil', 1926)

—Sassoon is obliged to use his own voice, a voice that has no absolute confidence in its rectitude, that in the laborious 'Lines' can only "declaim against vice". There is, elsewhere, the ironic voice, but then —with double irony—upon the dubious advantages of the very creed to which he had been disposed to commit himself. If, on the one side, he derides capitalistic exploitation and philistinism, on the other he strikes no fire from democratic *dullness* and philistinism. The feeling of 'Fantasia', 'A Stately Exterior' and 'Observations in Hyde Park' is ambivalent, but there is no doubt about the tendency of 'Utopian Times', one of the latest written, a facetious vision of the "Social State" on the "Seventieth Anniversary of Peace". The principal achievements of Socialism, apart from improving health and longevity, are the elimination of "'crimes'/Of the once-prevalent, punishable sort" (a few peculating financiers are "condemned to spade-work ... /By the Vegetable Growers' Board of Censure"—an anticipatory parody of Chinese Communist methods) and the suppression of the gutter-press. Empire, "inconvenient", has gone. It is ideal—and dull: the State has done its work all too well and approved uniformity reigns. The juxtaposition of this poem with 'Mammoniac Ode' illustrates the difficulty of determining where Sassoon's sympathies lie. In any case, he seems bored with both topics.

He is not, in today's jargon, "committed". Whatever his original intentions as a satirist of materialism and privilege, he discovers a deepening vein of sympathy—approaching identification—with many

---

8. *Argonaut and Juggernaut*, 1919.

of the people and things a less scrupulous Socialist would scarify un-
reservedly: the Electors of Bavaria, the dowagers who "Hearken in
pensive frumpdom to the chords/That thrilled flounced-muslin maiden-
hood to tears" ('Observations'), the civilised aura of Scutcheon Hall,
the "unhygienic dwelling" of 'An Old-World Effect'. His heart and his
mind run in awkward harness—a weakness in the satirist, though a
virtue in the man. He concedes more than a satirist ought; not least,
he lays *himself* open. Edmund Blunden has defended the *Satirical Poems*
on the grounds that they are not satires at all: "His title was *Satirical
Poems*. Flogging the town, in the style of Juvenal or Charles Churchill,
demands a degree of ferocity and self-certainty which he would not
claim. His sense is rather, even in his indignation, 'There, but for the
grace of God ...' He is anxious to make all allowances".[9] It has already
been shown that there is substantial truth in this, yet it cannot acquit
such poems as 'Afterthoughts', 'Lines', 'In the National Gallery',
'Mammoniac Ode' and 'Memorial Service' from being judged as
satires. And is not the distinction between' satires' and 'satirical poems'
debatable? Sassoon seems to have chosen the latter description to cover
the many poems which, though they contain elements of satire, might
better be described as ironic commentaries on the human scene. He
may not have attempted to "flog the town" in poems like 'A Post-
Elizabethan Tragedy', 'Some Portraits' and 'Concert-Interpretation',
but this is hardly because he is making allowances—the last of these
certainly makes none and succeeds the better for it.

If we call these poems "satirical", "not satire", we are making a
basic distinction between amateurism and professionalism: between
satirists like Sassoon and Belloc on the one hand, Dryden and Pope
on the other. Both contemporary satirists are well armed, yet neither
has complete mastery of himself or of his medium: when Belloc flays
the Jews and Sassoon the slaves of the cultural vogue, they involve
themselves too clumsily and succeed only in landing in the camp of the
Philistines.[10]

9. *Edmund Blunden: A Selection*, p. 319.
10. Belloc, however, was able to turn his doubts about democracy to satirical
purpose:

> The accursed power which stands on privilege
> (And goes with Women and Champagne and Bridge)
> Broke—and Democracy resumed her reign
> (Which goes with Bridge and Women and Champagne).

(*Epigram XX:* 'On a General Election' *Collected Verse*. Penguin, 1954, p. 156)
Unlike Sassoon at this time, he had a standpoint—the religious—from which to
launch such confident attacks.

There is, therefore, in the most satirical of these poems, no control-
ling attitude and no sustained attack. But Sassoon's use of the term
"satirical" comprehends a wide range, which takes into account, not
only public abuses and social follies, but also himself as characterizing
limited, often ridiculous, humanity. Signs of this have already been
noted: the diffidence, the inclination to express a qualifying judgment
or—an allied symptom—to press the adverse one too clumsily. This
uncertain attitude yields more positive results in a number of very
individual poems where, instead of standing back to pontificate, he
sketches an ironic picture of man's pretensions, often putting himself
inside it as the typical absurd figure—a strange humility in the
satirist. These poems are effortlessly controlled, simply because he can,
without violating the slightest moral scruple, view himself and his
doings ironically. The very role of the satirist is, as we have seen, held
tentatively: "While roaming in the Villa d'Este Gardens/I felt like
that ... and fumbled for my note-book" ('Villa d'Este Gardens').
He may represent himself as modern urban man, seemingly self-
sufficient, impervious to the uncontrollable elements that batter at the
confines of his orderly desert:

> A sallow waiter brings me beans and pork . . .
> Outside there's fury in the firmament.
> Ice-cream, of course, will follow; and I'm content.
> O Babylon! O Carthage! O New York!

> ('Storm on Fifth Avenue')[11]

Or, in similar vein, he presents us ingeniously explaining our existence,
then quietly punctures our pretensions:

> Beyond the college garden something glinted;
> A copper moon climbed clear above black trees.
> Some Lydian coin? . . . Professor Brown agrees
> That copper coins *were* in that Culture minted.
> But, as her whitening way aloft she took,
> I thought she had a pre-dynastic look.

> ('Early Chronology')

11. It is noteworthy that in *The Mercury Book of Verse* (1931) which contains a
selection of poems published in *The London Mercury*, 1919-30, 'Storm on Fifth
Avenue' is the only poem containing material drawn from the contemporary
world. The anthology also contains poems by such poets as Chesterton, Davies,
de la Mare, W. W. Gibson and J. C. Squire, but none by Eliot, Pound or Lawrence.
In his willingness to turn to the modern world for material Sassoon stands closer
at this time to the 'modernist' poets, though in the forms he employs (rhyming
decasyllabics and, occasionally, blank verse) he belongs undeviatingly with the
'traditionalists'.

—the Professor continues unaware of the mischievous analogy made
by the ironic observer, as if he were glibly classifying the moon; the
poet's voice is that of the sceptical plain man. But he is still part of
the audience: as he is again, now plumb in the centre, in 'In the Turner
Rooms':

> Bold
> With pursuance of the encharioted Sublime,
> I set my brains to work till closing-time;

and, in 'Evensong in Westminster Abbey',

> Ferrying through vaulted sanctuaries a head
> Calm, vesper-tolling, and subdued to shed
> Gross thoughts and sabbatize the intemperate husk.

In both cases we are presented with an ordinary, confused figure—the
conscientious worker-poet, determined to do Turner justice, the humdrum human being aspiring to spirituality—diminished by contrast
with the greatness he moves amongst and vainly seeks to grasp (the
'sounding terms' in the second quotation weigh him down ludicrously).
Sassoon is intrigued—and delighted—by his own absurdity, equally
with that of others:

> My music-loving Self this afternoon
> (Clothed in the gilded surname of Sassoon)
> Squats in the packed Sheldonian and observes . . .

observes a sweating, self-important collection of "cultured mammals"
(which cannot help, despite its soulful pretensions, being animal) and
reflects mischievously upon their mutual doom:

> Meanwhile, in Oxford sunshine out of doors,
> Birds in collegiate gardens rhapsodise
> Antediluvian airs of worm-thanksgiving.
> To them the austere and buried Bach replies
> With song that from ecclesiasmus cries
> Eternal *Resurrexit* to the living.

A mischievous, not a misanthropic, fancy; this is far from being the
voice of Swift. However ironically the performance may be viewed as
an optimistic human exercise, the poet too is carried away—"And
Benedictus sings my heart to Me" ('Sheldonian Soliloquy').

None of the poems in which Sassoon has depicted himself could alienate, chiefly because he has implicated himself in the human comedy: it is *amiable* satire—if, indeed, it merits the name—that prompts no sharper response than a rueful smile. His satirical country is truly what Professor Sutherland aptly calls "the no-man's land of the ironical".[12] This, not the war satire, typifies his normal self.

We discover also in these poems the lighter side of the radical re-appraisal of self which eventually supersedes his anatomizing of the world. It is revealing that he should append in the Second Edition of *Satirical Poems* (in 1933), not only the sceptical picture of achieved Socialism, 'The Utopian Times', but also two highly personal pieces whose inclusion stretches the meaning of "satirical" to the utmost. However, as rueful commentaries upon his unsettled condition of mind, 'The Facts' and 'The Traveller to His Soul' provide a valuable gloss upon his decline as a satirist. In 'The Facts', dated 1932, he ironic-ally juxtaposes his own case with those of Swift and Shakespeare:

> Oblivion was the only epitaph
> They asked, as private persons, having eased
> Their spirits of the burden that they bore.
>
> The facts of life are fierce. One feels a wraith
> When facing them with luminous lyric faith.

He craves a more substantial defence against "the jungle"—both within and without—"In this thought-riddled twentieth-century day" than the fragile power of poetry. 'The Traveller to His Soul" dated a year later, presents the issue in more precise terms:

> That problem which concerns me most—about
> Which I have entertained the gravest doubt—
> Is, bluntly stated, "Have I got a soul?"

He speculates upon this question in a quizzical, non-committal tone that dominates the first part of the poem; he banters with the soul:

> "O Soul, consider what you are," I say;
> "How seldom you exert your white authority
> On the bemused and sense-instructed way
> In which your apparatus spends his day"

12. *English Satire*, 1958, p. 77.

—and one wonders how seriously the matter concerns him. But the last two stanzas are serious enough:

> Souls have their Sunday morning, belled and bright;
> And in the night they move in landless light.
> (Skulls thus affirm their legend.) Souls arise
> Through flames of martyrdom, absolved and wise,
> And those who moved in gloom regain their sight.

There are strong echoes of the other-worldly imagery of Vaughan: "I saw Eternity the other night/Like a great Ring of pure and endless light,/All calm, as it was bright," ('The World') and "Should poor souls fear a shade or night,/Who came (sure) from a sea of light?" ('The Water-fall').[13] But Vaughan's "soulhood" is as yet only intellectually realised, albeit the heart is moved by it. He quotes Descartes' "The starry heavens above me ..." as inspiration to head and heart to "feel aware of wings/And soaring Gothic-aisled imaginings," but must end with the wistful query, "Soul, will you feel like that when I am dead?" Heart and head are willing, but not prepared: there is a disjunction between them and the soul.

   In spirit, if not altogether in tone, 'The Traveller to His Soul' belongs with *The Heart's Journey* and *Vigils*, but it is fitting to note it here as serving to illustrate the introspective concern toward which Sassoon had been moving throughout the nineteen-twenties. It defines the central "problem" which becomes his predominant theme in the years to come, rendering the satirical impulse, never strong in the absence of clearly defined targets, practically nugatory. The failure of *The Road to Ruin* is sad witness to this.

§ 2 *The Road to Ruin*

The Road to Ruin was published (in 1933) in its original form as a group of seven poems in which Sassoon rehearses[14] the dictum of Wilfred Owen: "All a poet can do today is warn." These poems, together with six later pieces, cover the vital pre-war period between 1933 and 1939. They prompt sad reflections upon the nature and the possibilities of

13. Quotations from Vaughan are as printed in *Vaughan's Works*, Ed. L. C. Martin (2nd Edition, Oxford, 1963). The spelling has not been altered.
14. 'Rehearses' in that Owen's 'today' referred to the time of war in which he was inextricably involved: we do not know what more he might have done 'tomorrow'.

Owen's "all". Their very manner seems to betray a depressed awareness of prophesying in the void. At least Sassoon *can* be single-minded
where the alternatives of peace and war are concerned, but only two
poems have real force; the remainder reveal an acute sense of strain,
of labouring wearily under a disillusioned certainty of the unregenerate
nature of man. His is the irascible voice of the Old Testament prophet,
and by it one is reminded forcibly of his half-Jewish ancestry.

The prefatory verses set the governing tone, a premonition of inevitable disaster. The prophet's voice begins thin and sad: "My hopes,
my messengers I sent/Across the ten years continent/Of Time." Time
passes, while "Like one in purgatory, I learned/The loss of hope."
But then a ghost struggles back to gasp out "from an agony of death,/
'No, not that way; no, not that way'." This is the burden of Sassoon's
warning—and this in itself is much, when reinforced by such poems as
'An Unveiling'. But what strikes the reader thirty years later, when
considering nine poems on the theme, is the abstract nature of the
warning. It lacks substance: timely though it is, there is no incisive
judgment or exposure of the contemporary symptoms and manifestations of approaching war.

Is there, in 'At The Cenotaph', a reference to the severity of the
peace terms imposed upon Germany at Versailles—"Lift up their
hearts in large destructive lust;/And crown their heads with blind
vindictive Peace"? Yet, if there is, who are guilty of "Men's biologic
urge to readjust/The Map of Europe"—the Allies, Germany, or
both? The attack is too sweeping; it is no more telling than its mouthpiece, the pasteboard figure of the Prince of Darkness, cloaked and
saturnine, complete with Mephistophelian laugh.

'Mimic Warfare' at first prompts more disturbing thought, rather
about the true meaning of war itself than about the imminence of war.
But the irony upon the grim earnest underlying the 'war-game' is not
sustained, and in the middle breaks down into explicit statement:

> Meanwhile in summer sunlight no one's finding
> Cause to disparage these unconscious provers
> Of nations pledged to war's traditional crimes.

As in the first poem, war is envisaged as a form of original sin to which
man is bound to turn, sooner or later: how constructive is it to assert
this, to generalize about "biologic urges" and neglect to anatomize
immediate causes? Could such satire serve any useful purpose, unless
it were to point little more than a conventional platitude?

Less generalized is the message of 'News from the War-After-Next', which was doubtless inspired by Hitler's accession to full power in January, 1933 (the poem was first published in the following March), but the impact is weakened by the use of a stilted Old Testament vocabulary. Phrases like "the creed of Anti-Christ", "Beelzebub's Cathedral", "Moloch willing" smother the sense of an immediate reality, not sharpen it. Even the construction falters; the final clause hangs listlessly in,

> we are pledged to live
> With Violence, Greed, and Ignorance as those in
> Controllership of Life.

The final couplet, burdened with the biblical, is wooden, the allegory too obvious to be worthwhile: "Thus, Moloch willing, we inaugurate/ A super-savage Mammonistic State." Whatever his primary intentions, T. S. Eliot's 'Triumphal March' (of the previous year), with its evocation of the appeal of the all-encompassing, all-redeeming Leader, far more subtly elicited the spirit of Nazi Germany: beside this poem, Sassoon's seems ingenuous.

'A Premonition' and 'The Ultimate Atrocity' warn that another war will destroy the laboriously constructed values of European civilization The latter poem is a plain, sober warning—there is no irony—that "The first bacterial bomb" will utterly destroy "the aspirations of the dead," of those "In whom the world's redemption dreamed and died— /To whom the vision of perfection came." A similar message is conveyed more forcefully in 'A Premonition', where the poetic imagination calls up a compelling picture of such destruction. "A gas-proof ghost", the poet leaves "the stilled/Disaster of Trafalgar Square" and enters the National Gallery to learn what has become of "time's eternities". He finds, we are told with laconic irony, "The claim/Of Art was disallowed": the gas knows no respect and is "tarnishing each gilded frame"; the Virgin of the Rocks may still dream "the secure/Apocalypse of peace"—a telling phrase—but, like many a dream, it lies under the doom of reality. The war to come will refute the old consolation, "Ars longa, vita brevis". This poem, unlike the others so far considered, succeeds by leaving much unsaid.

The most trenchant poem is the caustically ironic 'An Unveiling'. Here, Sassoon recaptures the tone and method of "'They'" and sustains it to the end. He parodies a future President's oration in honour of "London's war-gassed victims", endowing the clichés inseparable from such performances with bizarre irony: "We are part of them, and they of us"; "all did what/They could, who stood like warriors at their post/ (Even when too young to walk)"—a Byronic parenthesis. The number of victims is stated with a proud emphasis upon its impressive size: "'We honour here' (he paused) 'our Million Dead'," who "Are now forever London.'" In its barren futility, the memorial recalls that of 'Menin Gate' and bleakly inaugurates a gas-choked future:

> 'Our bequest
> Is to rebuild, for What-they-died-for's sake,
> A bomb-proof roofed Metropolis, and to make
> Gas-drill compulsory. *Dulce et decorum est . . .*'

The echoes of Owen and Brooke contribute to the impression of a monstrous perversion of human attitudes: this is a vision of an insanely war-engrossed puppet world, mimicking the old humanity. It is still disturbingly prophetic, more so today than when it was first published.[15]

When *Road to Ruin* was reprinted in *Collected Poems* (1947), 'Asking For It' and 'Litany of the Lost' were added. 'Asking For It', first published in November, 1934 (in *Time and Tide*), belongs by its prophetic purpose with the original group; so also do four other satires from later volumes: 'Memorandum' and 'Babylon', both first published in 1935, from *Vigils*, and 'Silver Jubilee Celebration' and 'Ideologies', which first appeared in *Rhymed Ruminations* (1939). 'Litany of the Lost' did not appear until November, 1945, and stands as a commentary upon the predicted conflict and its aftermath.

In 'Asking For It' Sassoon aims at too many targets and hits none cleanly. At one moment he seems to be attacking the misgovernment that allowed the drift into war—"Lord God of block-heads, bombing-planes, and bungle"; the next he castigates the deliberate aggressor— "Perfect in us thy tyrannous technique/For torturing the innocent and weak"; finally, with "Grant us the power to prove, by poison gases,/ The needlessness of *shedding* human blood," he indicts (with little finesse) a vein of hypocrisy that, where methods of waging war are concerned, can scarcely lie down with either "bungle" or "randomized damnations indefensible". One wonders whether the action of Nazi Germany in breaking off the Disarmament Conference at Geneva in

15. This poem alone merits the large praise Joseph Cohen accords *The Road to Ruin* as a whole, when he says Sassoon "was playing masterfully a rôle he had determined for himself years before", i.e. that of angry prophet (*Tulane Studies in English*, Vol. VII, 1957, p. 178.)

October, 1933, was the direct inspiration for this, but clearly Germany is not the sole target. Despite the apparent confusion, there is surely only one: Modern Man, still unregenerate, still the jungle beast.

'Memorandum', sub-titled 'Sonnet for Statesmen', is significant for its non-committal reference to the likelihood of God's existence— "If there should be some Power ensphered in light …". Again Sassoon comments in an abstract, rhetorical fashion upon sinful man, immersing the present in a homily upon man's inborn waywardness. 'Babylon' is another biblical allegory of man's pride and fall:

> Babylon the merciless, now a name of doom,
> Built towers in Time, as we today, for whom
> Auguries of self-annihilation loom.

Whatever its general truth, so conventional an analogy has little power to stir or illuminate.

In 'Silver Jubilee Celebration', on the other hand, he takes a concrete occasion that invites satire and draws out something of his old bitterness. It was, perhaps, in 1935, no very unrealistic piece of pacifism to inveigh against Kipling's anti-German speech and his exhortation to re-arm. Sassoon's indignation arises from the disillusioned perception that the only ideal the world he welcomed in 'Everyone Sang' has proved able to offer its youth is 'Arm or perish'. Since this is the case, let us have no cant, but openly confess what creed we live by:

> Let us at least be candid with the world
> And stitch across each Union Jack unfurled
> "No bargain struck with Potsdam is put over
> Unless well backed by bombers—and Jehovah!"

This is a racy, sarcastic poem; with a well-defined target to aim at, Sassoon still has the power to wound. But it reflects an emotional reaction rather than a consistent point of view, for years later we find him "preening" himself "on having printed in 1935 a poem in which I described the Nazi régime as 'a creed of crime'", and wondering why the politicians took so long to realize this.[16] The poem referred to is 'On Edington Hill', first published in *The Spectator*, November 22, 1935; 'Silver Jubilee Celebration' was not published till 1939. In

16. Letter to Sir S. C. Cockerell, May 7, 1945, op. cit. p. 154.

1940, with 'The English Spirit', he was of course to assume the mantle of Kipling himself.

Whatever the strength of his feeling against Nazism, in 'Ideologies' he generalizes again, employing the Swiftian analogy between man and monkey; the man-monkey has his clever ideas, but has not yet "learnt to make his mind"; meanwhile his works, the only tangible evidence of these ideas, decay beneath enduring Nature: "where Babels once were built we find/A spider in his web among the weeds."

The uncompromising picture of Fallen Man is preserved, hardened indeed by the experience of the past war and the prospect of a worse one, in 'Litany of the Lost'—a revealing title. Man is now straight-forwardly presented as fallen—"unregenerate still in head and heart" —and is characterized with lofty pity:

> World masterers with a foolish frightened face;
> Loud speakers, leaderless and sceptic-souled;
> Aeroplane angels, crashed from glory and grace.

He is reduced to Yahoo level, "Armed with our marvellous monkey innovations." Only by facing this truth and confessing to his deep imperfections and presumption, can he be delivered. The refrain "Deliver us from ourselves," though it carries the same burden as Milton's "Thy self not free, but to thy self enthrall'd," is chanted to no defined Being: in an Age of Unbelief this petition has a forlorn ring.

The forlornness is the poet's own: "My hopes, my messengers I sent"—hopes, rather than any positive conviction or antidote. That Sassoon seems inclined to adopt a somewhat Calvinistic view of man's crimes is evident from the biblical allegorizing—but this has only negative value, its effect is mechanical. Hampered by a profound sense of his own unworthiness (evident in the contemporary *Vigils*), he is not yet fully prepared to preach from a positive Christian position, unlike the younger religious poet, David Gascoyne, for example, in his long poem 'Miserere':

> Here is the hill
> Made ghastly by His spattered blood,
>
> Whereon He hangs and suffers still:
> See, the centurions wear riding-boots,
> Black shirts and badges and peaked caps,
> Greet one another with raised-arm salutes;
> They have cold eyes, unsmiling lips;
> Yet these His brothers know not what they do.[17]

17. *Poems 1937-1942* (1943).

Neither is he able to offer an alternative *of this world*, such as the Christian-flavoured Socialism espoused at that time by Spender and C. Day Lewis:

> Comrades, my tongue can speak
> No comfortable words,
> Calls to a forlorn hope,
> Gives work and not rewards.[18]

He has definite attitudes—a hatred of war, of man's inhumanity, of the hypocrisy of leaders—which do furnish two powerful satires against cant, 'An Unveiling' and 'Silver Jubilee', but these are primarily emotional. As in *Satirical Poems*, lacking a constructive standpoint (for pacificism alone is not enough), he damns the symptoms of modern degeneracy without probing the causes, and without offering more to counter them than the impotent anger of the disillusioned idealist. He is a prophet only in the old-fashioned sense: of a vaguely defined impending doom, no more.[19]

It is in the failure of this small group of poems especially that we see crystallised the reason why Sassoon was not an influence upon the 'Thirties poets, despite the fact that his rôle as war poet might have seemed to elect him for a peace-time one akin to that which related Hardy to the Georgians: it is that he is still the sad prisoner of the War, whose fair outside he had, ironically, destroyed. Not having discovered the means of his own release (he has to wait another twenty years to point the 'Path to Peace'), he cannot show the way for others.

His chief concern for the past twenty years, between the wars, had been the slow healing of the scars left by his war experience. This he had accomplished, creatively, in two ways: by withdrawing into his own earliest years, reliving them, finding in the process a healing power, and by a complementary endeavour in his *Memoirs* to re-enact his harshest experiences, seeking to give them emotional coherence and wider significance. This preoccupation involved a with-

18. 'The Magnetic Mountain', 24. (1933).
19. Briefly referring to *The Road to Ruin* in *Scrutiny* (June 1934), F. R. Leavis seems to have found similar fault with it: it showed, he thought, that Sassoon was not amongst those "expressing sensibilities of our time in verse", though, he added darkly, these poems have "in certain social *milieux*, their function." (This comment is chiefly remarkable as representing the only review of Sassoon's work to have appeared in *Scrutiny*.)

drawal from the rôle of public poet which he had tenuously sustained
in his post-war satirical writing: it is significant that the *Memoirs of a
Fox-Hunting Man* were begun in 1926, the year when the first collection
of 'Satirical Poems' appeared—and little more satire was to follow.
It also involved, as we shall see, an understandable tendency to idealise
the pre-War period, particularly apparent in the first two volumes of
'straight' autobiography and the nostalgic poetry of *Rhymed Ruminations*:
none of this would endear him to a generation reacting to fresh
challenges at home and in Europe. But in this process of retrospective
self-exploration Sassoon's George Sherston becomes the representative
figure of a lost generation and a lost world and its values. It is in his
prose, not in his poetry, that the memorable achievement of Sassoon's
middle years lies.

PART II

PEACE AND WAR RECAPTURED

THE SHERSTON TRILOGY (I)

Memoirs of a Fox-Hunting Man, Sassoon's first prose work, is also the one by which he is best known: "The peg," as he himself puts it, "on which my popular reputation finally suspended itself."[1] The idea for the book appears to have arisen from a suggestion made to the author by Sir Edmund Gosse that he should undertake a long poem which would give body to his reputation. "He suggested that I might draw on my sporting experiences for typical country figures—the squire, the doctor, the parson, and so on;" at the time this had not appealed to Sassoon who "believed that [he] ought to address the age on more startling and momentous themes," but the work that appeared some ten years later "was essentially in accordance with his [Gosse's] advice."[2]

It is perhaps as well that Sassoon followed Gosse's advice only so far as the subject-matter was concerned. A long poem using the same material would not, however well executed, have reached a fraction of the audience earnt by *A Fox-Hunting Man*.[3]

It was, writes Edmund Blunden, "a prose work acclaimed every-where."[4] It is one of those rare books which have a universal appeal in the sense that they please both the casual or amateurish reader and the literary expert. It appeals, as Blunden goes on to note, to "two races of men—those who did not catch its subtler beckonings, and those who did." It is tempting to try to account for so widespread a popu-larity, but for such a phenomenon there can be no single, inclusive

---

1. *S. J.*, p. 101.
2. Ibid, pp. 100-101.
3. Since its original publication on September 28th, 1928, it has appeared in eight English editions of various kinds (including a "School Edition"), with sales which must by now have reached 200,000. It also earnt Sassoon the Hawthornden Prize for 1928 and the James Tait Black Memorial Prize—aids to an international reputation and thus to a large printing (16,875 copies) in the United States (1929) and to translations into French, Swedish and German.
4. *Edmund Blunden, A Selection of His Poetry and Prose*, p. 311.

explanation. One can imagine why a book which looked back with such poetic evocativeness to a world obliterated by the First War should appeal to the peace-weary Englishmen of the late 1920s, fatigued by the struggles between class and class, between the trades unions and the government, and disillusioned by the disunity of the League of Nations. *A Fox-Hunting Man* was relaxing, too, after the astringent satire of a novel by Huxley or Waugh. It took the yearning reader back to an ideal rustic life where everyone was in his place and was, moreover, happy with his place (for young George's relationship with Dixon is as refreshingly human as the young Osbert Sitwell's with his father's butler, Henry Moat). Yet it would be superficial to dismiss the book as mere escapism, though there can be no doubt that Sassoon himself found escape—of a kind—in writing it; but it is no enchanted flight into the past.

Sassoon, in a retrospective piece written in 1946, recalls the feelings he experienced when writing *A Fox-Hunting Man*. This piece is worth quoting at some length for its deceptively pleasing expression not only of the feelings the writer had during composition but also as being representative of those which many of his readers—of his own generation especially—must have experienced in their enjoyment of the book; one says "deceptively pleasing" because Sassoon conveys here, too, hints of the unease which casts a faint shadow even upon some of the brightest passages:

I can claim, he writes, to have been one of the earliest authors to demonstrate that it [the period the book covers, roughly 1896-1915] was good literary material, and that the remembering of its remoteness was enjoyable. When, in 1926, I began to write *Memoirs of a Fox-Hunting Man*, I surprised myself by discovering that 1896 felt as though it were much more than thirty years ago. This, though it can hardly be described as a spectacular achievement, afforded me much intimate felicity. "Ten miles was a long way when I was a child," I wrote, and the thought produced a delicious thrill of enchantment. For the nineties had acquired an idyllic flavour. Recreating them was almost like reading *Cranford* or the 'Barchester' novels. They were as far away as the boyhood of Richard Feverel. Stabilized and detached, the past had become a charmingly perspectived late-Victorian picture. How happily humdrum, how exquisitely unperturbed by innovations it all seemed when reflected in the mirror of memory. Time went as slowly as the carrier's van that brought the parcels from the station, and international events were comfortably epitomised in the weekly cartoons of *Punch*. France was a lady in a short skirt, Russia a bear, and the performances of the county cricket team more important than either of them . . .[5]

The remembered qualities of this early world have a perennial appeal: the Arcadian remoteness, free from the pressing events that make time burdensome, free from "innovations" whose unfamiliarity disrupts the settled process of life and destroys our sense of continuity. Most of us desire "an intensely local and limited world", as Sassoon points out, though we would differ as to how we would wish it to be composed.[6]

Yet Sassoon has not simply indulged himself with remembrance of this world but has shown how it ultimately proves too limited for Sherston because, again like most of us, he has the nagging itch to 'do' which at first makes him uneasily conscious of the aimlessness of his youth and at last finds its outlet under the pressure of shocking events. Not for him the placid—and stable—satisfactions of the Aunt Evelyns of this idyll. Aunt Evelyn is sketched—and fixed—for us (together with many of her generation) in the first few pages: "She was fond of her two Persian cats, busied herself sensibly with her garden, and was charitably interested in the old and rheumatic inhabitants of the village. Beyond this, the radius of her activities extended no further than the eight or ten miles which she could cover in a four-wheeled dogcart driven by Tom Dixon, the groom. The rest of the world was what she described as 'beyond calling distance'". Her "social code" is equally an anachronism, "which divided the world into people whom one could 'call on' and people who were 'socially impossible'." A character like this might have stepped out of a 'Barsetshire' novel.[7]

5. *The Saturday Book Sixth Year* (1946), quoted in Keynes' *Bibliography*, p. 73. (Sir Osbert Sitwell, also looking back to late-Victorian and Edwardian England, views the period as being similarly "stabilized and detached": "Looking back at it was like regarding some previous existence of which we had once been part." *The Scarlet Tree*, 1946, p. 197).
6. "I wanted to be strongly connected with the hunting organism . . . And it was (though a limited one) a clearly defined world, which is an idea that most of us cling to, unless we happen to be transcendental thinkers" (*M.F.H.*, 'Faber Library' edition 1936, p. 227). In the remainder of this chapter, most of the quotations from *M.F.H.* are given without footnote references; for full references, see 'Page References', p. 307. Quotations from other books are, of course, clearly distinguished.
7. There is a family resemblance to Lady Lufton, of whom Trollope writes: "She liked cheerful, quiet well-to-do people, who loved their Church, their country, and their Queen, and who were not too anxious to make a noise in the world. She desired . . . that all the old women should have warm flannel petticoats, that the working men should be saved from rheumatism by healthy food and dry houses, that they should all be obedient to their pastors and masters—temporal as well as spiritual" (*Framley Parsonage*).

And so might several others, aristocratic, squirearchical or ecclesiastical in this book. The resemblance is not accidental, as the reference to the Barsetshire novels in Sassoon's reminiscences about writing *A Fox-Hunting Man* indicates.

Most of the people who hunt or bat in this idyll are 'flat' characters. The major exception is the hero, George Sherston. He alone is shown in the round: his reaction to the life he leads and has led becomes increasingly ambivalent, his dissatisfactions grow, he moves towards maturity. The other characters have, at best, supporting rôles: like Aunt Evelyn, as she is described for us at the outset, they cannot develop—they are immutably fixed in the period the War extinguishes and leaves behind.

Sherston is a germ of individuality and sensitivity that works with a growing irritant power to taint the "idyllic flavour" of the life he leads. It needs no stirring international events, no noisy scientific inventions to cast a shadow over the pastoral. The aimless youth that is Sherston does this. He is presented to us in such a way by the older, wiser Sherston that, to adapt a phrase of Coleridge's, we criticize him for he criticizes himself—and, in so doing, we criticize (perhaps more than Sassoon would wish) the way of life to which he so uncertainly belongs. So amiably, however, is this limited world presented to us, and so delicately are the strands of the older Sherston's thoughts woven into the narrative—there is no bitterness, no knowing hindsight—that the total effect is a complex one. It is the hero who both makes and breaks the idyll for us: but for him we might perhaps convert it into an escapist Arcadia, but he is too much like ourselves and will not allow it. He is convincing and complex, a remarkably skilful transmutation of Sassoon's youthful experience.

The Hero

It would be a disservice to Sassoon to give the idyllic quality of *A Fox-Hunting Man* primary emphasis. The book is an integral part of a trilogy and its artistic effect depends primarily on the successful delineation of George Sherston's development from the aimless young hedonist of this book into the compassionate and anguished figure we find in *Memoirs of an Infantry Officer* and *Sherston's Progress*. He is the refined product of an outmoded way of life exposed to the harsh tests of a new epoch.

Though one may be tempted at first to follow Sassoon in his description of the hero as "a simplified version of my outdoor self,"[8] too great an emphasis on the element of simplification would have destroyed the artistic continuity of Sherston's development throughout the three volumes. Certainly Sassoon ran the risk of doing so when he chose for his hero "an active young man who asks nothing more of life than twelve hundred a year and four days a week with the Packlestone". The mental condition of such a young man, as he observes through his mouthpiece, the reminiscent Sherston, "is perhaps not easy to defend". Sensibly, he makes no attempt to defend it.

There are two Sherstons in the book: the narrator—the older, wiser Sherston—looks back with a tolerant eye upon the younger, whom we can only see through this eye. It is essential that there should be no refraction: that the narrator and the youth from whom he develops should be more than cousins. The older Sherston is certainly sympathetic. In sensitivity in human relationships he compensates for the thoughtlessness of youth; thus, when the triumphant George basks in the glory of having won the Colonel's Cup, we are reminded: "And Miriam served the dinner with the tired face of a saint that seemed lit with foreknowledge of her ultimate reward. But at that time I didn't know what her goodness meant." This youthful insensitivity to others' feelings is again pointed out and compensated for in relation to Sherston's hunting activities. After the Coshford Stag Hunt Sherston merely notes in his dairy that the stag, Miss Masterful, was 'taken'. In what manner he does not say, but he complains that it rains on the way home, causing him some discomfort. "It may also be inferred," adds the older Sherston, "that poor Miss Masterful sweated and shivered in the barn with heaving sides and frightened eyes. It did not occur to me to sympathize with her as I stood at the entrance to watch them tie her up." Engaging, too, is the narrator's affection for people: from his insight into the pathetic mechanics of Colonel Hesmon's existence to his comradely affection for his groom, Dixon, or for the more distantly known village cricketers, with "shy solemnity in [their] faces".

But it is not enough that we should respond to the narrator's maturer sympathies. We need, too, to be able to share his tolerant attitude towards his younger self: "As I remember and write, I grin, but not unkindly, at my distant and callow self and the absurdities which con-

8. *S.J.*, p. 169.

stitute his chronicle." Can we "grin, but not unkindly" at the activities
of this selfish, self-centred, barbarous young philistine? If this were all,
we could not. But it is not all: young Sherston has many good, even
endearing, qualities, the seeds of his future self.

The young George Sherston epitomises unawakened youth. Psychologically, he suffers from that most universal of youthful disabilities
—an inferiority complex. Socially, his aspirations are inevitably limited
within an idle, pleasure-loving sphere: "Fantasies of polite society swept
through me in wave on wave of secret snobbishness ... I never doubted
the authenticity of those enjoyments ... It was the spectacle of vivid life,
and I was young to it."

We see him from the very beginning striving to overcome his psychological disability in the face of this world into which the vicariously
ambitious Dixon guides him. At his first meet he is made bitterly aware
of his own shortcomings when contrasted with the capable and cool
young Milden. But he has reserves of grit, a basic capacity for muddling
through which earns in the end the Master's praise: "he's quite a
young thruster". This quality is again shown when he reaches the
apogee of his riding career—winning the Colonel's Cup. It sets the
seal upon his doings in this limited world; it proves that he can master
himself and his most treacherous feelings, and this is no despicable
quality. But one feels that it is wasted in such a world—though this
would be a pointless comment if Sherston possessed nothing more
refined than grit and determination, and no possibility of love more
powerful than that for his horse.

It is precisely because this is not so; because his sporting life is only
a phase, albeit a very useful one, in the development of character that
Sherston provides a deeper interest than do the characters amongst
whom he moves. Fortunately, Sassoon has bestowed upon Sherston
enough of the endearing traits of his own character to enable us to
extend both tolerance and sympathy toward the unawakened youth.
Though Sherston occasionally comes close to alienating the sympathetic reader (as sometimes does Sassoon in his own voice) by flaunting
his philistinism in such asides as "I have never cared greatly about
highly sophisticated persons, although some of them may seek to en-
large their intellectual experience by perusing my modest narrative",
this note neither obtrudes nor convinces. For Sherston, however much
he may alienate us, does so largely because we realize that he has the
potentiality for better things. Doubtless many readers have afforded

Sherston tolerance because he is a youth—tentative, fumbling, hyper-sensitive to others' opinions, but with a stubborn and courageous streak when 'up against it'—with whom they can readily identify themselves. But there is more than this, although it must be conceded that in stripping Sherston, above all, of his own poetic aspirations, Sassoon has left him virtually uncultivated and apparently less sensi-tive. Whatever may be lost here is gained in the presentation of a more convincing 'ordinary man'—so far as many readers would be con-cerned. Nevertheless, Sherston is no ordinary 'fox-hunting man'. He is repelled by the typical 'blood', like Croplady and Jaggett, who "took no interest in anything except horses and hunting and it was difficult to believe that he had ever learnt to read or write".[9] Even if his own diversions are not of the most exalted kind, this is chiefly for the want of stimulation. As a child, he is imaginative and responsive to his surroundings. He creates for himself a "dream friend" to supply the want of brothers or friends. He has a sense of wonder: "I felt that almost anything might happen in a world which could show me twenty hop-kilns neatly arranged in one field." This element of sensitivity is one which he must learn to mask, if not crush, in the world he tries to enter. It betrays him at his first hunt when his instinctive reaction is a concern for the safety of the fox. He sits beside Denis Milden when the fox appears near them and looks at him with "human alertness":

Why I should have behaved as I did I will not attempt to explain, but when Denis stood up in the stirrups and emitted a shrill "Huick-holler", I felt spontaneously alarmed for the future of the fox.

"Don't do that; they'll catch him!" I exclaimed.

The words were no sooner out of my mouth than I knew I had made another fool of myself.

Dixon reproves him for this afterwards and tells him Milden, upon whom he had hoped to model himself, must have thought him "a regular booby"; young George promises "to be more careful in future". And, of course, he is more careful—with such success that he is even-tually able, as we have seen, to watch the terrified stag with equanimity,

9. Sherston may seem little better: "I esteemed books mostly for their outsides" (p. 94). But this *is* a beginning—common enough even amongst those who develop an absorbing interest in their insides.

and to dissemble his feelings at the digging-out of a leash of fox-cubs — ''for whom, to tell the truth, I felt an unconfessed sympathy''. And how many hard-bitten hunting men would dream about talking horses?

The more sensitive side is only dormant, or it emerges elsewhere. Above all, it appears in his love for the countryside: "I loved the early morning" are words that begin the most idyllic nature description in the book (pp. 55-6). At first this love is vague; it crystallizes slowly: "I was lazily aware through my dreaming and unobservant eyes that this was the sort of world I wanted. For it was my own countryside, and I loved it with an intimate feeling, though all its associations were crude and incoherent." His claim to this countryside is largely a sentiment; it is associated for him with an unattainable, rooted way of life which, because he is neither rich nor poor enough, he cannot share: "I was conscious of having no genuine connection with the countryside. Other people owned estates, or rented farms, or did something countrified; but I only walked along the roads or took furtive short cuts across the fields ... So I went mooning, more and more moodily, about the looming countryside ..." He fancies how pleasant it would have been to live a Cathedral Close life, as in a Trollope novel, "comfortable and old-fashioned." What he has not yet realized is that he loves this countryside for itself; youth does not count the nearest blessings. He finds another outlet for his emotions in the enjoyment of music (a pleasure he shares with his creator). His attendance at his first Kreisler concert affects him so strongly that "I knew then, as I had never known before, that such music was more satisfying than the huntsman's horn," but he is not wholly ready for it, his priorities are unformed: "On my way home in the train my thoughts were equally divided between the Kreisler concert and my new hunting things. Probably my new boots got the best of it." Such moments are few and, of course, not final. It is seldom, when involved in it, that he questions his way of life—as when, for example, during the sermon in Hoadley Church, reflection half-heartedly attempts to break through: "But who was I, and what on earth had I been doing?" This questioning is left to the older Sherston, but the potentiality for it is shown to exist in the younger. That it exists side by side with selfishness, self-centredness, callousness and irresponsibility is perfectly consistent with a true portrayal of youth. The important thing is that it should exist.

In the last two chapters of the book Sherston is torn out of his limited world and exposed to the shock of separation and of death in a world

full of bitter contrasts with the old one. His better self is forced into
contact with a new reality and he rapidly develops a heightened awareness: "Never before had I known how much I had to lose. Never before
had I looked at the living world with any degree of intensity. It seemed
almost as if I had been waiting for this thing to happen ..." One of the
first manifestations of this is his awareness of the value of close human
relationships, as shown in his new valuation of Aunt Evelyn—"My
sympathetic feeling for her now was, perhaps, the beginning of my
emancipation from the egotism of youth"—and in his first realization
of the meaning of death, brought home to him in the early deaths,
first of Stephen Colwood and soon afterwards of Dick Tiltwood. These
deaths and the appalling conditions of the Front Line into which he is
thrown give his mind a severe jolt. On the one hand, he begins to
question the old, easy assumptions about patriotism and Christianity
—though he is defensively sceptical about "the blue-blooded upper
ten's" responsibility for the war as explained to him by Joe Dottrell;
on the other, he is drawn towards an emotional escape through heroic
action, a kind of 'peace' from irresponsibility, which is given an edge
by the death of Dick Tiltwood: "I went up to the trenches with the
intention of trying to kill someone". The confused moralities of war,
especially as is soon obvious to him in the "war-time dilemma of the
Churches", are reflected in his own muddled, inchoate mind. His
sympathies are with the men who lack even his degree of understanding
or the possibility of emotional release through glory—"where was the
glory for the obscure private?" and yet the very release he seeks involves the killing of men like those. He is not yet able to view the rights
and wrongs of war: he is still learning what matters to him, his attitude
is yet to be formed in the heat of war-experience. Meanwhile, fatalism
is the only defence: "I had more or less made up my mind to die ...
In the circumstances there didn't seem to be anything else to be done."

Our view of Sherston in this book closes with him at a pause, before
the deeper involvement that is to come. He recalls the essential elements
of the past, the permanence and beauty of the countryside, his home
and Aunt Evelyn, the carrier's van (the past is now felt to be gone forever in the final imagined farewell he gives John Homeward). At the
Front, a symbolic bird sings "beyond the splintered tree-tops." It is
Easter Sunday: "Standing in that dismal ditch, I could find no consolation in the thought that Christ had risen. I sploshed back to the
dug-out to call the others up for 'stand-to'." The immediate peril is

all-consuming, the time for profound questioning has not yet arrived. But he is emerging, albeit belatedly, into manhood, "with blank discarded youthfulness behind him."[10]

The Idyll

So far the aim has been to establish the integrity of the hero as being necessary to the appreciation of the trilogy. It is now time to consider *Memoirs of a Fox-Hunting Man* in relation to the grounds on which it has been most praised: as an evocation of a vanished way of life. "They conjure up," writes Swinnerton, "the countryside of old peaceful days."[11] David Daiches is a little more expansive: "*Memoirs of a Fox-Hunting Man* is an impressive rendering of a kind of English life that has by now almost completely passed away—that of the cultivated squirearchy in the large country-house".[12] An anonymous reviewer in *The Times Literary Supplement* offers a narrower perspective: "Edwardian life in the shires, viewed through a golden haze as an idyll of hunting and cricket."[13]

The last and most limited comment seems the most accurate. Daiches' comment is surely misleading: if 'cultivation' is concerned with the development of mind and manners, it can hardly be said that this book reveals to us at all fully the cultivated qualities of the "squirearchy in the large country-house." It gives us too one-sided a picture, a highly selective and impressionistic one, concerned almost entirely with the sporting diversions of this class. It is true that their behaviour in the hunting-field teaches us much of their manners and ways of thought—though we would have reservations about even this because of the methods of characterization employed. But when we look beyond the hunting field we have in a few characters only glimpses of this kind of English life: we see little of their intimate human relationships, inter-family or inter-class relationships, domesticities or social and cultural aspirations. This is largely because Sherston himself, who is our sole viewpoint, only makes brief excursions into this complex life beyond the confines of the hunting or cricket field. For the kind of "rendering" Daiches speaks of we should go rather to the first two

10. From 'Progressions', *C.P.* p. 253.
11. Frank Swinnerton, *The Georgian Literary Scene*, Revised Edition (1938), p. 345.
12. *The Present Age: From 1920*, p. 202.
13. *The Times Literary Supplement*, August 5, 1960, p. 498.

volumes of Sassoon's 'pure' autobiographies than to this book (using *A Fox-Hunting Man* as a valuable complement).

Few characters (other than Sherston) are seen outside the highly coloured sporting context. The general effect lies somewhere between Surtees and Trollope. Like both these nineteenth century writers Sassoon indulges in amusing caricature, clearly defining his characters and placing them in a landscape (in his case, a sporting print). But he sometimes offers more reflection upon these characters, going beyond their idiosyncrasies, than Surtees ever does, though far less upon them than Trollope. Neither, of course, does he explore complex human relationships, which exist in Trollope side by side with the behaviour of the more mechanical figures. As in Surtees, the range of characters is limited, not by their origin—we have noblemen, squires, parsons, lawyers, colonels, members of parliament, as well as ordinary country-men—but by the fact that they are almost all seen solely in relation to their sporting activities.[14] Occasionally, Sherston comes to learn more, and his close sympathy for Colonel Hesmon and Captain Huxtable, or his warm (if somewhat reticent) comradeship for Denis Milden and Stephen Colwood and his affectionate attachment to Dixon, which provides an ingratiating view of the master-servant relationship, all give a true sense of life. Glimpses of country life below the levels dictated by class are tantalisingly brief. One wishes to know more of John Homeward, the carrier ("I used to wonder what he thought about while on the road, for he had the look of a man who was cogitant rather than vegetative"), or of Joey, the flint-breaker ("he always saluted me as I passed, but I never conversed with him and he never seemed to get any older"). There must, one feels, be many a Granfer Cantle and Timothy Fairway lurking in the shadows—but that is where they remain, apart from the few, like William 'Did-I-Say-Myself' Dodd, who emerge as sharply etched white figures in the Flower Show Match. Also tantalising is the glimpse we have of such a character as the genteel Miss Clara Maskall, whose activities are anything but sporting: "the menace of Roman Catholicism was her most substantial and engrossing theme; and up to the age of ninety she continued to paste on the walls of her bed-room every article on the subject which she could find in *The Times* and the *Morning Post*."

14. The major exception is Aunt Evelyn, who, besides being the very picture of kindliness and tolerance of youth's waywardness, unconsciously provides some richly humorous passages, e.g. her eccentric tea-making ceremony in the first-class compartment of a railway carriage.

Miss Maskall, whom we only see for three short pages, has all the hues and tints of a Jane Austen character; one can imagine her sayings and doings reverberating through a dozen nervous households anxious about 'keeping up appearances.'

Sassoon is chiefly concerned, however, with the "rich-flavoured collection of characters" who compose the Ringwell—and other hunts. They are an entertaining collection enough, described with an exuberant fancy and an eye for idiosyncrasy. Their names are inevitable, for Sassoon had imbibed his Surtees (at an early age) and Trollope: thus we have Lord Dumborough, Major Gamble, Mr. Gaffikin ("effusively cheerful"), Bill Jaggett (the boor), Fred Buzzaway (the hard rider) and Sir Jocelyn Porteus-Porteous, who has a "a pompous manner".[15] Their appearance and actions are as inevitable as their names. In a context so inherently colourful Sassoon is able to obtain striking and extravagant visual effects. The young Sherston had "taken it for granted that there would be people 'in pink', but these enormous confident strangers overwhelmed my mind with the visible authenticity of their brick-red coats." And so they remain, "enormous confident strangers," Olympian figures, larger than life: from Lord Dumborough, "a tall man in a blue velvet cap and vermilion coat," with his extremely red face and bawling, constantly angry, voice—"the most terrifying man I had ever encountered"—to the "terrific 'Boots' Brownrigg," who is introduced thus:

The terrific 'Boots' Brownrigg was puffing a cigar with apparent unconcern; his black cap was well over his eyes and both hands were plunged in the pockets of a short blue overcoat; from one of the pockets protruded a short cutting whip. His boots were perfection. Spare built and middle-sized, he looked absolutely undefeatable . . .

By way of contrast, there is "Mr. Bellerby, of Cowslake Manor":

Mr. Bellerby was mounted on a fidgety, ewe-necked, weak-middled, dun-coloured mare. He had a straggling sandy beard and was untidily dressed in new clothes which looked all wrong. He seemed to have put them on in a hurry—baggy black coat half-buttoned—spurs falling back from loose-fitting patent-leather boots, starched stock with a horseshoe pin insecurely

---

15. Trollope has, for a few, The Duke of Omnium, Mr. Quiverful, Captain Culpepper, Lords Boanerges and Dumbello and Mr. Slope (ancestral name formerly spelt without an 'e'). In Surtees we find Major Bouncer, Sir Giles Nabem ("the great police magistrate"), Lord Scamperdale, Parson Blossomnose, Squire Cheatum, Mr. Bangup, Mr. Apperley Nimrod and many more.

inserted—badly cut white corduroy breeches; and an absurdly long cane hunting-crop without a thong . . . He wore moss-green worsted gloves, and his mare's bridle had a browband of yellow and black striped patent leather.

Other figures are more economically portrayed: "He was a dumpy little man with a surly red face, and he wore a coat that had once been scarlet and was now plum-coloured"; "'Where are you going now, Master?' shouted a sharp-faced man with a green collar on his cut-away coat ... Mr. Gaffikin explained that the green-collared man was a notoriously tardy and niggardly subscriber". We do not need Mr. Gaffikin's explanation: the character is implicit in the matching face and coat. We know these men by externals: Lord Dumborough by his "very red" face, Brownrigg by his boots, Mr. Bellerby by his mare— burdened with her accumulation of pejorative epithets. It is no surprise to us to learn that the "dumpy little man" is a Master whose methods of hunting are dubious; he looks seedy enough for anything. One sees each character strongly in terms of colour: an irascible red—or a deeper, saturnine variation of this —a commanding, glossy blackness, a blundering, ill-coordinated grey, a sinister green. It would be impossible for these characters to wriggle out from beneath this brush —and it is not desirable that they should.[16]

Where Sassoon describes the handful of characters with whom he wishes to do something more—to engage our sympathy—he is careful to avoid caricature. In the case of Squire Maundle, for example, one of the book's most endearing characters, he prefaces a somewhat ludicrous comparison with a typical saving clause: "Without wishing to ridicule him, for he was always kind and courteous, I may say that both his features and his tone of voice have something in common with the sheep who lift their mild munching faces to regard him while he plays an approach shot in his cautious, regular, and automatic style."

Our response to such characters as Squire Maundle, Colonel Hesmon and Captain Huxtable, whom we see outside the sporting sphere, is more complex. In them we are allowed to see something of the virtues of this "local, limited world". Simple and kindly in their personal relationships, remote from "the outside world of unfamiliar and momentous happenings", they characterize all that was best in what is often dismissed today as an age of purblind paternalism.[17] Sherston

16. Appendix A, (7).
17. More will be said about the social aspect of this world in the discussion of the first two volumes of 'pure' autobiography (Part III).

takes Captain Huxtable as "an epitome of all that was most pleasant and homely in the countryfied life for which I was proposing to risk my own":

Chairman of the local bench, Churchwarden, fond of a day's shooting with Squire Maundle, comfortably occupied with a moderate-sized farm overlooking the Weald, he was a pattern of neighbourly qualities, and there was no one with whom Aunt Evelyn more enjoyed a good gossip. Time-honoured jokes passed between them, and his manner towards her was jovial, spruce, and gallant . . . His shrewd and watchful eyes had stocked his mind with accurate knowledge of the country-side. He was, as he said himself, 'addicted to observing the habits of the rook', and he was also a keen gardener.

It is difficult to imagine how a man could do better than pursue such a life to the full.

Less sympathetic is Sir Jocelyn Porteus-Porteous, the exemplar of the ugly rich: "Unwelcome, from the picturesquely feudal point of view, were the rows of industrial habitations which had cropped up outside his grandiose gateway. These, with the unsightly colliery chimneys, were a lucrative element in his existence, since they represented mineral royalties for the owner of the estate. Nevertheless, his attitude towards such plebeian upstarts was lofty and impercipient: not having been introduced to them, he had not the pleasure of their acquaintance, so to speak." This is a rare intrusion of Sassoon's somewhat erratic social-ist sympathies: more figures such as Sir Jocelyn would have destroyed the delicate fabric of this book. We are not brought too close to the (one supposes) greedy, insensitive and irresponsible characters such as Lord Dumborough, Jaggett and the Peppermore brothers—whose "reckless, insolent, unprincipled, and aggressively competitive" qualities they are allowed to exercise only on horseback; these are properly confined to the sporting comedy of humours. It is, however, their version of this world which dominates. We see little of Captain Huxtable's way of life *in action*: admirable one supposes it to have been, in many ways, but it is allowed to come to life hardly more than Emma Woodhouse's Highbury charity.

What we have instead, to move from a consideration of character to one of the broader effects of the book, is a series of pictures and evocations of Edwardian life in the shires.[18] The abiding impression is

18. "Are not pictures and evocations better than horology? What says Tristram?—'It was sometime in the summer of that year.'" (Edmund Blunden, *Undertones of War*, World Classics Edn., 1956, p. 25).

atmospheric, not concrete. Whether in the great set pieces, like The Flower Show Match of The Colonel's Cup,[19] or in the less epic moments, Sassoon saturates his descriptions with an atmosphere of ideal rustic beauty and peace, of slow and even life, of sunshine and permanence, which conveys the sense that Osbert Sitwell puts into these words: "Nothing had happened for so long, and nothing would happen again: nothing".[20]

This sense derives chiefly from the fact that Nature (still "the un-infected green country"), rules and hers is a kindly rule, whatever the season. Memory has done its work of transmutation; a fact which is early established:

Looking back across the years I listen to the summer afternoon cooing of my aunt's white pigeons, and the soft clatter of their wings as they flutter upward from the lawn at the approach of one of the well-nourished cats. I remember, too, the smell of strawberry jam being made; and Aunt Evelyn with a green bee-veil over her head . . . The large rambling garden, with its Irish yews and sloping paths and wind-buffeted rose arches, remains to haunt my sleep. The quince tree which grew beside the little pond was the only quince tree in the world . . .

Here is all the recollected timelessness of childhood: a collection of impressions of a stable life, rooted in the recurrent and dependable processes of nature and their nourishing effect on man's domestic life. Sherston draws a strength from this as natural and unreflecting (in youth) as the processes of eating and drinking. Before his Colonel's Cup race he feels "in some way harmonious with the mild, half-clouded April morning which contained me;" but the feeling is vague, no more at the time than a conscious sense of well-being: "To have understood the gusto of that physical experience would have been to destroy the illusion which we call youth and immaturity ..." He is alive to nature in much the same way as he is to his earthly ambitions; it is a pure, animal delight, and something of this purity is transmitted to us (who can see only through Sherston's eye remembering youth), giving us a sense of a refined world, beyond change:

When I unlocked the door into the garden the early morning air met me with its cold purity; on the stone step were the bowls of roses and delphi-

19. Three such pieces were included in a collection of extracts from the three *Memoirs* and *O.C.*: entitled *The Flower Show Match*, it was published by Faber and Faber in 1941.
20. Osbert Sitwell, *Left Hand, Right Hand!* (1945), p.v.

niums and sweet peas which Aunt Evelyn had carried out there before she went to bed; the scarlet disc of the sun had climbed an inch above the hills. Thrushes and blackbirds hopped and pecked busily on the dew-soaked lawn, and a pigeon was cooing monotonously from the belt of woodland which sloped from the garden toward the Weald. Down there in the belt of river-mist a goods train whistled as it puffed steadily away from the station with a distinctly heard clanking of buffers. How little I knew of the enormous world beyond that valley and those low green hills.[21]

But it is not the theme of the last sentence that we pursue. Inevitably, this "common dawn", in Wordsworth's phrase, heralds a perfect day, a day for one of this little world's epic events. Nature, we can see, has her business and goes about it with a brisk diurnal thoroughness; and a vital part of that business is to cater for man's diversions.

The Flower Show Match is carried on in an aura of timeless perfection and Nature's beneficence.[22] At eleven o'clock it is "a cloudless day" and all is set. The idle waggoners have gravitated towards the cricket field to look on and neglect their work (we know it will get done eventually). Meanwhile "Rooks would be cawing in the vicarage elms, and Butley, with its huddle of red roofs and square church tower, was a contented-looking place." All is neat, self-sufficient, enduring. At about noon the opposing team arrives to inspect the pitch: "Meanwhile Butley bells chimed sedately to the close of the mellow extra cele-bration which Providence allowed them every three hours without fail ..." There follows a fanciful reflection upon members of the Rother-den team, a fancy in which men and landscape genially merge: "when-ever I thought of Crump and Bishop, I comprehensively visualized the whole fourteen miles of more or less unfamiliar landscape between Butley and Rotherden. For me the names meant certain lovely glimp-ses of the Weald, and the smell of mown hayfields, and the noise of a shallow river flowing under a bridge." There are no misfits in this universe: yokel and farmer, cobbler and clergyman strike and are struck with impartial good cheer, "while the Butley Band palavered peacefully onward into the unclouded jollity of the afternoon."

The summer that follows this one is, not surprisingly, "extra fine". Its flavour is conveyed in one of Sassoon's most evocative images: "My memory of that summer returns like a bee that comes buzzing into a

---

21. P. 56. A closely similar passage occurs in *W.Y.*, pp. 39-40, where it has a poetic function in the evolution of the young man's sensibility.
22. Part Two: pp. 53-79.

quiet room where the curtains are drawn on a blazing hot afternoon."[23]
Nature presides over and mellows all, lending fragrance and colour
even to man's less unexceptionable activities: "... they took their
coats off in the dappling sunshine for a real good dig. The crunch of
delving spades and the smell of sandy soil now mingled with the redo-
lence of the perspiring pack, the crushed bracken that the horses were
munching, and the pungent unmistakeable odour of foxes. However
inhumane its purpose, it was a kindly scene"; and another morning
scene conjures up a vision of a cleaner time and place:

The mornings I remember most zestfully were those which took us up onto
the chalk downs. To watch the day breaking from purple to dazzling gold
while we trotted up a deep-rutted lane; to inhale the early freshness when
we were on the sheep-cropped uplands; to stare back at the low country
with its cock-crowing farms and mist-coiled waterways; thus to be riding
out with a sense of spacious discovery—was it not something stolen from
the lie-a-bed world and the luckless city workers—even though it ended in
nothing more than the killing of a leash of fox-cubs (for whom, to tell the
truth, I felt an unconfessed sympathy)? Up on the downs in fine September
weather sixteen years ago . . .

Was it not stolen—not just from the luckless city workers, but from
time itself? Do such moments no longer exist? They do, but it was a
time—the last time, so it seems in retrospect—of peace, and that
makes all the difference. The narrator himself has a strong sense of
this, which is communicated to us, giving such moments in the young
man's career a precious quality, an aura that clings to the simplest
things:

I can see the pair of us clearly enough; myself [returning from a day's
hunting], with my brow-pinching bowler hat tilted on to the back of my
head, staring, with the ignorant face of a callow young man, at the dusky
landscape and its glimmering wet fields . . . I can hear the creak of the
saddle and the clop and clink of hooves as we cross the bridge over the
brook by Dundell Farm; there is a light burning in the farmhouse window,
and the evening star glitters above a broken drift of half-luminous cloud.
"Only three miles more, old man,"I say, slipping to the ground to walk
alongside him for a while.

It is with a sigh that I remember simple moments such as these, when I
understood so little of the deepening sadness of life . . .

23. P. 212. This image is based on a small incident recounted, with similar effect,
in *O.C.*, p. 288.

In such passages as this, where the picture is sombre enough, and in others where a more clearly defined cloud trespasses upon the sun, this retrospect is imbued with a deep nostalgia. Everything described has a precarious, evanescent quality: we cannot quite believe in it, not because we know it is idealized and never existed in quite this way, but because we know that nothing remotely like it could ever exist again. We are also reminded that 'nothing happening' is not a permanent condition of life. With unobtrusive tact, the author scatters throughout the book hints and intimations of the future, which looms black against Sherston's total unawareness: "I inspected the village grocer's calendar which was hanging on the nail. On it there was a picture of 'The Relief of Ladysmith' ... Old Kruger and the Boers. I never could make up my mind what it was all about, that Boer War, and it seemed such a long way off ... Yawning and munching I went creaking up to my room"—this on the morning of the Flower Show Match. And again, at the approach of the last winter before the outbreak of war—it is a splendid autumn: "I did not dread the dark winter as people do when they have lost their youth and live alone in some great city. Not wholly unconscious of the wistful splendour, but blind to its significance, I waited for cub-hunting to end. Europe was nothing but a name to me. I couldn't even bring myself to read about it in the daily paper. I could, however, read about cubbing in the Midlands ..." He looks forward to the security of the Packlestone hunting fraternity and when amongst them has "a comfortable feeling that here was something which no political upheaval could interrupt." A more sombre intimation occurs when, for a brief moment, the amiable (and essentially pathetic) Colonel Hesmon is caught in an attitude of premonitory desolation. The Colonel has just taken leave of his—and Sherston's— young friend, Stephen Colwood ("one of the keenest young chaps I've ever known"), who is about to ride his horse for him in a point-to-point: "Colonel Hesmon looked almost forlorn when the horse and his long-legged rider had vanished through the crowd. He had the appearance of a man who has been left behind. And as I see it now, in the light of my knowledge of after-events, there was a premonition in his momentarily forsaken air. Elderly people used to look like that during the War, when they had said good-bye to someone and the train had left them alone on the station platform." Later, Stephen Colwood is to be one of the War's first casualties, removing from the Colonel's life the only real friend he has and from Sherston's the "sensitive and gentle" friend of his youth. Stephen it was who "liked soldiering well enough," but "the guns, he said, were nothing but a nuisance, and he, for one, had no wish to chuck shells at anyone."

With such carefully planted hints and forebodings, Sassoon keeps us always uneasily aware of what lies beyond the golden haze that wreathes this idyll of hunting and cricket.[24] And the first movements of War come in at the end to cancel out Nature's beneficent and tolerrant rule. In the last paragraph Sherston stands with a knobkerrie, not a hunting crop, in his hand and gazes, not upon "a confusion of green branches shaken by the summer breeze", but towards "the splintered tree-tops of Hidden Wood"—sinister name.[25] Throughout the book these ugly shapes have always been on the fringes of our consciousness —and would have been, perhaps, if the author had not tried to put them there at all; the forebodings might not, to some readers, be an essential element to stimulate their awareness. In any case, henceforward, there is to be, not an "intuitive and gleaming retrospect"[26],: but a remembrance of "All squalid, abject, and inglorious elements in war." Something, at last, has happened.

A Poet's Prose

By the time he came to take up serious prose-writing, Sassoon had already been publishing poetry for some twenty years: it is not surprising, therefore, that *Memoirs of a Fox-Hunting Man* should so often have been referred to as a 'poet's book'.[27] The style is, in the broadest sense of the word, poetic—it has an elevated quality. The texture of the prose is most carefully worked: as in the prose of Pater, which Sassoon has always admired, exceptional attention has been paid to

24. Cp. Bergonzi, *Heroes' Twilight* (p. 160): "there is no sense in these chapters [of peace] that the carefree scene is already overshadowed by the prospect of war." Bergonzi has, however, detected one "odd proleptic hint of the future . . . when the local Master of Hounds asks the members of the Hunt 'to do everything in their power to eliminate the most dangerous enemy of the hunting man—he meant barbed wire'."
25. pp. 24 & 344 respectively.
26. Blunden's phrase for *M.F.H.*: *Edmund Blunden: A Selection of His Poetry and Prose*, p. 311.
27. R. A. Scott-James writes: "his poetic temperament, reacting rebelliously against the cruelty, found its most ample expression in the prose works written later . . ." (*Fifty Years of English Literature*, 1951, p. 123). Critics as far removed from each other as David Daiches and Edmund Blunden agree on the quality of the prose: the former finds it "distinctive" (*The Present Age: After 1920*, 1958, p. 202), whilst Blunden uses the phrase "a prose masterpiece" (*Edmund Blunden: A Selection*, p. 311).

sound and to the selection of the precise word.[28] This could lead to
mere phrase-making: but Sassoon's style is a flexible instrument which
he turns equally to account whether he is describing the lighter and
more satisfying or the savage aspects of existence. Certain technical
characteristics of his poetic style which we have already noted—a
penchant for occasional Latinisms, fanciful coinages and a versatile
use of alliteration—lend variety to the narrative and gratify the ear.
In the two final chapters the sights and sounds of war are described in
a finely textured prose which sadly contrasts with the desolation it must
evoke.

In the early chapters, which are concerned with Sherston's gradual
initiation into the sporting world, Sassoon employs an underlying
minor comic epic structure by which small things are made great.
We view events through Sherston's eyes—the eyes of wondering childhood and callow youth—and what we see is inevitably magnified.
Young George's ambition is to be elevated to membership of "the
distant Dumborough Elysium" and to this end Dixon works with
elaborate generalship. The process is slow, the end a glowing but distant one: "sometimes he would tell me that we were 'on the edge of
the Dumborough country,' and he would pull up and point out to me,
a few miles away, some looming covert where they often went to
draw." But the country—the fastness of fabled heroes with names like
MacDoggart—is mysteriously empty; in his training for the ultimate
encounter the child is allowed to venture only to the verge of it. At
last, comes his day of trial and it is beyond anything he had imagined:
"these enormous confident strangers overwhelmed my mind with the
visual authenticity of their brick-red coats". "A gaunt, ginger-haired
man in a weatherstained scarlet coat" turns out to be "the legendary
figure" of Mr. MacDoggart whom, since he is bent upon some "mysterious errand", George can only gaze after in awe. The first encounter
ends with romantic justice, the most fabled hero, Lord Dumborough,
deigning to notice an aspiring one with the words: "'I hear he's quite
a young thruster ...' The great man glanced at me for a moment with
curiosity before he turned away ..." Thus, the first movement in this
minor epic comes to an appropriate climax. At later events, the mock-
heroic element is maintained. At his next meet, "everything appeared
a little larger than life: voices seemed louder, coats a more raucous

28. In *W.Y.*, after a short passage in imitation of Pater's style, he refers to "my
continued enjoyment of almost everything he wrote" (pp. 33-35).

red, and the entire atmosphere more acute with imminent jeopardy than at Finchurst Green. Hard-bitten hunting men rattled up in gigs, peeled off their outer coverings, and came straddling along the crowded lane to look for their nags. Having found them, they spoke in low tones to the groom and swung themselves importantly into the saddle as though there were indeed some desperate business on hand ..." The scene is observed entirely through the child's enlarging eye: even when the characters take individual shape, they retain this "larger than life" quality. This, considering the nature and significance of the events described, is a true perspective. Sassoon is unfaltering in setting the figures of his humorous narrative at a distance just sufficient to lend comic distortion without, at the same time, destroying their humanity. The Rotherden cricketers appear in a similar perspective: "How enormous they looked as they sauntered across the ground"; "Crump and Bishop! The names had a profound significance for me. For many years I had heard Dixon speak of them ... Heavily built men in dark blue caps, with large drooping moustaches ..." At the same time, we are told "Crump was an ordinary auctioneer who sold sheep and cattle on market days, and Bishop kept the 'Rose and Crown' at Rotherden". This prosaic addition adds a further dimension to the portraiture, as do the inevitably commonplace words of approval Lord Dumborough gives the awestruck George. The humour works by a process of comic inflation: we are aware at one and the same time of the rosy conceptions cherished by the naive George and of the humdrum reality. In passages like this George's reverent attitude becomes the focus of our amusement: "The winner of the Open Race was weighing in when we arrived, and I stepped diffidently of to the machine immediately after his glorified and perspiring vacation of the seat". We are made doubly conscious of the flesh and blood reality of this scene by its elaborate verbal dress.

This heightening of the tone for comic effect can be further illustrated by more detailed examples which reinforce the mock-heroic sweep of character and incident. As in his satirical poems, Sassoon chiefly employs Latinisms—'sounding terms'—and the weighty alliterative phrase for the sake of humorous or ironic contrast in description between the thing expressed and the expression itself. Phrases like "uncouth matutinal jocularities" for the early morning greetings of huntsmen, the description of Homeward the carrier as having "the look of a man who was cogitant rather than vegetative" and the expression of Sherston's diffidence about purchasing a proper pair of riding-boots—"the notion of my inexpert self acquiring such unfamiliar accoutrements seemed problematic and audacious"— achieve their effect by the amusing disparity between the humdrum nature of the subject-matter and the elaborate and uncommon form of its expression.[29] This effect either strikes at once or is delayed, to be rounded off—as in Homeward's case, by a piece of deflating information which follows: this cogitant man is only, we are told, "weighing the pros and cons of the half-crown bets which he made on races." The plainer prose underlines the contrast. Similarly, in his description of the unfortunate boots, he speaks of them first as "palpably provincial in origin," but rounds it off with the plain statement: "A boot can look just as silly as a human being." A further variation of this method is to state a fact once with mock solemnity and then to repeat it in plainer language that throws an ironic light upon it: "... I had made further progress in what I believed to be an important phase of my terrestrial experience. In other words ... I had averaged five days a fortnight with the hounds."[30]

The mnemonic alliterative phrase is employed to gain a variety of effects. It may, by describing some commonplace aspect of Sherston's world or doings with reverential care, throw a mild ironic light upon them, as when Sherston remembers the last hunting season: "The ruddy faces of the Ringwell sportsmen accompanied my meditations in amiable clusters"; or when he rides proudly home after winning the Colonel's Cup: "Aquamarine and celestial were the shoals of sunset as I hacked pensively home from Dumbridge." The blunt Anglo-Saxon "ruddy" and "hacked" neatly keep the complacent sibilants in their proper place. At other times, the extravagance of the phrase itself is enough: (of Sherston's horse) "He had become the equine equivalent of Divinity." The carefully worked alliterative phrase is often purely descriptive, a loving attempt to elevate the small detail of a scene to a poetic plane. Occasionally, this technique may draw too much attention to itself and produce a clotted effect: "As we rattled up the road the unpunctual train with a series of snorts and a streamer of

29. Surtees also luxuriates in extravagant diction, of which the following is a fair sample: "towards the hour of nine may be heard to perfection that pleasing assemblage of sounds issuing from the masticatory organs of a number of men steadfastly and studiously employed in the delightful occupation of preparing their mouthfuls for deglutition." (*Jorrocks's Jaunts and Jollities*, first publ. 1843).
30. Appendix A, (8).

smoke sauntered sedately away into the calm agricultural valley of its vocation."[31]

Less excessive are the neatly balanced sound effects of the following, where assonance unobtrusively maintains the impression of lightness: "The flitting steeds now revolved and undulated noiselessly beneath their gilded canopy, while the Butley Band palavered peacefully onward into the unclouded jollity of the afternoon." A like effect is shown in this example where the succession of short ' e' sounds, variously placed, gives the right sense of random movement; the dogs are released at the beginning of the hunt: "Even then I used to feel the strangeness of the scene with its sharp exuberance of unkennelled energy." There is no clotting here, nor in this, perhaps the most exquisite example of a scene caught in a few words; again, alliteration (with occasional assonance) gives the rhythm but the 's', 'p' and 'w' sounds mingle, there is no undue emphasis: "So we did outpost schemes at the forest's edge, and open-order attacks across wheat-fields and up the stubbled slopes, while sandy hares galloped away; and an old shepherd, in a blue frieze cloak with a pointed hood, watched us from the nook where he was avoiding the wind." Such pictures provide an indelible contrast with the pervasive scenes of desolation in the War chapters.

These last two chapters bring before us the sheer desolation rather than the horrors of war (the latter have their due place in the poetry, and, to a lesser extent, in *Memoirs of an Infantry Officer*).[32] In descriptions like that just quoted, in the paragraphs describing with loving precision the threatened serenity of Morlancourt[33] and in such brief glimpses as that of the "grey-roofed chateau, with its many windows and no face there to watch me pass", caught from his galloping horse, the narrator keeps us continually aware of the meaning and value of the harmony that is broken by war. Many of these glimpses are fleeting —as is inevitable, for the present business and the present scene com-

31. Their effect may sometimes be brittle, as here: "I acquired an exact knowledge of the ancestries of Vivian, Villager, Conquest, Cottager, and various other eloquent veterans whose music had made the ploughman pause with attentive ear on many a copse-crowned upland" (p. 260). This sentence contains too many self-contained alliterative groups, each of which attracts attention to itself, so that where in the latter half of the sentence a picture should be evoked we have instead slabs of sound. I have noted these two less satisfactory examples to illustrate the dangers of the technique: they are not typical.
32. ". . . as you read the latter end of this book . . . you become conscious of being spoken to in a voice of sadness and utter resignation. This sense seems to be conveyed almost entirely by the plain statement of the existence of things" (*Modern Prose Style*, Bonamy Dobree, 1934, p. 74.)
33. p. 320.

mand the mind as well as the eye, but the effect is continually to juxta-
pose the symbols of peace and war—the latter as finely described as
the former: "The shallow blanching flare of a rocket gave me a
glimpse of the mounds of bleached sandbags on the Redoubt. Its brief
whiteness died downward, leaving a dark world; chilly gusts met me at
corners, piping drearily through crannies of the parapet; very different
was the voice of the wind that sang in the cedar tree in the garden at
home ..." The dreary clarity of the rocket, the tormenting wind are
both seen and felt; felt, too, as warmth after cold is the soft voice of the
remembered peaceful wind. As in the chapters of peace we have a
predominant sense of summer, so here it is winter's turn: mud, frost,
hostile winds. Abetting these is the awful beauty of war's paraphernalia
—the flares and the bursting shells: "One of our shrapnel shells,
whizzing over to the enemy lines, bursts with a hollow crash. Against
the clear morning sky a cloud of dark smoke expands and drifts away.
Slowly its dingy wrestling vapours take the form of a hooded giant
with clumsy expostulating arms. Then, with a gradual gesture of
acquiescence, it lolls sideways, falling over into the attitude of a
swimmer on his side. And so it dissolves into nothingness." A grim,
compelling fancy, this: there is food for the observing eye even in time
of war; though "Perhaps the shell has killed someone," which is inevitable, and the immediate task is to scrape the mud off one's boots.
Man—"the patient dun-coloured column" is resigned to his fate, a
passive sufferer on the broken face of the earth. If he retreats below
ground, he cannot escape the desolation that shrouds him there, too,
smothering his pathetic symbols of civilization: "The air was dank and
musty; lumps of chalk fell from the 'ceiling' at intervals. There was a
bad smell of burnt grease, and the frizzle of something frying in the
adjoining kennel that was called the kitchen was the only evidence of
ordinary civilization—that and Barton's shining pince-nez, and the
maps and notebooks which were on the table ..." The inevitability
might be enough to render the mind blank, yet the mind continues to
record because it must (this being the only recourse to preserve one's
sanity). There is no sensationalism—no attempt to glorify, to produce
something truly epic—no impatient rejection: the "squalid, abject and
inglorious elements" are recorded with a sensuous exactitude equal to
that devoted to the more ingratiating subjects of the earlier chapters.
Little comment is needed. In the later *Memoirs* this prose-poetry will
be developed to the full.

THE SHERSTON TRILOGY (II)

M *emoirs of an Infantry Officer* and *Sherston's Progress* are in their distinctive features complementary to Sassoon's war poetry.[1]
Though not entirely absent from the prose account, the realism and
bitter irony that characterize the poetry are far less conspicuous. The
poetry had long ago served an immediate purpose: it had rubbed the
noses of the bloodthirsty and ignorant patriots in "a few rank physical
facts";[2] it had pilloried Government, Church and the Red-Tabbed
Staff, and voiced the soldier's resentment against the non-combatant.
Its denunciations had been thoroughgoing and extreme; those of the
Memoirs are tempered with concession: as the poem 'War Experience'
tells us, "Not much remains, twelve winters later, of the hater/Of
purgatorial pains."

Recollection in tranquillity lends the *Memoirs* a new poetry, which
gives form and significant meaning to the raw chaos of events, thus
transcending them. This cannot be claimed to be dominant, but the
tone is strong enough to give the impression of a broader vision underlying the continuing portrayal of Sherston at war. The poetic aspect
now speaks to us of war as a breach of order and harmony upon earth;
the portrayal of Sherston shows the disrupting effect that war, without
claiming his life, has upon such a man: these are the two notable
—and complementary—features of the narrative. In Sassoon's treatment of them, we shall see a quality of detachment and a concern
which extends beyond the purely individual or partisan. However,
before considering them, let us glance first at his treatment in prose of
the themes for satire which engaged him as a war poet to see how he
brings to them also a more detached mind.

Coming to the *Memoirs* from the war poems, one is struck by the

1. Appendix A, (9).
2. *M.I.O.*, pp. 262-3. For further references from this book and *S.P.*, see 'Page
References', p. 308.

relative infrequency of passages of raw realism; there are none that appear deliberately designed to shock. The lapse of time has enabled an all-embracing irony to replace the savage indignation of the earlier writing; the worst has been said already:

I noticed an English soldier lying by the road with a horribly smashed head; soon such sights would be too frequent to attract attention, but this first one was perceptibly unpleasant. At the risk of being thought squeamish or even unsoldierly, I still maintain that an ordinary human being has a right to be momentarily horrified by a mangled body seen on an afternoon walk, although people with sound common sense can always refute me by saying that life is full of gruesome sights and violent catastrophes. But I am no believer in wild denunciations of the War; I am merely describing my own experiences of it . . .

The tone of this is characteristic. Sassoon does not indulge himself —or us—with a detailed description of horrors: the sight was "perceptibly unpleasant;" there is no emotional outburst; he puts his own view with studied restraint, refraining with ironical deference from dogmatizing over "people with sound common sense." A passage similarly free from "wild denunciations" is the following, written more in sadness than in anger:

Alternately crouching and crawling, I worked my way back. I passed the young German whose body I had rescued from disfigurement a couple of hours before. He was down in the mud again, and someone had trodden on his face. It disheartened me to see him, though his body had now lost all touch with life and was part of the wastage of the war. He and Kendle had cancelled one another out in the process called 'attrition of manpower.' Further along I found one of our men dying slowly with a hole in his forehead. His eyes were open and he breathed with a horrible snoring sound . . .

The 'realism' is conveyed in a matter-of-fact tone, the commentary restrained, the emotion brought under control. When, elsewhere, the bitterness comes uppermost, it is because Sassoon has thoroughly recaptured the spirit of his younger self:

. . . I was cutting the wire by daylight because commonsense warned me that the lives of several hundred soldiers might depend on it being done properly . . . And I had entirely forgotten that tomorrow Six Army Corps would attack, and whatever else happened, a tragic slaughter was inevitable. But if I had been intelligent enough to realize all that, my talents would have been serving in some more exalted place, probably Corps Intelligence Headquarters.

Another passage describes Sherston's bitter reaction to seeing a proud, patriotic father visiting his disabled son in a convalescent hospital:

... I heard him telling one of the nurses how splendidly the boy had done in the Gommecourt attack, showing her a letter, too, probably from the boy's Colonel. I wondered whether he had ever allowed himself to find out that the Gommecourt show had been nothing but a massacre of good troops. Probably he kept a war map with little flags on it; when Mametz Wood was reported captured he moved a little flag an inch forward after breakfast. For him the Wood was a small green patch on a piece of paper. For the Welsh Division it had been a bloody nightmare ...

These passages are in character with the younger Sherston in their purism and the inclination they reveal to make the least charitable suppositions; at such points it would be wrong to identify the attitudes of the narrator with those of his remembered self. Their effect is mitigated by many others in which a broader tolerance and understanding are shown.

The old targets of attack still receive their share of ironic attention, but it is a pricking irony, not a slashing one: "But the contrast between the Front Line and the Base was an old story, and at any rate the Base Details were at a disadvantage as regards the honour and glory which made the War such an uplifting experience for those in close contact with it"; "It was a Sunday, and there was a Church parade for the whole battalion. This was a special occasion, for we were addressed by a bishop in uniform, a fact which speaks for itself." Beside these hits we must put some of the many passages which concede another side to the question. The Staff, too, had their problems: "this sort of warfare was a new experience for all of us, and the difficulties of extempore organization must have been considerable." There is good-humoured understanding even for the "scarlet-majors": "The large dining-room was full of London Clubmen dressed as Colonels, Majors, and Captains with a conscientious objection to physical discomfort. They were as much the victims of circumstances as the unfortunate troops ..." The narrator notes the inconsistencies of his younger self in his thoroughgoing detestation for civilian patriotism and its "callous complacency": "Must the War go on in order that colonels might become brigadiers and brigadiers get divisions, while contractors and manufacturers enriched themselves and people in high places ate and drank well and bandied official information and organized entertainments for the wounded? Some such questions I may have asked myself, but I was unable to include Captain Huxtable and Aunt Evelyn in the indictment."

Looking back in tranquillity, Sassoon casts the net of understanding and tolerance wider: guilt rests with no individual or group, but with the Christian civilization to which all belong. The following paragraph, with which he ends a passage describing the insomnia-ridden inmates of Slateford by night (a passage reminiscent of Wilfred Owen's poem, "Mental Cases"), well conveys the spirit of the *Memoirs*:

Shell-shock. How many a brief bombardment had its long-delayed after-effect in the minds of these survivors, many of whom had looked at their companions and laughed while inferno did its best to destroy them! Not then was their evil hour, but now: now, in the sweating suffocation of nightmare, in paralysis of limbs, in the stammering of dislocated speech. Worst of all, in the disintegration of those qualities through which they had been so gallant and selfless and uncomplaining—this, in the finer types of men, was the unspeakable tragedy of shell-shock; it was in this that their humanity had been outraged by those explosives wich were sanctioned and glorified by the Churches; it was thus that their self-sacrifice was mocked and maltreated—they, who in the name of righteousness had been sent out to maim and slaughter their fellow-men. In the name of civilization these soldiers had been martyred, and it remained for civilization to prove that their martyrdom wasn't a dirty swindle.

Humanity must look forward, beyond petty blame, and atone for crimes against itself by an effort of re-making.

The Hero

Sassoon's primary aim in writing *Memoirs of an Infantry Officer* was to show how the extraordinary events of the First World War tested and shaped the character of one of the many ordinary young men who were compelled to take part in it. He makes this clear near the beginning of the book: "those who expect a universalisation of the Great War must look for it elsewhere. Here they will only find an attempt to show its effect on a somewhat solitary-minded young man." One uses the word 'ordinary' deliberately, since there is no doubt that Sassoon wishes to portray—as in *Memoirs of a Fox-Hunting Man*—a character with whom many readers might find it possible to identify themselves. To do this, he has to omit a significant part of his own

II. Siegfried Sassoon, a cartoon by Sir Max Beerbohm, 1931.

ONE WHO WATCHES.

We are all near to death; but in my friends
I am forewarned too closely of that nearness.
Death haunts their days that are; in him descends
The darkness that shall change their living dearness
    To something different, made within my mind
    By memories and recordings and convenings
    Of voices heard through veils and faces blind
    To the kind light of my autumnal gleanings.

Not so much for myself I feel that fear
As for all those in whom my loves must die;
Thus, like some hooded death, I stand apart:
And in their happiest moments I can hear
Silence mending, when those lives must lie
Hoarded like happy summers in my heart.

28·10·27.

III. Manuscript (Poem).

identity: the poetic self. If, under the pressure of war experience, Sherston develops gradually into more than "a simplified version of my outdoor self," he is still, as Sassoon later recognised, "denied the complex advantage of being a soldier-poet."[3] Sherston is ordinary, then, only in this sense: he is not a public figure and thus, in his most significant action—his protest against the continuance of the war— lacks any sustaining power other than that of his own conscience. He is thrust wholly upon himself, as most of us would be.

At the same time, if his extraordinary protest is to be convincing, he must be seen to possess the qualities of sensitivity which we saw (in *Memoirs of a Fox-Hunting Man*) as latent in his immature self. No *absolutely* ordinary hero would do. If he is not a poet, Sherston has the English poet's traditional communion with Nature, now more fully developed under the pressure of opposing circumstances than in the previous book. We often glimpse him alone, detached from preparations for the march or for a battle: "For me, it was a luxury to be alone for a few minutes, watching the yellow irises, and the ribbon weeds that swayed like fishes in the dimpling stream." Later he writes: "From such things I got what consolation I could". So might all sensitive men, drawing strength from the small continuance of life amongst such chaos. He has, like all such men, the desire for an ideal harmony transcending the chaos. For Sherston this ideal is, as one might expect, enshrined in the past of rustic England (an escape that experience eventually renders inadequate): he goes to war, not only with Surtees', but also with Thomas Hardy's England in his haversack. He reads *Far from the Madding Crowd* and *The Return of the Native* not only, as he says, "to keep my mind from stagnation", but to preserve the spirit of old England in him—the spirit that so many of his generation idealised and yearned for. At another time it is the concentrated gentleness of *Lamb's Letters* that consoles. The poetic sensibility is present, if not the poet.[4]

3. *S.J.*, p. 69. As Bergonzi comments, Sassoon seems in the later book to feel "a certain unease" about the simplification of self in *An Infantry Officer*, which the critic shares when he writes that the earlier account of the anti-war rebellion "would have acquired greater resonance if we had been told that this was the action of the author of *The Old Huntsman* and *Counter-Attack*" (*Heroes' Twilight*, 1965, p. 159). Certainly the force of the protest was diminished in the first account and Sassoon felt compelled to fill in the gaps in *S.J.*—for this reason the least integrated of his autobiographies—but the artistic justification for this editing of self is that he thereby gave Sherston the convincing, sensitive 'ordinariness' of character which has brought him close to so many readers.

In the past, Sherston's love for nature has been a sentiment. Now, when it is threatened, it becomes more vital to him, at first as giving a sharper sense of sheer living: "Never before had I been so intensely aware of what it meant to be young and healthy in fine weather at the outset of summer". After the raid in which he is plunged for the first time into the thick of action he strides out above the trenches: "The landscape loomed round me, and the landscape was life, stretching away and away into freedom". His initial reactions are relatively uncomplicated, for the "outdoor self" is still dominant. However unwillingly he may have been plunged into war, he is not yet disposed to revolt. War is another contest, another challenge to one's courage and endurance. He wishes to lead the raid just as, formerly, it had been his ambition to win steeplechases: it was "a significant way of demonstrating my equality with my contemporaries ... if only I could get an M.C. I should feel comparatively safe and confident". His horizons are narrow; he sees the whole business of war only as it gives scope for the satisfaction of an elemental need: "My courage was of the cock-fighting kind"—a kind required by the time, of which there could be no surplus. The mind and the sensitivity are not yet fully awake, except as they make for him consolations for fear and ugliness. If he asks himself why he suffers—not at first why others do—the answer might pass as patriotic, but it is essentially escapist; he suffers, he tells himself in his nostalgic moments, for the beauties of rustic England: "dark green woodlands with pigeons circling above the tree-tops; dogs barking, cocks crowing, and all the casual tappings and twinklings of the countryside. I thought of the huntsman walking out in his long white coat with the hounds ... It was for all that, I supposed, that I was in the front-line with soaked feet, trench-mouth, and feeling short of sleep ..." This is his great consolation—that he will return to England as he remembers it—which war will shatter and prove that it was always only a dream; he must learn to face the present, though he may never learn to tolerate it.

"While writing these memoirs," the author tells us, "my interest in

4. Occasionally it might seem that Sassoon has played down the poetic self unduly: as in Sherston's dim responses to Jerusalem—"not a very holy looking place"—from which he escapes into the countryside, which he finds only "nicer than it had looked" (*S.P.* pp. 163-164), and Paris seen from the train: "It looked rather romantic and mysterious somehow, and a deep-toned bell was tolling slowly." (Ibid. p. 194). But these passages are taken from a diary and were presumably not refashioned later; they do convey the less articulate quality of Sherston's younger responses.

each chapter has been stimulated by the fact that I nearly always saw myself engaged in doing something for the first time." The interest for the reader, in watching the shaping of George Sherston, is somewhat similar. The experiences Sherston undergoes draw him out of his solitary self and lead him to many fresh perceptions, especially about his fellow-men. His sympathies are moving outwards. Through shared suffering he gradually develops a vital bond with the men he commands, which goes deeper than his callow heroics: "I couldn't save them," he reflects, "but at least I could share the dangers and discomforts they endured." This feeling, the older Sherston realizes, was intermittent—"vaguely altruistic". It lacked, at that time, a deeper foundation of thought: "in 1917 I was only beginning to learn that life, for the majority of the population, is an unlovely struggle against unfair odds, culminating in a cheap funeral ..." This feeling for his fellow-victims—and for "the humanity which was on the other side" —is the generous impulse of youth seeking an ideal: "Against the background of the war and its brutal stupidity those men had stood glorified by the thing which sought to destroy them ..." But *he* must be a part of the ideal and thus, as he comes to learn, is in danger of basking in self-created glory. The perceptions will be valuable only when rightly used.

That the motives which bring them into existence are not absolutely pure and that they are not lived up to with complete consistency should not surprise us. The subtlety of Sassoon's portrayal of Sherston derives particularly from the honesty with which he has delineated motives and conduct in all their contradictoriness. He has achieved this with greater success than he is willing to claim when he says, "our inconsistencies are often what make us most interesting, and it is possible that, in my zeal to construct these memoirs carefully, I have eliminated too many of my own self-contradictions."

Sherston never completely masters the 'happy warrior' attitude that sustains him throughout his early experiences of the war. It is at best a means of escape from the "bleak truth" of the "impermanence of [war's] humanities," by making "a little drama out of my own experience"; at its lowest an egotistic display of 'spirit'.[5] Even when,

5. However complex the psychological motivation for Sassoon's daredevildom, there is no doubt that his men were greatly impressed. This is attested enthusiastically by Frank Richards, who was at the time in Sassoon's Battalion and who, in his

convalescing after his first wound, he "[begins] to think" about the rights and wrongs of the War, his vanity still seduces him into a desire to wear a medal for his exploits. Receiving news in hospital of a "dud show" in which his Battalion has been involved, his pity centres upon Wilmot—"now minus one of his arms [who] wouldn't be able to play the piano again"—but he sleeps well nevertheless, for the fact is that "Altruism is an episodic and debatable quality." It is beyond ordinary human capacity to live indefinitely on a plane of high thinking. In the tranquil atmosphere of Nutwood Manor the instinct for self-preservation, to give way to "assuasive human happiness," competes strongly with his desire "to keep the smoke-drifted battle memories true and intense, unmodified by the comforts of convalescence." When at last he comes to the decision to voice his protest, though it derives from a true feeling of identity with the men from whom he feels guiltily separated, the form it takes is by no means selfless. He ignores Markington's counsel of prudence, blindly sets his face against his misgivings that he cannot carry it through effectively and derives from his decision "a glowing sense of martyrdom"; "I was in the throes of a species of conversion which made the prospect of persecution stimulating and almost enjoyable." He is fortified by the emotional conviction, held with the purism of youth, that he and all who have suffered like him are absolutely right. He sets his mind upon Ormond, his courageous brother-officer—"the typical Flintshire Fusilier at his best, and the vast anonymity of courage and cheerfulness which he represented": far removed from this pure figure are the politicians, the military caste, the profiteers, about whom his knowledge is extremely vague. Conflicting with this conviction of defending the right is the rational knowledge that he will be misunderstood by every "right-minded Butley man" in the trenches: "But I felt the desire to suffer ... gain some new spiritual freedom and live as I had never lived before." In seizing upon half-digested ideas[6] that chime with his emotional

lively and shrewd account of the War as a 'ranker' saw it, refers several times to the good impression Sassoon made upon the troops. (See *Old Soldiers Never Die*, 1964 paper-covered edition, pp. 227-8 especially, 221 & 271: "it was only once in a blue moon that we had an officer like Mr. Sassoon.")

6. Supplied by Markington (H. V. Massingham), the editor of *The Unconservative Weekly* (*The Nation*) and Thornton Tyrell (Bertrand Russell), the pacifist, but beyond his power to assimilate fully: there is no counterpart here to the Morrells' Garsington, where Sassoon acquired "a fomentation of confused and inflamed ideas" which were not talked out—"no one pressed me to divulge the harrowing details or indeed to describe the humanly rewarding aspects of war service" (*S.J.*, p. 22.) More so than his creator, Sherston is left too much alone with his thoughts.

idealism he is at the same time satisfying a temperamental need in a way akin to hisfr ont-line heroism. War has rapidly matured his feelings, but the mind has much to learn. His action is a compound of youth's extreme impulses: of its generosity and uncompromising truth to an ideal, but also of its selfishness and conscious rectitude. "We weren't life-learned enough," he reflects (of himself and Cromlech), "to share the patient selfless stoicism through which men of maturer age were acquiring anonymous glory."

Trapped, rather than argued, out of his extreme position by his friend 'Cromlech',[7] Sherston is forced to recognize that he is mentally ill. He is sent to Slateford Hospital (Craiglockhart), a convalescent home for neurasthenics and there, detached indefinitely from the strain of facing circumstances alone, he comes under the care of the neurologist and psychologist, Dr. W. H. R. Rivers. His problem now is to master himself and to achieve a balanced acceptance of the fact that it is beyond him to guide major events by individual action. With this the first part of *Sherston's Progress* is concerned.

* * *

Sherston experiences the inevitable reaction from the strain of making his protest, which elicits only a number of letters either agreeing or disagreeing with his views: "I needed a holiday from that sort of thing."[8] He lapses into a state of mental passivity, which Rivers deliberately does little to disturb. Their discussions of Sherston's action and his motives for it reveal gently to him that "the weak point about my 'protest' had been that it was evoked by personal feeling. It was an emotional idea based on my war experience ... I could only see the situation from the point of view of the troops I had served with ..." Rivers points out that he had omitted German militarism entirely from his calculations and that a negotiated peace now would only nullify the sacrifices made by Sherston's fellows.[9] With such arguments

---

7. 'Cromlech' is Robert Graves, whose account of his part in this can be read in *Goodbye to All That* (Penguin Edition, 1960, pp. 214-217) : it tallies in every important respect with Sassoon's. Graves was acting upon the advice of Edward Marsh who, as Winston Churchill's secretary, had first-hand knowledge of the harsh way the Government would handle the matter if Sassoon persisted in his insubordination (See *Edward Marsh*, by C. Hassall, 1959).

8. *S.P.*, p. 17. Sassoon himself had no such 'holiday': it was at Craiglockhart that he wrote most of the poems included in *Counter-Attack*, many of which were included in the hospital magazine, *The Hydra* (which is only briefly mentioned in *S.P.*). This was the most important means of sublimating his experience denied Sherston by his "soldier-poet" creator.

9. In *S.J.* (p. 57), Sassoon considers that a Peace in 1917 would "not have prevented a recurrence of Teutonic aggressiveness".

Rivers subtly brings Sherston round to constructive thought, but without pressing him: whilst "muddling on toward maturity" under Rivers' paternal wing, he spends most of his time "in pursuit of a ball" on the nearby golf links. Sherston's certainty is slowly eroded as he approaches intellectual humility: at the same time, a nagging sense of purposelessness grows now that he has lost the anchor of uncomplicated conviction. The old feeling creeps back—"Reality was on the other side of the Channel, surely"—vying with the old accompanying desire to preserve oneself whole, a temptation to postpone decision, "shortening the War" for himself. What at last asserts itself is a renewed awareness of the human values he had learnt in the front-line —"which really did feel as if it had been a better place than this where now I sat in bitter safety surrounded by the wreckage and defeat of those who had once been brave." In a long reflective passage Sherston reminisces about the comradeship, cheerfulness and fortitude of those with whom he had fought—but without reaching the sentimentalist's inevitable conclusion, "that death is preferable to dishonour." Instead, he comes to one more consistent with his own temperament: pride and his sensitivity to the doubts or hostility of others also reassert themselves—he regains a sense of self in a desire to prove his surviving capacity to be responsible for his own actions: "Humanity asserted itself in the form of a sulky little lapse into exasperation against the people who pitied my 'wrong-headedness' and regarded me as 'not quite normal'." Irrationality still rules his choice; had he been capable of intellectual consistency, he would have adhered to "the abstract idea that the War was wrong" on purely pacifist grounds. But he is not an intellectual: his mind gains no swift mastery over circumstances; the only thing he can do, having reached a mental block, is to avoid it, and to preserve his sanity he must *do*. It is the desire to regain a sense of self through action that carries him away from Slateford, a desire underwritten by the moral justification supplied by Rivers: "He had set me on the right road ... a strenuous effort must be made to take some small share in the real work of the world".

In his ensuing actions, as in this one, we see the often contradictory urges to fulfil needs of a basic, emotional kind and of a more complex, not readily satisfied, moral nature. The Middle Eastern interlude (Part III)[10] affords him an opportunity for sober reflection upon the

10. Part II of *S.P.* provides light relief: a return to the hunting-scene, this time in

War; though he still recognizes its futility, he begins to see it as a manifestation of human imperfection: "I dimly realize the human weakness which makes it possible." A weakness, that is, in man's failure to *govern* himself: only "the patience and simple decency ... in the ordinary soldier ... make it possible to go on". When, at last, he returns to France and takes up again his officer's rôle, in caring for his men he finds "I have, for the time being, escaped from my own individuality ..." Yet as he approaches the Line, with the prospect of immersing himself in action he feels "strong and confident in the security of a sort of St Martin's Summer of Happy Warriorism". For a while his moral repulsion is in abeyance. Back with the Battalion, he appraises the quality of his new fellow-officers without reflecting upon the fact that they, like the old, are to be sacrificed: "The old crowd are gone; but young 'Stiffy' and Howitt are just as good." Service in the line kills reflection, which would otherwise prompt indecision and doubt, an awareness of the "mechanical stupidity of infantry soldiering". He alternates between two moods: the Happy Warrior's— "the daylight of my activities"—and that of the rebellious soul "in the darkness", powerless to avert the tragedy of his fellows' destruction: "I know that I can do nothing." This is the crucial, tragic perception, but the mind is now more resilient—or rather, more capable of suppressing the darker side, fortified (albeit far short of the ideal) by its release from the sense of ultimate responsibility.[11]

Though still Sherston relapses into bursts of his old dare-devildom and foolhardiness, he has glimpsed something of the tragic vision that extends beyond the suffering self to suffering mankind. His mind has turned outwards. In pitying all, he no longer pities himself. Reflecting

Limerick, which centres upon the exploits of Blarnett, a full-blooded and endearing sportsman with an eighteenth-century flavour, reminiscent of Fielding's Squire Western. Though this interlude is entertaining, its presence is responsible for the diminished intensity of this final volume of the trilogy, when it is compared with its predecessors.

11. Graves testifies to the truth of Sassoon's portrayal of the two selves: "Siegfried's unconquerable idealism changed direction with his environment: he varied between happy warrior and bitter pacifist" (op. cit. p. 226). A non-combatant observer, Arnold Bennett, meeting him in June 1917, before his last overseas posting, found happy warriorism seemingly uppermost: "He is evidently one of the reckless ones. He said his pals said he always gave the Germans every chance to pot him. He said he would like to go out once more and give them another chance to get him, and come home unscathed. He seemed jealous for the military reputation of poets. He said most of war was a tedious nuisance, but there were great moments and he would like them again" (*The Journals of Arnold Bennett*, Penguin Edn. p. 304).

on the men's inglorious rôle in a diary entry made during the voyage to France from the Middle East, he writes:

> They are only a part of the huge dun-coloured mass of victims which passes through the shambles of war into the gloom of death where even generals 'automatically revert to the rank of private.' But in the patience and simplicity of their outward showing they seem like one soul. They are the tradition of human suffering and endurance, stripped of all the silly self-glorifications and embellishments by which human society seeks to justify its conventions.[12]

With these men he identifies himself as never before—"nothing matters except the Company." But his rôle is humbler than it was before; he is no longer deluded by thoughts that he can become their ultimate saviour. He sets himself now to bridge the gulf, not between the rights and wrongs of war, but between his desire to relieve the troops' sufferings and the practical limitations upon it—"all I can do for them is to try and obtain them fresh vegetables"; the simple act of successfully obtaining hot tea against odds for fatigued men going up to the line, is "more truly human" than anything else imaginable. He is beyond the grand gesture; martyrdom is no longer a purely personal matter. He has discovered the perfect means of self-forgetfulness.

This discovery cannot, however, provide a complete answer to his emotional needs. The suppression of fear and the strain of command continually re-create the urge for emotional release. He makes a lone, irresponsible foray into No-Man's Land ("Discarding all my obligations as Company Commander"), undertakes a voluntary patrol by night as "an antidote to my suppressed weariness of the entire bloody business," a patrol from which he is lucky to return only wounded, a victim of what some would term high spirits—seeking a "great moment"—and others over-wrought nerves. This wound finally puts

12. *S.P.*, p. 186. There is a close parallel in situation and writer's attitude between Sassoon's troopship reflections and those of an outstanding Second World War writer, Dan Billany (see *The Trap*, Faber and Faber 1950, Chapters XX-XXIII). A whole generation later, one finds Billany experiencing Sassoon's digust with his fellow-officers' upper-deck gluttony and seeking to identify himself with the men penned like forced pigs below. In the quality of his humanity, Billany sustains the spirit of Sassoon: but in social experience he is closer to the men and displays a more mature insight into their personalities; also, of course, he had the 'Thirties behind him. For Billany, as for the poet Alun Lewis, neither acceptance not protest was enough: he was extraordinarily sane, a builder of life around around him (well shown in his book about prison-camp life, *The Cage*); his death in 1944 was a tragic loss.

him out of the war and delivers the mind from its ceaseless efforts "to achieve, in its individual isolation, some sort of mastery over the experience which it shared with those dead and sleeping multitudes ..."

* * *

We have seen in these two volumes of memoirs, not only a mind trying to achieve "some sort of mastery over the experience," but also a mind striving to know and govern itself. It is appropriate that neither of these processes has a conclusive ending. Given the youth and immaturity of Sherston [13] it is improbable that they should. Sassoon leaves us with the impression that Sherston, forever divided from the old, pre-War world, must fashion for himself a new one, building as best he can upon the insight into human existence his testing experience has granted him. His awareness has been forced; it remains to be seen whether it will bear good fruit in the future:

I couldn't go back to being the same as I was before it started. The 'good old days' had been pleasant enough in their way, but what could a repetition of them possibly lead to?
How could I begin my life all over again when I had no conviction about anything except that the War was a dirty trick which had been played on me and my generation? That, at any rate, was something to be angry and bitter about now that everything had fallen to pieces and one's mind was in a muddle and one's nerves were all on edge ...

Faced with this end in which there is no ending, Sherston is type and symbol of the sensitive among his generation.[14] He is, too, ingenuous youth put to the test of life. In this rôle, he makes no extraordinary discoveries, but reaches instead those that enable him to see himself with greater clarity, both in himself and in his relations with his fellow-men. In this latter respect the War forces him into contact with the world of men as it is, not as he had imagined it to be in his limited, local experiences of *Memoirs of a Fox-Hunting Man*. His greater insight into self is the most vital thing: he learns to recognize the contra-dictoriness of motives and behaviour, how emotion governs action and how action is too often justified by spurious reasoning.

In this portrayal of youth fumbling towards maturity Sassoon main-tains, throughout the three books, a remarkably even tone. He has

13. "Youth" in no literal sense: "I was nearly thirty-two," he writes, adding "one wasn't as old as one's age"; one would, of course, put the accent upon "immaturity."
14. "We left the war as we entered it: dazed, indifferent, incapable of any creative action. We had acquired only one new quality: exhaustion" (Herbert Read, *The Contrary Experience*, p. 217).

resisted the natural temptation to impose retrospectively a self-grati-
fying pattern upon Sherston's conduct at war. There is no rapid
maturing, and to the very last Sherston oscillates between the two
selves—the daylight self of impulse and action and the darker self of
the anguished mind groping for the meaning of what he does. Sherston's self-contradictions are an integral part of his character (and of
Sassoon's character, especially when unformed): there is no contradiction in characterization. Wisely, Sassoon gives us no sequel: we take
leave of Sherston once more in the presence of Rivers, "in calm of
mind, all passion spent." If there is a lesson to be learnt, it is that we
must look within to discover what the world has made of us; then only
can we learn to live in the world: "And my last words shall be these
—that it is only from the inmost silences of the heart that we know the
world for what it is, and ourselves for what the world has made us".

This somewhat detached close reflects the feeling of the Sassoon of
Vigils (almost contemporaneous with *Sherston's Progress*), which lies
far beyond the confused position in which we leave the wounded
Sherston.

Men at War

In a phrase previously quoted, Sassoon explicitly renounces any
pretensions to having universalized the Great War. He emphasizes
instead the more limited aim of showing its effect upon one individual
amongst the many. There will be no attempt to prove Sassoon's dis-
claimer wrong; it is the purpose, rather, here to show that his treatment
of the war goes in some respects beyond the merely subjective.

Sassoon's narrative, in giving us a complex insight into one man's
response to war, inevitably gives us a diluted impression of War in the
universal sense. Wherever Sherston goes, bearing with him his tor-
mented mind, we must go: into hospital, convalescence, training
camp, for a light interlude in Limerick and on posting to the remote
and quiescent Palestine Front. Nevertheless, though the remembering
mind is concerned to portray the more self-engrossed self, it has now
achieved a broader vision. As in *Memoirs of a Fox-Hunting Man*, there
are two perspectives: the narrator looks back upon his youthful self,
seeking to recapture the old experiences and reactions and trying to
present them faithfully; but at the same time, he views the experiences
as a whole in a more detached and coherent way than was possible

during the conflict and tries to convey impressions which now seem to have enduring significance. Self-involved at the time, he appears to have collected—and retains—more material for the presentation of the first perspective, less, as far as *human* subject-matter is concerned, for the second.

Our comprehension of human involvement remains partial. We glimpse other man at war: what they say and do is seen only through the hero's eyes and from scraps of reported conversation. We are continually with Sherston and understand him: Barton, the potentially complex Cromlech, Durley, Ormand and many others make their several appearances, may be liked and prompt our interest, but they are never truly known. We have no deep conception of anyone's fears, struggles, aspirations and affections other than Sherston's.[15]

This loss is inevitable. Sherston's vision must be limited because of his immaturity. He is incapable of the degree of detachment a universalization of the War would have required—a detachment that would have been necessary in the thick of the War itself. Though in the later stages of his war-experience Sherston does, as we have seen, develop a capacity for a detached, yet compassionate, observation of the suffering around him, this is never a settled mood. Happy Warriorism returns, obliterating reflection and enabling emotional release. So the process continues, as the mind struggles to come to terms with the strains of war. What most engages our interest is the development of Sherston's response *towards* a broader vision: this would not be so if Sherston were endowed at any stage with a precocious awareness and with the ability to subdue self in the contemplation of other's sufferings that a 'universalization' of the conflict would demand.

Yet throughout, for Sherston is always sensitive to the sufferings of his fellow-victims as well as his own, there are flashes of the broader vision. It comes to him, most often, in moments of reflection, in a pause from the heat of battle or the numbing physical discomfort of the trenches. Near the beginning, he compassionately sees men on the march to the Line through sleeping villages as "the patient dun-coloured column"—a recurrent figure exactly appropriate in its deadness and nullity. At such moments, watching his men from a distance, he sees them as living shadows, more at one with death than

15. Had Sassoon been less reticent about his friendships, this might not have been so: who, for example, was the person "whose friendship I valued highly" who gives him the lump of fire-opal which he keeps as an affecting remembrance of Front Line associations? The first mention of this comes as late as *S.P.*, p. 53.

life: "Visualizing that forlorn crowd of khaki figures under the twilight of the trees, I can believe that I saw then, for the first time, how blindly War destroys its victims". The Battalion returning from battle seem to him like "an army of ghosts ... as though I had seen the War as it might be envisioned by the mind of some epic poet a hundred years hence." (This impression is movingly caught in the poem 'Two Hundred Years After'.) This feeling never leaves him; even so far from the Front as the camp at Kantara, he watches the "dim brown moonlit mass of men" at a variety concert and his imagination catches them momentarily in a universal sense: "It was as though these civilians were playing to an audience of the dead and the living—men and ghosts who had crowded in like moths to a lamp"—and then the erosive feeling passes: "But it was the voice of life that 'joined in the chorus, boys'; and very powerful and impressive it sounded." An erosive feeling: it is hard to carry the tragic vision. Sherston has continually to guard himself against its spiritually destructive effects, to keep his intelligence alive (though it seems useless) among men "like the dead ... in some dim region where time survived in ghostly remembrances." His own mind is not yet fortified to master the reality: our interest is necessarily focused rather upon Sherston's endeavour to come to terms with such perceptions than upon the man-and-man reality that gives rise to them.

This is not to say that we have no awareness of individuals other than Sherston. We do, but chiefly in intense, isolated moments, not—like the 'squad' whose individual experiences and reactions Barbusse describes[16]—in crowded day-to-day detail. More vivid than any characterization in the *Memoirs* are the inconsequential human actions that stand, without comment, in stark contrast to the unremitting massive destruction of humanity: "What we did in the Front Line I don't remember; but while we were remounting our horses ... two privates were engaged in a good-humoured scuffle; one had the other's head under his arm. Why should I remember that and forget so much else?" On another occasion, the order to march arrives in the middle of a cricket-match and he remembers "one of the Company Sergeant-Majors was playing a lively innings." Such moments have more significance as demonstrations of humanity's power to survive than have the named characters who, admirable as many of them are, remain in

16. *Under Fire* (*Le Feu*), Henri Barbusse (1916): for further reference to this book see Appendix C.

the mind as little more than types of courage, fortitude and stoicism. Kinjack and Velmore, Barton and Dottrell, Corporal Griffiths and Sergeant Wickham, remain as names, faces, actions; they call up *qualities*:

I was standing beside Corporal Griffiths, who had his Lewis gun between his elbows on the dew-soaked parapet. His face, visible in the sinking light of a flare, had the look of a man who was doing his simple duty without demanding explanations from the stars above him. Vigilant and serious he stared straight ahead of him, and a fine picture of fortitude he made. He was only a stolid young farmer from Montgomeryshire; only; but such men, I think, were England, in those dreadful years of war.

We can give little more than a formal assent to these words, for such characters make too brief an appearance—which is, considering War's dividing power, often only too appropriate—or else we know them by their outward behaviour as Sherston reports it. We do not feel we know them intimately: we know too little of what they have to lose and of what—not the world—but their families, their friends, will lose irreplaceably in losing them. They do not establish individual voices, however much physical presence they possess: their characters have no opportunity to unfold before us. The limitations of circumstances would almost certainly have precluded any such delineation, even had Sassoon wished to attempt it.[17] He achieves instead more shadowy intimations of individual human tragedy; infinite possibilities of exploring character through dialogue and situation lie behind this sketch of two young officers, new to the Line:

They were a well contrasted couple. Rees was a garrulous and excitable little Welshman; it would be flattery to call him anything except uncouth, and he made no pretensions to being a 'gentleman'. But he was good-natured and moderately efficient. Shirley, on the other hand, had been educated at Winchester and the war had interrupted his first year at Oxford. He was a delicate-featured and fastidious young man, an only child, and heir to a comfortable estate in Flintshire . . . I noticed that Rees kept his courage up by talking incessantly and making jokes about the

17. That he desired to attain to some all-embracing vision is shown by the following quotation: "I felt a great longing to be liberated from these few hundred yards of ant-like activity—to travel all the way along the Western Front—to learn through my eyes and with my heart the organism of this monstrous drama which my mind had not the power to envision as a whole" (*S.P.*, p. 248). The poet Sassoon also desires to return to the Line in 1918 to obtain material for "something on a bigger scale" (see *S.J.*, p. 70). (It is, however, by an intensive concentration upon experience within narrow limits that Barbusse universalizes the War).

battle; while Shirley, true to the traditions of his class, simulated non-chalance, discussing with Leake (also an Oxford man) the comparative merits of Magdalen and Christ Church, or Balliol and New College. But he couldn't get the nonchalance into his eyes ... Both Shirley and Rees were killed before the autumn.

After this description, Shirley and Rees only reappear in one of two glimpses: neither of them is ever *heard*—and merely turning over the pages of the *Memoirs* quickly reveals that this is a characteristic deficiency. The two characters sketched above are, of course, just two of a vast number, promising or otherwise, caught for a moment before extinction. One is perpetually aware that those mentioned are just a few figures shuffled into brief notice, of the many who lie behind. One recognises their individual meaning for Sherston, but each one is too little known to us, not close enough to enable us to feel, in the death of one, the enormity of the death of so many more who might have been as thoroughly known.

Nature's Rôle

If at the human level the range is disappointing, we are made deeply conscious through Nature's rôle—as also in the last two chapters of *A Fox-Hunting Man*—that War is a monstrous aberration, mindlessly wrecking Earth's essential harmony. This is done most effectively by juxtaposing the symbols of Nature and of simple things man-made for peace with those of War: the one constructive and creative, the other bent only on destruction. A pointed example of this occurs early in *Memoirs of an Infantry Officer*; Sherston has been attending a vigorous lecture on the use of the bayonet:

Afterwards I went up the hill to my favourite sanctuary, a wood of hazels and beeches. The evening air smelt of wet mould and wet leaves; the trees were misty-green; the church bell was tolling in the town, and smoke rose from the roofs. Peace was there in the twilight of that prophetic foreign spring. But the lecturer's voice still battered on my brain. "The bullet and the bayonet are brother and sister." "If you don't kill him, he'll kill you." "Stick him between the eyes, in the throat, in the chest ..."

Here, the contrast is made too explicit: "peace", "prophetic foreign spring", "sanctuary", the lecturer's bloodthirsty phrases are not all essential to the effect.[18] More impressive is a much later passage which points the same contrast; also following a lecture on "The Spirit of the Bayonet", heard again some two years later:

I have just been out for a stroll in the warm dusk along twilight lanes, past farms with a few yellow-lit windows, and the glooming trees towering overhead. Nightingales were singing beautifully. Beyond the village I could see the dark masses of the copses on the hill, and the stars were showing among a few thin clouds. But the sky winked and glowed with swift flashes of the distant bombardments at Amiens and Albert, and there was a faint rumbling, low and menacing. And still the nightingales sang on. O world God made!

In this passage the description does its own work: in the balanced contrasts between the warm twilight and the steady glowing windows and the nervous, abrupt and intense flashing of the guns, and between the clear song of the nightingale and the deep menace of the gunfire. The final brief exclamation is more than enough to convey the narrator's emotional reaction—the effect upon the reader has already been gained.[19]

The single observed detail, caught in the midst of action, may point the contrast even more sharply: "Shells were banging away on the rising ground behind Fricourt and the low ridge of Contalmaison. A young yellow-hammer was fluttering about in the trench, and I wondered how it got there: it seemed out of place, perching on a body which lay trussed in a waterproof sheet." "It seemed out of place": a live thing, belonging to life, amongst the dead or nearly so—a profound understatement. Elsewhere, comment may be dispensed with altogether; the observed fact is enough in itself, without "embroidering [it] with afterthoughts": "9.50. Fricourt half-hidden by clouds of drifting smoke, blue pinkish and grey. Shrapnel bursting in small bluish-white puffs with tiny flashes. The birds seem bewildered; a lark begins to go up and then flies feebly along, thinking better of it. Others flutter above the trench with querulous cries, weak on the wing." Such glimpses of natural life disrupted lend perspective to the scene of

18. One is reminded, by contrast, of Henry Reed's delicately ironic poem, 'Lessons of the War', especially of the first part ("Naming of Parts") in which the words of a lecturer on the use of the rifle are juxtaposed with comments on the natural mechanism of Spring.
19. These closing words are used again in the poem, At Carnoy, but to close the description of a different scene—camp-fires, the conviviality of the men and, again, a fine sunset—observed before going up to the Line (described in prose in M.I.O., pp. 79-80).

massive destruction, like a leaf or a twig in the corner of a landscape painting.

Nature is normality and ideal order: "Birds whistle and pipe small in the still morning air, flitting among the clematis and broom, alighting on fig branches or bright green thorn bushes. The hillside feels more like a garden than ever before—an everlasting garden just outside the temporary habitations of men. In half an hour I shall be trudging along behind the column with a lot of baggage mules, trudging away from Arcadia, with not much more liberty than a mule myself." Man is restless, wilful; though he yearns for Nature's peace, he abandons her or attempts to despoil her: she looks on, indifferently and suffers him to do as he pleases. He will be the first to tire: she is the unchangeable dimension by which his puny actions are measured and judged to be perishable and pitiable: "Two days later we vacated the camp at Heilly. The aspens by the river were shivering and showing the whites of their leaves, and it was good-bye to their cool showery sound when we marched away in our own dust at four o'clock on a glaring bright afternoon. The aspens waited, with their indifferent welcome, for some other dead beat and diminished battalion. Such was their habit, and so the war went on."

In a number of crucial passages the setting sun becomes a symbol and a portent of disaster, painting the landscape in ironically beautiful colours: "We had trudged that way up to the Citadel and 71. North may times before; but never in such a blood-red light as now, when we halted with the sunset behind us and the whole sky mountainous with the magnificence of retreating rain-clouds." This is a fitting prelude to the Battle of the Somme: as men mass to kill each other, and there is a pause, so the sky puts forward its whole strength to furnish a massive symbol of the red destruction of war. A later passage describes a remembered evening during the Battle (most of which Sherston escapes through illness):

I remember another evening . . . when the weather seemed awaiting some spectacular event in this world of blundering warfare. Or was it as though the desolation of numberless deaths had halted the clouded sky to an attitude of brooding inertia? I looked across at Albert; its tall trees were flat grey-blue outlines, and the broken tower of the Basilica might have been a gigantic clump of foliage. Above this landscape of massed stillness and smoky silhouettes the observation balloons were swaying slowly, their noses pointing toward the line of battle. Only the distant thud of gun-fire disturbed the silence—like someone kicking footballs—a soft bumping, miles away. Walking along by the river I passed the horse-lines of the Indian cavalry; the barley field above couldn't raise a rustle, so still was the air. Low in the west, pale orange beams were streaming down on the country that receded with a sort of rich, regretful beauty, like the background of a painted masterpiece. For me that evening expressed the indeterminate tragedy which was moving, with agony on agony, toward the autumn.

In this paragraph one has an overpowering sense of the solidity of the landscape, patterned by the heavy clouds and deeply incised by the beams of the sun piercing them. By contrast, the symbols of man's activities—the balloons and the gun-fire—seem insubstantial, irritating intrusions. It is not easy to grasp the reason why these ignoble things should matter: yet they have the capacity to destroy our perception of beauty; they are an ever-present menace dominating the immediate reality—and seeming, tragically, to usurp the ultimate meaning of existence. In a shorter passage, this time before the Battle of Arras, the sun's rays seem to mock the courage and delusive cheerfulness of the troops marching to the Line:

Among the troops I observed a growing and almost eager expectancy; their cheerfulness increased; something was going to happen to them; perhaps they believed that the Arras Battle would end the War. It was the same spirit which had animated the Army before the Battle of the Somme. And now, once again, we could hear along the horizon that blundering doom which bludgeoned armies into material for military histories. "That way to the Sausage Machine!" some old soldier exclaimed as we passed a signpost marked Arras, 32 K. We were entering Doullens with the brightness of the setting sun on our faces . . .

Here, the explicit comments of the narrator would stand bare without the last sentence, which evokes an emotional response. This common evening sun may be the troops' last: one imagines them closing their eyes against its brilliance, though they may never have the chance to see it again. It is such things the mind remembers; they crystallise a scene or situation, giving it an enduring reality: "the remembering mind refuses to forget, and imbues the scene of past experience with significant finality." These words introduce the most vivid of the sunset scenes, again caught in a brief interval of calm on the way up to the Line:

... when we marched away from the straggling village and out into the flat green fertile farmlands, the world did seem to be lit up as though for some momentous occasion. There had been thunder showers all the afternoon and the sunset flared with a sort of crude magnificence which dazzled us when our road took a sudden twist to the left. More memorable now, perhaps; but memorable even then, for me, whose senses were so teemingly alive as I gazed on that rich yet havoc-bordered landscape and thought of the darkness toward which we were going. The clouds flamed and the clover was crimson and the patches of tillage were vividly green as we splashed along between the poplars. And then, with dusk, the rain came down again as though to wash the picture out for ever.

The vivid tones of this remembered scene both correspond to the narrator's heightened emotional awareness, forcefully conveying the strength of his feeling, and throw the drab thread of marching men (of which he is one) into tragic relief. They seem to be caught in the dominant, brilliant landscape, and are illumined only for a few bright moments; they struggle on through the mud, fatally insignificant, until the rain comes again and seems mercifully to blot out them, too, forever. It was not for nothing that the writer of such passages went to war with *The Return of the Native* in his haversack.

If one derives from these contrasts an awareness of the vastness of the catastrophe, one derives from them also a conviction of the ultimate insignificance of man's destructive endeavours: and from this comes a sense of reconciliation. If, as in the last passage quoted, the sun and rain are seen to blind and blot out man's worst actions and sufferings, there must be also the possibility of reconstruction. The aberration is not the ultimate reality. The retrospective mind sees, in recapturing its significant impressions, the littleness as well as the enormity of man's sins: "The pine-trees are patiently waiting for the guns to stop"—a fleeting perception in the face of the bitter reality, but these recollections are imbued with its truth. It is in the *Memoirs* that Sassoon to a large extent redeems his frustrated desire, expressed in *Siegfried's Journey*, to describe the Western Front "in a more comprehensive way, seeing it like a painter and imbuing my poetry with Whitmanesque humanity and amplitude." [20]

20. This view is shared by the most thorough contemporary reviewer of *M.I.O.*, who wrote: "One finds duly an implicit and an explicit condemnation of the War in this long prose elegy; but something of the light of eternity falls upon every passage, and an even excessive modesty restrains the retrospective spirit from laying down the law on anything except pride and prejudice." (*The Times Literary Supplement*, September 18, 1930).

For further discussion of the *Memoirs* in a larger context see Appendix C, 'Some Books of the Great War Compared.'

RENEWED RETROSPECTION

VII

THE MAKING OF A POET (I)

Portrayal of Self

In his Preface to *Father and Son* Edmund Gosse warns of the dangers that autobiographers face in dealing with their own childhood: "The author has observed," he writes, "that those who have written about the facts of their own childhood have usually delayed to note them down until age has dimmed their recollections. Perhaps an even more common fault in such autobiographies is that they are sentimental, and are falsified by self-admiration and self-pity."[1] If it be admitted that in writing of one's early life the autobiographer runs these grave risks, then in *The Old Century*[2] Sassoon avoids the worst pitfalls. In describing his early childhood, he adheres to a true delineation of childhood's uncertain progress towards awareness of others: there is no precocious understanding, no 'pure' sensitivity. The period of early youth, likewise, is treated, as in the *Memoirs*, with an eye continually upon its contradictions and inconsistencies. So far as 'self-pity' is concerned, Sassoon is in no danger of falsification—rather, as he concedes, of the reverse: "... I feel the unbending visages of the realists reproving me for failing to imitate their awful and astringent example. Let me, therefore, be on the safe side, and offer a semi-apologetic confession of my inability to describe my early life in a dismal and dissatisfied tone of voice. All human beings desire to be glad. I prefer to remember my own gladness and good luck ..."[3]

In *Memoirs of a Fox-Hunting Man* Sassoon had given a more selective picture of childhood, and from which one is conscious of the narrator always standing back, making objective comment on the life he describes. Here, Sassoon approaches the subject differently. He tries to

1. Edmund Gosse, *Father and Son*, 1907, pp. v-vi.
2. Full title: *The Old Century and Seven More Years*, 1st pub. 1938; reference is made here to the Fifth Impression, pub. 1946.
3. *O.C.*, p. 233: all ensuing quotations in this chapter are taken, unless otherwise stated, from this book; most of the references are given under 'Page References', p. 309.

present past experiences much as the child saw them and reacted to them: "I have even made efforts to feel childish," he writes, "when childhood was my theme." A curious mark of his success in doing this is that his style of narration is even, quite often, childlike. He frequently recaptures the simplicity of childish comments upon people: "Mr. Arnold's house by the river was quite plain and very ugly; he had no time for being picturesque and had only built it to be a corn merchant in"; "Nellie Gosse was married to Mr. Gosse, who was the only author who had ever given me one of his books. I felt that he must be a nice man because he had put Mr. before my name in his inscription..."; and, of this tutor, "After tutoring me for a year he intended to start learning to be a clergyman, and in the meantime he occasionally practised intoning the service in his bedroom". As is obvious from the last example especially, there is a mixture of styles, the phrasing and more complicated vocabulary of the adult mingling with a child's naive expressions. This mixture suggests that the childish style may not be conscious (as it is in the first part of Joyce's *Portrait of the Artist*); sometimes the styles alternate with almost disconcerting rapidity, as in this paragraph: "Ever since I could remember, I had been remotely aware of a lot of rich Sassoon relations. I had great-uncles galore, whom I had never met and they all knew the Prince of Wales, who sometimes stayed with them at Brighton. One of them had been made into a baronet. Never having received so much as a chuck under the chin from any of these great-uncles, I couldn't exactly feel proud of them for being so affluent.." There are two voices here: in the first sentence, one of adult recollection, in the second and third a childlike one, while the tone returns in the fourth to an adult objectivity. Sometimes the childlike voice is remarkably pure: "When we got there we had a glorious time with our grown-up girl cousins and their schoolboy brother Tom, who had a little sailing boat of his own and had built himself a crow's nest at the top of a lime tree and knew all about birds' eggs." This is a close approximation to the breathless language of childhood. Although there are many examples of this style in Book I, it never becomes a mannerism —as might be the case if it were deliberate. It contributes subtly to one's impression of childhood recaptured in actuality.

As, in these features of style, Sassoon recaptures something of the inconsequential nature of childish expression, so he recalls much of the random development of a child's deeper awareness and sensitivity. This is best shown in his descriptions of childish reactions to tragedy

and change, in which we see the competing elements of raw feeling
—selfishness, pity, fear, love—being shaped and attuned to life's
demands. Sassoon does not romanticize childhood, whose memory is
brief: "Poor old Grandmama, we said, as we laced up our boots and
went out to build a snow fort on the lawn; and we wondered when we
should be out in the sledge again, and how soon after the funeral
'Mamsy' would be able to skate." At one moment the child can love
and suffer an inexplicable ache for the loss of a loved one, the next he
can deny this love, prompted by another contrary impulse. So the
young Siegfried tells his lie against the departed Mrs. Mitchell, to feel
almost at once the pricking of that other elemental thing, conscience,
which is reinforced by conditioned fears of hell: "Miserably I resigned
myself to everlasting perdition; all I could do was to put it off as long
as possible by living to be about a hundred." For a while the child's
natural buoyancy reasserts itself, the fears suppressed: "Meanwhile I
continued my career as an interesting invalid in the best bedroom
with the wash-basin which had the big blue fish on it." But the fear
is too basic to kill, and conscience combines with cunning to bring
about a gratifying emotional release: "At any rate I could burst into
tears and tell Batty all about it .." It is hard for the child to adjust to
the possession of complex human feeling and to learn to balance the
claims of self against those of others. An early trial of this kind was the
death of Sassoon's father, which causes mingled feelings of selfish loss:
"I felt desolate, because of so much happiness which could never
happen now that he was dead ..."; and of protective love: "It horrified me to think of poor 'Pappy' being buried in a place where people
behaved like that ... I felt death in a new way now ..." Fortunately
for the child, the intensity of such impressions is blurred by the ever-
new experience of life. But in Sassoon's case they appear to have
produced, at an early age, a strong sensitivity to human loss and suffering. This awareness is, however, not exaggerated; but properly related
to the limitations of his understanding, as when he pities his invalid
uncle Beer for whom, in her refusal to recognise his extreme sickness,
his wife has bought a complete cricket outfit: "Even then I was
haunted by the pathetic futility of those cricket things which she had
purchased for him"; and there is pity, too, for the wife, Aunt Rachel,
but in a child's measure: "... there was a sense of sadness that she had
gone back to her joylessly opulent Mayfair mansion where even the
clocks seemed to have nothing to do, while I played cricket with my

brothers ..." There is no precocity of feeling here, no ultra-sensitivity, no suggestion that the child can imaginatively share the adult suffering; he stands outside, only half-aware, measuring the misery upon his own scale.

The scale is, in every respect, convincing. Just as he recaptures the nuances of childish feeling, so he seems able to re-enter the child's world of make-believe and wonder. He seems to have retained the child's eye view, as in the quotation cited in the last paragraph where the remembered detail about "the wash-basin which had the big blue fish on it" is the kind of observation that is likely to be indelibly printed on the child's mind. Such minute details fix a scene when the faces and actions are forgotten, as when recalling the *tableaux vivants* produced in their house by his mother, the principal features he recalls about the setting reflect the child's response to the outlandish: "the footlights were only candles, aided in special effects by a sort of magic-lantern, worked by the Tonbridge photographer from where the Sheraton sideboard stood in everyday life (with the cat's dinner plate underneath it);" of himself, he remembers, "I wore red shoes with twiddly toes to them". He recounts what is most meaningful to the child without condescension; in such passages as those describing the significance of "Moocow" and his "friends and relations" with whom he used to communicate "down a small hole in the cement between the blue and white Dutch tiles on the bathroom wall" (pp. 29-31) — a consoling contact in time of need — or in the longer one describing his activities in the orchard pond and the wood beyond, he re-creates the child's world without intrusive adult comment or moralising.[4] The latter passage especially (pp. 93-100), where he remembers the solitary world he made for himself, though it is typical childish make-believe, is related with a seriousness befitting its serious meaning. Sassoon does not nudge the reader, inviting him to say 'how amusing'; this is a meaningful world: "Alone with my tin of bait and my wool-gatherings, I was in an undisturbed world of my own, localized and satisfying as such worlds always are." The child makes "a snug little port" in the pond: "In squelching self-absorption I talked to myself as I thought it all out, adding one improvement after another and ignoring the irresponsible behaviour of the water-boatmen and other inhabitants." The comments on the "personalities" of the tadpoles and snails are

4. "The fantasies of childhood cannot be explained or analysed in the rational afterthoughts of experienced maturity" (*M.F.H.* p. 17).

not precious, but imbued with affectionate remembrance of the child's fantasies.[5] Tired of the pond, the child climbs over the hedge into Gedges Wood, "which quite easily became something else." He skirts the wood, reconnoitring, and glimpses a familiar dogcart go by; two worlds come together, but without conflict: "... the groom-gardener was on the back seat, and he'd got ... *The Globe* on his knee. The stop-press scores of today's county cricket were in it; these I should have liked to take a squint at. But I'd just been on the banks of the Zambesi River, where anything might happen ..." The cart passes out of sight, and the child again becomes a Rider Haggard character: this easy transition between the worlds of reality and fancy is a true mark of childhood, something we lose and desire to regain. This passage well recaptures childhood's double vision.

So far the emphasis has been upon the verisimilitude of Sassoon's recollections and upon their moderation: his refusal to exaggerate the significance of what he recalls or to moralize unduly. This approach extends to what, for most readers, will provide the leading interest: the growth of the poet's sensibility. To begin with, Sassoon treats this theme as an integral part of the child's developing awareness; it receives no concentrated attention—and there is certainly no reverence, no presentation of the poet born. The first stage in the child's development of a deeper awareness arises, as is often the case (H. G. Wells and Osbert Sitwell bear witness to a similar effect) from the experience of a prolonged illness; the convalescent child is carried downstairs to sit outside again:

To be out of doors again at that time of year was indeed like coming back to life. But it was more than that, for illness had made my perceptions detached and sensitive. I know how memory idealizes things; but I think, all the same, that this was my first conscious experience of exquisite enjoyment . . .
I was beginning to discover that solitude could quicken my awareness of aspects within me and around me.

Lying there alone, day after day, the child begins to hear "the sounds of life going on around me", of birdsong, of scythe upon stone, of the trotting pony: "Thus I lay, reposefully reviving in convalescent quiet-ude, aware—and yet unaware—of the blue evening distance of the

5. A passage in *Father and Son*, p. 205, provides a close parallel to this (p. 98) in description: one need not, however, suppose that Sassoon was influenced by it— this form of child's make-believe is common.

Weald beyond the tree-tops and the green tangles of our terraced untidy garden ... There it all was—looked at by the uncomparing eyes
of a child whose mind had so little in it to remember that the landscape
was like life, empty as yet and almost unlearned." He does not write
poetry about it, albeit an Aeolian harp on the crab-apple tree made a
sound "like poetry; for even then poetry could just stir my mind—as
though it were some living and yet mysterious spirit—touching me to
a blurred and uncontrolled chord of ecstasy." This is enough; it could
hardly be more. Like the young Wordsworth, he "[holds] unconscious
intercourse with beauty": "linking with the spectacle/No conscious
memory of a kindred sight"; there is "no need of a remoter charm/By
thought supplied ..."

These early perceptions may not be common, but they are not
enough to make the poet. They have to cross with other needs of the
personality and the contrary pressures of life. At the age of ten, the
vaguely aspiring poet is ignorant of what his true perceptions are: "I
had a tendency to expect all the best poetry to be gloomy, or at any
rate solemn". So he tackles, somewhat waveringly, *Queen Mab*, but
comes to rest with exquisite romantic enjoyment upon 'The Lady of
Shalott'. It is the dream world that draws him most strongly ("never
suspecting that the moral of the poem was a warning to people who turn
away from wholesome realities"): the child must answer to the demands
of his nature. The poet is not born; he evolves from the lucky accidents
of temperament and circumstance. Looking at two manuscript books
of poems written in 1897 (his eleventh year), Sassoon writes:

There is a transition from the serene simplicity of childhood to something
uncontrolled, and wilfully lugubrious. The poetic impulse in me had become
more impetuous, while the artistic sense, which so many children possess
up to the age of twelve, was about to leave me to my own devices until such
time as I was old enough to call it back. Meanwhile, not being aware
of Nature's arrangements for the artistic development of the species, I
continued to think of myself as what I called 'an infant prodigy' ...

Unconsciously, the choice is right: consciously, poetry is the means by
which the child chooses to express his urge for display. The poems he
writes to impress his mother must not be "insipid and unimaginative";
he wishes to please her with the sensational, whilst also indulging his
childish fascination for horrors: "Eternity and the Tomb were among
my favourite themes, and from the accessories of Death I drew my
liveliest inspirations." So far, the young poet has developed alone, but

now the external forces of human existence intervene to curtail—
though ultimately to promote—his poetic activity. He attends his
first school, where "no one suspected me of having written poetry in
past years. I now looked upon that as an occupation to be almost
ashamed of." For a time we lose sight of the poet, who remains in
abeyance until in answer to a fresh need of the personality he is given
renewed life.

Sassoon's account of his school-days plays a relatively small part in
this volume, and it is clear that his experiences at school played no
decisive part in his development. He passes quickly over his life at
preparatory school and devotes the most attention to his time at Marlborough. In dealing with this period, he shows even less inclination
than elsewhere to follow "the awful and astringent example" of the
realists. Here are none of the seamy revelations about public school
life which form so notable a part of such contemporary memoirs as those
of Cyril Connolly, Robert Graves and Osbert Sitwell. From the beginning, the recollections are in a low, but sensitive key: the touching
parting between mother and child at the station, the child's lonely
walk about the town, wondering what face he should put upon things
before his fellows, the painful episode of the recalcitrant stick-up collar.
This last is recounted with the same sympathetic understanding for the
magnitude of childish misfortunes as Sassoon displays in recounting
earlier experiences. These apparent trivialities deserve the most careful
notice: "... for me the whole episode ... remained for fully twenty
years afterwards in my repertoire of unpleasant dreams, in spite of the
fact that, like most of our poor little mistakes in life, it only ended in
my being told not to do it again".[6] Similar episodes—being publicly
accused by his housemaster of learning the organ to get out of games,
and his unwitting playing of a forbidden hymn, which lent itself to
comic variations about the matron, in prayers—are dealt with in a
tone in which humour blends with understanding, whereas it might
easily have been arch or moralizing.

At Marlborough the poetic impulse returns, after a lapse of three
years, and this time by chance. A master happens to offer half-crown
prizes for the best poems written by his pupils, and the young Siegfried,
who has failed to distinguish himself at his books, at the organ, or on

6. "These failures in trivial things loom much larger in childhood and affect us
much more deeply than any backwardness in learning manners or facts, for they
reflect on our physical capacity, and that is much more real to us than any mental
power" (Herbert Read, *The Contrary Experience*, Part I: 'The Innocent Eye', p. 27).

the hockey-field, turns his attention to winning them. His effusions are characteristic of his years—"portentously solemn"—but now once more they can be made to serve a need of his nature, a basic need in any human being. One day, alone in the library, he picks up an anthology at random and opens it at Hood's "Bridge of Sighs": "... here was a direct utterance which gave me goose flesh and brought tears to my eyes. It wasn't so much the subject of the poem which thrilled me as the sense of powerful expression and memorable word music. For the first time since I had been at school I felt separated from my surroundings and liberated from the condition of being only a boy". He is moved now with the conviction that he possesses a secret gift, which one day will give him mastery: "Down there [in the school] I was an unprivileged nobody. But up here, with this book in my hand and this poem in my head, I was alive with some power which I would some day put into words. And those words I would find, said I to myself, that the spirit within me might be made manifest". There is here a rare lapse into rhetoric, which produces a too portentous effect; on the other hand, this may well convey the nature of the child's feeling at the time. We see that, at this point, the original childish perception of the meaning of poetry is renewed, but it is hardly more firmly based. It answers now to a vaguer romanticism, feeding the adolescent desire for singularity.

The *idea* of being a poet is the thing upon which he now grounds his life. Opportunity to indulge this romantic conception of himself is given, once more, by illness. Convalescent, lengthily, once more, he sets himself to collecting books—the concentrated and visible symbol of his new feeling: "The smell of such books appealed to me and suggested leisurely lives in days when authors had odd handwriting and did their work very slowly in panelled parlours while their wives made home-made wine or sang sweetly to the lute." Actual endeavours fall short of this, though he achieves publication of a poem called 'The Extra Inch' in *Cricket*—a poem he reproduces, with humorous apologies, for the reader's amusement. The remaining four terms at Marlborough are passed over in as many pages, until Siegfried's unavoidable "superannuation at the age of eighteen," with the parting advice from Mr. Gould, "Try to be more sensible." The valedictory words upon his educational experience—"moderately pleasant but mentally unprofitable"—stand in striking contrast with Sir Osbert Sitwell's: "I liked Eton, except in the following respects: for work and games, for boys and masters ..."[7] It is evident that, at this age, Sassoon was in every outward respect the normal, even 'average' boy, with a predilection for games which, even if he was not an outstanding player, would have ensured his acceptance by both staff and boys. Non-acceptance might well have caused him to develop more rapidly, but in fact this was largely a fallow period so far as the development of his sensibility was concerned.

Sassoon is fully aware of this. He is even, as was pointed out at the beginning of this discussion, somewhat defensive about it: he has, he confesses, no "doldrums of precocious disillusionment" to describe, and neither would he do so if he could, for: "Turning the page, you would sigh and hope for something better to follow." He retains no dominant impression of himself "at [his] adolescent worst" and sees no reason why he should indulge in a specious realism.

For him, youth was "heedless and happy," and he expects the (perhaps jaded) reader to be thankful for it: "Be grateful, therefore, and share my gratitude that I lived in such a pleasant region. For in those days I found no fault with the world, and did not foresee that it would, in my lifetime, alter much." If, in recollecting childhood and youth, Sassoon "tried to feel young again," he never pretends that this is an easy matter, and, as he draws closer to that period of life in which people are expected to become "sensible", retrospection becomes imbued with a more serious note: "... when describing my approaches to manhood I have sometimes been prematurely aged by sensations reserved for those of riper years." Thus, much of the latter part of Book II is devoted to recollections of those human contacts at Henley House (the crammer's) which supported him more than he ever realized at the time (this aspect will be further discussed later). Meanwhile, we observe the youth dreaming, drifting, perhaps too secure in the life that surrounds him, ignorantly planning an epic in twelve books or escaping on his bicycle from the as yet arid questions in Paley's *Evidences*. Cambridge comes, and there is no apparent change for the better: "'In three months I shall be twenty, and I don't seem to have done anything at Cambridge except buy books in vellum bindings,' I thought, while the clock watched me with its hands at half-past five and I overheard my thought as though it were a repetition of some previous experience." Once more, he has surrounded himself with the trappings of the artistic life; once more, he enjoys imaginatively a

7. Osbert Sitwell, *The Scarlet Tree*, p. 257.

wished-for existence: "Far away from factory chimneys, Rossetti would be reading me his latest sonnet, or Morris showing me the carp in his fish-pond, and my own poems would be being exquisitely printed by the Kelmscott Press and bound in limp vellum with woven silk ties." The Law Tripos is abandoned, History undertaken—with equal ill-success. He abandons Stubbs's *Constitutional History* and applies himself to producing the prize poem for the Chancellor's Medal, as formerly his path to self-esteem had been competing for half crowns at Marlborough. This fruitless endeavour to compose a poem on a subject—Edward I—which he finds intractable in prose anyway, is described with humorous detachment. Sassoon wastes no time upon superfluous apologetics, for either this piece of misplaced industry or the youthful egotism that later drives a privately-printed volume of callow poems into existence. There is no need for apology or censure, though those who judge only by externals might think otherwise. However erratically, the youthful Siegfried is following his star, a fact his mother recognizes when she agrees to his leaving Cambridge without graduating: "She thought that I should be wasting my time by trying to learn things which didn't interest me, and should do better by educating myself in the art of poetry, which was obviously the only thing for which I had a natural gift." If, though fortified by this sympathetic understanding, he retires into the ivory tower of his book-ornamented studio and proceeds to *trifle* with poetry ("I was planning a longish dramatic poem which was to be about either Orpheus or Apollo—I hadn't yet made up my mind which"), what of it? These are the irresponsible years: "There was only the dazzling daydream of visible existence, and the serenity of poems and pictures, and past and future meeting in a siesta of weather which was neither summer nor autumn." If youth is fortunate enough to have maintained such a vision of life till the age of twenty-one, it is the duty of its chronicler to recall faithfully its origin and nature by showing the interaction of circumstances and temperament as they are. He must do this without impatience or superior hindsight—for every kind of life has its value, and this is what Sassoon has done. Life makes youth what it is: youth cannot make life. In the autobiographer's art the making is what matters most.

"Commemorative Affection"

The portrayal of the autobiographer's self is, within the limits he has set himself, frank and clear. However, when one turns to consider the other principal subjects of autobiography, one receives a picture more coloured and qualified by retrospect: this applies to both the portrayal of the people the poet knew and that of the time in which he lived.

The author portrays none of his contemporaries in any detail—not even his brothers—at home, school, or university. This may well be because he describes himself as leading a relatively solitary life— though only so far as his mental activity was concerned. In other respects, physically and socially, he seems to have been involved in a normal way. His portrayals of people he remembers are noticeably strongest where his human contacts appear to have been most fruitful: at home, throughout childhood and youth, and during his period at Henley House, the crammer's; we have only glimpses of the more exalted way of life of his rich Sassoon relatives.

Though most of the people he remembers, however briefly, have an individual quality, one's final impression is of a group portrait. Firmly occupying the centre are the people of his county home and neighbourhood: his mother, the children, the neighbouring squire's daughters, the gentlemanly landowner, Major Horrocks. Grouped about these are the children's tutors and the family servants and, on the periphery, the masters and instructors of Marlborough and Henley House, with the shadowy figures of the Sassoons and Thornycrofts in the background. The range suggests great variety, but the picture, it has been said, is a composite one; the reason for this lies in the author's general approach to his subject: "I have spoken of my desire not to remember unpleasant things too clearly. My intention in this book has been to commemorate or memorialize those human contacts which supported me in my rather simple-minded belief that the world was full of extremely nice people if only one could get to know them properly." One receives an impression precisely corresponding to this intention. If some of these people have their asperities, foolishness, and prejudices, these are never emphasized: fundamentally they are "nice" —harmless, well-meaning, dutiful, often loving and self-sacrificing to a high degree.

At the centre, we have a much clearer impression than in *A Fox-Hunting Man* of what, referring to that book, Daiches calls "the tone and rhythm of a kind of English life that has now almost completely passed away—that of the cultivated squirearchy in the large country-house."[8] Sassoon's mother, Major Horrocks, and the daughters of the local squire, May and Bessie Marchant, epitomise this way of life. The mother is gentle and understanding, cultivated—a lover of gardens, painting, her Meredith, and good talk. The Marchant girls complement each other: May active and practical-minded, a sports-woman (she plays golf), but not mannish; her sister, Bessie, to the uninitiated like a survival from the period of Jane Austen: "In her serious and romantic moods she practised her violin and read poetry; but she was as good as May at finding bird's nests and told amusing stories about the cottagers, imitating their way of talking." "In these days," Sassoon points out, "people who lived quietly in the country were much more dependent on their neighbours than they are now." And thus we find Sassoon's mother jogging twenty miles on a visit to her friend, Florence Branwell, for the sake of a lively conversation; of this friend he writes (with a rare moralizing note): "... she had spontaneous and original phrases for the most ordinary matters, and her downright opinions were the delight of all who knew her. [De-lightedly, Sassoon's mother compares her to Meredith's Diana.] Time teaches one to admire such people, who refuse to pull a long face how-ever deeply life may have hurt them, and whose cheerfulness is born of courage as well as being the outcome of their abundant aliveness." Nearer home, there is old Major Horrocks, jovial, bumbling, kind-hearted, but no fool: "... a well-connected country gentleman who farmed a few hundred acres, was an authority on rock-plants and flowering shrubs, and loved good music and the fine arts in an un-affected way." And then there is 'Wirgie', Helen Wirgman, paying frequent visits, sensitive, intellectually curious, a balanced person with a fine sense of fun, also artistic—a reader of poetry and an excellent pianist. These people are the core of the life Sassoon recalls, a life from which he excludes the often boorish figures who jostle the pages of *A Fox-Hunting Man*.

If, extending our consideration to the less central characters in very different spheres of life, we ask ourselves why the picture still remains a composite one, the answer seems to be that Sassoon "memorializes" not just characters he admires, but ones he admires for their common qualities. Each of them—Ellen Batty, Uncle John, 'Moony', Mr.

8. *The Present Age: After 1920*, p. 202.

Gould, 'The Teacher' and many more—possesses one, or more, of the qualities of sincerity, simplicity, gentleness, lack of affectation. The overmastering moral impression one receives becomes evident if one places side by side a number of extracts in the form of comment upon people of differing backgrounds:

(i) of Uncle John Thornycroft, the famous naval engineer: "he seemed to spend most of his time cutting roses or pulling up weeds; when I passed him he would look up, pink-faced and fluffy-bearded, smile seraphically, and stoop again to his gardening."

(ii) of Mr. Moon, the obscure tutor: "Affectionately nicknamed 'Moony', he was one of the mildest of men. Nobody could have been more like an indulgent tutor and less like a stern taskmaster . . . with his silver hair and straggling moustache—a tall, tired, stooping man, who never spoke fast and always wore the same black tail-coat."

(iii) "Dear Ellen Batty, with her wide mouth and rather sallow face which wrinkled and puckered like a tomato under her black hair that was streaked with white; who always dressed in brown and wore queer shapeless hats that got on one side, whose port-manteau key usually got lost on the journey, and who did everything one asked her . . . If Heaven can be made real by trusting in it, hers was never far away, and it was full of happy children . . ."

(iv) 'The Teacher': "He always wore a high single collar, even when he played his steady rounds of golf, or when, in the summer, he bicycled slowly about the country by himself. And from behind that high collar I see him now, looking at me in his mildly quizzical way, and wondering perhaps, like old Mr. Gould, whether I shall ever learn to be more sensible . . . He had no great things to hope for; next year, perhaps, he would buy a new bicycle. Frugal and unenvious, he watched us go our ways, little knowing that one at least would return to him long afterwards with commemorative affection."[9]

These quotations demonstrate the qualities of character toward which Sassoon feels drawn: gentleness above all and an undemanding simplicity; Uncle John and 'Moony' could easily exchange places, it seems, and Ellen Batty and 'The Teacher' typify the selfless persons who "supported me in my rather simple-minded belief that the world was full of extremely nice people if only one could get to know them." For Sassoon, it is a labour of love to remember these people; as in *A Fox-Hunting Man*, we see that he is highly conscious of the impercipience of youth and wishes, so far as he can, to compensate for it. This appears from the words with which he prefaces his affectionate remembrance of his instructors at Henley House, of which 'The Teacher' was one:

9. These quotations can be found on pp. 57, 58-59, 51-52 and 249-250 respectively.

"... I have found myself wanting to be back there so that I could just for once, communicate my fellow-feeling to some of those people whose grey hairs I took for granted—and perhaps made slightly greyer." He relishes remembering the modest and unassuming, to recall them (as the sentence in the quotation about 'The Teacher' shows) from their undeserved obscurity.

It is quite unnecessary for him to point the moral of this. Many of the people he recalls are distinguished for their unaffected goodness; and he brings to his recollections of them a matching spontaneity of expression that perfectly conveys the strength of his feeling. A fine example of this is his unaffected tribute to his mother in his recollection of his feelings at parting from her on his first day at Marlborough: "With an unsympathetic whistle the little train disappeared down the branch line to the junction, carrying away from me that loving heart, whose anxieties and agitations I was too young to accept with responsive understanding. My devotion to her was so comprehensive that I had never given any thought to it." His memories of others less intimately known are strengthened with a loving recollection of what mattered to them: "Dear Ellen Batty" and her simple belief in children's goodness; "Good old Gould" is remembered for both his idiosyncrasies and the gruff kindliness that lay beneath an exterior roughened by years of exacting schoolmastering; "Uncle", with his boyish pride in his golf and his "gentle, unemphatic voice," is a successor to Mr. Moon; "The Teacher's" poignant action of going to the window to listen to the blackbird's song, which must arouse in him feelings utterly different from the hopeful young poet's—his lonely bicycling is the pathetic symbol of his life. Looking back, Sassoon realizes how lucky he was, and these warm remembrances of the people who contributed to his good luck form the most sympathetic element of the book.

But of the people remembered we know 'Wirgie' best, for she is to us, as to Sassoon, "different from other people in a different way." She is a more many-sided character than the others. She is adaptable, with a temperament partly childlike, and with a great enthusiasm for whatever activity she is involved in: "she would crawl and sprawl and bawl as if dumb crambo were the only thing in the world worth doing." From the beginning, the young Siegfried feels a strong sense of identity with her: "Wirgie was more than forty years older than I was ... it did seem strange to think of her having lived all that time without my knowing what she was doing." She keeps pace with his growth, her enthusiasm for poetry and music having a strong influence on his development, whilst in childhood she sympathetically encourages his efforts and later helps him to correct his youthful excesses. She alone exists a little outside the 'gentle' picture: 'nice', yet with a volatile temperament that makes her less predictable than the rest; the portrayal of her deepens in *The Weald of Youth*.

'Summer Not to Come Again'

We have seen that the recollections of people in *The Old Century* are highly selective, consciously, it seems, arising from "my desire not to remember unpleasant things too clearly"—though it might also be said that their ideal quality derives largely from the author's fortunate life.

A parallel narrowing of focus governs the narrative as a portrayal of the age. If *A Fox-Hunting Man* presents the Edwardian Age as an idyll of hunting and cricket, *The Old Century* is a complementary idyll of a serenely cultivated existence carried on, like the former, in the atmosphere of perpetual summer. That this should have seemed so when Sassoon looked back upon it in 1938, with so much destruction intervening and so much more imminent, is hardly surprising. Nor it is surprising, when one remembers the happiness that his early human contacts had given him, that his recollection of those should lend colour to the whole.

The whole book breathes an unashamed desire for the past—the past as he knew it at the time; the very title breathes it. Sassoon allows no subsequent knowledge of the time he may have gained to intrude and mar the limited, ideal picture that he gives. He does not look outside its limits at facts about life, public or private, as they were for ordinary Englishmen between 1886 and 1907. He gives no hint that any such knowledge disturbs his ideal view; the only disturbed note is that which we also find in *A Fox-Hunting Man*, of the brief and doomed nature of this life in relation to the coming Great War: "No-one could tell what was going to happen any more than I could see beyond our safe-looking hills. While Wirgie played the piano after dinner people were jingling out to the Opera in hansom-cabs. A brilliant season was in full swing around them, and they knew as little of their future in-

security as my tortoise Joey, who died the next winter of being dug up
to see how he was getting on while hibernating." This note is recurrent,
reminding us of the disaster imminent for all, but it is the only contrast
with the ideal that we are offered (of this more will we said later).

Even in dealing with his educational experiences that lay outside the
idyll of country-life, Sassoon recounts little of general interest. In
reading of Marlborough and Cambridge we gain little impression of
the place, and there is no significant mention of his contemporaries,
famous or otherwise. By contrast, other roughly contemporary autobiographers, such as Chesterton, Osbert Sitwell, Graves and Cyril
Connolly, describe their school and university life in considerable
detail, ranging widely over both masters and pupils, moving forward
and back in time to give depth—and also dimension to their own
individual experience. Sassoon further differs from these writers in
treating his relatives only as they are important to him personally, or
as they seem to the child who observes them: it matters nothing to his
narrative that Uncle John Thornycroft invented the tubular boiler
(though he mentions it), that Uncle Beer owns both the *Observer* and
The Sunday Times, or that his rich Sassoon relatives are very well
connected in high places. They meant nothing to him in these ways
when he was young; and they mean nothing now—or at least his
curiosity about them has not been of the kind that would lead him to
suppose his readers would be greatly interested. His knowledge of them,
however interesting, could only be second-hand; he does not recount
what he never knew or what was not significant to him in the past
anyway.

By the exclusion of these factors, especially of a broader reference to
the conditions of the period for the sake of contrast and proportion,
the past world Sassoon recalls seems utterly detached; it has the quality
of a dream. A dream, if it is pleasurable, is something we wish to
retain in its entirety. We do not reject it impatiently with our wakened
mind, because it did not happen—except in our sleep. We retain it
as a positive form of experience, ignoring the fact that we slept as
irrelevant: this is what Sassoon has done. He offers us a dream only,
which he himself uses, when he can, as a means of escape, to satisfy
"my queer craving to revisit the past and give the modern world the
slip." The dream was, for a time, the reality; now, it is irrecoverable.
The whole of *The Old Century* is written in the nostalgic spirit of the
chapter in which the author describes his sentimental journey of return

to Edingthorpe, the Norfolk holiday village of his childhood.[10] For once, the past seems truly resuscitated—or rather it seems as if here life has retained an essential continuity:

> . . . I was relieved to find that the lane was as narrow and unassuming as ever. The wild convolvulus still twined exuberantly over the low hedges, and the level landscape receded as prosily as it had done in 1897, when it really was a long way from anywhere, and looked like it—as indeed it still did. Edingthorpe, thank goodness, was still a straggling hamlet a few miles inland from the east coast, and the almost unidentifiable post office had merely been moved from one dear old cottage to another.

He wanders round, delightedly recapturing the small familiar details, mingling with the present scenes recollections of the past. Though one sight is a sombre one—the lych-gate at the church which is dedicated to the memory of a young soldier killed in the Great War—even that seems no disfiguring mark; many wars cannot destroy this place: "It seemed to be aware that it had never been anything but a thorpe and would remain one in perpetuity. This, perhaps, was its appealing quality—that it had no expectancy of being sought out again by any-one who had known it in days gone by. It was friendly, but quite content to be lost sight of and forgotten, not speaking until it was spoken to." The crucial appeal of this place is at one with that of many of the people he remembers; it is at one, too, with the author's own retiring temperament, his muted expectations of life and his distrust of display. It also embodies a way of life utterly removed from the present, a way which, as he gazes at the village church, seems to possess an essential continuity: "... it evoked in me a sense of local England and of the simple old centuries behind it—the harvests it had seen, and the pathos of those humble folk who had toiled and died and had been 'of this parish'."

Here, Sassoon's view of the past tends toward sentimentality. There is a wistfulness of tone, an inclination to mourn the passing of a life which only existed for the very few, which harks back to the Edwardian spirit as it is sometimes seen to be epitomised in "The Old Vicarage, Grantchester": "... And then we came into the courtyard, where the gilded stable clock was striking the hour and their brother Dick was giving his falcons some raw meat while his golden setter sat watching him; and the evening sunshine was on it all—as it is now in my mind,

10. Book I, Chapter VIII.

at the memory of those young voices in that dawdling homespun world of long ago." And the unhistorical bias of the following quotation will hardly bear comment: "Behind him was that wonderful view of the Kentish Weald which one got from his big meadow, and a good picture of a man of Kent he must have made as he stood there, in the prime of life, long before the world became the troubled place it now is." No explicit comparisons to the disadvantage of the modern world are made, but an unfavourable contrast clearly underlies the preference for simplicity, slow time, solidity and dependability. In human terms, the book ends with a passage in which two figures representative of the Old Century, old Major Horrocks and his sister, are given an honoured place, gentle—and genteel—exemplars of unaffected taste and refinement. We are not invited to lament, 'A dying breed!' but the invitation is implicit.

Positive and admirable as are the human qualities he commemorates, and appealing in its charm and simplicity though the country-life he describes may have been, many contemporary readers will be dissatisfied because Sassoon does not question the basis upon which they way of life he has depicted rests, and because he makes neither apology nor defence of it.[11] The only disquieting element in the narrative—the undertones of impending war—directs attention to what accidentally precipitated, not caused, the disintegration of this way of life. There is no hint that, but for the War and the troubles that followed it, it would not have endured.

But *The Old Century* can be allowed to stand apart from its fellows in the autobiographical trilogy in that it gives no destructive licence for criticisms of this kind. It matters little to our appreciation of this book whether Sassoon has deliberately suppressed any doubts he may have had—or any inclination to argue—about the defensibility of the way of life he describes. Nor does it matter greatly whether he sincerely sees the life depicted as ideal. *The Old Century* seldom provokes such questions and has sufficient artistic unity to be accepted for what it is: a frankly escapist idyll of rural life, narrated by one who is sensitive, humane and generous-minded. But in the two books that follow our interest is gradually engaged less completely by the portrayal of the writer's developing personality and increasingly by the nature of the wider society in which he moves. A stricter critical appraisal of that

11. See Appendix A, (10).

society and of the writer's retrospective valuation of it then becomes unavoidable.[12]

"Spots of Time"

The Old Century has the scrupulous finish that we have noticed in *A Fox-Hunting Man* and the descriptive passages of the war *Memoirs*. There is no looseness of expression, nothing jarring or inappropriate in its context. One marks especially Sassoon's penchant for the alliterative phrase, used variously in both humorous and serious passages, and his choice of the precise word or sound that conveys the sense. As in *A Fox-Hunting Man*, latinisms are frequent, especially in a humorous context, but there are fewer coinages than one would expect from reading the poetry of this period.[13]

The most distinctive and memorable feature of the style[14] is the recurrence of carefully composed and detailed descriptive passages which seem to stand out in the narrative as, to use Wordsworth's phrase, "spots of time"—though they do, of course, lack Wordsworth's heightened visionary quality. Like the similar, but fewer, passages in *A Fox-Hunting Man*, they establish the atmosphere of tranquillity and slowness and, for many of them are devoted to natural description, mellow fruitfulness under nature's beneficent rule. In them the past is indelibly defined for us in a number of recaptured moments which fix, so far as it can be done in words, the texture of time. In a way that is impossible in the thematically more restricted *A Fox-Hunting Man*, these moments punctuate both the life of the child and youth and the time during which he grows; in them, we perceive how these two merge as the remembered "spots of time" seem to symbolize stages in the growth of the young sensibility.

12. See on *W.T.*, Chapter VIII, 'Coloured Retrospect', p. 152 et. seq., where objections are made to Sassoon's uncritical idealisation of English (rural and urban) life as it was during his childhood and youth and in earlier times: this nostalgic conservatism is also expressed with particular clarity in several poems in the contemporaneous *Rhymed Ruminations*, e.g. 'In Heytesbury Wood', 'A View of Old Exeter' and 'Doggerel About Old Days.'
13. Examples are: the compound "mind-sight" (p. 117), which recurs three times in the reflective poems, is probably derived from Hardy who uses it in the poem 'Often when Warring'; "memorialize" (p. 248) seems unnecessary, since Sassoon has already used "commemorate" in the same context; "havocked" (p. 133) is more successful. The sonorous word "bombilations" is redeemed from disuse (p. 83). There is a pun, worth noting for its rarity: "I found the *Works of William Penn* impenetrable."
14. Reference has already been made to the childlike tone of the prose in parts of Book I.

This symbolism is early established in the vividly detailed well- and sowing-scenes which form the Prelude to Book I. These scenes show the child close to nature, wondering, and finding wonder in the common sights that later will form the unquestioned background of his life. They provide a poetic metaphor for life heralded in its beginnings: "And the purpose of this book is to tell whither the water journeyed from its source, and how the seed came up." In the narrative of childhood that follows we glimpse intensely remembered scenes which correspond to the child's feeling: of desolation, "... the blank hours in bad weather when I sat on the window-still in the nursery passage, and the texture of time consisted of a smell of ivy and elder bushes, and the noise of sparrows quarrelling, and an intense longing to be grown-up and able to do what one liked"; but more often of sheer physical enjoyment and absorption in pleasant surroundings: "I see her showing me a robin's nest in the hedge-bank, just before we crossed the lane and passed the old orchard and the farm buildings behind their house. And then we came into the courtyard, where the gilded stable clock was striking the hour ... and the evening sunshine was on it all ..." It is seldom that we see the first kind of scene, with its ominous shiny dark ivy and irritable sparrows, for it seems never to be winter—and in the summer, "Idle white pigeons cooed and scrabbled on the skylight", and all is gentle movement: "Very gently the night air stirs and sways the tall white window curtains, bringing the surf-like sound of a train going along the valley." Like all country-trains, this one is completely assimilated to the landscape.

The most complete 'period picture' is the passage—a companion to the sentimental journey to Edingthorpe—in which the author visits Weirleigh in his imagination "on some ordinary-looking morning in August 1897."[15] The family has gone away for a holiday, but the place lives on, though "rather pauseful and absent-minded," continuing to accommodate the small activities which humanise it: "Peter, our plebeian old tabby cat, would be crouching intently under an Irish yew near the pigeon's bath while the white fantails pecked up maize. Lizzy the housemaid would be shaking her duster out of an upstairs window. Mrs. Battersen the cook ... would be making plum jam and singing to herself in the kitchen ..." As at Edingthorpe, the author wanders, marking these trifling details which in their sum make life. In one especially he catches an undertone that the picture is essentially

15. pp. 115-118.

dead or, if it lives, it is imprisoned in the past: in the studio "an imprisoned butterfly fluttered drily against the skylight." Here, the author
simply remembers ordinariness — the ordinary tranquil day, not
distinctive in itself: this crystallizes the past as a simpler unity than
anything experienced since. The memory is poignant in that, though so
ordinary, once so commonplace, it is forever irrecoverable: "In mind-
sight we return: but even if in more than mind-sight we could somehow be there in the actuality of outlived experience, we should be
strangers, invisible, and powerless to avert so much as the overwinding
of a clock." Nevertheless, Sassoon has set before the reader an abun-
dantly lifelike picture of this past, which corresponds in its appearance of placid and uneventful continuity to the life lived in it and once
felt to be endless.

There are other scenes that make vital perceptions concrete: the
bonfire "on a dry frosty evening" with which the Sassoon children not
only welcome the new century, but unwittingly burn the old;[16] another, "somewhere in the early part of June 1906, and about five
o'clock in the morning," in which a faded group photograph is recalled, with all its perishable vain preliminaries, in the making.[17] A
low-toned glimpse of youth, this last, which well complements the
following thematic picture inaugurating his twenty-first birthday:

Coming of age merely meant that I woke up and looked out of the window
and observed a heavy dew on the grass, and a green woodpecker stumping
about on the tennis lawn among breakfasting blackbirds and thrushes.
It was evidently going to be another gloriously fine day. The air smelt
faintly of autumn; there was a white mist along the valley; and the horizon
seemed, as usual, to be suggesting that I should start out on my travels . . .

Uneventful the scene; uneventful the life—a life that rests its elbows
upon the window-still and only dallies with going further: "altogether
it seemed that I was fonder of the Kentish horizon than I was of the
places beyond it."

Into the account of this birthday[18] are gathered recollections of the
scene that late summer morning which concentrate all the scents,
sounds, colours, marks of the life, like the season, approaching a turning-point. The scene is still that of the Old Century, but now recaptured
more amply than before at a moment, it seems, of 'never to return':

16. pp. 179-80.
17. p. 252.
18. "Seven More Years", Chapter VI.

I had always accepted such familiar phenomena half-consciously, but today the place was drawing my attention to its intimate aspects, almost as though I were revisiting it, after an absence of many years, in a mood of mellowed acquaintanceship . . .

Year after year the sunshine had come and gone, slanting across the floor and along the walls and taking a little more colour out of the rugs and curtains, while the grandfather-clock, with its tuneless strike, ticked slowly on but never kept the right time.

Such are his reflections within the house, as he notes the traces of his childhood, and of his parents' life, each carried on in much the same way beneath the mellowing sun. Meanwhile, without: ". . . the warm air was aromatic with the musky smells of the autumn garden; trails of gossamer wavered silkily across vistas of sunshine, and everything seemed imbued with reluctance to do more than doze on into an idle afternoon." An unending scene—and all seems unending: it seems that people haven't changed much either, his mother humming over her lavender, Major Horrocks and his sister paying a neighbourly visit as they have done ever since he could remember; the cat basks in the sunshine, the pigeons croon contentment. Continuity seems absolute: "The Major stopped to inspect a bird-cherry tree which he had planted for my mother in the 'eighties. It was doing nicely, he observed; and the hum of insects from its foliage concurred with his opinion." The elements of this scene have been with us from the beginning, as they have with the author in his childhood and youth, both nourishing his life and forming an apt symbol of it.

VIII

THE MAKING OF A POET (II)

A Lucky Life

In *The Weald of Youth*,[1] Sassoon brings the record of his early life up to the outbreak of the First World War, covering the years 1909-early 1914, from his twenty-third to twenty-eighth year.[2]

This work might aptly be sub-titled 'The Growing-Pains of a Poet' a title that would suggest its dominant (though not entire) lightness of tone. It continues the story of a lucky life, a life which has known no tragedy, struggle, or deep misfortune throughout its first twenty-eight years. It is a life that can afford failure—at school, at university, in the practical business of living—and yet survive to grope its way toward a romantically conceived goal. But it is also a life bedevilled by its good fortune, for it is the life of an aspiring poet who lives in a manner comically unsuited to furnish him with the stuff of poetry.

The situation invites light treatment: the only alternatives in describing a life in which there is no significant development during a period of five (usually vital) years, would be dullness—or silence. The opening paragraph leaves us in no doubt as to how Sassoon intends to approach his subject. There, we find the same callow youth of *The Old Century*, jogging home in his dog-cart, a cricket-bag under his seat: "And beside me, below my straw hat, which I had placed over it for safety's sake, was this week's number of *The Academy*."[3] He is flushed with success and hope, for this magazine contains his sonnet on Villon (an unavoidable irony). Comfortably, he looks toward "the low-hilled blue horizon," which seems to promise the realization of his ambition

1. An edition of 10,000 copies was published on 15th October, 1942; and an edition of 2500 copies was published in the United States in the same month. The edition to which reference is made here is the First Edition, Third Impression, 1944. (For further details see *A Bibliography*, pp. 107-109).
2. Continuity with *O.C.* is not complete. Two years are missing between *O.C.* and *W.Y.*
3. p. 7. This, and all ensuing quotations in this chapter are taken from *W.Y.*, unless otherwise stated: references are given mainly under 'Page References', p. 310.

—"that I might someday be a really good poet." All the aspects of youth that most attract Sassoon are present: spontaneous enjoyment, health of body, simple awareness of beauty, a lofty and ingenuous ambition. Though his humorous treatment of the last predominates, he also (as we shall see) ascribes serious value to every one of these aspects.

The very fact that Sassoon does see positive value in his youthful life liberates his mind to treat it humorously. He feels no need to be self-defensive, to mask his weaknesses or falsify the picture out of a retro-spective sense of responsibility for his immaturity. It is another self that he is describing, with curiosity and even wonder: "what is most appa-rent to me is an utter ingenuousness" (he writes of his *Sonnets and Verses*); "I rediscover simplicities which move me—not deeply, but with a sort of selfless wonder." This attitude enables him to be utterly frank about his youthful absurdities (there is no doubt, too, that this approach will come more easily to a man who has demonstrably outgrown them than to one who has not).

Hitherto, the youth's contact with human affairs has, in the author's words, been "narrow and unenterprising." His endeavour suddenly to widen this contact and to become more adventurous leads him into situations that comically expose his unreadiness for the life he desires. Many of his blunders are of the perennial kind: socially he is always putting a foot wrong, taking "Hermitage" for "hermitage", writing an appreciative letter to Doughty in which he tactlessly assures him that he has read *The Dawn in Britain* "all through", sitting through *Les Sylphides* under the illusion that he is watching *The Legend of Joseph*. There is an amusing disparity between the kind of person he wants to be (a poet) and the kind of person he oddly thinks it necessary to be to achieve this end. He enters a circle where social proprieties and cultural exactitudes are much prized: thus, he finds it necessary to keep a London flat in style (as formerly, he had kept four horses for a season), to wear a top hat on fine days and white spats on occasion—which made the feet feel "more consciously important." When he has adjusted himself fairly well in the material sense, he has to be on his guard in the presence of the Marshes and the Gosses, making a mental note of new and im-pressive-sounding words like "daycore" and "Veronese style" for future use. He is feeling his way and to us, who know he is on the wrong tack, it is a comically painful process: "My appearance, I felt, was creditable enough, for I was wearing my buff linen waistcoat, with spats to match, and there was nothing countrified about my irreproachable dark summer suit. Thus attired, I ought to have had a self-possessed and reticently distinguished personality; but even my best clothes could not prevent me from being excessively shy and self-conscious." Such are his preoccupations before attending, for the first time, one of Sir Edmund Gosse's 'At Homes'; they are an amusing repetition of his unhappy struggles with his collar on his first morning at Marlborough.

However absurd he may be, one never pities or despises him; it is clear that he is out of his element. But in his way, he is strong and confident, blessed with a resilience—as well as an innocence—that carries him through. If he has an unsteady foot in the literary world, he has a firmer one in the sporting world where he has enjoyed his victories; and he is as yet too immature to realize how little either matters. He may mumble wretchedly in the house of Sir Edmund, but he can always strut at a point-to-point and indulge a private satisfaction in being recognized as a race-rider. He has in reserve qualities of determination and courage which, given some fresh obstacle to surmount, will serve him well. But he is not the person to make things happen by stepping outside his own range. His most unconventional step towards "leading an enterprising existence which would give me something real to write about" is to take a bus to Hornsey Rise—"whence I returned unrewarded." He is too diffident; if only, one wishes with his older self, he had followed his intuition and gone a second time to see Ralph Hodgson, who "would have set my mind alight." Though he desires, for the sake of both his poetry and his self-respect, to meet life's challenges, he is not an indiscriminate taster of experience. "London was around me": yet he betakes himself like a day-tripper to the National Gallery, the British Museum, the Victoria and Albert (he denies himself Lord's and the Oval) and finally, in a richly comic scene, to the Zoological Gardens—on two successive days. The Zoo "made me feel more solitary than ever, and its inhabitants appeared to be filling-in time as listlessly as I was." But Sassoon does not allow the situation to get out of hand: Wirgie's presence at the Zoo on these two occasions provides us with a counter-balance of feeling. Her permanent loneliness, her life behind her, enables us to measure the youth's in its true proportions. If the youth's situation arouses pity, it is the emotion the older and wiser may feel pitying him for his ignorance of his good fortune and for his unfounded despairs. We can afford to laugh at youth, but not at age.

Sassoon does, however, feel seriously about youth, and serious feeling is seldom far beneath the humorous surface. In an earlier chapter he lightly sketches his gauche self at a county-house dance: "'Do you reverse?' ... How those words bring my silly self back to me, with my inability to make my white ties look as effortless as other young men's, and my white gloves which always would split in at least one place ..." This is the beginning, but there is nothing frivolous about the note on which the scene ends. Abruptly, we are made to see through older eyes, not twinkling at the follies of youth, but glistening perhaps under the poignant sense of its unabashed confidence: "those who took the floor triumphally and carried the music along with them in their controlled and graceful career—exemplifying, for older eyes that watched them, the momentary conquest of youth and the pathos of its unawareness." In this and in the Zoo passage mentioned above there is a graver inflection than we find anywhere in *The Old Century*. This seems to be because Sassoon's theme is now youth at the full, a time when all things appear possible—yet a time, he sees in retrospect, when there is the widest gap between what we desire and what we can achieve. Never again shall we be so confident; never again will our emotions and aspirations be so strong.

Thus, he approaches the characterisation of his younger self, not only humorously, but with an admiration—even a certain reverence—for the irrecoverable qualities of youth that underlie the silliness and the selfishness. It is the feeling of his poems on the theme,

> A youth, impassioned by he knows not what, exploring
> Delusive labyrinths in errors age will pardon,—
> A youth, all ignorance, all grace, his dreams adoring.[4]

The ignorance is a perishable thing, and can be treated humorously. The selfishness allied to it is excusable, a by-product of youth's heady preoccupation with its own remarkable aims. Recalling his selfish reaction to the news of the death of his mother's maid, Miriam, he says: "Later on in life one accepts and admits the fact that youthful conduct can be unfeeling in a way that demands our tolerance. Young people don't take things to heart unless their own interests and enterprises are affected by the events."

The ignorance and the selfishness are susceptible to change for the better: not so the "grace" and the capacity to dream; these disappear

4. 'Progressions,' (*C.P.*, p. 253).

for ever. By "grace" it seems that he means unconscious charm, spontaneity, unaffected behaviour. He looks back with pride to those moments of youth's supreme unawareness, of absorption in the moment —himself, for example, at the finish of a winning race on Cockbird:

... I watch myself passing the Judge's waggon. Finishing in nice quiet style, one hopes—hands well down and eyes looking straight ahead. Not a bit of it! The successful rider is actually waving the stirrup-iron above his head and grinning exultantly at the Judge—a genial and popular ex-Master of Hounds. Not what I ought to have been doing, of course, but how revealingly characteristic!

Such are his "open-air memories": he finds that "they make easier and more enjoyable recording than my activities as a man of letters." For psychological reasons alone this is understandable: there is more of youth's essential freedom to wish for in them than in the "cabin'd, cribb'd, confin'd" self struggling to enter London literary society. Though *The Weald of Youth* is in the main complementary to *A Fox-Hunting Man*, Sassoon devotes three light-hearted chapters to the activities of the "outdoor self". But now he is anxious to stress their value, to show that the two worlds which in his youth he found difficulty in reconciling are, in fact, compatible: to show his youthful energies were not diverted from poetry for nothing. It is part of youth's good fortune to be able to enter freely into the physical life; this life should not be depreciated:

I take it—with a certain momentary sententiousness—to be highly significant of human affairs that a man like myself, who has done reasonably well in the arena of literature, should feel an almost equal regard for the sand-dunes among which he formerly straddled and swung and for those with whom he shared his enjoyment of the game ... "Homo sum; humani nil a me alienum puto." To which I would add that when you get close up to life, little things are just as important as big ones.

Naturally Sassoon wishes to defend the worth of those pursuits in which he spent so large a part of his youth against the sneers of those whom he calls elsewhere "highly sophisticated persons", but it is a pity that his own hostility to literary exclusiveness should make him adopt this sententious attitude (even if he attempts to disarm by confessing to it). He shows us clearly enough that the outdoor life has advantages far beyond sheer physical enjoyment: by its competitive tests, and its necessary human contacts, it helps to shape character quite as much as other ways of 'wasting' one's youth. It is a tangible life; it can be grasped and entered into: perhaps the only life in which youth can find immediate and satisfying outlet for the spontaneity Sassoon admires.[5]

There is also the less definable life which nourishes the spirit. Sassoon's youth is "bursting with something to express," but he can only grope towards its realization in the actual world. His blunders and despairs can be humorously treated; so also can his embryonic literary achievements. Yet underneath these things is the sensitivity—a precious essence: outwardly, this takes the shape of unreal and imitative poems, but, however honestly Sassoon may criticize these, he never tramples upon the state of mind which gave rise to them. "What need was there to worry ... about literary originality," he asks, "when one's whole being felt like some grand mysterious chord of music?" Age may reject youthful romanticism—the "Debussy World", "some illusionary lover among the fountains, cypresses, and statues of a moon-vista'd garden"—which it has proved false, but in so doing it must also reject "the integrity of our acceptive innocence." What is the reality as opposed to this? The harsher reality has little place, but when it appears Sassoon puts it in such flatly contrasting colours that there seems little room for argument: "Better for youth to be falling asleep with a snatch of *Papillons* still dancing in his head than to be acquiring disillusionment in that dazzling limbo [a "grand party" given for the composer Strauss] of the coldly clever, the self-seeking, and the faithless." This is Sassoon's characteristic opposition between simplicity and sophistication. But it is equivocal that, in this context, he should draw so sharp a distinction, since at the same time he admits the validity of the youthful urge to *do*, to become involved in stirring life. He admits, too, that his enlistment in the Army enables him to escape from "a deplorably unfertile future"—unfertile, one might add, because of the unnatural prolongation of the simple, dreaming state. The involvement in war will destroy "innocence", but that will be replaced

---

5. Edmund Blunden, in *Cricket Country*, and Leonard Woolf in *Sowing*, write simply of the value of the sporting life for reasons similar to Sassoon's, but with no strained apologias.

Sassoon retained a youthful enthusiasm for cricket. For many years he led a team of Heytesbury men and we find him writing to Sir Sydney Cockerell at the age of 52: "We have had an idyllically quiet summer, punctuated by cricket matches in which I make rather fewer runs than I could have wished. But I hit a six at Devizes last Saturday and smashed 3 panes of glass in the pavilion window! How many poets have done that at my age?" (*The Best of Friends*, p. 60).

by values more positive, not only than those of the "limbo", but also
—and more significantly—than any he has so far discovered. As in
his opposition between the narrow intellectual man and the 'whole'
man (of both mind and body), Sassoon over-stresses the contrasts. This
has the unfortunate effect of obscuring, or even distorting, the values
he defends.

What is least satisfactory about his reverence for youth's 'dreams' is
that he seems to sentimentalize the dreaming state itself. One thinks of
other ways the youth might have taken — not necessarily into the
harsh awakening of the War nor into the "limbo" of ultra-sophistica-
tion — but into reality, to re-shape it if he can in the light of his
"dreams". One compares, for example, the young Rupert Brooke
—two years younger—already by 1910 taking great interest in Fabian
reform. For Sassoon this was to come—to some extent—much later,
and he is certainly aware of his youthful deficencies in this respect. Of
his mental condition in 1914, he writes: "I was starting with a clean
mental slate, uncomplicated by intellectual scruples. I had lived my
way to almost twenty-eight in what now appears to have been an unquestioning confidence that the world had arrived at a meridian of
unchangeableness." It is hard to reconcile this with Sassoon's idealization of a state of prolonged immaturity, unless we are to infer that
he would consider it better if the awakening had never been. It is surely
not youth's capacity to dream that matters most, however much the
world-weary mind may yearn to regain it, but the form this dreaming
may take. If, in youth, dreams take the form of idealistic action, only
to be crushed by contact with reality, we may lament their passing and
the disillusionment that follows. But it is hard to lament, as Sassoon is
prone to do, the dissolution of an "acceptive innocence" which he
himself admits to have been infertile.

Fortunately, this objection gives no fundamental cause of dissatisfaction with Sassoon's portrayal of self. Nevertheless, it must be said
that the author's self is less interesting than in *The Old Century*, since he
shows no significant development. That he matures so little is a telling
criticism of the society which cossets him—though Sassoon, who idealizes this society in which "innocence" could survive so long, would
doubtless take the opposite view. But since the author's self is not so
narrowly the focus of interest as in the previous book, his slow development is not fatal to the book as a whole. The strong humorous element
and the varied collection of characters diversify the interest. Other-

wise, the reader might be forgiven for feeling an impatience with the hero which the autobiographer himself never (to his credit) shows, "while watching him begin yet another self-engrossed little journey toward nothing in particular."

Portraits and Sketches

In *The Weald of Youth* the figures in the ambience claim equal attention with the author himself. They are not greater in number than those in *The Old Century*, but they are drawn from a wider range and have more diverse characters. Previously, we saw a general similarity between characters, whatever their background, and that they tend to coalesce in the mind as representatives of what the author sees as a kindly world. Now there are two worlds: the old one, of home and country-life, the new, of literary life in London. These two worlds cannot be continuous, and neither can Sassoon's reaction to them: whilst there is a firm underlay of characters that epitomize the original world, the new is peopled with individuals who live more in their own right and who, indirectly, break the old unified picture.

The characters fall into three groups: those of the intimate personal life, those associated with the "outdoor self", and the third, the largest, a miscellaneous collection who form a fair cross-section of London literary life in the five years immediately preceding the First World War.

The characters in the first two groups continue, as the representatives of an admired stable existence, to suggest qualities rather than clearly defined personalities. One is more conscious of their meaning for the author than of themselves as individuals. The salient example of this is Sassoon's mother. One is always conscious of her presence: but it is a shadowy presence, spoken of as accompanying her son to a tea-party, sitting out-of-doors with him on a perfect summer's evening, mentioned as taking a quiet pleasure in her gardening or in reading Meredith, and once, being considerate to the servants. We learn almost nothing of her opinions, mannerisms—or even appearance. When Sassoon writes, as late as page 176, "It now occurred to me that I hadn't told her about my curious encounter with Crosland, so it wouldn't be possible for her to be with me in spirit at lunch-time next day ..." one suddenly realizes that no sense of so strong an understanding between mother and son has been sufficiently established for this comment to be taken for granted. One has a similar impression that too much has been left untold for the reader's feelings to be deeply engaged when he refers to the death of Miriam, his mother's maid, in terms so strong as these: "Miriam had been with us for many years, and even then I realized her almost saintly willingness to do everybody else's work in addition to her own. It was the first time her heart had failed anyone ..." One recalls that Miriam is also mentioned—and is as highly praised— in *A Fox-Hunting Man*, but there is no continuous sense of her presence in the autobiographies; she is not mentioned in *The Old Century*.

As in *The Old Century*, of the characters closest to the author, it is "Wirgie" who emerges most strongly. She falls into no easily labelled category: she is responsive to youth, full of fun and joy in life, yet with an undertone of seriousness that evokes respect: "Even her inimitable flippancies were somehow attuned to regretfulness." She, if anyone, was good for the young poet: she avoids fulsome and useless praise and makes shrewd suggestions which gently lead him to an awareness of his limitations. We both see and hear her, with "that vibrant low-pitched voice and the wistful drollery of those querying eyes", and learn of her mannerisms, such as her little tricks of speech: "'If a burglar were to nobble my ear-rings,' she remarked, 'I should be absolutely done for as a duchess,' (She was rather addicted to using the word 'nobble' at that time.)" In the Zoo scene in Chapter XV, Sassoon devotes space to *showing* us the nature of her unselfish kindness. There is her fellow-feeling for the confined animals, whose loneliness is so much like her own, and her patient and kindly treatment of the discontented young man. The scene in his flat, when he takes her home to tea, is imbued with the pathos of her own lonely, straitened existence, which is accentuated by the shallow and uncomprehending presence of the youth whom she knows she cannot reach. We catch her feeling perfectly as we imagine her "soliloquising in urgent under-tones", overheard by the foolish young poet whilst he makes tea in the kitchen and wonders "why she should be so upset by my saying that nothing ever changes enough to make any real difference." With these characteristically felicitous words of praise Sassoon pays her a tribute we can fully appreciate: "Lonely and sociable, complex and single-hearted, she came and went among her submissive friends, lighting up their lives by the imaginative vitality of her spirit."

The part played in *The Old Century* by such characters as Allen Batty, Mr. Moon, "The Teacher" and others, is here carried on by the sport-

ing characters. There are none of the caricatures of *A Fox-Hunting Man*:
each of the sportsmen recalled is praised for positive qualities—and it
is for these that the reader also remembers them. The author's way of
seeing them is exemplified by the description of the "friendly foursome"
in Chapter IV, whose members are "gallant old General Fitzhugh,"
Captain Ruxton with "stocky upright figure," Mr. Watson, "well-
liked by everyone," and Squire Morland—to whose amiable qualities
ample justice has already been done in the person of Squire Maundle.[6]
All these are "kindly ghosts"; they seem to be "memorialized" as the
last such men in the world. More is said of closer sporting associates, of
"my friend Thompson" the golfer, of Norman Loder the huntsman,
of "Camel" Kelsey the captain of the cricket-team, but whoever it
may be the effect is not an individual one. Of a golden sovereign won
from Thompson after a round of golf he writes: "The coin would remind me—not only of our many happy days together—but also of the
sterling metal of his character—a fact which nobody can be any the
worse for hearing about, although its significance, like the result of our
match, remains private and personal." Norman Loder receives a
similar tribute: "He was one of those people whose strength is in their
consistent simplicity and directness, and who send out natural wisdom
through their mental limitations and avoidance of nimble ideas ...
He was kind, decent, and thorough, never aiming at anything beyond
plain common-sense and practical ability." And lastly, "Kelsey—a
tremendous club cricketer—was tall and unhurrying, with a drawling,
kindly voice. The voice was the man— uncensorious and totally likeable." In these graceful tributes Sassoon is paying the scores of friendship; in his own phrase, their significance is "private and personal."
Collectively, they are meaningful to us as a reflection of the author's
human values: a consistent reflection, for he has written with the same
warmth and affection of their forerunners in *The Old Century*. But they
are given no scope to live for us as they do for him.

If we turn to the 'literary' characters, our pleasure consists in
variety. The range is wide, from Sir Edmund Gosse and Sir Edward
Marsh, the 'dictators' of the day, Rupert Brooke and George Moore, to
the disreputable and diverting T. W. H. Crosland. They command a
prior interest the more obscure figures cannot possess, though they
receive by no means rounded—and some not even adequate—treatment. It is, for example, irritating rather than entertaining to receive

6. *M.F.H.*, pp. 90-91.

o brief a glimpse of George Moore: "On this occasion Mr. Moore monopolized the conversation, indulging in a long jeremiad against the incivilized habits of dogs on door-steps. He had lately returned from he Holy Land, and gave us a memorable description of the blisters he got on his behind while riding from Joppa to Jerusalem on a mule. He had struck me as being a peculiarly unpleasant old gentleman who also happened to be doing his best to be at his worst." This is all, and one s left wondering whether Sassoon has, owing to the dislike the last sentence reveals, been unduly niggardly of his memories. It is tantalizing, too, to have W. H. Davies consigned to a digressive paragraph in he middle of the reminiscence of Rupert Brooke. It is, nevertheless, a finely rounded paragraph on him, not slurring over his weaknesses, ending with a typically handsome tribute: "The personal charm of Davies, however, was the abundant happiness and contentment which s so beautifully apparent in his imperishable poetry." There is also the noteworthy description of his eyes as having "an expression of child-like nobility."

Three of these characters—Gosse, Marsh and Crosland—are much more fully drawn, whilst Rupert Brooke is deftly sketched in a single scene. The odd man out here is obviously Crosland, the raffish and combative editor of *The Academy* and the publisher of a number of Sassoon's earliest poems, but he is, strangely enough, the most rounded character. Both consciously and unconsciously Sassoon makes his youthful self a foil to Crosland. The scene in which the precisely attired young poet presents himself and his sonnets for inspection at the editorial office is reminiscent of that where H. G. Wells appears before Frank Harris. Appearances are slightly reversed: whereas the young Wells appears with a decrepit top hat that he has vainly refurbished for the occasion, it is Crosland who possesses the hat—upon his head—but his manner matches that of the editor of the *Fortnightly Review*[7]:

He greeted me abruptly and without geniality, half rising from his chair and pointing me to another one with a half-smoked cigar. A noticeable thing about him was that he had his hat on. It was one of those square high-crowned bowler hats which one associates with judges at Cattle Shows, and while he was talking it was tilted over his nose. Crosland was evidently a man who never wore his hat on the back of his head, possibly because he had long since lost all hope of wearing a halo. He had a dark heavy moustache, side-whiskers, a strong harsh voice with a Lancashire,

7. For the description of H. G. Wells's interview see his *Experiment in Autobiography*, 1934, pp. 356-358.

accent, and a truculent blood-shot eye . . . even his nose looked antagonistic to the universe.

Perhaps because Crosland lends himself so readily to extravagant description, Sassoon gives us a stronger visual impression of him than of anyone else. Crosland reappears on two other occasions, both all too brief. On the first, now incredibly without his moustache but escorting a mysterious woman in a bright red hat, he accidentally meets the poet at the Hippodrome and invites him to lunch—this despite the fact that Sassoon had ignored a hard-luck letter he wrote from Monte Carlo. One wonders why, in any case, he does this, since it seems that no two 'literary men' could have less in common—except bad blood about publishing. The lunch itself is orgiastic and is described with comic exaggeration, but Sassoon's account of the conversation, or rather Crosland's monologue, is less satisfying. There is a self-defensive note and even a pomposity in the disapproving paragraphs upon Crosland's character which seem disproportionate to the subject.[8] Clearly, Crosland had invited Sassoon to lunch in order to make one whom he regarded as a spoilt young man the target for an envious diatribe. Whatever Crosland's faults, he is undoubtedly a 'character', complex enough to be on the border-line between the comic and the pathetic: by adopting a superior tone, Sassoon spoils the possibilities of Crosland as a player in the human comedy. One cannot agree with him when he writes: "Crosland's character must have been mainly composed of contradictions. How many of the ingredients were honourable ones *it is needless to inquire* [my italics] . . . I never saw him again or felt any further inclination to communicate with him." The enquiry *would*, one feels, have been worthwhile. Presumably, the younger Sassoon withdrew from Crosland as a compromising and incalculable quantity, who offended his concern for gentlemanly behaviour and propriety; it is a pity—and oddly uncharacteristic—that the older sees fit to write him down so strongly.

Sir Edmund Gosse and Sir Edward Marsh are naturally described in a milder key, and they also make a fainter impression. What Sassoon does best is to suggest the aura in which they move. They epitomise a literary epoch: when a literary breakfast with Marsh, an 'At Home' with Gosse might open the way to success. The obscure and aspiring young poet is lucky to get a word with either—for someone more im-

8. See pp. 188-189.

portant is invariably present—and we ourselves are unlikely to be
rewarded with more than the occasional glimpse of them. The angle of
vision is primarily that of the younger Sassoon—who did not, one
supposes, keep a very thorough notebook. On every occasion when he
meets Gosse he is tongue-tied and awkward. He listens, something of
what he hears is reported, but one doubts whether the whole man is
captured. He makes Gosse too much the *grand seigneur*. We have Gosse,
the oracle, the phrasemaker—tediously the latter: Gosse's "conversational virtuosity" seems to be caricatured rather than parodied.
Whereas for the youth "he seemed to enrich the room with a glow
reflected from ideal regions of classical achievement", for the reader he
emerges as pompous and a bore, forever fashioning his allusive, weighted sentences. One can see why Gosse dominated—and even intimi-
dated—the literary world of the day: one is not shown why he was
also loved, though as Sassoon says, "He had befriended and encouraged
me ..." It is a pity that the only details of his first private conversation
with Gosse Sassoon reports are the great man's prim inquisition about
Crosland and yet another laborious *mot*. Had Sassoon chosen to paint
Gosse's portrait from his more mature angle of vision, this deficiency
would doubtless have been overcome.[9] No such limitation applies to
the portrait of Marsh—"kind Eddie"—whose ability to reach the
young is pleasantly conveyed. In his flat Sassoon observes "the Gosse
atmosphere in a different guise": and in Marsh himself we observe a
different and more congenial type of literary patron. Where the young
poet is concerned, it seems that Gosse will wait, courteously and kindly
enough, for blossoming time: it is Marsh, on the other hand, who takes
immense pains to bring him out. Though a busy man, he takes it upon
himself to (literally) move Sassoon into London life. He finds him a
flat and even has it decorated. Having lodged him, he persists in trying
to launch him, however frustrating the task must have been, introducing him to well-known writers and to refined pleasures such as
classical ballet. One would have liked to see—and hear—more of
such a man.

It is through Marsh that Sassoon meets Rupert Brooke. Though
Brooke appears only once, he leaves a more distinctive impression of

9. In his much fuller portrayal of Gosse Sir Osbert Sitwell writes: "No account of
Gosse, then, should omit the sheer quality of fun which he possessed in the highest
degree, and which his presence never failed to impart to any occasion or gathering,
large or small. Yet it is precisely this attribute which I have seen most seldom, if
ever, mentioned in descriptions of him ..." (*Noble Essences*, 1950, p. 161).

personality behind than do the other figures. His meeting with Sassoon has a marked dramatic quality, though it had none at the time: "There is no need," says Sassoon at the end of the chapter, "to explain that our one brief meeting had a quite unpredictable significance. Nor need I underline the latent irony of the situation." Without insisting upon it, Sassoon makes us conscious of the irony from the beginning by lending himself to telling contrasts with the other poet. Brooke is introduced as self-contained and composed, unconventional in appearance—while his contemporary notes "his gold-brown hair ... was, I thought, just a shade longer than it need have been." He is lively and adaptable: watched by the envious Sassoon, who admires his unapproachable, easy brilliance and feels himself to be ordinary and unadventurous, he jokes on equal terms with W. H. Davies and Marsh, seemingly unaware of Sassoon's existence. When the two younger men are left alone, Brooke sits by the window "serenely observing the trees of Gray's Inn gardens." Perhaps he is bored, but Sassoon stays out his time—in print as in actuality—seeking to make some impression, the clumsy foil to an ideal presence. He utters his banalities, blundering into the calculation that they must have been at Cambridge together into 1906, recalling seeing Brooke in the *Eumenides*—as far from him as then: "I was only one more in the procession of people who were now more interested in him than he was in them." Of the meeting itself we have only the occasional word or look, but by eking these out with reflections on his own contrasting immaturity, on the serenely impressive quality of Brooke's presence and on Brooke as others were privileged to know him, Sassoon transmits to us his deep sense of loss. He conveys, too, his retrospective understanding of Brooke's feelings in the situation. So many meetings in life are like this, but they are seldom recorded: it is a shadowy sketch, tinged with romantic regret, a fitting reminiscence of one whose life achieved little more fulfilment than does this ironic meeting.

Coloured Retrospect

The setting of *The Weald of Youth*, like the figures we have discussed, is more diverse than that of either *The Old Century* or *A Fox-Hunting Man*. In the earlier books the country-life has been self-contained and seemingly insulated from destructive forces or alien influences of any kind. Sassoon has left us in no doubt of the high valuation he puts upon this state of affairs: it is a treasured state of ignorance, of illusory stability. He has tried to make the reader see the years of his youth as he saw them at the time—a partial view, which has the effect of a dream.

It has been said, with regard to *The Old Century*, that the exclusion from that book of all unpleasant realities (except the undertones of impending war) may be artistically defensible. One can also accept the escapist paradise of the peace-chapters of *A Fox-Hunting Man* for the sake of a lighter kind of fiction. In these books the occasional note of idealization does not fundamentally disturb what one regards as a holiday from the harsher aspects of reality anyway. Acceptance becomes more difficult where *The Weald of Youth* is concerned, largely because the paradisal unity is broken and the world as a whole comes more into view. It is no longer just a "local, limited world", but one that includes London and glimpses of 'County' life on the grand scale. The author still takes arms on the side of this enlarged world—so far as he saw it—but in such a way as to elicit a more serious response from the reader, who is now more strongly aware of what has been omitted.

It is quite understandable that the impressionable youth should be as uncritical as he is shown to be in fashionable sporting, or superior literary, society; his criticism extends little further than envy and he solaces himself with despising fashionable people for their "shallow sophistication". It is natural, also, that the author should remember all that was good—courtesy and good fellowship, refined tastes, the gentlemanly kindness of such people as Sir Edward Marsh. But it is strange that a writer who has been an active socialist should see no reason either to qualify his idealized view of the way of life he describes, or, assuming that he has abandoned his socialism, to defend it.

The whole range of life is idealized, from the stately dowager to the rustic cricketer. Writing of the young dancers and the "sedately watchful dowagers" at a country-house ball in 1910, Sassoon asks: "Would one willingly invite them back, to be as they then were in the world darkness of today? I cannot think so ... more than once I have thought that it was well for my old friends that they went when they did." What appeal, one wonders, can such sentiments have to any but those who live in the past? They are life-denying. And is it unfair to retort: if one would not have the dowagers face the world of today, what of the many less fortunate who had to face it yesterday? We see little of the latter, except in the more idealized postures, as country cricketers, for example, of the homely stamp: "For some reason it gave me peculiar pleasure when I was told that in everyday life he was a wheelwright." "Old Walter Humphreys ... used to appear in a pale pink flannel shirt—made for him, I hope, by his wife ... It seemed more like home-made cricket in those days." These are comfortable reflections, and no doubt Baldwin and Humphreys were comfortable enough men.

Comfortable and unquestioning, as perhaps were the men mentioned in this quotation: "I was already keeping four horses, Richardson, and a stable helper, on an income of less than six hundred a year ..." Unquestioning, too, was the youth—and unquestioning, it *appears*, his mature self. Sassoon never probes the material basis on which his youthful way of life rests. This omission is not for the lack of opportunities. For example, there is a rare reference to the servants, whom his mother considerately decides not to trouble by having them set dinner on the lawn, followed almost at once by: "It was one of those summers which one associated with people sitting out of doors after dinner— their voices murmuring on and on until it wasn't worth while to light the lamps in the drawing room." '*Some* people!' one is inclined to add, but Sassoon takes it for granted, as at the time: a passage such as this reminds one of the nature of the audience Sassoon assumes—a (once) comfortable enough middle class readership who would naturally feel that 'people' included them. Again, he reports with an unqualified pride how, during his Atherstone season, "for the first time in my life I could claim that I had half a valet." Uncritically he relates the following anecdote about his (albeit likeable) philistine friend, Norman Loder—they are inspecting the 'country' together:

Now and again he would volunteer a comment of his own. For instance, after skirting a straggling and ill-favoured town which was, I had gathered, mainly addicted to the manufacture of boots, he suddenly exclaimed— "They never ought to have built a place like that so near Burbage Wood!"

The phrase "mainly addicted to the manufacture of boots" is unpleasant: Sassoon appears to endorse Loder's limited view. Apart from recalling that he deplored the thinness of their conversation in moods of youthful intolerance, he is content in his recollections of his fashionable fellow-hunters to reproduce the awe, even reverence, he felt for such figures as "the Squire of Blankney,", "who had run through his fortune in the grand style." [10]

Sassoon tells us that his fox-hunting friends looked unfavourably upon his "Socialist experiment" with *The Daily Herald*. They must indeed have been puzzled, and puzzled too must be the reader who, bearing this reference to Socialism in mind, comes to the author's reminiscence of "that dizzyingly good dance at Thorpe Hall, when the whole county assembled for the climax of a period of peace and prosperity". The climax, one might prosaically add, of a period of industrial unrest, which included the National Rail Strike in 1911, the Coal Strike in 1912, and the threat in 1913 of a 'general strike', only put off by the War, not to mention the threat of civil war in Ireland. These things cannot be irrelevant to one's response: clearly Sassoon had little awareness of them at the time, but it is impossible to justify—there is no irony—so sweeping a retrospective view. It is a pity that the imperceptiveness of the young Sassoon in London is also left unqualified: "I was," he says, "acquiring a liking for its back-street smells and busy disregarding of my existence ... Sunsets beyond these roofs and chimneys, those miles of bricks and mortar, affected me with a newly-discovered emotion ... There was a sort of poetry behind it all ..." Not, however, the poetry seen by W. H. Davies:

> These people have no work, thought I,
> And long before their time they die[11]

Nor is it the prose of Tressall's *The Ragged-Trousered Philanthropists* (1914) or of the historian, who writes of London in 1914, "men were still sleeping out on the Embankment in large numbers, queueing up at the soup-kitchens, running after cabs in order to earn a tip for

---

10. On the subject of Blankney in this period Sir Osbert Sitwell provides an entertaining contrast; the male hunting guests, he writes, "would probably have felt more at home in the court of Tamerlane the Tartar than in the contemporary world, and would have formed the most appropriate leaders of a new Golden Horde" (*The Scarlet Tree*, p. 175). Sir Osbert Sitwell is as disrespectful to the 'County' as to the hunting fraternity; its social life, he says, "suggested the seventeenth century, but a seventeenth century suffering from arrested mental development, elephantiasis and consumption, overgrown yet undeveloped, hectic yet weakly" (*Before the Bombardment*, 1926, p. 151).
11. From 'The Sleepers' (*Complete Poems of W. H. Davies*, 1963, p. 159). cf. Sassoon's "the prosperous prime/Of your well-ordered distant mid-Victorian time" ('In Heytesbury Wood') and "In 1909 the future was a thing desired" ('Doggerel About Old Days').

opening the door." [12] There is no reason why Sassoon—like an earlier sensitive handler of genteel society, Jane Austen—should not exclude such things, but it is a pity that he should make large assertions which suggest that they did not exist. Of his youthful self he says: "No one could have been more unaware that he was in for one of the most unrestful epochs in human history, and that the next twenty-five years would be a cemetery for the civilized delusions of the nineteenth century." *The Weald of Youth* gives no evidence of a later awareness that one of these "civilized delusions" was the assumption that a civilization could rest indefinitely upon the toil of a largely poverty-stricken mass.

One cannot escape the conclusion that, in his understandable revulsion against a brutal present, Sassoon has idealized the past *against* the broader insight he had expressed a decade earlier in *An Infantry Officer*: that life in the years he writes of was, "for the majority of the population ... an unlovely struggle against unfair odds, culminating in a cheap funeral". In the discussion of *Siegfried's Journey*, an attempt will be made to explain how this conclusion squares with Sassoon's "Socialist experiment." [13]

Atmosphere

Owing to the more varied subject-matter of this book, we do not receive so integrated an atmospheric effect as that given by the "spots of time" passages in *The Old Century*. This distinctive technique is still evident, but the scenes it evokes are more suggestive of isolated, significant moments; there is no continual thread throughout the book. But there is continuity with the atmosphere of *The Old Century*: a harking back to tranquil pictures of the past, with an even deeper nostalgia for what can only be glimpsed in the mind and never recaptured in actuality.

Three of these scenes occur in the first three chapters and carry on directly the tenour of *The Old Century*. The 'dawn-rising' scene (pp. 37-40), upon which the author lavishes loving description, is a favourite subject; it is an enlarged version of a description in *A Fox-Hunting Man* [14]

12. H. Pelling, *Modern Britain: 1885–1955*, London, 1960, p. 57. Another historian of the period, Guy Chapman, writes: "The first 14 years of the twentieth century show an ostentation of wealth and a vulgarity unknown since the days of James I" (*The Victorians and After* (ed. Batho and Dobrée), London, 1938, p. 128.
13. Appendix A, (10).
14. pp. 55-56.

and contains many elements of poems so early as 'Daybreak in a Garden' and the much later 'Childhood'. In this version Sassoon devotes more space to wistful recollection and to describing the house in every common, friendly detail—a painfully sweet memory, for: "The house was like an old person resigned to uneventfulness and nothing new, unmindful of my transient immaturity which was haunting it with heart-ache for freedom and fulfilment." The pendant to this darker side of the picture is the fresh dawn of an unused day, an evocative setting for still innocent youth: "And here was I, unconsciously lifting my arms to welcome the glittering shafts of sunrise that went wide-winged up through the innocent blueness above the east."

Following this, are two "gentle revisitations", in the manner of those to Weirleigh and Edingthorpe in *The Old Century*. They are indeed gentle scenes, in which are gathered together wistfully remembered scraps of "vanished life". It is a summer morning in a Queen Anne country house, with the sunlight gradually spreading through the quiet rooms, as it has always done, whether one watches it or not: 'where the cushions along the window-seat have had the colour faded out of them by many a morning such as this".[15] Below, a girl plays Grieg's *Schmetterling*, whilst "I", leaning at the window, "must enjoy my final stare at the garden; listen to the stable-clock striking twelve; hear the clink of a bucket as the stable-boy finishes washing the carriage-wheels, and then one of horses neighing and snorting while the coachman goes to the cornbin with his sieve. From somewhere beyond a yew hedge comes a murmur of voices, talking contentedly as people do while sitting out of doors on a fine summer day." The scene recalled here almost seems a composite picture, in which the author assembles all that memory holds most affectionately; only regret blurs the picture, "The past ought always to be like this." The next scene, allied to this, is the one which takes us outside to dawdle a little longer upon Squire Morland's golf-course, to catch across the chasm of time, a last glimpse of the pottering "friendly foursome".[16] There is birdsong and sheep are munching contentedly by the homely course; all is green harmony—and after the game, it will be back "to the House for tea and a stroll in the garden to admire the daffodils."

These scenes all contribute to a single effect: as in *The Old Century*,

15. pp. 45-47.
16. p. 53. We have been there before, in *M.F.H.*, pp. 90-92, and Sassoon disarmingly begs indulgence for this.

they represent the distilled essence of a peaceful and forever sunlit past. But now they are seen for the last time: they are no longer continually recaptured for us, as in the previous book, but are the fleeting images of the idyll from which the hero is now forced to separate himself, however much in his heart he does otherwise. This is evident in the last of these "spots of time" at the very end of the book (an ending more pointed than the abrupt transition from dozing Butley to Yeomanry life in *A Fox-Hunting Man*) where the author is seen cycling home through the familiar Kent landscape after he has taken the momentous step of enlisting in the Army. The well-known surroundings pass in review before him and all seems the same as ever, fruitful and friendly, the sky cloudless: "The landscape wore no look of imminent doom." But now, for the first time, he is no unquestioning part of it; his life must take a different course, merged dormant no longer with peace and tranquillity. For the first time, he sees no certainty in the present:

But the aspect of things was within me, imbuing what I beheld with significances of impending disaster. Those two hop-kilns on rising ground above the road—in the past there had never been anything noticeable about them. Now they seemed half-tragic in their homely simplicity. Standing away from their lengthened shadows, they were transfigured by the low-shot light of this heart-absorbing evening. In the reddening glow of the setting sun their kindly cowls were like sign-posts pointing toward the ominous continent of Europe.

IX

SIEGFRIED'S JOURNEY

There is no exact continuity between *Siegfried's Journey*[1] and *The Weald of Youth*, in chronology or style. In *The Weald of Youth* we take leave of the hero in August 1914, at the time of his enlistment in the Army; we do not meet him again until exactly two years later, in convalescent hospital in Oxford. The intervening period has been covered by the narration of Sherston's experience, mainly at the Front Line, which covers the last two parts of *A Fox-Hunting Man* and the first four of *An Infantry Officer*. Thus a vital and transforming part of the hero's experience can only be understood by reference to the earlier books. Sassoon assumes the reader's knowledge of these and so repeats nothing, not only from the intervening period, but also from that between August 1916 and July 1918, when his experience of the War is terminated by a wound in the head. He begins instead by filling in the gaps necessitated by his having made Sherston "a simplified version of my 'outdoor self'"[2] Approximately a third of the book is devoted to this, from Chapters I to VI. For this reason, the early chapters make sketchy and somewhat disjointed reading: they do, however, supply the material one needs for a more complete understanding of the author during the War years, and it is from this viewpoint that they will be discussed.

The remainder of *Siegfried's Journey* is devoted to the author's experiences and the development of his attitudes in the two years immediately following the Armistice. Parallel with this subject-matter —and interwoven with it in places—is a series of vignettes of well-

---

1. *S.J.* was published by Faber and Faber on Dec. 7, 1945 in an edition of 31,350 copies; a further 6000 copies were published in the same month under the imprint of Faber and Faber and The Book Society. An American edition of 3500 copies was published by The Viking Press on 25 March 1946. References here are to the Faber and Book Society edition. (For further information see *A Bibliography*, pp. 110-111.)
2. *S.J.*, p. 69, from which all quotations in this chapter come, unless otherwise stated: page references may be found on p. 311.

known literary, and other, figures whom the author encountered at that time. These sketches are so numerous and possess so much intrinsic interest, especially those of Wilfred Owen and Thomas Hardy, for example, that *Siegfried's Journey* is as much a 'book of personalities' as an autobiography. It is, as it were, a pendant to the earlier books, in a similar way to Sir Osbert Sitwell's *Noble Essences* and L. E. Jones's *Georgian Afternoon*, in each of which the remembrance of people known bulks large.[3]

Owing largely to this varied—even miscellaneous—subject-matter, the narrative is more discursive than is the case in either of the two previous volumes. The manner of reminiscence is more straightforward: there is no need for the careful building of atmosphere, because there is, in fact, no coherence, no singleness in either the setting or the experiences and feeling of the hero. Style is no longer closely integrated with feeling—as it is in the nostalgic evocation of a stable world-picture in *The Old Century* and *The Weald of Youth*. There is relatively little description of the setting, natural or otherwise (this is most noticeably lacking in the 'American chapters') and no memorable all-embracing tone. Of the three autobiographies, *Siegfried's Journey* gives, on the whole, the least satisfaction as a work of art. It has plainly suffered from the psychologically disturbing conditions in which it was written, a time when the stress of personal difficulties combined with the extreme depression into which he was plunged by the Second World War made it a labour for him to write at all.[4]

Sherston Sophisticated

The first six chapters enable us to form a more many-sided impression of the author's personality than that given by the *Memoirs*. Temperamentally, Sherston's and Sassoon's true self are akin. The difference lies in the latter's greater intellectual sophistication. This is seen first in their differing intellectual backgrounds: whereas Sherston has little more sustaining power for his pacifist convictions—when away from

3. *Noble Essences* is the fifth and final volume of Sitwell's autobiographies; *Georgian Afternoon* (London, 1958), the third and last by L. E. Jones, the others, covering the same period and a somewhat similar background to Sassoon's, being *A Victorian Boyhood* and *An Edwardian Youth*.
4. The letters for the period 1943-45 included in *The Best of Friends* give some indication of this state of mind. In one he writes, nearing the end of his work on the book, "I've struggled on with my MS. though my mind was very unwilling to work, and I'm terribly stale on the book" (p. 148).

the Front—than his lonely, emotional kinship with his fellows, his creator has the flattering encouragement of the Morrells, more than a single meeting with Bertrand Russell (cf. the 'Thornton Tyrell' interview) and the help in composing his 'protest' of Middleton Murry, all grounded upon the fact that his poems have already earnt him admiration and respect. Under such influences as these, though taking into account also Sassoon's excitable and self-dramatising self, the form that his protest takes has greater inherent probability than is the case with Sherston. In his poetry he has kept up a long-standing 'war on the War'; he hopes that in this war his protest will prove the most telling shot: "I went up to London resolved to write something more definitely antagonistic than satiric epigrams in *The Cambridge Magazine*." The naivety is there, and the state of acute mental tension, but the action seems less hectically conceived; it gains moral strength from the fact that, in this context, Sassoon has not played down his intelligence, as he is inclined to do in describing Sherston's encounters with 'Markington' and 'Thornton Tyrell'. It becomes possible to share his disagreement with the verdict of the Under-Secretary for War, who "told the House of Commons that I was suffering from a nervous breakdown, unavoidably ignoring the fact that people in such a condition don't usually do things requiring moral courage." There is no boastfulness here; Sassoon's frankness about his shortcomings and inconsistencies earns him the right to say this.[5]

The period at Craiglockhart, fully dealt with in the first part of *Sherston's Progress*, rightly receives no recapitulation. The important thing is that Sassoon adds an account of his close relations there with Wilfred Owen, which reveals an influence almost as strong as that of Rivers in enabling him to make up his mind to drop his 'stop the War' attitude: "His [Owen's] hero being in sore need, he could bring him gentle and intuitive support, tiding over inevitable moods of bitterness and depression." That Sassoon should at that time have held the friendship and respect of Wilfred Owen speaks for itself: it is another valuable corrective to his tendency elsewhere toward self-depreciation.

Though the early chapters bring into focus much that is concealed from view in the *Memoirs*, Sassoon does not disturb the balance of his self-portrayal in the earlier books. The temperamental characteristics

5. Sir Osbert Sitwell, another pacifist poet at war, brackets Sassoon with Bertrand Russell as the two especially "for whose courage I then was able to feel an admiration" (*Laughter in the Next Room*, 1949, p. 112).

which, in *The Weald of Youth* especially, have been treated with a mixture of pride and humorous indulgence, are still allowed full scope. He lets it be seen that his protest was not pure idealism: "my action was the climax of a progression of ideas and emotions which had begun almost a year before, and ... my behaviour was in accordance with the temperament which had led me to perform reckless exploits in the front line." In the continuation of the story beyond the point at which Sherston's ends, we see that after recovering from his wound he still wishes to return to the Front, for a similar mixture of motives: on the one hand, to indulge his morbid desire for "tragic emotions about human existence"; on the other, "to acquire further material which would broaden and vitalize what was already in my mind," in other words to universalize the War in his poetry. In one of his temperament, the first motive might have defeated the second.

Despite his war experiences, he remains in many ways the callow young man, full of vanities and inconsistencies. He postures before the impressionable Lady Ottoline, takes romantic pride in his Byronic portrait, yet reacts huffily to the "fashionable exploitation in a Kensington drawing-room" which his behaviour invites. All of this is psychologically convincing; he has yet to know himself. Though "I could now safely admit that army life had persistently interfered with my ruminative and quiet-loving mentality," circumstances prevent him from exploiting this perception. Released from the War, he has yet to find release from the condition in which it has left him. There is still the backwash: the pent-up emotion, the search to relieve it by positive action, the unfixed mind. Circumstances do not help: he is being lionized as a War poet in a hectic atmosphere which cannot last indefinitely. His social behaviour at this time, as one would expect, is "deplorably chameleonic", and the impression given by the accounts of the part he plays in contact with people as different as Lady Ottoline, Thomas Hardy and the golfing 'George' bears this out: at times self-effacing and awkward almost to extinction, then a creature of impulse, often engagingly unpredictable and endearing, sometimes priggish and swollen-headed. At an Armistice-night party, for example, he involves himself in a high-minded argument with a young man who has spent the War assisting on the Central Liquor Control Board, asserting "that the War had been a loathsome tragedy and that all this flag-waving couldn't alter it"; the next night we find him, the fiery pacifist, attending a dinner in uniform, gratified to feel

hat "it suited my personality when I was being trotted out as a soldier-
poet." There is, on the other hand, his impulsive initiative in honour-
ng Thomas Hardy's seventy-ninth birthday—"my eagerness would
not wait for his eightieth birthday"—a warm and sympathetic
impulse. Another spontaneous action, also understandable though less
firmly grounded, is his gratuitous castigation of the "prosperous and
complacent" Jewish congregation whom he addresses during his
American tour. Yet this is the man who, not long before, has snobbishly
revelled in dinner at Brook's on the third night of the Armistice:
"the dinner was such that I felt myself to be celebrating Victory with
delectable exhilaration, reminded that there was more to be said for
privileged than for proletarian standards of behaviour."

The contradictions are manifold, but underneath there *is* a constant
thread, though only in brief interludes is the hero himself able to
catch hold of it. In England, he does so once in the company of the
golfing 'George', the symbol of the human values of *The Old Century*:
'When with him I became the impulsive and unaffected person he
had known in the past, glad to be guided by his integrity and good
sense ... His deductions, like his drives and his iron-shots, were
sound and unspectacular, well in the middle of the fairway." George
remains this shadowy ideal of homespun wisdom—but perhaps
Sassoon is wise to give him no more life than this. In America, there
is the lucky contact with the wealthy Edward Warren who, though
scholarly and high-minded, has an effect similar to George's—he is
unaffected and undemanding. In their company he recovers something
of his essential self.

Apart from these isolated interludes, Sassoon's history at this time
perfectly reflects the dilemma of his contemporaries who had endured
similar experiences and whose feelings were akin to his own. He is
wound up, as it were, and no-one gives him the chance to run down:
instead they give extra twists to the screw. First he is invited to speak
in the elections, next to go on an anti-War lecture tour in America.
In each case, he plunges in, both out of a desire to do something of
comparable significance to his experience at the Front and as a
(largely unconscious) means of escape, or deferment of re-adjustment
to normal conditions. Of his decision to tour America he writes:

In the first place I had pledged myself to expose war in every way I could;
and here was my opportunity for an active campaign. I may even have told
myself that it was a solemn duty to open the eyes of the Americans to those

realities of which they needed to be made aware. My second reason emerged
in a sudden impulse and longing to escape from the post-war complexities
of my existence.

The aims were noble, however mixed the motives. What is the attitude
of the "elderly quietist" who looks back on his 'Journey' at that time?
Naturally it is indivisibly associated with his immaturity—or rather
a period of aberration from his true self. He is now so completely
detached from any such condition of mind that he is able to recount
his poetry readings, his Socialist oratory, his sometimes intemperate
pacifist addresses with gentle irony. He neither idealizes his younger
self, nor fails to assess his activities at their true worth. He balances
his account of them with more moderate views on some of the issues
that once inflamed his mind. His pacificism has become qualified:
he was right, he thinks, to expose "the amateurish mismanagement and
incompetence" which caused the loss of so many lives in the First
War, but this had the incidental advantage of teaching England how
to wage modern warfare. For him there are righteous wars. We can
see, too, why he came to doubt his temperamental aptitude for politics,
and that he was justly disillusioned by the spectacle of the disunited
idealists in the intellectuals' organisation *Clarté*.

But the core of Sassoon's attitude in 1945 is one of acceptance of
the inevitable slowness of change and qualified disillusionment about
the progress of civilization. He is remembering here "the trivialities
of twenty-five years ago": they count for little against "a realization
of the unassuming littleness of life in relation to the stately progress of the
centuries." The standpoint of the elderly self is as fixed as that of the
younger is fluid and inconstant. On the one hand we have the passionate,
muddled idealist, involved in action: on the other, the "elderly quietist",
who in Tennyson's words advises us "to stick to [our] trust that somehow
good will be the final goal of ill," having clearly followed a path at
some time divergent from the earlier one. The modification of the
pacificism and the abandonment of active politics are comprehensible
within the context, but what remains puzzling—at least on the surface
—is the development of Sassoon's socialism, which plays so large a
part in his immediately post-war life. Though he introduces mature
feeling about life and experience in general, he fails to express his
later attitude on this subject.

The reader must infer what he can. Fortunately, Sassoon writes so
frankly about his conduct during his "Socialist experiment" in its

early stages that it is possible to attempt some explanation of the apparent conflict between it and the attitude we have found in the earlier volumes where he idealizes the pre-First War world without any trace of Socialist feeling.

Socialist Experiment

The Sassoon we see before the 1919 election campaign is a most improbable Socialist. At Garsington, he hobnobs, most impressionably, with Lady Ottoline Morrell: "to be hobnobbing about my poetry— however clumsily—with the sister of a Derby-winning Duke was one of the last things I had ever expected to do." The tone of this—there is no irony or external comment—and of the subsequent reference to the contrast between 'privileged' and 'proletarian' standards of behaviour already referred to (p. 163) give no hint that Sassoon's retrospective attitude is any different. (But it is not impossible to be both a snob and a Socialist, as Labour leaders themselves have shown.)

It is not surprising, considering his background and attitudes such as these, that his first contact with the Labour Party should be accidental. He supports Philip Snowden at Blackburn as "an uncompromising pacifist" rather than as a Socialist. It is not until he reaches Blackburn and really looks at an industrial town for the first time that he gains some idea of the political issues at stake. His reaction is spontaneous and sincere: "I had been spouting about freedom of thought, emancipation from social and industrial injustice, and the need for a clean Peace. But what use was a clean Peace to people whose bodies were condemned to such dirty conditions? How could the plans and promises of politicians have any meaning for their minds until Social Reconstruction had improved these places?" In this belief, he now backs Snowden to the utmost and is bitterly disappointed when they lose the election. Soon after this, he meets Rivers again, who points out the inconsistency between his being an ardent Socialist and at the same hobnobbing with their political adversaries at sumptuous dinner-parties. Sassoon sees the point of this—"For, after all, the Blackburn episode had shown me which side I was on"—and resolves to make himself into an intellectual Socialist as previously he had sought, and failed, to become an intellectual pacificist. He goes to Oxford with this purpose, but makes little headway in giving his idealistic feeling prosaic foundations.

Nevertheless, though he continues to dine with the aristocracy, he conducts himself with moody reserve, trying to remember that he is 'theoretically inimical' to them. He is fired once more with indignation by the Labour-inspired riots in Glasgow, where he goes to report for *The Nation*. Here again is the possibility of action, but he arrives to find all quiet and the union leaders in jail. The most he can do is to receive another bitter taste of the slums: "Cold as the stones we trod was the bleak inhumanity of those terrible tenements." He also goes to court and admires the workers' leader, David Kirkwood, from afar: "He looked strong, kindly, and sensible. I should have liked to shake him by the hand."[6] But he has been unable to achieve anything more positive; even his report is written, with an irony unremarked by Sassoon, by John Langdon-Davies, who was later to become one of the *News Chronicle's* notorious communist correspondents. Returned briefly to Oxford, he continues brashly to exploit his patently under-developed Labour personality. The next and final stage is his appointment as Literary Editor of *The Daily Herald*. This, too, leads to nothing conclusive: he was soon to hand over the editorship to the poet W. J. Turner, "tired", Swinnerton plausibly suggests, "of the paper's futility".[7] Tired also, one hazards, of the weekly grind of journalism, with so little immediate effect to show for it.

Sassoon's most positive political action during this period is probably the composition of "Everyone Sang", and upon this he makes comments whose irony is revealing:

The singing that would 'never be done' was the Social Revolution which I believed to be at hand. In what form that Revolution would arrive I cannot now remember foreseeing—possibly because its form was invisible to me. No doubt I anticipated that there would be some comparatively harmless rioting, but on the whole I merely thought of it as the sunlight of Liberty spreading across the landscape and Everyone being obliged to admit that the opinions of *The Daily Herald* were, at any rate, worthy of their serious consideration. Most of my arguments in favour of it were denunciations of the Rich, supported by extremely imperfect acquaintance with the Poor.

6. There is an account of Sassoon's visit to Glasgow in Jack Lindsay's *After the 'Thirties* (1956, pp. 25-27). Lindsay quotes William Gallagher's view that Sassoon "came to Glasgow ready to welcome a change whatever course it took": if this is true, Sassoon does not say so, but he might well have expressed such sentiments without, at that time, realizing their full implications.
7. *Figures in the Foreground*, p. 210. (One positive effect of this journalistic interlude, no doubt, is Sassoon's sympathetic treatment of Meredith's hard labour in the newspaper world: see *M.* pp. 66-67.)

It astonishes me now that I could have felt so strongly about it, or have been so oblivious to the obdurate unprogressiveness of semi-civilized mankind.

These are his last published words upon his Socialism, looking back upon it as the quirk of a romantic young idealist who was naïve enough to believe the millenium of equality and fraternity was at hand in 1919. Instead of the "sunlight of Liberty" there were to be the storm-clouds of violence (not just "harmless rioting"); the admirable men he had commanded and fought with during the War were to turn into an obdurately unprogressive mob.

Sassoon's temperament craved for quick results; his fragile idealism needed men to be better than they were. His Socialism was at first a generous impulse, but later was to falter for the lack of a clear objective and eventually to weaken in face of bitter realities. His last significant chance of action was at the time of the General Strike in 1926 and it is worthwhile to consider how his behaviour then bears out this view. According to Sir Osbert Sitwell's account,[8] he and Sitwell feverishly used what influence they had—on both sides—to bring about an end to the Strike in the belief that: "The supreme national asset we possessed was ... that there had never been war between the classes: that, at all costs, must be avoided." Though we do not, unfortunately, have Sassoon's account of this, Sitwell seems to have represented Sassoon's attitude consistently with that conveyed by the half-statements of *Siegfried's Journey*. The paramount feeling was a dislike for violence and a conviction that class-warfare would carry change beyond all reasonable limits. In the view of Jack Lindsay, Sassoon's behaviour on this occasion was a question of the blood rather than the brain: "The clash which he had hoped for in 1918-19 was now the last thing he wanted. He had lost faith in the power of the working class to change things for the better; and when the up-sweep of the political struggle did emerge on a national front, he saw it as a threat to be averted. He had regained a sense of unity with the society which he had once detested."[9] Lindsay's diagnosis is not entirely convincing: Sassoon never "detested" the society Socialists were seeking to change. His hatred has never been so thoroughgoing, except in time of war.

But his hatred of violence has been enduring and needs little more

8. *Laughter in the Next Room*, pp. 208-231.
9. *After The 'Thirties*, p. 27.

psychological explanation than that the War had given him his fill of it. Why this should have caused him, seemingly, to reject what Socialism stands for altogether—in his swing of sympathy wholly towards society as it existed before the First War—is more debatable. In a paragraph of reflection upon the gulf of understanding that would exist between his earlier, altruistic self and "sedately-compromising maturity", Sassoon says ruefully, "Seeing all round a subject doesn't always produce illuminating results". There is, however, insufficient published evidence here or elsewhere (the *Satirical Poems* of 1926 contain, as we have seen, only a handful of emotional 'Socialist poems' and nothing like them appears after 1928 in poetry or prose) that Sassoon has "seen all round" Socialism. In mature years he has certainly been fair to those he terms "the Rich", in such books as *The Old Century* and *The Weald of Youth*, but "the Poor", with a few individual exceptions and then not as subjects for 'social comment', have provided no material for his creative pen. Disillusionment had, in the brutal and bitter nineteen-forties, brought about a total rejection of "the clamorous mutability of the modern world" and a consequent idealization of an earlier world in which such a man as he could live at a pace that would enable self-discovery, the preoccupation of his mature years.[10]

Like Wordsworth and Tennyson before him, Sassoon served his apprenticeship to radical ideas, with generous feeling, only to abandon them on realizing how poor were their immediate prospects. The reaction is a familiar one—when it came to the tearing down of Hyde Park railings, even so radical a thinker as Matthew Arnold was not proof against it. It is felt that the innate folly of man soils the highest ideals and must be controlled; the unity of the old world is preferable to the chaos of the new:

> A nation yet, the ruler and the ruled,
> Some sense of duty, something of a faith,
> Some reverence for the laws ourselves have made,
> Some patient force to change them when we will,
> Some civic manhood firm against the crowd—[11]

10. This earlier world (as he knew it) he sought to keep alive at his home in the Wiltshire village of Heytesbury. Writing to Sir Sydney Cockerell, shortly before the outbreak of war, he says: "'cultivating one's garden' . . . seems to be the only sensible thing to do in these times. Mentally, we live in such a hullaballoo of ideas and inventions and non-reticences that the perennial undertones of decent humanity are having a very bad time. Our life here really is a sort of oasis of simple doings in beautiful surroundings." (Letter dated 12.8.39, *The Best of Friends*, p. 69).
11. 'The Princess', Conclusion, 11.53-57.

Tennyson's reaction to an earlier state of change is much akin to that underlying Sassoon's treatment of English society in these volumes of autobiography.[12]

Portraits and Sketches

The pages of *Siegfried's Journey* are crowded with famous figures, who together form a fair panorama of the literary world of the time. The description of famous people he has known is one of the autobiographer's most challenging tasks. It provides a test which the 'literary man' does not always pass with credit. Envy or the rankling of old rivalries may tempt him, however unconsciously, to score a posthumous victory. Sassoon, though he has strong personal affinities, cannot be said to have belonged to any literary clique; he has neither the inclination nor the temperament to titillate his readers with the more pungent variety of literary recollections. This is not to say that he is one "who praises everybody", but he is never malicious. To mitigate the rare depreciatory phrase, he allows something praiseworthy or makes it clear that his knowledge is too limited for definitive comment. He makes no literary gossip: his sketches might well be called, to employ Sir Osbert Sitwell's sub-title to *Noble Essences*, 'Courteous Revelations'. In dealing with a remarkably wide range of figures, from the well-loved Wilfred Owen and Thomas Hardy to the far less congenial (to him) Ronald Firbank and John Drinkwater, he displays a broad generosity of mind.

Sassoon has set himself no special task of commemorating the well-known; he is most concerned with the well-loved. One of the most attractive aspects of the previous volumes has been the manner in which he has paid his debts of friendship, whether it be to the famous or to the obscure. In remembering those who mean most to him he unselfconsciously reveals the depth of his affection in warm yet strong phrasing. He is never stilted or pompous, and is not reluctant to use terms which have gone out of fashion today. Of Robert Ross he says: "My heart went out to him, as it always did, and as it does now; for he was one whose memory lives on through his gaiety and courage and the friendship which never failed those who benefited by it." His tributes to the still living have an unvarnished dignity: of Edmund

12. See Appendix A (11).

Blunden he tells us, "he has since brought me one of the best and most fruitful friendships of my life", and of S. N. Behrman, "The years have made that face a map of kindliness and temperate sagacity." "How *generously*," to paraphrase Hazlitt's praise of Lamb, "he serves up his friends!"

Sassoon has a similarly old-fashioned capacity for admiration— hero-worship would be an invidious word, for he does not make his idols more than human. This is particularly evident in his sketches of Robert Ross, Wilfred Owen, Thomas Hardy, Walter de la Mare and Wilfrid Blunt, each of whom, however they differ from one another, possesses qualities of character for which he has developed a mature respect. His judgements of them are expressed in firm and clear language that evokes a positive sense of their characters and denotes a mind that has long weighed their value. He recalls them with great humility, using himself—so far as he allows himself to appear at all— as a foil to their distinction.

His recollections of Robert Ross are imbued with pathos: we are made conscious of the contrast between the robust, only half-seeing young man that Sassoon was and the ailing, kindly Ross who taxes his strength to the utmost to serve his friends.[13] Sassoon crystallizes this perfectly in their final moment of (unknowing) farewell: "He said nothing; but took my hand and looked up at me for a long moment. His worn face, grey with exhaustion and ill-health, was beatified by sympathy and affection. The memory of it will always remain with me. How should I forget that look, with what afterwards seemed to have been its presentiment of final farewell?" There is nothing inflated about these words, for in recalling numerous actions—of chivalry, patience and generosity—Sassoon has given life to his subject. Part of the final paragraph, with its graceful play on words, recalls his tribute to Miriam in *The Weald of Youth*: "The next evening, while resting before dinner, he died of heart failure. It seems reasonable to claim that this was the only occasion on which his heart failed him, either in personal courage or in generosity towards his friends." This unaffected tribute contrasts favourably with the stilted obituary periods Sassoon quotes from Sir Edmund Gosse.

13. See pp. 83-84. "Ross was, more than anyone else, the stimulator of the anti-war verse by which Siegfried Sassoon became known" (Introduction, *Robert Ross Friend of Friends*, Ed. Margery Ross, 1952).

The sketches of Owen and Hardy are truly commemorative.[14] Sassoon plays down the importance of the mentorship Owen granted him and recaptures instead the human basis of their relationship —their shared humour and sympathies—whilst at the same time firmly defining the distance between them as writers. Owen is not romanticized, as is shown in the sensitive description of his face: "He wasn't a fine-drawn type ... Under ordinary conditions it wasn't a spiritual face. It was of the mould which either coarsens or refines itself in later life. I cannot say that I ever saw what is called 'a look of genius' in it. His mouth was resolute and humorous, his eyes long and heavy-lidded, quiescent rather than penetrating. They were somewhat sleepy eyes, kind, shrewd, and seldom lit up from within." Eyes are perhaps the most challenging aspect of description; in Sassoon's words we have the eyes of a man, whereas Sitwell gives us the generic eyes of the poet when he writes of: "the message of his eyes—deep wisdom, and dark in their meaning".[15]

Hardy, "my main admiration", is celebrated in simple, strong phrases such as "homely strength and ripe integrity" and "simplicity of true greatness", but this is not all. Sassoon's appreciation of Hardy's view of life and sustained liveliness of mind is defined more tellingly by a few pages of vivid description and anecdote than would be possible in pages of critical exposition: we see Hardy at 84 running upstairs to fetch his First Folio to check an arguing point, with childlike pleasure practising his initials preparatory to inscribing copies of *The Owl*, or hobnobbing over the fire of an evening with an impetuous young poet who thought him "the nearest thing to Shakespeare" he would ever meet. In his accustomed way, Sassoon distils a significant picture from his memories, a fireside scene in which Hardy becomes "genius made visible", the seer, yet still the homely figure that he was:

Here was the real Hardy, unmeasurable by intellectual standards, who will haunt the civilized consciousness of our race when the age he lived in has become as remote as the Roman occupation of Britain. He was sitting with one arm round his old friend 'Wessex'—that unruly and vociferous sheep-dog whom he has enshrined in a poem. But when he gazed down at 'Wessie' he ceased to be Merlin. The face of the wizard became suffused with gentle compassion for all living creatures whom he longed to defend against the chanceful injustice and calamity of earthly existence.

14. The Owen chapter earned a just tribute from an unlikely source—Dylan Thomas, who wrote: "Siegfried Sassoon has a lovely chapter about [Owen] ... in his latest book" (*Letters to Vernon Watkins*, 1957, p. 134).
15. *Noble Essences*, p. 103.

In the short poem 'At Max Gate',[16] Sassoon returns to this scene,
further distilling from it the two faces of Hardy as he saw them: the
one of an amiable and inoffensive old man, the other of "the Wessex
wizard", rapt in thought over the flickering fire.

Most memorable is the compassionate vignette of Wilfrid Scawen
Blunt, who is made a poignant symbol of the inevitable decay of the
strongest life.[17] In recalling his meeting with Blunt, Sassoon's poetic
intuition and capacity for admiration have been more conspicuously
at work than elsewhere in the book.[18] He prefaces the first sight of
Blunt with a comparison between Blunt's house and Thomas Hardy's,
which imaginatively suggests the contrast in temperament between the
two writers. Blunt's house becomes a beautiful shell, the symbol of the
sick man's romantic past; it is stilled into sympathy with him: "It had
now become a house of settled habits and restricted happenings,
dependent on the bodily condition of an old man." The peacocks
preening themselves in the gardens and the Arab stallions that stamp
in the stables are the symbols of the man Blunt has been. The bed-
ridden old man still has an obvious distinction—the comparison
with his horses is pointed by phrases like "thoroughbred human-being"
and "high-bred majesty of mind"—but the eyes, to which Sassoon
frequently recurs, alone hold a sure grasp upon life: "His dark eyes
observed me steadily with the mournful scrutiny of a proud spirit
resenting age and infirmity when confronted by unimpeded youth."
The bitter contrast is underlined (perhaps unconsciously) by Sassoon's
incidental recollection of how "when strolling out with Cockerell
before dinner—in a sudden access of energy I had swung myself to
the topmost branches of a large oak." In a later scene there is a touching recollection of Blunt lying out in the garden whilst his robust
friend Belloc sings "Ha'nacker Mill" to him, "and Wilfrid Blunt,
listening with half-closed eyes, his face touched to tenderness and regret

16. *C.P.*, p. 263.
17. pp. 153-159.
18. He wrote to Sir Sydney Cockerell on August 11, 1944, "[I] shall soon be doing
the chapter containing the New-buildings episode, which I shall enjoy," and again
on October 15, asking if Cockerell could refresh his memory with details of the
house and confirm his impressions of the man: "the main thing is that my portrait
of Blunt should not be idealised by memory—I saw him as a proud, many-sided
spirit, but capable of tenderness and tolerance. I should like to believe that I
saw the essential Blunt—the poet & chivalrous rebel against stupid conventions and
political injustice & misgovernment" (*The Best of Friends*, pp. 127 & 134-5).

by the power and pathos of the words." At the end, Sassoon is careful to emphasize the best of Blunt, to enter a last word for a courageous man whatever his reputation may have been; the pathos of seeing this man forced to bow to the body's imperfections is more than enough: "Nothing can alter that impression of high-bred majesty of mind which I took away with me when he had relinquished my hand, lay back on the pillows, and turned his life-renouncing eyes to watch me go."

So great is the sympathetic and imaginative quality of the pages on Blunt that one cannot but regret the sketchiness of Sassoon's comments on the many other interesting people he met during his lionizing period. Nevertheless, the tone is always right: whether it be in the amusing encounters with Lady Ottoline Morrell, Ronald Firbank, Hilaire Belloc and Dr. Liveing, in all of which he adopts the approach of *The Weald of Youth* and freely uses his own impetuous, gauche and rombustious personality as a foil to others; or in the scrupulous tempering of criticism with generosity in his comments on the exhibitionistic John Drinkwater or the fanatical anti-Germanism of Robert Bridges. No detraction or injurious anecdote is allowed to stand as a final impression—fairly enough when one considers how tangential most of these contacts were: yet many memoirists would have yielded to the temptation to make smart capital out of a fleeting contact with a well-known man by writing him up—or down. This is the positive side of Sassoon's anxiety to make allowances which, as we have seen, was a weakness in his peace-time satire.

If many figures do pass too much in the shadows—one thinks especially of De la Mare, the brothers Sitwell, T. E. Lawrence, and the American poets Robert Frost, Carl Sandburg and Vachel Lindsay— it must be remembered that these are random recollections written in an intimate, discursive manner: what they would have gained in literary interest, had he attempted more set pieces, might have been a loss in freshness. The haphazard nature of his comments upon the great figures of the literary scene during the period 1916-1920 only underlines the essentially personal character of these reminiscences. They bring the autobiographical account of the author's experience and development up to a turning-point in his life, the point where we see him beginning to withdraw from his public rôle: it would have not only blurred the self-portrait but also been inconsistent with his valuation of such performances had he treated the literary scene in the

manner of the professional man of letters. As always in his autobiographical rôle, his affections and sympathies guide his pen.[19]

THE AUTOBIOGRAPHIES

A Summing-Up

The present age ... is one which appears to be advancing most rapidly
through the courageous resolve (of its best intellects) to elucidate the subtle
mechanisms of the human mind. It believes that the noblest man is he who
can reveal himself most completely. Too much cannot be known of a great
man. And if a man does not gain ultimate dignity through efficient self-
revelation, he ceases to be great. For the last thing that a writer learns is
to be himself. And his final artistic achievement is the natural and faithful
expression of that essential self.[20]

These words, which Sassoon wrote some years before he published his first
Memoirs, show his keen awareness of the exacting demands likely to be
made by the branch of literature in which he was to make his own
chief mark. It is in the light of this awareness that his achievement may
be judged.

The autobiographer's highest aim must indeed be to show himself to
us as he really is, with all his imperfections—or a convincing number,
at least—upon his head. But it is doubtful whether any autobiographer
has ever achieved this. Apart from the ever-increasing difficulties of
self-knowledge, the temptation to dress himself up for posterity's
partial eye is one that no man can completely overcome: every autobiographer must be something of an egoist. He may falsify the facts, as
George Moore does, but the more common practice is simply to omit
the embarrassing or unpleasant ones. This does not matter—or
rather, it is to the purpose; the very act of concealment or avoidance
reveals the man. Whatever twists and turns the writer takes, we shall
still ask the question, "Do I feel I know this man as he is?" The purport
of this vital question is likely to differ according to whether the expectations of autobiography involve psycho-analytical complexities or not.

19. A reviewer who also wished for more about the literary men nevertheless con-
cluded: "As for the proportion observed between what the outside observer would
call important and what he would rate as minor incident, that is a question for the auto-
psychologist himself, who knows best what the younger man felt vividly in his
original journey" (*The Times Literary Supplement*, January 5, 1946).
20. *The Daily Herald*, 28th March 1923: review of *Tennyson*, by Harold Nicolson.

This is not merely a matter of generations: Sir Osbert Sitwell and Richard Church do not even incline the head towards Freud: their close contemporaries, Edwin Muir and Leonard Woolf, are very conscious of having to take him into account. Freud does not make the only difference: there is also the question of 'taste'—Rousseau's *Confessions* is one thing, Trollope's *An Autobiography* quite another.

Despite the implications of his remarks on the psychological investigations of "the present age", Sassoon takes cognizance of neither Freud nor Rousseau: not for him 'frank confessions' in either the traditional or the modern sense. It might be thought odd that so reticent a man, according to his own profession,[21] should have elected to take up autobiography at all. Certainly, this reticence precludes anything of the stamp of 'startling revelations,' but it is a qualified reticence: in discussing his behaviour, socially and intellectually, and the emotional springs of action he is open and sincere; if he idealizes the past, he does not idealize the self who lived in it. The omissions are obvious: there is no account of sexual experience or feeling, nothing to titillate about the people closest to him—his family; nothing on the 'subconsious self' which plays so conspicuous a part in the autobiographies of Herbert Read and Edwin Muir.[22] He is still old-fashioned enough to consider these matters private property and he is entitled to assume that many of his readers, of his own generation especially, share this attitude: his contemporary and a writer much akin to him, L. E. Jones, says in the Postscript to the third volume of his autobiography, "That I have wanted to write little or nothing about my own family goes without saying."[23] The revelations of Caitlin Thomas—or even of Helen Thomas —lie far outside the scope of such writers as these.

Nevertheless, though it is clear that his approach is less modern than his words of 1923 might lead one to expect, surely the degree of "frankness" desired by modern taste is a debatable quantity. Whatever the autobiographer's success in this respect, he should possess certain positive qualities of character and temperament if we are to be impressed at all by his vision of life. These need not be qualities in the strictest sense of the word, but they must be positive; we may be excused for supposing that George Moore, Rousseau and Frank Harris

21."This instinct for anonymity has been with me all my life" (*W.Y.*, p. 13).
22.Muir writes, "No autobiography can confine itself to conscious life ..., sleep, in which we pass a third of our existence, is a mode of experience, and our dreams a part of reality" (*An Autobiography*, 1954, p. 49).
23.*Georgian Afternoon*, p. 267.

would have made trying friends, but they are enlivening book-companions. Their autobiographies are not only combative; they have the additional advantage of being accounts of eventful lives—Sir Osbert Sitwell's and G. K. Chesterton's, though more 'pleasant', also benefit by this. Sassoon's autobiographies can claim the advantages of neither combativeness nor—apart from the feverish interlude of the War years, mostly confined to the *Memoirs*—eventfulness. The qualities they possess are quieter, though nevertheless positive; they stem from attributes invaluable to the practitioner of this most personal form of literary art: intimacy, a Lamb-like warmth of affection, compassion and sympathy, humour, expressed in a sensitive and sensuously satis-fying prose. It is, from a strictly autobiographical viewpoint, a pity that the *Memoirs*, though they are complete in themselves and exhibit the same qualities of mind and art as the later books, do split the autobiographical sequence; they must be used guardedly to fill out the 'life.' *The Old Century* possesses the greatest artistic unity: as a sensuous evocation of childhood it deserves to stand beside Sir Herbert Read's much-admired *The Innocent Eye*; in its humorous and sympa-thetic treatment of a sensitive child's fears and delusions, it has the flavour of a book by a master of this subject, L. P. Hartley's *The Shrimp and the Anemone*.

There are, in a broader view, certain other limitations. "If one has the temerity to write an autobiography," says Leonard Woolf, "then one is under an obligation not to conceal. The only point in an auto-biography is to give, as far as one can, in the most simple, clear and truthful way, a picture, first of one's own personality and of the people one has known, and secondly of the society and age in which one lived. To do this entails revealing as simply as possible one's own simplicity, absurdity, trivialities, nastiness."[24] If this be accepted as a com-prehensive statement of an autobiographer's primary obligations, Sassoon achieves considerable success on the first count, but only equivocal success on the second. Perhaps Woolf's demands smack of the political historian, but it is reasonable to expect that an autobiographer, as one who deliberately reveals himself to a public audience, shall have a strong, even passionate, involvement in the life we all live. Unless he is a mystic, this is likely to entail a concern with his "society and age". Many autobiographers have made it their primary aim, not to portray themselves, but to laud, castigate or reform their time; others

24. *Growing*, 1961, p. 148.

have wished to show the part they have played and to express their hopes for the future. Sassoon's autobiographies show no such involvement, but go instead to the opposite extreme: the truth of the *Memoirs* must be weighed against the nostalgic idealization of the pre-War period. Valuable as they are as an evocation of a local aspect of Edwardian society and of a way of life, the first two 'straight' autobiographies convey a partial view of that life, little related to the age and society in general.

As a picture, therefore, of "the society and age" they cover, the autobiographies are severely limited: they are surpassed in these respects by such books by near contemporaries as the first three autobiographies of Sir Osbert Sitwell, (*Left Hand Right Hand!*, *The Scarlet Tree* and *Great Morning*, the first two of Leonard Woolf, *Sowing* and *Growing*, and of L. E. Jones, *A Victorian Boyhood* and *An Edwardian Youth*, and H. G. Wells's *An Experiment in Autobiography*), which have wider scope and, in the cases of Woolf and Wells, greater objectivity. Yet none of these books excels Sassoon's in the sincere exploration of self, and it is arguable that the least of an autobiographer's sins is to show a 'disproportionate' concern with self. The autobiography which is detailed and comprehensive upon both the author himself and his times has probably not been written. Sassoon wrote according to the needs of his temperament; the autobiographical theme represents a stage[25]—and not the final one—in 'Siegfried's Journey' in search of positive values.

---

25. A stage—or a blind alley: it could have led no further. There is a similarity between Sassoon's lingering at this period upon the enclosed and inviolate past and that observed by Graham Hough in Pater's *The Child in the House*. Hough writes:
Pater's longing for emotional security characteristically finds its satisfaction in the physical image of a familiar childhood spot, "a place 'inclosed' and 'sealed'", as he calls it with pre-Freudian simplicity, from which it is yet possible to look out upon other fields and other ranges of experience: "a womb with a view", in the crisper idiom of Palinurus (*The Last Romantics*, 1949, p. 163).
But Sassoon has been a restless seeker: and if he has an affinity with Pater, it consists more in decorative prose than in decorative thinking.

PART IV

A RELIGIOUS CONCERN

X

PROLOGUE: VIEWS ON POETRY

"Grey, friend, is Theory—true though Theory be,—
And green the foliage of Life's golden tree."

(Goethe, quoted in *Meredith*)

The main purpose of this chapter is not to lay claims for Sassoon as a critic but to give an outline of his *credo* as a poet: firstly, in order to establish his position in relation to the English poetic tradition and to contemporary English poetry, considering chiefly his views of these matters as expressed in his lecture *On Poetry*, which is the only place where he has discussed them at any length[1]; it also serves as a preface to the religious poetry of almost forty years, which has developed in accordance with these views.

With regard to a poet's criticism, T. S. Eliot observes: "At the back of the poet's mind, if not as his ostensible purpose, he is always trying to defend the kind of poetry he is writing, or to formulate the kind he wants to write."[2] This could be applied with particular truth to Sassoon, as he would readily concede. His critical—'appreciative' is a word he would prefer—method differs greatly from any now widely regarded as ideal or even desirable. Conscious of alienation from contemporary attitudes, he appears before his Bristol audience as "an old-fashioned defender of direct utterance" and pointedly disclaims the 'professional' approach: he is giving, he says, not a lecture, but "the diffident divulgement of a few personal opinions."[3]

In his lecture, in *Meredith* and in all minor pieces elsewhere he shuns verbal or structural analysis—the modern search for the most difficult meaning—social significance, psycho-analytical method, and makes no claim to exact scholarship. He wrote to Sir Sydney Cockerell shortly after giving his lecture, "As criticism it doesn't amount to much; but the audience didn't want a learned discourse; and I could only tell them the sort of poetry I like—and couldn't have been erudite if I'd tried!"[4] As often, Sassoon is unduly self-effacing here:

1. Appendix A, (12).
2. *The Music of Poetry*, p. 8.
3. Appendix A, (13).
4. *The Best of Friends*, pp. 63-64: Letter dated 19.5.39.

whether as criticism it "amounts to much" or not is unimportant for our purposes and unimportant to Sassoon himself, who meant what he said and thought it worth saying.

On Poetry is a personal defence of the Wordsworthian tradition of "simplicity". It is a plea for the primacy of a poetry which will arouse "immediate pleasure" in dealing with the undying theme of love, friendship, mortality and all that can "touch the heart." Concomitant with these themes should be passionate observation of natural scenes and objects. Nature is *the* source of imagery since it is with what Wordsworth calls "the beautiful and permanent forms of nature" that man has his most vital relationship outside those of the human world.

On Poetry has historical interest (some twenty years later) if regarded as a more explicit 'Defence' for the *best* of the poetry in the 'Georgian Poetry' anthologies than Sir Edward Marsh himself ever provided in his Prefaces. The ideals of matter and manner it propounds look back through Hardy to Wordsworth and have continued to animate the poetry of the few surviving 'Georgians'—Sassoon himself, Andrew Young, Edmund Blunden and, until their recent deaths, Wilfrid Gibson and Ralph Hodgson.

The discussion that follows has been arranged under the headings Art and Inspiration, Simplicity and Directness, "The Language of the Heart", The Visual Element—which four "elements" Sassoon distinguishes as "essential"—and Poetry and 'Purpose', concerned with the didactic element, which he certainly does not consider essential.

§ 1 *Art and Inspiration*

Sassoon opens his lecture on poetry with a number of generalisations about the relation between poetry as art and poetry as the utterance of 'inspiration', a something beyond precise identification: "The art of poetry is, of course, the development of a tradition of exact and metrical use of language"; "A man may be born a poet, but he has to make himself an artist as well"; "I entirely agree with Rossetti's dictum about the need for 'fundamental brain-work'"; and finally, "In the poetry of an inventive genius . . . there is some quality which cannot be explained or analysed, something which transcends artifice and belongs to the secret chemicals of emotional aliveness."[5]

The first of these generalisations is probably basic enough to satisfy all but the most rabid of free versifiers, though the word "exact" would beg too many questions for some. It is more satisfying if we interpret it as stressing the need for some degree of control whilst, at the same time, not enforcing a rigid obedience to 'rules'. "A man may be born a poet, but he has to make himself an artist as well." The poetic faculty is innate, but there is what Hopkins called "the common teachable element." Though elsewhere he confesses his perplexity when faced with the intricacies of prosody[6], Sassoon consistently adheres to the view that there is much to be learnt. The poetry may, usually does, come raw; then workmanship must begin. In *Siegfried's Journey*, he criticises the "loose impressionism" of Sandburg which "resembles the provisional scenario or preliminary ingredients of expression rather than the finished work of art." He adds, "'Explanations of life' should be evolved and stated once and for all, not incontinently ejaculated in blissful immunity from the restrictions of versecraft."[7] Polish matters: the bardic poetry, the minutely wrought harmony of such a poem as Collins's 'Ode to Evening'—which he sets against Sandburg's in this passage. He prefers it, he writes, to "the seething poetry of the incarnate Now." It is a significant choice: a poem in which the poet's personality is subdued to an expression of universal feeling, a poem, furthermore, written in the consciousness of a tradition, not "incontinently ejaculated". (It has, too, a marked visual quality, of which Sassoon has much to say later in his lecture.) In these respects—an emphasis upon control of both self and style and a consciousness of tradition—there is an obvious connection with the exceptional restraint of his own later poetry. Being an artist involves having, above all, a capacity for "disciplined statement", for "clarity and control of outline."[8]

Poetry, then, does not spring fully armed from some mystical source —not *fully* armed: but it does spring—"there is some quality which

5. All quotations given in this chapter are taken from *On Poetry*, unless otherwise stated: fairly liberal quotation has been made, owing to the scarcity of the text of the lecture.
6. *S.J.*, p. 108: "I have always found prosody a perplexing and unassimilable subject."
7. Ibid, pp. 198-199.
8. Foreword, *Piers Prodigal*, by Ian Davie, 1961.

cannot be explained or analysed, something which transcends artifice and belongs to the secret chemicals of emotional aliveness." The Intellect is called in—consciously—after the act of composition, "with his critical suggestions and luminous emendations."[9] He quotes the well-known passage from Shelley's *Defence* in which the mind in the act of creation is compared to "a fading coal, which some invisible influence, like an inconstant wind, awakens to transitory brightness." This is not to suggest, as Shelley does in his misleading appeal to Milton's claim in *Paradise Lost* that the muse "dictated" to him "the unpremeditated song", that poetry is *all* mystery. (Shelley was overlooking the convention of the Muses.) But it is hard for the poet to exaggerate what this mysterious quality means to him: if Wordsworth wished to correct the inspiration theory by pointing out that "elaborate and painful toil" is necessary, he was also aware that there *is* a spontaneous element in "spontaneous utterance". Sassoon, in tune with contemporary thought, speaks of this unanalysable quality as arising in "that unchartable element the subconscious mind" which, he humorously observes, "knows a lot more than the conscious one!" In the light of Sassoon's general approach to criticism, it is perhaps justifiable to discern a note of scepticism as well as humour in this remark: he is interested rather in the end product than in the process of creation itself or in delving into the origins of a poem. He nowhere concerns himself with psychoanalytical interpretations of the kind advanced, notably, by I. A. Richards and Maud Bodkin: he has an aversion to the minutiae of such contemporary criticism, as will appear more fully later.

There is a point "where technical accomplishment ends and imaginative modulation begins." The "best poets" have found themselves unable to rationalise it, to explain how it was that "meanings and metaphors of which they knew nothing while composing them" have found their way into their work. Imagination is the vital quality, but he is not concerned to define it, as Coleridge was, or even to offer half-definitions like Wordsworth. The question in the twentieth century is, of course, immensely complicated, even if Sassoon considered it of prime importance to explore the springs of creativity. In his concern

---

9. Though Sassoon relates one notable example of 'inspiration'—from his own experience: he writes of 'Everyone Sang' that there was "no apparent mental process during its composition"; furthermore, it "was composed without emotion, and needed no alteration afterwards" (*S.J.*, p. 140-141).

to emphasize the mystery rather than the possibility of deeper understanding (of such apparently 'simple' poets as Blake, for instance),
he is closer to the Romantics than the Moderns, and amongst the
former to Shelley rather than Coleridge. He comes close to the words
of the elder Romantics in speaking of the "secret chemicals of emotional
aliveness" to which the unanalysable "something" belongs: here, he
seems to refer to the poet's heightened degree of responsiveness to all
that comes within his purview. Thus, Wordsworth's poet is "possessed
of a more than usual organic sensibility", Coleridge's has "a more
than usual state of emotion." Like Shelley who, in his *Defence*, begins
by asserting what Coleridge attempts to prove—the power of imagination to penetrate to essential meaning—Sassoon is content to take the
poet's special faculty for granted:

> How I caught it, found it, or came by it,
> What stuff 'tis made of, whereof it is born

are questions that do not concern him.

He is more concerned with effect than with cause, and with the
technical means to the effect ("Without clarified construction and
technical control no poetical communication can be effective"). He
is interested primarily in what the poet should communicate and in
how best he should do it: he is not interested in complex interpretations
of the thing communicated, least of all in cases where the explanation
of the effect must be sought in an understanding (or theoretical understanding) of the cause.

§ 2 *"Simplicity" and "Directness"; their absence from "modernist verse".*

I. In the third part of his lecture Sassoon has more to say about the
nature of the "art" of poetry. Without "art", he says, "my 'responses'
would be playthings of the faculty which we now call 'free association'".
Art, this implies, is to make poetry intelligible—but how if the poet
does not himself understand the true significance of his 'responses'?
This is a question he nowhere considers: for him, the inmost self can
be known and expressed in such a way as to move immediately. We
may not know *why* we are moved, or we may be unable to define what
exactly moves us: this does not matter. The poet can speak to us
directly and, presumably if we ourselves are attuned properly, he will
arouse in us something akin to his own feeling.

"Art", therefore, is at its best in "direct utterance": "a great poet is most moving and memorable when he speaks the simplest language of the heart." His definition of "direct utterance"—the common denominator of all the poetry he "[likes] best"—is "a full and living voice, seemingly natural, though often using the language of a personal poetic idiom. I mean the true vocal cadence of something urgently communicated—the best words in the best order—yes—but empowered also by sincerity and inspiration."

Sassoon does, in writing on Meredith, grant poetry a *licensed* complexity, though his lecture might give the opposite impression. This is, however, a complexity of a kind which can be ascribed to the imagination that creates what Shelley called in the *Defence* "vitally metaphorical language", to show "the before unapprehended relations of things." Thus it was "permissible" for Meredith to translate "looking at the stars causes profound thought" into

> To deeper than this ball of sight
> Appeal the lustrous people of the night[10]

The complexity he advocates is, as we shall see, primarily concerned with "the visual element". There are, for him, certain traditional complexities of poetry and the "modern", factitious ones.

II. Before we consider his objections to some contemporary writing, we should try to obtain a clearer view of what in practice he means by "directness". Like the earlier poet-critics, Sidney and Shelley, he calls evocative similes to his aid: "by 'direct' I also mean something as inevitable as the rising of the sun, something spontaneous, like the unfolding of a flower." Also like the earlier poets, he can do little more than assert a feeling in the best language he can muster. He is not concerned to argue his audience into acquiescence. Analysis will not do. One points to it and says, "There—there it is. That's what I mean." In *Meredith* he continually adopts this approach in commenting upon his favourite poems. Meredith's 'Dirge in Woods' and 'Woodland Peace' are described as having "a profound simplicity which defies analysis"; 'The Lark Ascending' has an "incomparable aloofness from the ploddings of the journeyman critic"; of 'Hymn to Colour' he writes "I refuse to lay a finger on it"; he asserts a preference for the concluding lines of 'My Theme' and impresses the reader, if at all,

10. *M.*, p. 208.

by the strength of his own regard for them—"These lines mean more to me than many of his longer poems, lock, stock, and barrel."[11] These are poems where he considers the metaphysical Meredith did not overpower the imaginative one. His purpose in *Meredith* is to draw the reader's attention to his own enthusiasms: he makes little attempt to induce, much less force, a response. Such criticism has its value— Sassoon's rare quality is that of enthusiasm, of freely giving praise where it is due. But it is a method that has serious limitations for a reader apt for conversion, but sceptical, who will not be carried away; and more so for the reader who wishes to be led to see *more* in the poem than he can by his own unaided effort.

Sometimes, one wonders whether Sassoon is not himself content with a surface meaning lest analysis should destroy: "I refuse to lay a finger on it." If he is averse (as I shall show) to a good deal of modern writing, he is equally opposed to modern critical methods. I have already noted his tendency to treat critics as a lesser breed, as if all were of Empson's second class of "barking dogs", who set about scratching up the flower when it has had barely time to unfold. But if, as Empson points out, a 'good' poem is subjected to analysis, what loss can there be? "You think the poem is worth the trouble before you choose to go into it carefully, and you know more about what it is worth when you have done so."[12] If Sassoon considers one should circumscribe one's endeavours to appreciate the full ramifications of a poem, so also should one not be too eager to interpret it in relation to the state of the poet's mind. This can be illustrated by a comparison of his remarks on Meredith's 'The Lark Ascending' with those of another modern critic of Meredith, Norman Kelvin.

I quote the comments of the two critics in full:

Sassoon,

... 'The Lark Ascending', a sustained lyric of one hundred and twenty lines which never for a moment falls short of the effect aimed at, soars up and up with the song it imitates, and unites inspired spontaneity with a demonstration of effortless technical ingenuity. At a first reading it may seem breath-taking. As usual, Meredith demanded a *tour de force* of mental concentration. But on this fortunate occasion he was so completely successful that one has only to re-read the poem a few times to become aware of its perfection. The lark-song he says, is

11. *M.*, pp. 105, 164, 205, 173 respectively.
12. *Seven Types of Ambiguity*, 2nd Edn., 1961, p. xii.

> The song seraphically free
> From taint of personality,

and he himself, in the first eighty-four lines, comes as near as is humanly possible to disproving his assertions that

> Was never voice of ours could say
> Our inmost in the sweetest way,
> Like yonder voice aloft, and link
> All hearers in the song they drink . . .
> We want the key of his wild note
> Of truthful in a tuneful throat

But to write of such a poem is to be reminded of its incomparable aloofness from the ploddings of the journeyman critic, however much he may be uplifted with the lark . . .   (*Meredith*, p. 164)

Kelvin,

. . . he compares the song of the lark with the utterances of man. Meredith's intention is heavily symbolic:

[Here follows the quotation Sassoon gives, only with the first couplet he quotes in its proper place and without any omission]

> Was never voice of ours could say
> Our inmost in the sweetest way,
> Like yonder voice aloft, and link
> All hearers in the song they drink.
> Our wisdom speaks from failing blood,
> Our passion is too full in flood,
> We want the key of his wild note
> Of truthful in a tuneful throat,
> The song seraphically free
> Of taint of personality.

For Meredith, the lark's song is a symbol of the lack of egoism, lack of self-awareness, lack of desire for individuality, that is the mark of all creatures of nature except man. Presumably the lark is content to be a minute particle of the organic entity that is nature herself, and the lark has no need to be distinguished from other such particles. Her song is a single note in a symphony of sound, and we are to understand that the symphony, not the single note, is important. Significantly, though the song speaks of the lark's "inmost", its function is not to give the lark 'self-expression' but to "link all hearers in the song they drink." Like the seraph, the lark is self-forgetful to the utmost. But unlike the seraph, she occupies no special place in the universe.   (N. Kelvin *A Troubled Eden*, 1961, p. 118)

Here we see a marked difference in critical or, as Sassoon might prefer to put it, *appreciative* method. Sassoon gives his whole attention to asserting that the poem is a triumph of pure sound—expressing an inwardness of harmony in a human being fit to match the lark's song, so finely disproving the poet's "Was never voice of ours could say . . ." The poet has presumably freed himself of the limitations of 'personality' and become a pure, harmonious voice. Man, too, can create a thing of sounding beauty. Yet, how if we consider, with Kelvin, what the poem actually *says*? How will this affect our reaction to "the word music"—does it, when fully understood, bear continued re-reading for the pleasure of pure sound? Or may we not find that the "heavily symbolic" intention gradually overmasters and even destroys this pleasure? I shall not attempt to answer these questions, but merely wish to point out that *meaning* is relevant to the full appreciation of this poem: it is a case where meaning, in the light of Meredith's consistent concern with anti-egoism,[13] must have some relevance to the reader's response, beyond mere sound and impressionistic meaning. It is odd that Sassoon, who so often complains of the obtrusiveness of the didactic element in Meredith, should have failed to note its presence here.

The advocate of 'simplicity' and simple appreciation rarely attempts to defend his preferences systematically, and this is the case with Sassoon, not only in the limited compass of his lecture but also throughout *Meredith*, where there would have been scope for argument. What he says on the subject of simplicity and directness must rest, as is usually the case with one who writes in support of this viewpoint, on the assertion of personal preferences.

III. A dogmatic assertiveness is particularly evident in his comments upon contemporary poetry. These occur chiefly in the fourth section of his lecture, where he digresses to glance in a general way at the contemporary practice. "For the last decade and a half" [he was speaking in 1939] "the writing of straightforward and whole-hearted verse has been increasingly out of fashion, and indirect utterance has been indulged in to an unprecedented degree. Its most earnest

13. Nowhere in *Meredith* does Sassoon bring out the strength of this governing idea— it would not, in any case, be part of his intention to do so: the cardinal weakness of his treatment of Meredith's poetry is his reluctance to come to grips with the thought of one whom C. Day Lewis, a younger Meredithian, has eulogised as "the highest intelligence at work upon poetry in modern times" (*The Poetic Image*, 1947, p. 82). In marked contrast, Sassoon believed that to promulgate the Meredithian spirit it was necessary first to jettison the 'philosophy.'

practitioners appear to regard verse-writing as a science, and emotional expression as a scientific exercise." One can only guess at whom he means by "its most earnest practitioners", since he offers no names. But by his standard, it is "direct utterance" that matters: we may, therefore, suppose that he has in mind writers as allusive and concentrated as Eliot, Pound and Empson, and metrical and linguistic experimenters such as Edith Sitwell; elsewhere, more explicitly, he deplores the lack of "sustenance" in "symbolist mystification."[14] In the statement quoted previously "science" is used pejoratively, as in some of his poems, to be contradistinguished from "art". The choice of words is emotive: "straightforward and whole-hearted"—and further on he describes himself as ''an old-fashioned defender of direct utterance". This is 'the plain man's' approach which sometimes blows fresh through his writing, as when he utters his frank enthusiasms; but too often seems like the veiling of an insubstantial argument, as when he compares Meredith's 'The South-Wester' unfavourably with what Shelley, "who called a cloud a cloud . . . and used plain Wordsworthian language", would have made of the subject.[15] Certainly Shelley would not have called a cloud a "brine-born issue", but he called it a great many other things in his 'Ode to the West Wind' (with which Meredith's poem naturally invites comparison), using a vividly metaphorical language—not "plain Wordsworthian"—that has set commentators puzzling over which metaphors refer to clouds and which do not.[16] However, Sassoon prefers a generalised emotional impact and would see little value in such investigations.

As an "old-fashioned defender" of his standpoint, he abjures detailed analysis and exemplification: "I have", he observes of contemporary poetry, "wrestled with large quantities of modernist verse and have found in it considerable ingenuity, verbal audacity and compression of ideas. But I am discouraged by its ambiguity, euphuistic indirectness, and a sort of dehumanizing logic in it." One needs only to say 'Empson' to remember that "ambiguity" and "euphuistic indirectness" are neither modern weaknesses nor absent from such poems as Blake's 'The Tiger' and Shelley's 'Ode' which Sassoon admires. What of "dehumanizing logic"? He can hardly mean by this a dislike for design, which would be utterly at variance with his demand for

14. Foreword to *Collected Poems of Anna Gordon Keown*, 1953.
15. *M.*, p. 202-3.
16. Notably F. R. Leavis in *Revaluations*.

careful artistry: "Who can deny", he asks apropos of Meredith's
'Seed-Time' and 'Outer and Inner', "that precision of statement and
shapeliness of design are more acceptable to posterity than diffuse
declamation?"[17] No: it is that he sees nothing but "logic" — the fault
is in the poet, who has nothing "human" to give. Poetry has become
"a scientific exercise", without power to move. What Sassoon really
desires is a moving simplicity of both manner and matter, such as he
finds in the "homespun strength of sobriety" of Robert Frost.[18] In
considering his comments on the technique of modern poetry, one
should bear in mind that his antipathy is grounded in his lack of
sympathy with current attitudes of mind. His dislike for these attitudes
leads him to speak of obscurity—unhistorically—as their peculiar
product.

We can consider as a symptomatic case the significance of his
disparaging reference to one contemporary poet—Edith Sitwell. He
complains of "the cult of incomprehensibility" that has arisen from
an approach to writing that is too "technique-conscious". He traces
the main influences to Hopkins and Bridges—for whom he confesses
a deep admiration—and rejects their theories, together with Edith
Sitwell's, which he sees as leading to an unjustifiable confusion between
the arts of music and of poetry. "To Miss Sitwell", he observes tartly,
"a syllable may be a chromatic semi-tone, but I much prefer to regard
it as a unit of pronunciation." This may seem inconsistent if it is
remembered that the younger Sassoon was one of the few reviewers
who welcomed the deliberate dissonances of *Façade*, Edith Sitwell's
series of poems written especially for music and performed in 1922.
In his *Daily Herald* article, he had pilloried the typical 'fat-headed'
reactionary with the airy humour characteristic of his reviewing at
that time:

"What would Coleridge say to such asylum-stuff?" ejaculates some exasperated gentleman, flinging *Façade* on to the floor.

Question:
"What would Mr. Coleridge say
In Nineteen Twenty-two?"

Answer:
"Miss Edith Sitwell's verses ought to be
Admired for their originality."

17. *M.*, p. 204.
18. *S.J.*, p. 183.

Chorus:
"And that's what Coleridge says to you
In good old Nineteen-Twenty-Two."

Probably Mr. C. would add that Miss S. writes for her own ears and sees with her own eyes, which is a rare and exquisite achievement. The results are, of course, totally unexpected! To the intolerant and purblind the results are "all damned nonsense." All fantastic art is "nonsense," until we have got over our astonishment.[19]

In 1922, then, Sassoon had sympathised with Miss Sitwell's reaction against the debased Tennysonian versifying which still, despite Eliot and Yeats, held the popular field. A little earlier, he had written to Edward Marsh, then preparing *Georgian Poetry IV*, exhorting him to ask Edith Sitwell for a contribution, since her work was "far stronger" (than that of Fredegond Shove, whose verses Marsh liked) "and quite original"; in the same letter he argued against including Edward Shanks's work, which, though "delightful" was all "based on echoes from the past."[20]

The interesting thing is that he did not maintain this earlier tolerance for experiment and oddity—in reaction against Georgian flaccidity—and extend it to the poetry of the 'Thirties, though that poetry was, in part at least, symptomatic of the same kind of reaction as Edith Sitwell's. The explanation for this changed attitude lies in Sassoon's gradual withdrawal, over the twenty years intervening, from the present. In 1939 he could no longer welcome the revolutionary. Too much was in turmoil: the technical influence of such writers as Edith Sitwell had led to "dehumanising logic", a baneful mechanism that struck at the very "language of the heart." Complexity for complexity's sake was symptomatic of a deep-laid sickness: much like his "exasperated gentleman" who flung *Façade* to the floor, he felt that the present did not belong to him nor he to it. Neither did that earlier self, who had written to Robert Graves of "You and me, the poets who mean to work together some day and scandalize the jolly old Gosses and Stracheys."[21] Perhaps such things as the *Façade* review realized this aim for a time, but the essential conservatism of Sassoon's temperament was bound to come uppermost. This he himself sees, as when in *Siegfried's Journey* he comments on how in the early 'Twenties the Sitwells had laid siege to that conservatism and, for a time, had

19. 'Too Fantastic for Fat-heads': review of *Façade*, *The Daily Herald*, 24 May, 1922.
20. *Edward Marsh*, by C. Hassall, p. 467.
21. *Goodbye To All That*, p. 210.

provided "a wholesome antidote to my intolerance of the unusual and my instinctive preference for the traditional."[22] He may speak of his preference humorously, but there is no doubt that it is deeply held and that, consonant with his religious viewpoint, that which is modern represents a decline from "tradition", no enrichment of it.

§ 3. '*The Language of the Heart*'

Like Wordsworth and the Pre-Raphaelites before him, who were each writing at periods of what they conceived to be emotional dessication, Sassoon reasserts the primacy of true feeling. He enlists contemporary support from the eloquent words of A. E. Housman: "I think that to transfuse emotion—not to transmit thought, but to set up in the reader's sense a vibration corresponding to what was felt by the writer—is the peculiar function of poetry" (*The Name and Nature of Poetry*). But the line of descent for this attitude may be traced back through Hardy, who thought that "the ultimate aim of the poet should be to touch our hearts by showing his own",[23] to Wordsworth, who laid it down that the object of poetry is truth "not standing upon external testimony, but carried alive into the heart by passion," and who elsewhere yoked the simple and the wholehearted in a fashion Sassoon would entirely approve: "In the higher poetry, an enlightened Critic chiefly looks for a reflection of the wisdom of the heart and the grandeur of the imagination. Wherever these appear, simplicity accompanies them . . ."

Writing then in this respectable tradition of feeling (it may also be extended back to the Johnson who reacted against the Metaphysicals much as we have seen Sassoon doing against innovating modern poets), Sassoon complains that critics have lost the capacity for a simple response. Lamenting that of the numerous critiques of 'The Thrush in February' he had read "none appeared aware that poetry is the language of the heart as well as the head",[24] he asks, doubtless with the scalpel-wielding critic in mind, of the last line he quotes from that poem ("The young time with the life ahead"): "Is it thought which causes that simple, concluding statement to touch one at the source of tears?" He would consider this question unanswerable, as a

22. p. 163.
23. *The Life of Thomas Hardy*, p. 128.
24. *M.*, p. 198.

further supporting quotation, this time from Leigh Hunt, is meant to show: in which Hunt distinguishes "feeling" from "the mere conclusions of the understanding" as "a sort of thought without the process of thinking, a grasper of the truth without seeing it." But is this process so very mysterious? Surely it depends closely on the individual reader's reaction; it will be worthwhile to consider what it seems to mean in Sassoon's case and how convincingly it can be shown to be superior to vicious analysis.

He offers a concrete example of his preference in the lyric "Tell me not here, it needs not saying" from Housman's own *Last Poems*. The merits of this poem he summarises as: "simple statement"; completeness—"a vision of 'the world seen once for all'"; "intensity; every word contributes something to the whole"; there are "verbal surprises, yet every image is recognisable, friendly, and unaffected"; "form and style fit the meaning; it is a beguiling lyric about earthly beguilements." The language of the poem consists largely of "ordinary words", yet these are so transformed by emotion as to produce an effect of intensity transmitted through the perfect combination of the elements he distinguishes. So far as they go, these comments are unexceptionable— and, inevitably in a lecture—brief and concise. One objects, however, that the remarks that introduce the poem ("to transfuse emotion —not to transmit thought . . .") cannot be strictly applied to it. This lyric, like 'The Lark Ascending', is an unfortunate example, though not until one reaches the concluding stanza which opens with a forceful claim upon our "thought":

> For nature, heartless, witless nature,
> Will neither care nor know . . .

—these lines draw their force from their contrast with the muted cadences of the preceding stanzas and compel us suddenly to brace ourselves at the onslaught of an idea. Housman is making a point here and giving it prominence: our emotional reaction will depend to a great extent upon whether or not we see nature in the Tennysonian way. Seen in the Meredithian way, the conclusion to such a poem would have been very different:

> Death is the word of a bovine day,
> Know you the breast of the springing To-be.
>
> ('Seed-Time')

But Meredith's is no more simply "the language of the heart" here than Housman's: the intellect has pushed its way to the fore and 'thought' stands naked. *Both* poets have failed to transmute emotion.

As William Empson justly points out, "the language of the heart" is not necessarily a simple matter: "whenever a receiver of poetry is seriously moved by an apparently simple line, what are moving in him are the traces of a great part of his past experience and of the structure of his past judgments."[25] A predisposition towards Housman's view of nature seems to have blinded Sassoon to the obtrusive 'thought' in the lines I have quoted—or rather he takes for granted a conception that would challenge a reader differently disposed. Naturally, we are inclined to eulogise poetry with whose feeling we sympathise and in *Meredith* Sassoon repeatedly does so. For example, of the concluding lines of Meredith's 'My Theme',

> I say but that this love of Earth reveals
> A soul beside our own to quicken, quell,
> Irradiate, and through ruinous floods uplift

he writes "Those lines mean more to me than many of his longer poems, lock, stock, and barrel." Yet these lines are not by any means Meredith's best upon this subject: their movement is stiff, the presentation of the concept trite. But the concept itself, which might be interpreted to suggest a belief that God works through Nature, would be more sympathetic to Sassoon than the idea of 'Earth and Man' (which I think Meredith also intends in the lines from 'My Theme'), where Earth is, virtually, God:

XXIX

> If he aloft for aid
> Imploring storms, her essence is the spur.
> His cry to heaven is a cry to her
> He would evade.

XXX

> Not elsewhere can he tend.
> Those are her rules which bid him wash foul sins;
> Those her revulsions from the skull that grins
> To ape his end.

25. *Seven Types of Ambiguity*, Preface p. xv.

XXXI
And her desires are those
For happiness, for lastingness, for light.
'Tis she who kindles in his haunting night
The hoped dawn-rose.

The implications of this are more ambiguous; one cannot so readily extract from them a religious interpretation as from the lines from 'My Theme' which Sassoon eulogises. He is moved, I think, by the sentiment of those lines, not by their poetic quality where, to adapt his own words, "form and style should fit the meaning."

We have, unfortunately, no objective method of determining where "the simplest language of the heart" is being spoken: we can, however, determine with some accuracy when it is not. And we can only attempt to do this by trying to show *why* we are moved—whether it is by something in the poem, something in ourselves, or by a fusion of the two. We read carelessly, with an alertness to what we are predisposed to accept; only by analysis can we discipline ourselves to a careful reading for both our own satisfaction and a due appreciation of a poet's achievement.

"The simplest language of the heart" is bound to be a variable quantity: it is a dubious critical test. I have already glanced at his disapproving comment on the critiques of Meredith's 'The Thrush in February': "none appeared aware that poetry is the language of the heart as well as the head." This is undoubtedly a strong point, but it must also be said that Sassoon's enthusiasm for this poem—a very personal one, he admits, carries him too far in the contrary direction. He confesses his bias frankly enough: he has no time for the poem's (admittedly chilling) philosophy—"It is the thrush that makes the poem memorable, not the moralisings." He extracts from the poem the stanzas which are most evocative for him (one is reminded of his own 'Awareness of Alcuin')—the first five stanzas that treat of the thrush's song as a welcome portent

. . . out of Winter's throat, [of]
The young time with the life ahead.

Clearly he finds the 'thought' of the poem repugnant and dismisses it without discussion purely on the grounds that it is disagreeable— "Why is it so inexpressibly more satisfying to read those opening

stanzas than to be told that 'We breathe but to be sword or block'?"
Torn from its context this line offers the reader no inkling of the
Meredithian idea of the relationship between Earth and Man behind
it. Sassoon does not interpret what he finds repugnant—he leaves it
alone. His comments on the Meredith poem are no more *critically*
valuable than those on the Housman: in the first he finds alien, and
therefore obtrusive, thought, in the latter (as in 'My Theme') he
welcomes congenial thought without seeing it as the false note of
what we might call 'head-language'. His critical comments stem from
personal preferences for certain attitudes, not from an objective consideration of both feeling and *form*. In both poems the 'head' plays
an obvious part: on the Housman he passes too smoothly over pro-
tuberances of thought and speaks vaguely of "the simplest language";
from the Meredith he extracts "the simplest language" and rejects the
thought.[26]

This contradiction is inherent in Sassoon's subjective approach to
criticism, a type of criticism congenial to those whose response to
his 'I know what I like—and here it is' attitude can be to agree
warmly 'I like it too.' But no useful standards can be established if our
predisposition to certain ways of feeling leads us to apply no consistent
principles to what we read. The attitude of writers like Sassoon,
nevertheless, must always be an essential corrective to 'analysis for
analysis' sake'. His affirmation of the primacy of feeling in poetry has
no *theoretical* effect, any more than Wordsworth's had: in their two
cases, it is their poetry that must justify them.

§ 4 *The Visual Element*

I. Humphry House notes that for Coleridge as a poet "the strength
of impression of external nature on the mind is the essential starting-
point."[27] It was equally so for Wordsworth and Keats, as for Hardy,
Housman and Meredith, and the visual expression of this—going
on from the question of feeling—is a further vital aspect of the poet's
response as Sassoon sees it. He devotes a third of his lecture to the
subject and has much to say of it elsewhere, especially in *Meredith*.[28]

26. See Appendix A (14).
27. *Coleridge*, 1953, p. 54.
28. His concern with visual imagery, strong though it is, should not be abstracted
from his general statement of the qualities he requires from poetry; it is just one
of those he finds in the Housman poem—in combination with "simple statement",
"intensity" and "wholeheartedness".

"From my earliest years", he writes in *The Old Century* (p. 140) "I was interested in words, but their effect on my mind was mainly visual. In a muddled way I knew that they had derivations, but my spontaneous assumption was that a mouse was called a mouse because it was mouse-like." And in *On Poetry*, he makes it clear that he has always found it natural to conceive of ideas in pictorial terms: "Thinking in pictures is my natural method of self-expression. I have always been a submissively visual writer." He is little attracted by "ideas for their own sake"; it is the poet's business to consider the dress of thought—though this dress should never be extravagant. Primarily, he regards visual imagery as a means towards heightened, yet clarified, expression. It is another of the aids to communication at a poet's command: "the ear is not enough. There is also the eye . . . the mind's eye; by which I mean the faculty of inward visualisation."

"The ear is not enough": but it is an important element, as we have seen. Though he shares his contemporaries' interest in revitalising visual imagery, he is concerned to maintain a tradition rather than add to it. He would applaud Hulme's powerful advocacy of imagery in poetry: "The direct language is poetry, it is direct because it deals in images. The indirect language is prose, because it uses images that have died and become figures of speech . . . while one arrests the mind all the time with a picture, the other allows the mind to run along with the least possible effort to a conclusion." He would *not* join with Hulme in saying that verse should resemble sculpture more than music ("word-music" is a common phrase of his), nor would he see rhythm as anything but indispensable.[29] "The harmonious hymn of being" becomes, for Hulme, a trap for the unwary. A further sharp difference between their attitudes is that Hulme's theory is concerned with restricting the 'damp', emotional appeal of poetry: "The great aim is accurate, precise, and definite description." This theory was a reaction against poetry in which Hulme considered diction and rhythms had become ossified: but it would make the process of creation appear excessively conscious and deliberate to one who is concerned with "wholeheartedness". There is, we shall see, an intimate relationship between Sassoon's demand for the 'simplest language of the

---

29. "[Poetry] builds up a plastic image which it hands over to the reader, whereas the old art endeavoured to influence him physically by the hypnotic effects of rhythm": taken, with the previous quotation, from Hulme's *Lecture on Modern Poetry*.

heart' and the appeal that he discovers in certain kinds of visual imagery.

In *On Poetry* Sassoon applies the 'visual test' to three poets chiefly, Dryden, Donne and Vaughan. He finds Dryden grossly deficient: "He makes us see words and nothing else." He qualifies this by saying that this is a failure of communication—a technical deficiency—and admits that it might have little significance to another reader.[30] He supplies two concrete illustrations, with comment, of Dryden's "deficiency": the line, "And straight the green fields laugh with promised grain" and the lines,

> Orpheus could lead the savage race;
> And trees uprooted left their place,
> Sequacious of the lyre,

which he sets side by side with Shakespeare's on Orpheus,

> Everything that heard him play,
> Even the billows of the sea,
> Hung their heads and then lay by.

He comments, of the Dryden, that it lacks "visual spontaneity"; of the Shakespeare, that "the curve of a breaking wave suggests that the billows 'hung their heads.'" In parenthesis, he adds "'To take arms against a sea of troubles' is another example of his visual evocativeness." By contrast, Dryden's 'sequacious' is tartly dismissed as a "ludicrous Latinism". These just and explicit comments upon concrete examples, of which two are chosen for comparative judgment, are more convincing (because more constructive) than anything he has to say elsewhere in the lecture. He ends his comments upon Dryden with a suggestive (visual) idea: "When we think of his works the man whom they represent sits beside them as uncommunicative about himself as his own portrait." It is implied that had Dryden made us see more, we should have seen the poet himself more clearly.

Sassoon turns next to a very different kind of poet, Donne, who certainly is not impersonal—"a self-investigator who delights in

30. He praises Dryden handsomely in other respects: "His cadenced control of the rhymed verse paragraph was magnificent; and his command of the poetic diction of his day was masterly . . ." (He makes a just distinction in the phrase "the poetic diction of his day": Dryden was the supreme *manipulator* of language). He even grants, with a generosity that few writers on Dryden have shown, "rich humanity and lucid common-sense" (in his *Epistles:* which pleasantly reminds one of Lamb's praise of Pope's "friendly epistles and compliments").

pulling his consciousness to pieces, a vehement talker whose whole mind seems voluble with vitality." But this mind is not projected in vivid colours: "His compelling voice carries me along with him all the way, but his eloquence moves in darkness." His poems "abound in references to night, darkness, twilight, and shadows"; "his tenebrous poems are full of torches and tapers, candles and kindlings—contrasts between gloom and radiation": but nature is seldom delineated in her true colours—"he would have called a rose anything before he called it red". Thus, wittily and concisely, Sassoon draws attention to what many readers must have felt to be a deficiency in Donne without being able to put it into words. At the same time, he points out that what, from his standpoint, is a deficiency, arises from a positive and indivisible way of seeing: "when his genius was active, he instinctively exploited his visual darkness, as being an inherent element of his intensely personal poetic idiom." His preference does not blind him to the peculiar intensity Donne's 'dark poetry' achieves.

With Donne's use of conceits he is not concerned, though these surely have a visual impact, as in the two 'Valedictions'—'Of Weeping' and 'Forbidding Mourning'. He is clearly thinking of the religious rather than the love poems, in any case, but above all of imagery drawn from the most common source—nature. 'He would have called a rose anything before he called it red"—or, one might add, "before he called it anything at all." It is Donne's choice of visual imagery to which Sassoon cannot respond; it is not that—even in the religious poetry—there is a marked absence of it.

This accent upon nature imagery is confirmed by what, in the light of his own religious poetry, seems his inevitable choice of poet to contrast with Donne—Henry Vaughan. He commends Vaughan's choice, following Herbert, of "the sudden homely image or epithet."[31] He notes an affinity with Donne in that they "shared that intense awareness of darkness and light", but finds in Vaughan a visionary power of illumination, whereas "in Donne's midnights you cannot see

31. "Homely"—a characteristic word of approval. Thus, he finds Housman's imagery in 'Tell Me Not Here' to be "recognisable," "friendly and unaffected." Meredith, too, receives highest praise for his "homely and intimate" 'Ballad of Past Meridian', for "the homely and beautiful elegy on Mrs Meredith," 'Change in Recurrence,' and for the "glowing spontaneity and visual richness" of 'Ode to the Spirit of Earth in Autumn,' whilst he is reproved for the "oppressively didactic" 'Earth and Man' which Sassoon compares unfavourably with 'Rabbi Ben Ezra' ("From that I can get something visual and kindly") (M., pp. 205, 202, 170, 168 respectively.)

your hand before your face until he calls for a candle." Vaughan's "illuminated vision" as Hutchinson calls it, is a critical commonplace; one need only remember here that a sense of light is strong in Sassoon's own religious poetry—the preference is a vitally personal one. He embroiders his remarks on Vaughan's "mental imagery inwardly illuminated" by quoting, without comment, the first three stanzas and the seventh of 'They are all gone into the world of light!' (It is perhaps significant that he should choose a poem concerned with the death of friends.) The rapt and serene imagery of the second stanza—on the living quality of the memory of his friends—is particularly appropriate to his purpose,

> It glows and glitters in my cloudy breast
> Like stars upon some gloomy grove,
> Or those faint beams in which this hill is drest,
> After the sun's remove.

Having, in his lecture, indicated the importance to him, as appreciator and poet, of visual imagery drawn from nature as the fittest dress of thought, he adds a rider that it must be employed sparingly. "Simplification of visual imagery is essential to the best poetry. Strength and simplicity always go together ... mindsight eliminates what is inessential, and achieves breadth and intensity by transmuted perception." The necessity to eliminate redundant imagery is a consistent theme in his criticism of Meredith's poetry. Though Meredith's nature-imagery strongly attracts him, he finds fault with Meredith for "leaping from image to image ... regardless of the visualising faculty of the reader."[32] "Controlled visualisation"[33] is essential if the writer wishes to communicate—and Sassoon considers that he should carry out this aim with a high degree of "simplicity and directness." He praises his protegé, Ian Davie's "intrinsic gift for disciplined statement of visual and philosophical particularities—mood and meaning combined."[34] We have already noted his preference for "the controlled tranquillity" of Collins' 'Ode to Evening' to "the seething poetry of the incarnate Now." Imagery is to serve the poet's thought by bringing it vividly into focus; it is not to claim the whole attention for itself. The emphasis has an eighteenth-century flavour:

32. *M.*, p. 201.
33. Ibid. p. 172.
34. Foreword, *Piers Prodigal*.

> No single parts unequally surprize;
> All comes united to th'admiring eyes.

II. Sassoon's concern with this question is, to modern taste, somewhat restrictive. The ideal visual imagery is sensuous, drawn from nature, non-intellectualised—simplified—and homely. It is difficult to see how it could be demonstrated that such qualities adequately distinguish poems like 'Ash Wednesday', 'Kubla Khan' or Keats' 'Ode to Autumn' where, though the impression is strongly visual, it can hardly be said that "strength and simplicity go together." He never considers the complex problem of the interpretation of symbol. What, using his standard, are we to say of the uniquely personal symbol—Eliot's rose, his ocean and river, the private (though visually common) symbols of Shelley—the boat, the isle, the dome and the star? Are we to rest satisfied with the deceptive straightforwardness of 'To Autumn' and regard it simply as a sensuous description of the season? The simplicity may be apparent, not real. In considering nature imagery, although it is drawn from the most familiar source of images, we must allow—as we do with all other kinds of imagery—for the transmuting effect of the poet's unique imagination. "The shaping spirit", writes Coleridge, must "dissolve, diffuse and dissipate, in order to create." Sassoon concedes the reality and importance of this process, together with the fact that it operates chiefly in the subconscious mind: can the "simplification of visual imagery" be entirely consistent with the preservation of the precious essence that results from this process? Are we, furthermore, to receive the poetry no more consciously than the poet does in the act of creation? One can concede too much to the necessity to "communicate". "The machinations of ambiguity," writes Empson, "are among the very roots of poetry."[35]

Sassoon treats complex imagery first and foremost as an obstacle to comprehension. He ignores Donne's metaphysical imagery and complains (with some justice) that Meredith's is too often clotted and obscure. His complaint against the "ambiguity and euphuistic indirectness" of contemporary poetry has already been noted. His preference for nature-imagery admits no place for contemporary writers such as Eliot and Auden who, as Donne had done, used the new sense-data afforded by contemporary life, so giving, as Eliot writes of Baudelaire, "new possibilities to poetry in a new stock of

35. *Seven Types*, p. 3.

imagery of contemporary life."[36] He is not concerned to evaluate
what such poets have tried to do, to consider whether the importance
of their poetry is "not merely in the use of imagery of common life,
not merely in the use of imagery of the sordid life of a great metropolis,
but in the elevation of such imagery to the *first intensity*—presenting it
as it is, and yet making it represent something much more than it is."[37]
The dusk-imagery of 'Preludes' and 'Rhapsody on a Windy Night',
the terrifying childish symbols Auden uses, symbolize modernity and
thus go beyond the mere sensationalism Sassoon implies the contemporary poet is aiming at. Eliot's was not, for Sassoon, a desirable task:
he reacted, in the 'Twenties, from the fragmented modern world to seek
something meaningful through things known, permanent, simple and
kindly. These are the qualities that he desires in both subject-matter
and expression.

§ 5 *Poetry and 'Purpose'*

I. In his mature writings, Sassoon has no sympathy with 'commitment'
in the restrictive, political sense of the word. "Can there really,"
he asks, "be such a thing as a Marxist Muse? Does a man liberate his
poetic afflatus by calling it 'proletarian'?" This question was of vital
importance to a young undergraduate audience in 1939. It cannot
be said that Sassoon attempts to answer it with much sympathy.
Poets who attempt to preach politics through poetry are little more
than "acknowledged tub-thumpers": "if they *must* be political, let
them stick to satire."

"If they *must* be political . . ." Clearly, he had reached the opinion
that to concern oneself with politics is to turn to something of only
minor importance. He was administering the chill, middle-aged
sponge. His earlier self had set out upon the political path, as the
young poets of the 'Thirties were doing—and for reasons similar to
theirs. His abandonment of this involvement with politics and the
reasons for it have already been considered and need not be discussed
again here. But it seems that by 1939 he had reached a position so far
removed from his earlier self that he was no longer able to bring his
disillusioned mind to bear at all sympathetically on the attitudes of his
younger contemporaries.

36. *Selected Essays*, 3rd Edn. 1951, p. 425.
37. Ibid. p. 426.

Nevertheless, he is aware that his young audience is looking to the present—"Republic Spain—and dictators." He offers, as an alternative to "acknowledged tub-thumping", the Republicanism of Swinburne's 'Songs before Sunrise': "One admires his impassioned affirmations of the ultimate victory of the soul of man—his faith in

> "The woundless and invisible thought that goes
> Free through time as north or south wind flows!"

Sassoon's preference is for the Rhapsody of Revolution, not for the local manifestations of it: "is one profoundly stirred," he asks, by his [Swinburne's] reference to "a certain august personage" as: "The one most poisonous worm that soiled the world"? Such things are not timeless—though he concedes, somewhat inconsistently, that we might now apply this description to "a certain living dictator." It is hard to acquit him of a further inconsistency here: he has recommended that political poets should "stick to satire", but he depreciates the one example he quotes. Doubtless, the Swinburne couplet is more stirring, but its purpose differs from that of his line on Napoleon III: each has its proper effect. The essential Sassoon, of course, is not a 'good hater'.[38] It is partly a temperamental preference, but chiefly that he is concerned with unworldly ultimates—"the ultimate victory of the soul of man" preached in 'Songs before Sunrise'. His eye sees no possibility of perfection in the present and sees with too much sense of its own weakness to look ruthlessly through the villain, whoever he may be. He was, inevitably, out of sympathy with such 'Thirties poems as C. Day Lewis's 'The Road These Times Must Take', with its ennoblement of Today's limited man:

> Mark him [the Communist], workers, and all who
>   wish the world aright—
> He is what your sons will be, the road these times
>   must take.

Political writing, however outstanding, cannot be of the first importance. Swinburne's republicanism is of academic interest now: "Meanwhile, [his] elegy on Baudelaire continues, timeless in its beauty and eloquence." "Beauty", "eloquence"—technical perfection—

38. Of course, his poetry written under the abnormal stress of war qualifies this statement, but, as has been shown in discussing his post-war satire, a capacity to hate did not become an enduring part of his "satirist-self".

have been subordinated in contemporary political writing to the
"message", a message conveyed in an essentially transient form:
"Unlike Swinburne, their ['the political poets'] imaginations col-
laborate with Press photography, radio-stations, and cinema news-
reels." Here Sassoon is no doubt referring to the strong 'documentary'
element in the Left writing of the 'Thirties. But he seems to have made
no distinction between pure documentary—purely propagandist
verse—and the best work of such poets as C. Day Lewis, Spender and
Auden, which, though far from great, is more than mere propaganda.
It is the poetry of inner struggle, of men's sincere efforts to reach an
accommodation with themselves and others; it shows a concern with
a country and a people. Such poems as C. Day Lewis's 'The Conflict'
and 'You That Love England', Spender's 'In Railway Halls' and
'After They Have Tired' and Auden's sequence Look, Stranger! cannot
be crammed, willy-nilly, into the mouth of the Marxist Muse. These
poets knew that what they were writing was largely ephemeral: in
A Hope For Poetry C. Day Lewis admits that "propaganda verse is to
be condemned when the didactic is achieved at the expense of the
poetic." Where Sassoon differs from C. Day Lewis is that, for him,
"propaganda verse' is not worth writing at all. He gives the impression
that it is *inevitably* poor stuff. His condemnation of the political poetry
of the 'Thirties is sweeping and total. This attitude stems rather from
his reaction against the politics espoused (and the *tone*—dogmatic,
aggressive, "tub-thumping"—of this espousal) than from a critical
appraisal of the relative merits of the poems produced by the "proletarian afflatus."

II. "To be non-political is, consciously or not, to be conservative; to
turn from social and political problems to individual and moral ones is
to become, in some sense of the word, religious": these words of
David Daiches [39] are applicable to the development of three contemporary writers as different from each other as Sassoon, Auden and Eliot.
It would be difficult for the first, who makes no philosophical statement
of his position, to put forward a valid alternative 'purpose' to the
political one. It was, when he lectured on poetry and for long after
that—some twenty years—impossible for him to speak from an
achieved position of faith. He would not now think it proper to do so:
his poetry, the record of a quest for meaning—in religious terms—
speaks for him. If this record is instructive, it is only so in the sense

39. *The Present Age: from 1920*, p. 12.

that the reader will take from it whatever he desires or can discover. His religious poetry does not exhort; it is the expression of a mind temperamentally averse to disputation.

As in his poetry, so in his criticism. Sassoon's statement of what he would have poetry offer must have seemed lamentably ineffectual to many of the young students who heard his lecture: "When we are old", he tells them, "we hear it ['the harmonious hymn of being'] most through simple and long familiar things—through remembered doings transmuted by memory—and in the recurrence of life-learned experiences." These are the words of a contemplative, a storer and interpreter of accumulated personal experience, not of a reformer or adventurer in ideas. The preference in subject-matter is frankly 'conservative': it concerns the personal life—self-discovery and an undemanding pleasure in what little the world offers, in a few highly valued friendships. His exploration of this subject-matter led him eventually to a religious standpoint: he was not prepared to rest in what might have seemed to his hearers a nostalgic and irresponsible quietism. They might well have contrasted his attitude with the younger self-reproof for such 'indulgences':

> . . . we
> Whom hunger cannot move,
> From gardens where we feel secure
> Look up, and with a sigh endure
> The tyrannies of love . . .
> ('A Summer Night 1933'; from *Look Stranger!*)

It might have seemed to them that Auden began where Sassoon was content to rest. Yet Sassoon was not at rest: he had abandoned the path that Auden was following, certainly, but he was casting about for an alternative direction not pointed by man—as Auden himself was to do. Like Eliot, he was seeking non-worldly reality, probing the truth of his own dictum that "The spirit of poetry looks beyond life's trench-lines."[40] Eliot's conversion to Anglo-Catholicism was seen by some as an avoidance of the issue—social usefulness. Social usefulness is not an absolute criterion of literary value: it is a pity that Sassoon did not feel able to speak, in 1939, with greater authority from his alternative position.[41] Only his poetry can do this.

40. Foreword to *The Collected Works of Isaac Rosenberg* (1937).
41. But see Appendix A, (15).

XI

THE WAY OF DISPOSSESSION

The three volumes to be considered in this chapter, *The Heart's Journey*, *Vigils* and *Rhymed Ruminations*, are the early stages of Sassoon's meditations upon "that problem which concerns me most," to which our attention is drawn at the end of *Satirical Poems*: it is, "bluntly stated, 'Have I got a soul?'" ('The Traveller to His Soul').[1]

In an essay, 'Soldiers' Writing', first published in 1944, the Catholic novelist Charles Morgan asks this question about the Second War poets: After the protest, what? It is a question equally, perhaps more, relevant to the case of their First War forerunners. Morgan finds in the writers and aspiring writers he visits at the Front a classical spirit of endurance and stoicism, "a mood purged of many extravagancies by which, in hope or fear, our world is beset." He considers that this should lead in the best of them to "the highest effect of tragedy; it swings the soul of man full-circle from his terror and nothingness and enables him, if he does not harden his heart against it, to proceed from despair, through rebellion, through curiosity, to contemplate order and atonement." He asserts the necessity of this in a world riddled with "the contempt of life."[2] It is doubtful whether the truth of this could be demonstrated with regard to Second War poets (of whom the best, Keith Douglas, Alun Lewis and Sidney Keyes, were killed), or such survivors from the First War as Edmund Blunden, Robert Graves and Herbert Read: but the entire process Morgan describes is reflected in the Catholic evolution of Sassoon.

Sassoon had always been temperamentally disposed to a withdrawn, meditative way of life, an inclination which became clear to him soon

1. Though the search for "selfhood's essence" ('The Tasking') is the main theme of these and all subsequent volumes, we still find in these earlier collections a noteworthy number of poems upon other themes: of these, the satirical poems and those related to the War poetry have already received particular mention; others have earned incidental comment.
2. *Reflections in a Mirror, Second Series*. London, 1946.

after the end of the First War. He narrates in *Siegfried's Journey* how, escaping to "quietude" from the rigours of his 1920 lecture-tour in America, he was allowed to browse amongst the old manuscripts in the Pierpoint Morgan Library. On one occasion he found himself before the manuscript of Pope's *Essay on Man* and read,

> This light and darkness in our chaos join'd,
> What shall divide?—the God within the mind.

He comments: "Whispering the words I found them applicable to my own temporarily disordered existence, in which the God within the mind was being obliterated. It was a relief to be reminded of one's own unimportance."[3] These two sentences are vital clues to an understanding of the nature of his religious poetry. In the first place, he possessed, even then, an inward sense that the spiritual was real, and secondly, an ingrained humility about the significance of the worldly self.

It may be thought that these psychological factors were likely to ensure the success of the spiritual journey upon which he embarked in the nineteen-twenties. Yet so scrupulous is the search that it issues in no firm belief until more than thirty years have passed. At the same time, the humility, the sense of the limitations of mind and heart are, from the outset, so strong that he rarely runs into extremes of feeling: the self-torment of Donne, Hopkins's terror of God, the utter desolation of 'The Hollow Men', are all alien to his nature. The transitions from a wish to believe, to hope, to positive belief are gradual: belief comes with the slow inevitability of organic growth, not in a passion of conversion. In Arnold's words, "A fugitive and gracious light he seeks, / Shy to illumine." His affinities are with the quieter metaphysicals, especially Vaughan—he describes himself as "Zealous to walk the way of Henry Vaughan" ('The Trial')—and Herbert, though he never rises to the gleaming heights of the one or the more complex imagery of the other. Few poems, though in the later volumes they have an increasingly refined brevity, are individually memorable: each volume, the last three (to be considered in Chapter XII) most compactly, is essentially a sequence of lucid meditations, bound together by a unity of mood and integrity of feeling.

3. *S.J.*, p. 184.

§ 1

Though *The Heart's Journey* (1927-1928) is only loosely a sequence—
there is no clear development of a single theme—it has a marked
unity of mood. Sassoon has set out upon the time-honoured way to
belief pointed in these words of Donne: "Seek we then ourselves
within ourselves."[4] It is, perhaps, more appropriate to describe the
poems in this volume as *preparations* for the journey: setting the house
in order, checking its contents, deciding what will be needed and
what can—and must—be left behind,

> In order to possess what you do not possess
> You must go by the way of dispossession.[5]

The journey is envisaged at first as a return—to what, under the
stress of being forced to take a false direction—has never been explored: the soul, the essential self, whose voice will be his poetry:

> Soul, be my song; return arrayed in white;
> Lead home the loves that I have wronged and slain:
> Bring back the summer dawns that banished night
> With distant-warbling bird-notes after rain . . .
> Time's way-worn traveller I. And you, O song,
> O soul, my Paradise laid waste so long.   ('I')

The dawn, a recurrent symbol, is associated with both fresh birth
and the pure instinctive knowing of youth and childhood. Vitally
important is the power to be moved by the "simple spells":

> the pang
> Which first I felt in childhood when I woke
> And heard the unheeding garden bird who sang
> Strangeness of heart for me while morning broke.
>   ('Strangeness of Heart')

Cleanness, freshness, a new beginning; this is naturally associated also
with spring, traditionally a symbol of innocence. The heart reawakens
like "patient birds / Who all this weary winter wait for spring"; the
winter is conventionally the symbol of the anguished, earthbound
spirit. Some "inward solemn influence, / Invisible, intangible, un-

---

4. 'To Mr. Rowland Woodward.'
5. T. S. Eliot, *The Four Quartets.*

kenned" is felt to be watching and waiting for the readiness of heart and mind, to unite him "with song that has no end / And with that stillness whence my spirit came" ('II') — the words recall 'Everyone Sang', but not the end to which they are directed. The "stillness", the place of departure and desired return, is reminiscent of the ideal early existence of Wordsworth or, amongst his contemporaries, de la Mare,[6] rather than of Vaughan's more explicitly religious idea of an "Angell-infancy" that could not "fancy ought / But a white, Celestiall thought" ('The Retreate'). The images of dawn and spring unite ('III') with the description of a cold dawn purity, "Cold was the music of the birds; and cold / The sunlight, shadowless with misty gold"; the two images of reawakening coalesce in, "A sense of wakening leaves that filled the air / With boding of Elysian days to be", producing as in youth a feeling that "some annunciation" is imminent, bringing "ultimate spring / Whence all that life had longed for might emerge."

Though in expression these nature poems hark back to the pantheistic 'Before Day', there is a lucid sense of being upon the threshold of a new and more vital life than any known before. Yet this life cannot be entered upon with the old innocence: that, once lost, cannot be regained by shrugging off the knowledge and experience of harsh life already undergone. This better knowledge must be seen *through*.[7] This idea is conveyed by the contrasting star-imagery of 'XII': the Morning Star symbolizes the young vision, "that youth's awakening eyes have seen"; he prays that its influence may last and sustain, but there is also Hesperus, the unseen Evening Star, obscured by the

6. Whereas Sassoon does eventually free himself of its spell, de la Mare never ceased to look back to childhood with a sad-sweet sense of irreparable loss:
> When then in memory I look back
> To childhood's visioned hours I see
> What now my anxious soul doth lack
> Is energy in peace to be
> At one with nature's mystery:
> And Conscience less my mind indicts
> For idle days than dreamless nights.
('Dreams': *Collected Poems*, 1961, p. 321.)
7. "For one who knew death as intimately as Sassoon did in the trenches, this [the feeling of a poem like 'Strangeness of Heart'] would seem to be little more than a superficial pose. Yet it was that close association with wholesale human destruction that crystallized for the poet what was of fundamental importance to him: the pleasures of a youth spent in a pastoral setting" (Joseph Cohen, op. cit. p. 181). Cohen is, of course, referring to the transitional stage during which the recovery of the poet's youthful relationship with nature is all-important, as a balm and succour, but not an end in itself.

clouds of an unknown and feared future, and to this he prays for compensation for the loss of early certainties: "make serene / Our loss of this loved heritage of light." It is the debased self that stands between him and some primal vision. This essentially religious conception is set out with particular clarity (in the way of the medieval, "O what a piece of work is man!") in 'VII':

> In me the cave-man clasps the seer,
> And garlanded Apollo goes
> Chanting to Abraham's deaf ear.
> In me the tiger sniffs the rose.
>   Look in my heart, kind friends, and tremble,
>   Since there your elements assemble.

(There is a clear echo of Shelley's 'Ozymandias'—"Look on my works, ye Mighty, and despair!'—the same message, but aimed at all of us.) These apparent contradictions must be reconciled or subdued by means of radical self-examination. Faced with the paradox of our dual nature, though we may be moved by "Those imageries of peace which men behold/Through inmost prayer in world-encircling white," how are we to know, for ourselves, which is the essential, or dominant, part: "who shall say to which we most belong?" ('XXVI'). Sassoon is preoccupied with the seemingly impenetrable nature of self. A true contemplative, he takes himself to be the strangest company: "I thought how strange we grow when we're alone, / And how unlike the selves that meet, and talk." Only by facing the self alone does one begin to approach the vital insight into one's capacities and limitations: "Alone ... the word is life endured and known"— endured, for this coming to terms with the self must reveal one's inmost nature and leave no stay "but inmost faith" ('XI').

Yet this "inmost faith", this will to self-knowledge and ultimately to belief, is strong. In 'X', the belief that the answer does lie within is for the first time couched in an apt image that becomes central to these meditations: standing outside his room, the arena of so many struggles with self, he feels that its "tranquil-toned interior" symbolizes the inner being whose nature is felt but not fully grasped, for "I stand outside you in the night." If the searchings the room has embodied could be unified, the unknown self might become clear:

> Could I condense five winters in one thought,
> Then might I know my unknown self and tell
> What our confederate silences have wrought.

Outside he must remain, but with a mind and heart seeking continually to make themselves fit for admission. 'XVI' is superficially a melancholy and conventional farewell of one, like Coleridge, "in city-pent," a farewell to vanished youth and instinctive communion with nature; but the town, so alien to the life within, also symbolises the spiritual "homelessness," "Where all's uncertain but my will for power/To ask of life no more than life can earn." He desires the power to ask for nothing except what may be won in the way of the true seeker after faith, by abstraction from ephemeral concerns and by subduing one's more strenuous nature with "quiet-toned persistence" ('XVII').

This state is to be attained by a clarification of one's thoughts and desires, shedding all gross impedimenta, and opening the mind to wonder—in everyday simplicities. In 'A Midnight Interior', the poem here which best exemplifies his personal imagery, "my patient lamp" shines "like a strange flower"—it is seen, an image of pure seeing, for the first time, and the common

> White flowers were in a bowl beside my book;
> In midnight's miracle of light they glowed,
> And every petal there in silence showed
> My life the way to wonder with a look.

He prays for "strength to find/From lamp and flower simplicity of mind." Flowers and light frequently provide Herbert and Vaughan also with images of wonder; as with these poets, his images are usually embedded in simple everyday reality. The affinity with Vaughan is acknowledged in the sonnet 'At The Grave of Henry Vaughan', a poem that has a luminous beauty. The phrases with which he commemorates him are appropriately imbued with Vaughan's own peculiar vision—the purity of light and stream, of dawn and unearthly whiteness:

> Here Vaughan lies dead, whose name flows on for ever
> Through pastures of the spirit washed with dew
> And starlit with eternities unknown.
>
> ***
>
> The skull that housed white angels and had vision
> Of daybreak through the gateways of the mind.

His personal image—of daybreak—is merged with those reminiscent of Vaughan. The grave speaks to him of peace and tranquillity, which he desires to achieve: "And here stand I, a suppliant at the door."

This echoes Carew, conscious of his "unwasht Muse": "Here, humbly at the porch she listening stayes,/And with glad eares sucks in thy sacred layes."[8] "Unwasht", Sassoon feels (though not in Carew's sense), is his own muse; he is responsive to the earthly consolations and inspirations of music and poetry, but these are not enough:

> If this in itself were enough, I am crowned with the best.
> But the vision in silence has vanished: I know but my need
> To be clearing my lofts of their lumber . . .

Thus, (using domestic imagery such as Herbert rather than Vaughan might have chosen) he reflects in 'From a Fugue by Bach', alone with the intimations of immortality—"voices from vastness divine"—such music arouses; yet, however strange this feeling, he is left "Praying I know not to whom in this musicless room."

The seeking and aspirations these poems proclaim are still far from ultimate reward, though upon a superficial reading 'All-Souls' Day' and 'The Power and the Glory' seem to assert positive faith. Yet it is a faith in a power for good, somewhere at work, asserted in the face of the worst, to

> quell the obscene derision
> Of demon-haunters in our heart
> Who work for worms and have no part
> In Thee, O ultimate power, who art
> Our victory and our vision.
>
> ('All Souls' Day')

This elevated *idea* of God issues in 'The Power and the Glory' in a preparedness to attest the truth of God in "This hour, this quiet room, and my small thought/Holding invisible vastness in its hands." Again, he defies whatever power dares to mock "my glorious angel" who stands willing "To fill my dark with fire, my heart with faith." But there is no settled faith; it is an act of will. It does, however, spring from the conviction that the reality is "inward vision winged with mysteries," the delusion the worldly wisdom that says, "*There is/No other wisdom but to gulp what time can give.*" With true love, loyalties to "ghostly friends" (a strong theme in the next two volumes) and the deepest sureties of the heart "to find my gloom I go,/Companioned by those powers who keep me unafraid." "To find my

8. 'To My Worthy Friend—Master George Sandys.'

gloom"; 'my death' and, with hope, 'my life'—an implicit paradox, a form of expression rare in his poetry. There is resolution, not revelation: "those powers" are not clearly defined.

The strength of the "inward vision" is most effectively suggested in two of the latest poems (included in the 1928 edition). The brief 'XXVII', in its visual simplicity, conciseness and clarity is reminiscent of the metaphysicals' assertions of sheer 'seeing':

> I cannot pray with my head,
> Nor aspire from bended knees;
> But I saw in a dream the dead
> Moving among green trees.
> I saw the living green
> Uprising from the rock.
> This have I surely seen,
> Though the morning mind may mock.

This is a vision of life resurrected, a snatched glimpse of a living principle: it is offered for what it is worth and no claims for its meaning are made. 'Nativity' testifies to a second birth of perception, as if much of the burden has been shed. This is symbolized by the image of a spring flower opening silently to sudden perfection in the heart. It is a "simple, secret thing," a sense of inward, inviolate peace— but its meaning is "secret", a recurrent word in this volume:

> Heart's miracle of inward light,
> What powers unknown have sown your seed
> And your perfection freed? . . .
> O flower within me wondrous white,
> I know you only as my need
> And my unsealèd sight.

For Vaughan "the flower of peace" was planted firmly in "a Countrie / Far beyond the stars" ('Peace'). For Sassoon it is, as yet, more earthbound: but the heart is lightened, the need defined.

§ 2

The emphasis in *Vigils* (1934-1935) is upon the uncertainty of the direction heart and mind must take in search of the true self. Though Sassoon opens boldly with "Poet, plant your tree / On the upward way," that man may see "through boughs divine / Freedom bravely blowing" ('An Emblem'), the burden of the whole is that there can be no freedom till the rebellious self is subdued, whilst, paradoxically, the self—as consciously realized—seems, upon analysis, nothing. He must wait withdrawn; he has made the more obvious preparations, outgrown "the pride/Of temporal trophydoms" (though not, he will find, a more intractable kind of pride) and chosen, he uses Hopkins's phrase, "Elected Silence" as "the ultimate guide." The destination remains remote; beyond the night of waiting—of man's "decay"— the vigilant watcher can only hope to find at length "peace, remote in the morning star" ('Vigils').

The Morning Star had previously (*The Heart's Journey*, 'XII') symbolized the youthful vision, vouchsafed to a mind clear and open, which he desires to regain. There is now a deepened feeling that this vision can never be regained by a mind darkened by mature experience. The mood alternates between a sad realisation that this is so, however much the heart may desire otherwise, and a nostalgic desire to make "dreams" the true reality again. The memory of them remains powerful: "dreams have secret strength . . ./They haunt the quiet house through idle afternoon"; the old house is a symbol of continuity, a storehouse of knowledge and intuitions only partially understood, to which he returns again to seek to penetrate to the truth of the vision:

> But in remembered eyes of youth my dreams remain.
> They were my firstling friends. I have returned again.
> (*Vigils* '7')

In 'Past and Present', the house image recurs: "My past has gone to bed. Upstairs in clockless rooms . . ."—but now when memories of the former self return in the shape of "sleep-walkers empty-eyed" to the living self who "sits brooding here/In the house where I was born," they throw light only upon the barrenness that has come after them:

> Me they did not foresee. But in their looks I find
> Simplicities unlearned long since and left behind.

If only the mind could recapture simplicity, could 'see' as once it saw in the dawn of life, "Seeing, beyond his limits,/Loveliness veiled and vast": but, paradoxically, that seeing was always associated with a kind of blessed blindness; it was, to employ Traherne's line on

"unexperienc'd Infancy", "A *Seeming* somewhat more than *View*."[9]
The older self, "laden / Head and heart with your years" recalls having
once exulted in "the vision splendid":

> Yet in this moment's vision,
> Youth at the window stands,
> Unforeboding, enchanted,
> Holding the world in his hands.

('Long Ago')

What in innocence he held was insubstantial; it had to fade in the
light of Wordsworth's "common day." Though he struggles against
it, he is forced to recognise that, while seeing with the youthful eye
might provide consolation, it could be no final answer: self will not
stand still. 'Farewell to Youth' is a moment of deep despair at being
insufficiently alive, cut off from the free breath of life (it is again
spring and "the leaves rejoice"), whose "secret spell I may not share."
The consolations seem flimsy against the overwhelming apprehension
of a blank future: "I see tomorrows grey like stone / Where virtues
walk as weary men." The essential alienation is crystallized in the
keenly visual,

> And while the lenten twilight falls
> On silent room and hand-propped head,
> Within my heart's mysterious walls
> The dreamer that was Youth lies dead.

He is self-imprisoned.[10]

He may, in one mood, recapture briefly a feeling akin to the exalted
pantheism of youth:

---

9. 'Shadows in the Water.'
10. The content of the poems discussed in this paragraph is closely paralleled by
that of Edwin Muir's single poem, 'The Return', in which the poet cannot bring
himself to re-enter "the house/Of my own life":
> for all within
> Rises before me there, rises against me,
> A sweet and terrible labyrinth of longing,
> So that I turn aside and take the road
> That always, early or late, runs on before.

(*Collected Poems*, 1960, p. 166)
In the quiet tone of his seeking, and in the lucidity of his expression, Muir has
much in common with Sassoon, particularly in poems of reminiscence or reflection
upon age and change; but he has a mystical insight, a complex preoccupation with
the real stuff of dreams, which sets them ultimately far apart.

> How solitude can hear! O see
> How stillness unreluctant stands
> Enharmonised with cloud and tree . . .
> O earth and heaven not made with hands!
>
> ('Elected Silence')

But he finds now in nature, not so much cause for exaltation, as strength to endure in his self-imposed journey: "December stillness, crossed by twilight roads,/Teach me to travel far and bear my loads" ('December Stillness'). Though world-weary, he is not earth-weary: in Meredithian manner, he yokes "the love of earth that is my law" with "the love of life," which is "my religion still." Nevertheless, the secret of this life is to be sought, not now "beyond the hill," but in solitude, "companioned only/By what I am and what strive to be" (*Vigils* '6').

Hitherto, his seeking has been primarily concerned with adjustment, and with clarifying "the need." The process has been one of intellectual self-abnegation and of charting the heart's will: yet, though much has been discarded and the limitations of self more clearly seen, little of a spiritual nature seems to have been gained to answer the need. What has evolved is indefinable, even disturbing: in a short poem which has the hitherto rare quality of quarrelling with inward experience, he complains that his mind is plagued with "presences" which even the light of day cannot dispel: "in that garret of uneasy gloom/Which is your brain, the presences persist." ('Presences'). The nature of these presences is given more friendly interpretation in "'We Shall Not All Sleep'"; may they not, he wonders, be beneficent spirits, for,

> if shriven self survives,
> Might not a hint be given, a warning uttered
> By ghostly vigilance, to troubled lives?

The living self is compared (further compressing the room image introduced in 'A Midnight Interior') to a shuttered room into which a ghostly power may "send one shaft of radiance." Though such beneficent spirits may be believed in,

> Unvouched are visions. But sleep-forsaken faith
> Can win unworlded miracles and rejoice,
> Welcoming, at haggard ends of night,—what wraith—
> What angel—what beloved and banished voice?

This hope is strong at this time, and with it grows an accompanying belief in the possibility of survival, nourished by the spiritual strength drawn from these "presences." The world of spirits manifests itself in many ways: there are the spirits of place,

> I hear you, vanished voices, where such peace
> Imbues my being as when your gladness breathed;
> And now like leafy whispering it is,
> And now slow shadows of the towering trees
> On lawns that your experience has bequeathed.

('Vibrations')

There is the inspiration derived from the light-givers of the past, whose influence is felt both to illuminate the struggling mind of the present and to awaken, by its very strength, hope of survival: "Through spirit alone/They triumphed, the makers of mankind." ('Presences Perfected'). There is also the immediate sense, born of affectionate memory, of the enduring presence of the beloved dead—remembered most powerfully in the poem commemorating Dr. W. H. R. Rivers:

> What voice revisits me this night? What face
> To my heart's room returns?

The "room" does receive the "shaft of radiance" desired ('"We Shall Not All Sleep"'). The presence is felt within—whether more tangible,

> I know not. Only I feel
> His influence undiminished.
> His life's work, in me and many, unfinished.

('Revisitation')

These many presences especially, no doubt, those of his many war-time comrades, are invoked in poem '22':

> Again the dead, the dead again demanding
> To be, O now to be remembered strongly—
> The dead, reminding mindsight of their darkness—
> The dead who overhear us, listening longly.

These strongly-stressed lines, with their repetitions and the contracted "longly" ('longingly' and 'for a long time') have an emphatic urgency rare in Sassoon; one hears in them rather the voice of Hopkins than his own:

No worst, there is none. Pitched past pitch of grief,
More pangs will, schooled at forepangs, wilder wring.
Comforter, where, where is your comforting?
Mary, mother of us, where is your relief?[11]

Sassoon does not maintain the strenuous tone, but it returns towards
the end with this plea from the blind living to the knowing dead, the
musician, the poet, the "dead youth": "How can you be believed in,
how made certain,/How sought beyond the silences of learning?"
"Visions," he realizes, may deceive: "designed by man's death-fearing
mind/To hallow his carnal heritage with healing" ('Heaven').

Meanwhile, it is no easy matter to wait for the mind to grow into
awareness at the pace of a tree seeking the light:

> The lowly growth and long endeavour of will
> That waits and watches from its human hill,
>   A landmark tree looming against the night.
>
> (*Vigils* '30')

The mind knows that Heaven is, and must be, accessible only through
long seeking and suffering:

> ... the reward of racked renunciation,
> When from the body's broken wayside shrine
> The spirit in its ultimate aspiration
> Shares the world-sacrifice and dies divine.
>
> ('Heaven')

And there is the nagging sense of one's own unworthiness, a feeling
that the search itself may be presumptuous; at his least hopeful for
self, he sees its continuance as being possible only in a higher mankind:

> ... through brutish Me made strong and fair and free,
> The dumb forgotten dead will be the ground they tread,
> And in their eyes will shine my deathless hope divine.
>
> ('Credo')

This mood is consonant with the disillusionment with Man expressed
in the contemporaneous *The Road to Ruin;* he is already conscious of
possessing a "fallen" mind, a Catholic strain traceable from these
early years onwards.

11. *Poems of Gerard Manley Hopkins*, Ed. Bridges & Gardner, p 106.

In a short poem partly reminiscent of 'Dover Beach', his aspiration is presented as frail and groping, inhibited by "worldhood":

> Something we cannot see, something we may not reach,
> Something beyond clairvoyant vision of the years
> Our senses, winged with spirit, wordlessly beseech.
>
> Meanwhile rife rumourings of the earth are in our ears,—
> The lonely beat of blood, the immanence of ghosts,
> And foam's oblivion whitening under crumbling coasts.
>
> ('Ultimatum')

But the sense is not Arnold's: the "lonely beat of blood" could be his, that human love might mask, but not "the immanence of ghosts." Sassoon has more than the will to believe: he is obsessed, not by a feeling of irrevocable loss, but rather by an instinctive urge to recover what has only been mislaid in ignorance. His desire comes from the heart as well as from the mind: it is, therefore, the more liable, he fears, to run past the truth. If he is never tempted to make his heaven upon earth, he knows the temptation to build it elsewhere according to his own wishful design. The final poem in this collection, 'Ode', reveals a wariness of the validity of "inward sight;" he wishes to guard against spiritual relaxation. Man constructs the City of God from the materials of his own desires and thus falls into the cardinal error of spiritual pride:

> How dares he in a dream's deceiving
> Link that vision with love unknown,—
> Out of the dark in his blind believing
> Claiming the City of God for his own?

He makes no such bold claim to know God as appears in the concluding poems of *The Heart's Journey*. He has achieved, rather, a negative declaration of faith, a humble acknowledgement that many false directions are bound to be taken by unaided man; these he wishes to renounce:

> Sense-confined in his brain existence,
> Not for him to deny his doom;
> Not through dreams does the soul outdistance
> Death who knocks at the listening room.
> Not from time shall he look on heaven;
> Not through hope shall his faults be healed . . .
> City of God, to redeemed forgiven
> Radiant life, be on earth revealed.

The prayer, significantly not directly addressed to **God,** is a prayer for revelation.

<h2 style="text-align:center">§ 3</h2>

There is, in *Rhymed Ruminations* (1939-1940), a marked slackening of spiritual tension. There is no fresh direction, no increased urgency concerning the questionings and doubts previously expressed. The title is apt in its suggestion of unambitious, unpretentious reflection: Sassoon seems to be seeking, to adapt Donne's injunction, to "settle [his] soule in such an infallibility as this present condition can admit."

The "present condition"—of the world—has become increasingly intrusive, unsettling his detachment. The opening poem, 'Brevities', in which he portrays himself as one who "Thinks harshly of the world —and corks it down," is in fact one of the last written[12]: it does not set the mood for the whole volume. It was not be to expected that one whose mind had been so deeply scarred by war should have found it easy to withdraw from a world in which a worse war was daily growing imminent. Though in '878-935' he just resists the temptation to idealize the more modest conflicts of Alfred's time, he rejects the present with utter repugnance (whose strength is unconsciously expressed by the strained and inadequate simile): "Yet I have wondered, when was Wiltshire more insane/Than now—when world ideas like wolves are on the run?" The physical manifestations of that world are inescapable: "Now in a world of books I try to live content,/And hear uneasily the droning aeroplane." Unease is the dominant note.[13]

Against the present reality the "sense-confined" mind can raise only flimsy defences. The quiet meditations on the insignificance of the personality in the face of nature's unheeding and uncomprehended continuity,

> We nothings use a name,
> Nor ask whence acorns came
> Before the oak was planted;
>
> ('Property')

12. Published in *Life and Letters*, September 1939.
13. "At present I find I can only keep going by seeing as few people as possible, & relieving my mind by reading civilised literature" (Letter dated 5.6.40: *The Best of Friends*, pp. 78-79).

and the quasi-pantheistic consolation that oneself will be absorbed at
the last into the flux of Greater Being,

> And in your greenery, while you last,
> I shall survive who shared your past
>   ('Outlived by Trees')

—hold an uneasy balance with such bleak forebodings as this:

> We are souls in hell; who hear no gradual music
> Advancing on the air, on wave-lengths walking.
> We are lost in life; who listen for hope and hear but
> The tyrant and the politician talking.
>   ('A Prayer from 1936')

He prays to the "heaven of music" to restore harmony and fullness
to life—but the prayer itself and its direction are as yet tentative.
There is no surety, only hope, a hope resting upon the evidence in
this world of goodness in men, if not in nations (a goodness obscured
beneath his many sad reflections upon the collective worst):

> O if there be that other world, that grace
> Of souls redeemed, we breathe it like the air;
> And angels are about us everywhere
> In love's good deeds, in life's transfigured face.
>   ('Earth and Heaven')

"If there be . . ." He can bring no message of absolute consolation;
his journey is not yet complete. The pace has slowed, and the mind
is disposed to accept this, "responsive to my world," as he tells us in
one of his conversation-pieces, 'Thoughts in 1938', "without resistance."
But the ending of this poem is enigmatic:

> Though sign-posts pointed toward the dread of war,
>   ourselves, of course,
> Were only hundrum joggers on through time.
>   Remembering it one smiles.

The world is not so easily shrugged off—and does he smile too for
the war poet of twenty years before? Now become the man upon a
horse, going his unspectacular local journeyings, to rest beneath
'Blunden's Beech', perhaps, where,

> The thought of Poetry will dwell, and bring
> To summer's idyll an unheeded grace.

(The diction of this poem—the poet is "contentful", and the birds
are "a flitting crew," reminiscent of Pope's "finny tribe"—suggests
the self-conscious diversions of a man of affairs turned week-end water-
colourist.) Returned home, he ruminates—'The Thrush in February'
in minor key, unlike Meredith, not daring to look ahead—on the
tranquillizing value of the little, local joys:

> Ruminant, while firelight glows on shadowy walls
> And dusk with the last leaves of autumn falls,
> I hear my garden thrush whose notes again
> Tell stillness after hours of gusty rain.
>
> ('November Dusk')

"*My* garden thrush"—and the first line is, perhaps intentionally, a
homely variant of Tennyson's "The splendour falls on castle walls."
These recurrent domesticities affirm continuity, the cycle of growth
and renewal; they are always present, producing "tranquillity
intense":

> And I've no need to travel far to find
> This bird who from the leafless walnut tree
> Sings like the world's farewell to sight and song.[14]

He feels at one with the rhythm of nature,

> One with these garden silences that pass,
> I know that life is in my saturate sense
> Of growth and memories of what lifetime meant.

Yet the feeling, he knows, is common: "And still, where trees like
sentinels look for day,/I feel what all have felt and know what none
can say" ('Wealth of Awareness'). The mono-syllabled alexandrine
hammers home the wearisome truth. He is not tempted to Earth-
worship, however seductive it may be, not trusting in its ultimate
significance; it springs from the heart too much in love with sheer life.
  The disjunction between heart and soul, like that between feeling
and believing, remains unresolved:

14. Not surprisingly, it was the tranquillising element in the "quietened cadences"
of *Rhymed Ruminations* that a reviewer welcomed in war-time: "It is good to be
reminded," he wrote, "'Beyond bewildering years/How little things beloved and
held are best'" (*The Times Literary Supplement*, November 2, 1940).

Soul undaunted and heart death-haunted
Dwell together, estranged yet one.
    (Starlight lonely and firelit room.)
Heart, be brave as you go to your grave;
Soul, be girt for the race unrun.
    (Holpen both by ghosts from the gloom.)

                                                      ('Heart and Soul')

The language of this—with the wooden archaisms 'girt' and 'holpen'
—and the neat parentheses produce a crabbed effect: it has the air
of a stoic manifesto, albeit a rhythmic one. The 'room' is stripped of its
old furniture, like the actual room in his house that reminds him all
too vividly how time immerses the dream, leaving behind a poignant
sense of loss:

Now, in empty room and evening,
I, that grieving vision facing,
Stand in memory's moment halted,
By my dreams no more exalted.

                                 ('A Picture of the Muses')

But there are two kinds of 'dreams': the dreams of youth, a confident,
visionary sense, and those, perhaps delusions, of age, age seeking for
an answer consciously, without the confidence of youth. Having
brought himself at last to admit the inadequacy of the first, it is the
second kind whose value he must measure now. 'Tragitones' wearily
voices both the inward necessity for separation and the uncertainty
as to where to build anew:

I have not sought these quietened cadences,
These tragitones, these stilled interior themes,
These vistas where imagined presences
Lead me away from life,—loved ghosts or dreams?

Look where the light of June is in the leaves,
And how the world with laughter hurries on.
The grass is golden; yet my faith perceives
No foot-print where felicity has gone.

More conventionally (the stiff, sententious 'perceives' illustrates one
of the tyrannies of the rhyme Sassoon prefers), the second stanza
images the necessity for renunciation of life's least blameworthy joys
in terms similar to Eliot's:

> Blown hair is sweet, brown hair over the mouth blown,
> Lilac and brown hair;
> Distraction . . .[15]

But this way of renunciation is by no means so thoroughly worked out in Sassoon, either now or later: the external challenges to sense are far less urgent than the inner contradictions of his nature. The title itself, 'Tragitones', is muted and tentative.

If "felicity" leaves no footprint, neither has there been vouchsafed him anything he is prepared to claim as a sure mark of more lasting life. 'Progressions' reviews four stages of life—childhood, "singing to himself serenely," youth, "all ignorance, all grace, his dreams adoring," man, "confounded by the facts of life that bind him," and lastly:

> A mind, matured in wearying bones, returning slowly
> Toward years revisioned richly while fruitions fail
>   him,—
> A mind, renouncing hopes and finding lost loves holy.

"Fruitions fail," hopes must be renounced, but there remains (as in *Vigils*) "lost loves holy": and the stored memories of these are his strongest stay; they have become part of him. This is expressed in a poem which gathers up and unifies the images of 'A Picture of the Muses'; the room is now the darkened mind, but the pictures of memory can bring life and light, unlike the sad reminder of lost youth in the earlier poem:

> Like the note of an old violin,
> Thoughts talk to me within
> My mind, that shuttered room.
> Like luminous portraits, hung
> On walls where I once was young,
> Dead friends pervade the gloom.
>
> ('Old Music')

The mind is mellowed to "calmed content," "mental vintagement" (an idea reinforced by the characteristically muted violin image), and no longer thirsts for "youth's harsh-tasting wine"—this conventional metaphor, however, jars, since it is at variance with any tendencies his poetry of youth has suggested. He repeats it in "the wine of dangerous desires" ('Acceptance'): in both cases the effect is

15. *Ash Wednesday,* III.

merely rhetorical; his most personal images choose themselves, as in the above quotation, but for expressing an idea not deeply felt—he is no Donne—he tends to use the obvious.

His "content" still does not stem from a certainty of the ultimate significance of his 'visions' (which formerly he had doubted as possible wish-fulfilments), but from a concentrated awareness of vital human values, a link between the living and the dead, indestructible at least during life: a stoical faith to which, somewhat ironically, he had looked forward over fifteen years before, in a poem reprinted as the last in this collection:

> For life sits faithful in old eyes, alone
> With mortal frailty and magnificence
>
> ('Eyes')[16]

16. 'Eyes' was first published in *The Decachord* (Exeter),v., November 1924.

XII

SEQUENCES

§ 1

ommon *Chords* (1950) was the first collection of poems to be published after an interval of ten years, during which Sassoon's main effort was devoted to the autobiographies and the critical biography of Meredith.[1] It contained only eighteen poems, of which twelve had been published in periodicals, seven of these during the years 1948-1950. None of the most significant of these poems appeared in print before 1948. His poetic output, especially during the early part of the decade, was thus very small if compared with the frequent publications between 1919 and 1940. One inference to be drawn from this is that there was no significant evolution of feeling so far as the earlier years of the decade, including the War period, are concerned.

During those years, we find him in the autobiographies returning with undisguised nostalgia to the world of his youth, re-living an idealized past, giving the modern world "the slip." In the immediate world, he lives on as best he can, clinging to the faith that time must heal and, like Hardy before him, seeing in nature's continuity a chart against which to measure the mad fevers of men. This is the theme of 'A 1940 Memory' — though, unlike Hardy, he places more emphasis on the value of the small perception to himself as an individual who seeks in life a meaningful pattern:

> Yet, every walk I pass that way,
> A sunless mid-September day
> Will faithfully recur, and I
> Stalk that slow loitering butterfly.

Allied with this is the theme of 'Man and Dog' where, in the down-to-earth voice of a Robert Frost or W. H. Davies, he lays claim to the positive value of a humble, time-honoured communion:

1. Appendix A, (16).

> Here's anyhow one decent thing
> That life to man and dog can bring;
> One decent thing, remultiplied
> Till earth's last dog and man have died.[2]

In only one poem, 'The Hardened Heart', does he recur to a mood of the previous volumes. It embodies no fresh attitude, but rather formalises an old one: youth, the period of "life beloved" and the "dream", is seen as "circumstance-led" and cannot know how maturity inevitably brings with it a numbing of the heart to "know/ The ugly facts of night." Youth (morning) and maturity (night and the darkness of the spirit) are placed side by side, in essence far apart. Except for a new feeling of compassion for youth, this had been more vividly expressed in the earlier 'Farewell to Youth'.

If one excepts the sad comments on man's inhumanity ('An Absentee'—a poem that surprisingly recaptures a trace of the old satirical bite—and 'A Post-Mortem'), 'The Hardened Heart' is the only 'dark' poem in the whole collection, and then, as has been said, merely in a formal way. The remainder to be considered here, all dating (in publication) from March 1948 at the earliest, breathe a spring-like spirit far removed from that of the previous volumes. The morbid preoccupations with "ghosts" and the wrenching loss of youth's vision, the stoical tone of resignation, of waiting "without hope", the interior atmosphere—confined to the house, the room, at best only *looking* out—suddenly give way to a lightness of spirit; the gloom is dissipated and the poet goes out to weave nature more fully into the texture of his "seeing" than ever before. The poetic pleasure is incidentally increased (though what the earlier volumes lack in variety is compensated for by their integrity of feeling).

The introductory poem, 'Release', signalises both a fresh voice and a new departure:

> One winter's end I much bemused my head
> In tasked attempts to drive it up to date
> With what the undelighting moderns said
> Forecasting human fate.

---

2. Cohen finds this poem banal, an example of the danger of Sassoon's seeing too little "outside of his immediate association with nature" (op. cit. p. 183): if this is sometimes a real weakness in Sassoon's writing (as in the extreme nostalgia noticed in the prose) 'Man and Dog' is a poorly chosen example. It is a slight poem, but as the tone of the stanza quoted shows, aspires to express nothing more than unpretentious natural feeling.

> And then, with nothing unforeseen to say
> And no belief or unbelief to bring,
> Came, in its old unintellectual way,
> 　　The first real day of spring.

This contrast—between the winter barrenness of heart, given over to the mind's futile government, and the spring lightness and un-questioning delight—was common to both Vaughan and Herbert. Herbert asks "Who would have thought my shrivel'd heart/Could have recover'd greennesse?"[3] Echoing this is the voice of the aptly entitled 'Euphrasy':

> The large untidy February skies—
> Some cheerful starlings screeling on a tree—
> West wind and low-shot sunlight in my eyes—
> 　　Is this decline for me?
>
> The feel of winter finishing once more—
> Sense of the present as a tale half told—
> The land of life to look at and explore—
> 　　Is this, then, to grow old?

Unambiguously related to nature—here neither mere consolation nor stay—is the disturbed mind, a mind in the grip of winter: but only temporarily, for the sense of the infinite, lying through and beyond this, keeps expectancy of the coming spring alive. This is the first poem in which we have a more particularized natural scene than is the case in the earlier volumes (if one excepts the affectionately re-worked dawn-scenes): the "untidy" skies, the "screeling" birds and the "low-shot" sunlight image the change.[4]

　　He does not demand from nature more than she can give, nor does he exact too pretentious a message from her. 'An Example' is a moment of insight in which his senses confirm the promptings of the inner self:

3. 'The Flower': Herbert quotations are made from *The Works of George Herbert* (Ed. F. E. Hutchinson. Oxford, 1941).
4. "Low-shot light" occurs in William Barnes's *Rustic Childhood* (*Poems Partly of Rural Life*, 1846), which Sassoon would probably have read; on the other hand, he might well have coined the word independently. Though the more particularised natural description is refreshing, one regrets that it recurs only spasmodically in a mere handful of poems: in this respect, one receives from Sassoon's poetry no continual pleasure comparable to that given by Edward Thomas, Edmund Blunden or Andrew Young—or even by his own prose, where he is lavish of description. In his own practice, he adheres over-strictly to his prescription of "controlled visualisation" (*M.*, p. 172).

> I stood below a beech
> And said to stillness, teach
> Tranquillity. I told
> Dumb patient earth to hold
> My unquiet mind from speech.

"Dumb patient earth"—not Meredith's Mother Earth: he makes of its mute signs no more than a reminder of what is already felt within. He watches the feeding bird:

> The moments passed; and I
> No self-concernment knew
> But one small purposed thing
> Which from my presence flew
> On deft unstartled wing . . .
> And I was tranquil too.

Such freedom, emancipated from questioning, living in a world limited and known, is what he desires: it is not an end itself. He is never tempted, in Herbert's words, to "rest in Nature, not the God of Nature."[5] In 'The Message' he checks himself from wishfully perceiving something divine in the face of nature, seemingly "Transfigured as by beneficence fulfilled"; he adds: "Thus Nature's countenance. The thought was merely mine." He never comes nearer than this modest approach to the sublimities of Wordsworth. It is not that he thinks such 'seeing' absurd: he desires such a vision so strongly as to feel distrustful of his desire. He is still, like the Hardy of 'On Christmas Eve', at a rational distance from belief, whilst being acutely sensitive to the possibility of an uplifting experience. His wistful end, "Thus, childlike, I imagined. Yet it might be true," echoes Hardy's "I should go with him in the gloom,/Hoping it might be so."

In 'In Time of Decivilisation'—in title and theme, except for the personal element, again echoing Hardy—he gazes from the "twilight windowed room" of the mind on to a natural scene of unhurried change and fruitful tranquillity:

> In August evening west
> No sign of world unrest.
> Goldening with gentle glow
> The crowns of crowded trees,
> Blue days decline and go
> Bourdened by bumble-bees.

5. 'The Pulley.'

So he, now divorced from youth and action, must achieve a comparable rightness within; the muted image of the viol recurs:

> Only as viol to string
> Vibrant, I would accord
> With time's importuning.

> Stillness, man's final friend,
> Absolve this turmoiled thought
> Of ills I cannot mend . . .

In 'Elsewhere' the way by which thought must be "absolved" is pointed by the assertion that, since one man can do nothing to mend the world's evils, he must look elsewhere to be "Defended and befriended and resigned/And fortified and free." If this seems a selfish view, it must be remembered that it rests upon a belief in a transcendent spiritual reality, however ill-defined, "Beyond found formulas of scientists."

In his claims to spiritual reality, Sassoon shows a fresh vigour and confidence. The words Edmund Blunden uses in commenting generally upon *The Heart's Journey* may, with greater aptness, be applied to the less strained mood of *Common Chords*: "It is his good fortune always to understand that man cannot wholly understand, to accept the ins and outs of the prodigious current of evolution, and to possess accordingly an impulsive and humorous freedom."[6] The lightest side of this "freedom" is shown in 'The Unproven', where he sketches a picture of "unbelieved-in angels" waiting hopefully in Heaven for mentally befogged man to see his way clear to true knowledge:

> Listening outside Eternity for Knowledge
>   And divination of Death
> Stood Science. Hushed was Heaven; and all those angels,
>   Still hopeful, held their breath.

Naturally suggested by this is the question, why does Heaven not lend a hand? And it is this that Sassoon tackles in three vigorous questioning poems in which the "Primordial Cause" is approached with a new directness. In 'Praise Persistent' and 'An Asking' he ponders the comedy of man's relationship with the divine. In the first, "Alone with life," he reflects upon how men have offered prayers to "the unseen/Essence which rules redemption", and imagines this praise resounding through "cathedral'd centuries," becoming on the

6. *Edmund Blunden: A Selection*, p. 312.

"gloom-girt winds of time" audible "with dwindling resonance." Men are at fault for pursuing "phantasms"—"Yet mindful of the Maker they would meet": it is implied that man has erred in forming an image of God according to his own desire, yet the conclusion is sceptical:

> Thus, praise persistent, year beyond wrought year,
> Those paeans rise and fade and disappear—
> Held to what infinite heart—heard by what
>   immanent ear?

'An Asking' opens with a question naturally prompted by this— whatever man's errors of direction, *some* force drives him: what are its origin and meaning? How did man come to possess a sense of soul, "beyond his death-environed care"? The stilted address—to the "Primordial Cause"—points the intellectual barrier that has yet to be crossed and prompts wry reflections upon the problem of giving spirit divine sanction.

But he remains an aspirant to belief, questioning self more than God. What, he asks himself in 'Resurrection', if truth were to be revealed and he be called to judgment?

> What, for the spiritual service some foresee
> Beyond probational breath,
> Would then emerge from marred and mystic me
> To stand with those white presences delivered through
>   death?

The setting of this poem is similar, though much less particularized, to that of Vaughan's 'Regeneration': he does not develop, through natural imagery, a parable of spiritual journeying, but the 'message' is, like Vaughan's, related to spring in "a primrosed wood":

> It was high-spring, and all the way
> Primros'd, and hung with shade;

But whereas Vaughan hears a reassuring voice, he hears none and can only suppose the effect of "the word heard within" and doubt his preparedness for it. 'Redemption' again points a similarity and a contrast with Vaughan. It expresses an earnest desire for illumination:

I thought; To the Invisible I am blind;
No angels tread my nights with feet of flame;
No mystery is mine—
No whisper from that world beyond my sense.

I think; If through some chink in me could shine
But once—O but one ray
From that all-hallowing and eternal day,
Asking no more of Heaven I would go hence.

This might almost be taken for the voice of Vaughan, but the echoes
have weaker emphasis. Vaughan could speak confidently of following
"A way where you might tread the Sun,"[7] and he could see some
amongst Sassoon's "host of souls redeemed," "walking in an Air of
glory,/Whose light doth trample on my days"—a sure vision of an
existence infinitely beyond the earthly. And, at the end of 'Regeneration', he asks in a moment of exalted certainty,

> "Lord," then said I, "*On me one breath,*
> *And let me dye before my death!"*

Sassoon's plea can echo this but faintly: it must be made for a sign
and to "the Invisible," unclaimed as God; whereas though Vaughan's
God may sometimes hold himself invisible (to the "vile and low" dust
of man[8]) his existence is never in doubt.

§ 2

One would not expect *Emblems of Experience* (1951), published only
a year later than *Common Chords*, to show any marked change of mood
or attitude. It is likely that almost all the poems included were written
later than those of the previous volume: only three, 'On Scratchbury
Camp' (*Country Life*, June 1943), 'Cleaning the Candelabrum' (*The
Listener*, May 1944) and 'Ultimate Values' (*Enquiry*, September 1949),
can, on the evidence of *A Bibliography*, be definitely assigned to an
earlier date; the remainder had not previously been published.

If *Common Chords* denotes a new tranquillity, born of a mind no
longer *struggling* for "stillness" (though stillness in the absolute sense
is not yet achieved), *Emblems of Experience* is a series of reflections

7. 'The World.'
8. 'The Dawning.'

naturally springing from an achieved centre of self-control. The key-note is acceptance born of humility. In 'Acceptance', he characterises man in three stages, "Simpleton, accuser, and acceptor," and it is the last he has himself reached and must enact,

> Till, in the presence of his one deliverer, death,
> "Take not Thy Holy Spirit from us, Lord," Man saith.

He doubts the validity of his intellectual strivings, since they are liable to lead him back only to what he himself desires. He presents this dramatically in 'A Dream', where he conjures up a vision of the earlier self who seems a stranger—"Hooded he stood, whose eyes acknowledged sorrow"; he joins this stranger and together they go (one remembers 'To One Who Was With Me in the War'), driving themselves on toward the future upon a "way . . . cragged and steep," like the hill on which Donne's "Truth" stands, only to discover at last that they are one and the same:

> "Stranger," I said, "since you and I are one,
> Let us go back. Let us undo what's done."

It was, too literally, a search for self. Now, in age, he ponders with rueful humour upon the handiwork such egotism has produced:

> What an old library of life I am!
>
> *What self's been shown?* What self had learnt from
>   selves
> While multiple they merged, each into each;
> This, for the central student they could teach,
> Remains most valued volume on my shelves.
>
> ('Travelling Library')

The old problem with which he began, aspiring to self-knowledge, remains, and must do so to the end; but he is now able to tell himself this with the unabashed simplicity which arises from grasping at least one small certainty:

> "This afternoon, as you remember, came
> And flew round your room a Jennie Wren . . .
> Not till that nimble creature knows its name
> Will you have learnt your meaning among men."
>
> ('Wren and Man')

There is no complacency about this acceptance, for it leaves him still alone. Though he can still bring to mind "beloved or valued ghosts,"

> They, once my wise and faithful, have no being:
> No supersensual agency can bring
> Those presences from silence and unseeing:
> They dwell secure from world's importuning.
> Meanwhile myself sits with myself agreeing
> That to be sixty is no easy thing.
>
> ('Solitudes at Sixty')

The mind must live increasingly upon its memories or its treasured human values, with little taste for aged life—"remaining, since I must" ('Ultimate Values'), but this, from one of the earlier-written poems, is a more sombre note than that which characterizes the whole. The acceptance achieved is neither resigned nor dismal. There is no reason why a feeling of release from "selfhood" should be. He embraces the conviction of his own insignificance in a way deeper than the intellectual, without regret. His life is but an episode in a greater continuity, both human and universal, "from traceless mystery" toward "times unknown"; man plants, he passes through, and even his creations die; and whilst he ponders this,

> He twirls a white wild violet in his fingers
> As others may when he's no more beheld,
> Nor memory of him lingers.
>
> ('A Proprietor')

The action has a touching, evanescent beauty: the violet is life itself, frail and briefly held, with which man toys as he teases its meaning.

But he himself has teased long enough: he is now ready to accept— rather than to *ask*—of life no more than it can give. The traces of "Ultimate Spring" can be enjoyed in spring itself, with the freedom of detachment:

> Designlessly in love with life unlived, I go
> Content with the mere fact that fields are drying fast
> And tiny beads of bud along the hedge foreshow
> The blackthorn winter that will come too late to last.
>
> ('Early March')

This enhances the mood of 'Euphrasy': the delicate observation is impregnated with a harmonious sense of nature's pattern, of time, change and renewal; he concludes,

> Meanwhile I'm thankful for this almost dusty road,
> Celandine's lowly gold, and daylight lengthening
>   when
> The winterbournes, like time, past February have
>   flowed.

The long lines run as evenly as the thought; he feels no need to argue the sense of essential continuity that flows strongly, in spite of what man does, like a stream beneath the ice. This tranquil certainty gives the tone to the whole of 'On Scratchbury Camp', but especially in these lines:

> I walk the fosse, once manned by bronze and
>   flint-head spear;
> On war's imperious wing the shafted sun-ray gleams:
> One with the warm sweet air of summer stoops the
>   bird.

He simply juxtaposes a recollection of the primitive weapons, now vanished and without trace, with their modern counterpart, "war's imperious wing," setting against and above both the bird in harmony with life's continuum, a harmony he now feels within himself. A comparison between this and the anxious and diffident 'Thoughts in 1938', where one feels conscious of a detachment desired rather than achieved, or the ponderous moralizing of such poems as 'Antiquities' and 'Gloria Mundi', illustrates the considerable evolution of feeling: the later poem is imbued with a sense of place as central, with the watcher himself a part of it. Though he may, in 'Cleaning the Candelabrum', still meditate pleasantly upon times past, when all is said, meditation "leaves us not much wiser than we were": "Meanwhile, for me, outside my open window, / The twilight blackbird flutes, and spring arrives." 'A Fallodon Memory' and 'Old-Fashioned Weather' are further examples of this preoccupation with continuity, but less memorably expressed (the latter poem hardly escapes with Sassoon's disarming admission that it is "obvious" and "trite"). In 'Awareness of Alcuin', more strikingly than in 'A Fallodon Memory', he celebrates a fellow-spirit attuned, as he desires to be, to the spirit of the universe. The poem is infused, like his sonnet to Henry Vaughan, with the quality of its subject, the quality of assured and peaceful serenity; this appears in the quiet rhythms of the opening,

> At peace in my tall-windowed Wiltshire room,
> (Birds overheard from chill March twilight's close)
> I read, translated, Alcuin's verse . . .

and of the reflective end, in which the movement grows firmer with
the suggestion of the goal, the ultimate renewal of self, to which every
visible sign of continual growth, change and remaking seems to point:

> Alcuin, from temporalities at rest,
> Sought grace within him, given from afar;
> Noting how sunsets worked around to west;
> Watching, at spring's approach, that beckoning star;
> And hearing, while one thrush sang through the rain,
> Youth, which his soul in Paradise might regain.

Here his favourite loves of spring and youth are together embodied
in a mature spiritual conception. The "beckoning star" is perhaps the
"evening star" of 'XII' (*The Heart's Journey*), symbolising the goal
toward which the seeker moves. Now, it is not "storm-hid", but
visible.

The star of 'Befriending Star' is not simply the goal toward which
he strives, since he prays that it will inspire his "lowly faith" by
appearing as a guide in a shape less awesome, whose sublimity will
not overwhelm the humble seeker:

> Heart-simplified, appear
> Not in ferocity of elemental fire,
> But, for my lowly faith, a sign by which to steer.

The star suggests, rather, the complex attributes of God—beneficent,
and yet remote and even fearsome. He also prays, "Empower my
human frailty to conceive you kind." 'The Need' is a variation upon
this theme, and more clearly a plea to God. He still hesitates to invoke
God outright—"O God within me, speak from your mysterious
morn"—the conception is deistic, but the "God within" has the
attributes of the Christian God:

> Act, as of old
> That we some dawnlit destiny may behold
> From this doom-darkened place.
> O move in mercy among us. Grant accepted grace.

Sassoon is never seriously inhibited by modern scepticism about the

beneficence of the God he seeks; he is never tempted to imagine
Hardy's Vast Imbecility. His belief that man has free will and is
therefore fully accountable for his crimes—that he is "fallen"—dates
back to *The Road to Ruin*.

The final confirmation of revelation may still be denied, but there
remains within, as always, "the idea of God," the "Holy Spirit" of
"Acceptance', as integral to his nature as man or creature:

> I see myself, one body on that invisible road;
> Brief bird on air, blind burrowing mole, dumb
>   fish in stream.
> I trust Eternity as being's elect abode,
> Where the idea of God pervades our daunted dream.
>
>   ('World Without End')

"Daunted"—unsatisfied; he cannot yet embrace the whole of
Vaughan's conception:

> Thou art a toylsom Mole, or less
>   A moving mist
> But life is, what none can express
> *A quickness, which my God hath kist.*
>
>   ('Quickness')

—But the elements of this bold assertion are present, waiting to be
fused into a whole. The witness must be deferred, for the mind continues
sluggish in its mortality, slow to accept from the soul ("in all God's
world, most welcome guest") "rumours and reportings from the
whole." If it now lacks the power, he prays that at the last this will
not be so:

> Poor mortal mind, when you, in me, decay—
> When once delighting faculties grow dim—
> Cry on the parting soul for power to say,
> With passion, "I befriended was by Him."
>
>   ('The Messenger')

In the final poem, he gathers together the homely images of his quiet
vigils—beneath "an evening lamp" that now fitly suggests age seeking
in solitude for light—and stresses once more what in *The Tasking*
he will assert with greater force,

How little, in life employed and planned,
The gnomic head may understand.

Thought-haunted room; and one for whom
Departure and disfleshment loom.
The ticking clock at evening's end;
And sleep,—thwart self's enfolding friend.

('The Present Writer')

§ 3

In the two volumes so far discussed, Sassoon was working towards a greater austerity of style: in such brief, compressed pieces as 'Release', 'Euphrasy' and 'An Example' (*Common Chords*) and 'Wren and Man', 'A Dream', The Messenger' and 'The Present Writer' (*Emblems of Experience*). Each of these earlier poems crystallizes a thought or perception within brief compass: words are spared—inessential verbs, the introductory participial phrase, explanatory transitions between thought and image—and imagery, too, is sparing. When imagery and an allied pleasure of poetry, natural description, are sparse— as now becomes markedly the case in *The Tasking* (1954)—it is hard for the poet to avoid dullness. Sassoon has escaped this, in the majority of the poems, by limiting himself to what has to be said, without elaboration; he also varies the movement sufficiently by alternating long and short lines and preserves harmony by selecting his words for the sake of binding alliteration and assonance. Within so small a compass (only one important poem exceeds 14 lines) the vitality of the insight, for this is a series of insights rather than, as previously, speculations, is communicated immediately. There is no need now for the longer breath: the ground is new (except in 'The Half-Century' and 'The Welcoming', like 'The Hardened Heart', poems of age looking back compassionately on youth); the old questionings are either resolved or pronounced invalid. It remains only to proclaim, without ambiguity, discoveries made.

The increasing relaxation of tension evident in the two previous volumes is now complete. In those volumes, there was a growing sense of freedom, especially in the poems of spring; the mind was less disposed to labour, more willing to accept its limitations and to wait in stillness, taking illumination when it came. Now, it has abdicated altogether:

> Toward kindled flames to come
> Your divination is dumb:
> Little the mind remembers,
> Sighed the shifting embers.

('Sic Sedebat')

And in 'The Humbled Heart' he writes: "I am but the brain that dreamed and died." He is content, for "the question that concerns me most" can now be given, for the first time, unequivocal reply:

> I know a universe beyond me;
> Power that pervades the fluctuant soul,
> Signalling my brain it would unbond me
> And make heart's imperfection whole.

('Human Bondage')

He freely acknowledges the soul's ascendancy:

> Go your seeking, soul.
> Mine the proven path of time's foretelling.
> Yours accordance with some mysteried whole.
> I am but your passion-haunted dwelling.

('The Humbled Heart')

These are the central truths achieved: mind has ceased its questionings, having somehow (there is still mystery) at last recognised soul and admitted its predominance. His task is henceforth, "To put world sounds behind and hope to hear/Instructed spirit speaking." ('The Tasking').

And we ourselves hear a new voice: "speaking" seems the appropriate word for these poems, in which he communicates directly with both self and reader with confident ease. Some of the quotations already cited illustrate this: the downright "I know . . .," the direct "Go your seeking, soul." Hitherto, he has usually opened tentatively, in the voice of groping or, at best, tranquil meditation: "At peace in my tall-windowed Wiltshire room," "Sexagenarian solitudes, I find," "One winter's end I much bemused my head"—from such beginnings we have expected no absolute certainties, some clarification of attitude, perhaps, but no more. Now, our attention is arrested by a more forceful voice, demanding, asserting, or simply communicating a truth unvarnished and whole; above all communicating, in the confident tone that heralds a conviction: "Just now I stared out on a star-

IV. Siegfried Sassoon in 1954. *Courtesy of Mr. D. R. W. Silk*

IV. Heytesbury House, Wiltshire. *Courtesy of Professor Edmund Blunden*

strange night," "Someone else I know of—neither young nor old—,"
"I know a night of stars within me." He may also address himself
challengingly, in the brusque tone of one about to convey a home-
truth: "Little enough you've learnt" and "What am I then?" This
new sureness and directness issue naturally from the "still centre".
It is no longer necessary for him to wind his way into the poem; the
issues now present themselves to his mind with sharpness and clarity,
dictated by a presence that has no need of the old groping brain:
"Clocked occluded self wrote never lines like his" ('The Visitant').
An unqualified series of mystical assertions answers the old wearying
question of the many selves: "What am I then?" (In an age of more
fundamental certainties, Crashaw could begin his 'Charitas Nimia'
with "*Lord*, what is man?" For him, *self*-examination was a less basic
problem):

> What am I then? A consciousness that cries
> Good morning and good night;
> A brevity whose eyes look once on light:
> One thought in all the unmindful mind of nature;
> One face in multitudes a moment seen;
> Eternity's quick creature, born of what has been.
>
> ('The Question')

This says "I am" in a purely religious sense, resolving the tyrannies of
individuality: formerly, in 'World Without End', he had written, "I
see myself, one body on that invisible road," "I trust Eternity . . ."
and had clung to "the idea of God." Now he can truly speak with
Vaughan,

> But life is, what none can express
> *A quickness, which my God hath kist.*

The spirit is now sure and dominant: this is more effectively expressed
by the agency of another voice, the voice of dramatic opposition—
between the doubting, fearing self, misled by the Devil, and a correc-
ting God; the method recalls Herbert, but the opening line echoes
Hopkins ("No worst, there is none . . ."):

> Then came a cry, "No spirit—none—
> Within your deathward being dwells:
> The will of darkness must be done:
> Take this, and make the most of what your timepiece
>   tells."

I knew, unknowing; I heard, unhearing,
A voice beyond my bodily boding,
"The faithful found me without fearing:
Learn this, and look forever toward your soul's
unloading."

('The Contention')

By means of the paradoxical "I knew, unknowing . . ." he distinguishes
between limited bodily and intellectual awareness and the prompting
of the spirit: this idea is imaged in the "harmony unheard" of 'A
Chord'. 'The Contention' is the only poem in which he presents a
conflict in Herbert's manner; elsewhere the "clues" from "selfhood's
essence" occur less dramatically. In 'Another Spring', which recalls
'Early March' and 'Resurrection' in mood, his method resembles
Vaughan's, though with a less exalted voice than that which ends
'Regeneration'. He portrays "Aged self, disposed to lose his hold on
life," looking down and marking "Continuance in some crinkled
primrose leaves"; this humble reminder moves to an inner recovery:

> Look, listen, live, some inward watcher warns.
> Absorb this moment's meaning: and be wise
> With hearts whom the first primrose purifies.

In 'An Epitome', a crucial insight comes, in what Eliot calls "the
unattended moment," when he is "Just thinking," and takes the
form of an authoritative voice that,

> Spoke the one word in all my time
> To make endured existence known
> Even as it is. Accept your soul.
> Be evermore alone.

In 'The Alliance' he sets body and soul in a dialogue against each
other, to attest his feeling that their interests are indivisible: the soul
has the responsibility to "cherish and control" the body. Life is still
to be accepted; he would not be "all soul." 'Sic Sedebat' and 'The
Humbled Heart' are complementary addresses to mind and soul, both
familiar friends, the one treated with compassion, the other—
"Stranger, loved of body's humbled heart"—with grateful love.

Though in the face of these serene certainties he raises, for the
first time, some of the most formidable obstacles to belief in a beneficent
God, he does so only to surmount them cleanly with the confidence

born of absolute faith, leaving no trace of doubt or dissatisfaction
behind. In 'The Making' he asks "What work was His, where mind
its self must make?" He answers:

> *It is He that hath made us, and not we*
> *Ourselves.* One moment's aftercome I live,
> Flawed with inherited humanity,
> And fooled by imperfections wrought through race.
> This He first fashioned; this He can forgive
> When granting His unapprehended grace.[9]

God gives: he takes away; his grace is "unfeared"; he will not punish
his repentant creature. The intermediate problem—how are the
"imperfections wrought through race" distinct from God's making?—
is passed over; Sassoon's theology is not systematic. He is highly
conscious of the limitations of Reason: though in 'The Trial' he grants
that rational enquiry raises apparent contradictions concerning God's
justice and mercy—"how he justifies fang, swamp, and claw"—
whilst the mere living eye, seeking a sign, registers only the incomprehensible vastness of the universe—he is content to set above such
doubts the inward knowledge he feels:

> Nature and knowledge daunt with dire denial
> The inward witness and the innocent dream.
> On such rough road must faith endure its trial,
> Upheld by resolution to redeem
> The soul, that world within an ignorant shape
> One with the solar system and the ape.

Thus, he uncompromisingly lifts the validity of the soul clear of man's
evolutionary and physical theories, which are the clumsy fumblings
of "an ignorant shape." His long-held idea of man as "fallen" recurs in
'The Worst of It' in the Promethean and Satanic images:

> Here's Man, empowered by armaments of flame,
> Unfuturing his future; self-assigned
> To suicide, through the secrets which he stole.

Aspiring to nothing of this, "Here's Me; who neither ask nor aim to
be/More than the mote in heaven's revealed ray."[10] His is the surety

9. See Appendix A (17).
10. Hopkins uses the same image in "*Thee, God, I come from*" (op. cit. p. 82):
> All day long I like fountain flow
> From thy hand out, swayed about
> Mote-like in thy mighty glow.

of revealed truth, not rational conviction: he has always distrusted
'mind'—there has been no passionate dualism of faith and reason—
and it is not remarkable that the faith he achieves is truly submissive.
One is reminded of Tennyson, warmed by the "heat of inward
evidence", but to tranquil—not fevered—conviction.

The new certainty is imaged in the way dear to Herbert and
Vaughan—by analogy with the stars. In 'Retreat from Eternity' he
is more akin to Herbert, by an everyday analogy reducing "the old
lonely question" prompted by gazing at the "star-strange night" to
the humble scope of human understanding:

> Then, while the firelight flickered, musing here,
> I saw, in mimic constellation shown,
> Reflected sparkles on the chandelier,
> And was no more benumbed by the unknown.

It is an insight into the infinite possibility of pattern and harmony
within the universe: it is an instinctive answer to the plea of 'Befriending Star', for an accommodation between the human and the
infinite. In 'The Best of It' he goes on to claim the infinite boldly
as no longer remote, the country that lies beyond the winter of age:

> Star-sown eternity for mindsight old.
> Winter endured. Time past a tale retold.
> Wisdom and wonder, faithful to enfold
> Life, that by no disaster is undone.

This impregnable "Life" embraces that which is eternal and within
him, here and now—and he believes it has always been latent:

> I know a night of stars within me;
> Through eyes of dream I have perceived
> Blest apparitions who would win me
> Home to what innocence believed.
>
> ('Human Bondage')

For once, if one takes a close parallel, his conception is not exceeded
in amplitude by Vaughan's,

> For each inclosed Spirit is a star
> Inlighting his own little sphaere,
> Whose light, though fetch and borrowed from far,
> Both mornings makes, and evenings there.[11]

11. 'The Bird.'

Yet it is more appropriate to end consideration of this crucial stage in
"The Heart's Journey" upon the characteristically quieter note of
revelation, expressed in a way completely in accord with a pilgrimage
less ecstatically rewarded than Vaughan's. It is, rather, the homelier
strain of Herbert in 'Employment' (1), "Lord place me in thy consort;
give one strain/To my poore reed":

> On stillness came a chord,
> While I, the instrument,
> Knew long-withheld reward:
> Gradual the glory went;
> Vibrating, on and on,
> Toward harmony unheard,
> Till dark where sanctus shone;
> Lost, once a living word.
>
> But in me yet abode
> The given grace though gone;
> The love, the lifted load,
> The answered orison.   ('A Chord')

The long-felt desire for spiritual certainty has been answered. He has
throughout fashioned himself into an instrument apt to respond to
the merest touch: "Only as viol to string/Vibrant, I would accord/
With time's importuning" ('In Time of Decivilisation'). The touch
comes, fleetingly—the mind has been so stubborn—but will remain
for the still "sense-confined" body an enduring link with "harmony
unheard."

XIII

RESOLUTION

§ 1

With *Lenten Illuminations and Sight Sufficient*, which appeared with characteristic unobtrusiveness in a small private printing in December, 1958, Sassoon set the seal upon his spiritual journey by proclaiming for its end the orthodox sanction of Roman Catholic belief.[1]

After the lucid brevities of *The Tasking*, 'Lenten Illuminations' is a surprising return to the manner of *Satirical Poems*. It is a conversation-piece addressed to the "old self", in which he looks back upon his spiritual search, comparing the "unconvert self" unfavourably with the new, and expresses his deep sense of the peace he has won. It moves at a ruminative pace, for some eighty lines of irregular, and sometimes extraordinary, length; he uses rhyme, but there seems no inner necessity for it. The leisurely kind of movement is appropriate, but the familiar tone only rarely comes through with sufficient freedom and clarity: successful examples are the easy opening of the first part, "Not properly Catholic, some might say . . ." and the jocular way in which he begins his self-examination, "What were you up to—going into Church all those years . . ." and continues, applying the familiar to the sublime, with "While you were in your purgatorial time, you used to say . . ." The ending of Part I has the affectionate warmth with which he has always treated his lesser being, "O unforeseeing/ Sad self, let's be together . . .", and the ending of the whole has the same quality: "You could have said this simple thing, old self, in any previous year."

Had this "plain Wordsworthian language", to employ his own phrase from *On Poetry*, been typical of the whole, this poem might have been a fitting corollary to *The Tasking*. Its overwhelming defect is that the familiar style is submerged beneath "a general turgidity of diction."[2] The free flow of speech is impeded by such ponderous

---

1. Appendix A, (18).
2. The fault Coleridge identified in his early poems: *Biographia Literaria*, Chapter **I.**

coinages and Latinisms as these (taken from the 18 lines of the first part only): "meditationment", "meditational consciousness', "unconvert", "wheretoward", "unforeknowing Ego, visitant in thought." Compression seems to be the aim, but, (as sometimes in Hardy, whose influence is perhaps strong here) it is achieved at the expense of both euphony and straightforward communication. Neither can meaning justify the use of "meditationment" where 'meditation' will serve, or of "announcements" for 'annunciations'.[3] The choice of diction is also heavily Miltonic, as if in tribute to the solemnity of the occasion: the near cousins "resultancy", "renunciant", "indubitant", "frustrate", "abidant" occur, heavily accented, too close together for comfort. An inflated effect is thus produced, inconsistent with the poem's purpose.

One turns, with regret, from style to content. Sassoon makes a church interior, visited one quiet afternoon during Lent, the setting for a meditation upon the pattern of his years. He sees them as a period of "faith unfaithful"—a faith desired and willed, not achieved. They were years of sympathetic response to "the aids" to faith, "anthems, organ-music, shaft-aspiring stone", and of deep feeling for Christ's sacrifice, but a sense of unworthiness had always kept him outside,

> From your default His face seemed ever turned aside.
> Not then for you the arisen Word—not then the
> wrought remedial gift of tears

—this phrase is strikingly compressed.

He then asks what brought about the new state, "This close, child-minded calm?" Instead of answering directly, he turns to the simple, cheap candles—"Two pennies for each. But Candlemass tells purity" —the symbols of absolution. "Their innocent radiance will remit/ Our errors": yet "at our broken orisons we kneel, unblest, unbenefited"; the faithful must strive to emulate their clear perfection, but he will never feel himself more than a sinner. He then reminds himself of the pride of "your purgatorial time" when, in the midst of worldly troubles, he "implored illumination", but lacked the obedience and humility to receive it (as in *The Road to Ruin* he was too

3. A penchant for noun coinages like these has already been noted as a minor characteristic of Sassoon's later poetry, (see Appendix A, 17): though in the shorter poems also they may not always seem justified by either sound or sense, they are used more sparingly in the individual poem and so attract no disproportionate attention to themselves.

much a part of the man he castigated). At last, the "Outcast and unprotected contours of the Soul" received "Influence, relief, result-tancy from Rome." He asks why this came about, and points once more to a visible image of "relief", "earth's best-loved Lady", whose name "Shines to intercede." Now, humbly, he has gratefully accepted her all embracing love: "Is it not well, that now you call yourself her child?" The next few lines are among the most successful, suggesting by their bare and broken construction the confused and indeterminate thought and action that preceded conversion:

> This day twelve months ago—it was Ash
> Wednesday—one
> Mid-way between us two toward urgent hope fulfilled
> Strove with submission. Arduous—forbidding—
> then to me
> Inflexible Authority.

In the remainder of the poem, he celebrates the "new making", harking back to his earlier analogy with the simplicity of the child, forever wondering and forever learning, but this is now a simplicity born of knowledge, not ignorance: "One road before us now—one guidance for our gain—/One morning light—whatever the world's weather—wherein wide-eyed to waken." Allied with this sense of "life breathed afresh", as if just begun, is the return of spring, now heard with utter joy, as a sure promise of the envisioned Whole:

> I never felt it more than now, when out beyond
> these safening walls
> Sculptured with Stations of the Cross, spring-
> confident, unburdened, bold
> The first March blackbird overheard to forward
> vision flutes and calls.

In 'Sight Sufficient', he attests once more the achievement of a kind of faith that needs no spectacular manifestation to sustain it:

> God, on the gloom divine wheretoward I pray,
> You send no sign, no doubt-redeeming ray;
> Nor manifest, for this unwisdom'd one,
> The faith that blest his pilgrim path begun.
>
> O purpose of my prayer, breath of my being,
> Your inward light I share through sightless seeing;
> Your love can but be told beyond blind thought
> That knows your peace enfold believement brought.

For the first time, he employs a paradox dear to the metaphysicals, by which man's earthbound blindness to the divine brightness only his spirit apprehends is suggested: "There is in God (some say)/ A deep, but dazzling darkness."[4] The proof of his "sightless seeing" (a variant of the "harmony unheard" of 'A Chord'), if proof there must be, is "The peace of God, which passeth all understanding."

It would be supererogatory to comment upon Sassoon's movement from a theistic to an orthodox belief: the history of this, unlike that of his quest for God, is too much compressed within one poem and yields no poetic results to compare with the simple and clear wedding of form and meaning which distinguishes *The Tasking*. That he would not be adept at decking his soul or his faith with the jewels of rhetoric is well shown by the unhappy marriage of the familiar and the exalted in 'Lenten Illuminations'—and he is temperamentally incapable of the ecstasies of a Crashaw. Neither has he ever shown a strong inclination to pursue doctrinal questions: Resurrection, Incarnation, Passion— he seems content to accept all that his Church embraces. Poetically, the most shapely end would have been *The Tasking*, the rounded conclusion of his quest for "selfhood's essence." It must be left for a Catholic writer to say, "Here is the story of a soul as shapely as any poet could want his verse to be."[5]

§ 2

In 1960, there appeared *The Path to Peace*, a volume designed to give retrospective shape to Sassoon's spiritual journey. It included twenty-nine poems, of which all but six had been previously published.[6] The title points to this selection having been designed to improve at last upon the negative admonitions of *The Road to Ruin* of almost thirty years earlier. The *Proposal* issued before publication adequately describes the pattern: "Although observing no chronological order, a designed sequence traces his spiritual pilgrimage from the somewhat

---

4. Vaughan, 'The Night'.
5. C. E. Maguire: 'Harmony Unheard: The Poetry of Siegfried Sassoon' (*Renascence*, Vol. XI, No. 3, Spring 1959). Frank Swinnerton, on the other hand, an old friend of Sassoon's and a rational sceptic, describes himself as "one who appreciated the love of quietude which produced the beauty of his rhymed ruminations, but one who had no sympathy with his final acceptance of clerical supervision" (*Figures in the Foreground*, 1963, pp. 211-12).
6. For the titles of the poems included see Appendix A, (19).

dreamy pantheism of youth through long years of lonely seeking to 'life breathed afresh' in acceptance of the gift of faith."

Little need be added to what has already been said about most of the poems in this celebratory volume. Of the six previously un-published, two, 'Unfoldment' and Arbor Vitae', are in his best manner, whilst the remainder are colourless devotional pieces more or less spoilt by the devitalising diction observed in 'Lenten Illuminations'. Whereas his leaning to the Latinate liturgical can betray him into this, whose clotted alliterative and assonantal effects defeat the tongue,

> Wisdom remote from reason, mysteried Word
> Shrined for reverberant precincts of the soul,
> Above blind-led belief be held and heard,
> Need of the nescient, radiate and enrol—[7]

his unforced poet's instinct for the "simplicity and directness" he has so often advocated can still produce the graceful 'Arbor Vitae':

> For grace in me divined
> This metaphor I find:
>   A tree.
> How can that be?
>
> This tree all winter through
> Found no green work to do—
>   No life
> Therein ran rife.
>
> But with an awoken year
> What surge of sap is here—
>   What flood
> In branch and bud.
>
> So grace in me can hide—
> Be darkened and denied—
>   Then once again
> Vesture my every vein.

This poem has clarity, economy, "controlled visualisation": yet it was written in the same year as 'Rogation' (1959) and after 'Lenten Illuminations'. In the one we have the true, illuminated poet of *The*

7. From 'Rogation': the manner (not, of course, the matter) of Hardy is especially recalled in lines like these; comparable in Hardy's writings are the speeches to the Spirits and Choruses in *The Dynasts*, e.g. the 'After Scene' closing Part Three.

Tasking, in the other the laboured, pious versifier: these are the extreme poles of Sassoon's religious poetry—and, for he is not unusual in this, of much written by those who attain to orthodox belief.

"Once one knows what really matters one tends to stop talking"[8]— Goethe's words are apt enough here. Since *The Path to Peace* Sassoon has kept silence; his desire to do so is expressed in the short poem, 'A Prayer at Pentecost', which closes that volume:

> Master musician, Life, I have overheard you,
> Labouring in litanies of heart to word you.
> Be noteless now. Our duologue is done.
>
> Spirit, who speak'st by silences, remake me;
> To light of unresistant faith, awake me,
> That with resolved requiem I be one.'

---

8. *Wilhelm Meister's Travels.*
9. Since this chapter was written, I have learnt that a further group of eight recent devotional poems is to be printed and published by private subscription to celebrate Sassoon's eightieth birthday. Entitled *An Octave*, it is to be printed by the Shenval Press and will contain an introduction by the poet Charles Causley.

XIV

ACHIEVEMENT

There is no universally accepted sliding-scale of values by which a writer's achievement may be measured. According to one viewpoint, a writer's stature is virtually determined by the extent to which he endeavours to grapple with and reconstruct the disordered world, material and intellectual, of the particular fragment of time in which he happens to have been born; according to another, it may be important that he has refused to touch the broken images of the present, but has instead explored the ramifications of the microcosmic self; yet a third—most exacting—viewpoint will demand that the search for "selfhood's essence" be seen to have taken place under the pressure of the time and that this agonising union result in an ordering of reality (as it may seem) that will be important to others.

Sassoon's writing has, at different times, responded to the first two demands, but never to the high intensity of the third. This failure to achieve what to many seems the ideal synthesis is inherent in the very success of his war poetry: a local, qualified success, of style and feeling, not of vision. Though his achievement at that time chimed with the freshest modern spirit, it cannot be claimed as an original influence upon the development of contemporary writing. Before 1914, D. H. Lawrence and Kipling had already revived the tradition of colloquial verse far more vigorously than either Sassoon or the begetter of *The Daffodil Murderer*, Masefield; whilst the Eliot of 'The Love Story of J. Alfred Prufrock' and the Yeats of *Responsibilities* needed to learn nothing in technique from their contemporary, and they it was who, for good or ill, would be the models for later poets. Certainly, the healthy effect of his war satires upon Owen's writing is well attested, but there can be no doubt that so critical an artist as Owen would soon enough have taught himself Sassoon's lesson anyway: most fruitful, one supposes, was the mutual sharpening and clarification that sometimes results from the meeting of minds at a crucial moment, as was the case with Wordsworth and Coleridge.

The quality of Sassoon's war poetry is remarkable, not when it is compared stylistically with the work of his more original contemporaries, but when its content is viewed in relation to the cramping Edwardian social and literary context in which Sassoon himself was reared. Looking back, one must wonder at how, by sheer truth and force of feeling, he broke out of the constricting mould of dead poeticism which, at nearly thirty years old, had almost stifled him. If he was no prophet, his famous war poetry makes him a portent. In his raw and heated satires the emasculated versifying of an outworn society is betrayed from within—his contributions to the 1918-1919 volume of *Georgian Poetry* give the lie to its heart. They are symptomatic of a new vitality which was to undermine the irresponsible rule of Marshianism.[1] Sassoon's revival of the Byronic protest vigorously renewed the involvement of the poet with society *at the centre of society.* The excellence of his war satire was, like that of much Byron wrote, one less of form than of "sincerity and strength."

Yet his example had to wait another decade for effective followers— who were not, however, to take their leadership from him or to earn his sympathy. After the First World War, he rapidly lost his hold upon his time. He could not sustain the indignant protestant's rôle in the peace-time world. The Pacifist Muse is a noble one, but she is apt to repeat herself: though she was briefly revived in *The Road to Ruin,* it was to speak with baffled feeling rather than force. Social issues were many and blurred: humanitarian feeling could distinguish no plain target. His satire in the 'Twenties, like that of Osbert Sitwell and the embittered prose of Richard Aldington, was primarily an emotional outlet. So far as it can be traced to identifiable causes, it arose from the frustrating denial of the old positives: unquestioned peace, an apparently assured future, and, when garnished with Socialism, the war's solitary fruit—the uplifting experience of men's capacity for kinship—had a bitter taste. It was marginal satire, directed upon social and political aberrations: beside the slick surgery of Auden, the leader of an unwearied later generation, it seems exhausted and querulous. "Perhaps . . ." writes Stephen Spender, "the qualities which distinguished us from the writers of the previous

1. Though the Marshian taste still had a sizeable readership for a few post-war years in J. C. Squire's *The London Mercury*—to which Sassoon himself was a frequent contributor. For the term 'Marshianism' see Appendix A (20).

decade lay not in ourselves, but in the events to which we reacted. These were unemployment, economic crisis, nascent fascism, approaching war ... The older writers were reacting in the 'Twenties to the exhaustion and hopelessness of a Europe in which the old regimes were falling to pieces."[2] War-weariness underlay everything Sassoon wrote in the post-war decade: the suffering he had endured and striven to repress could not be ordered so soon. Had another straightforward crusade presented itself, a sublimation of that haunting experience might have resulted: but the tortuosities of politics, the mean distrust and fear dividing the classes, could not be cut through by one of Sassoon's cavalier temperament.

He was not, in his brief attachment to Socialism, either a sentimentalist or a fanatic, but he was ill-fitted for practical politics. Unlike the acutely class-conscious 'Thirties poets, he laboured under no harrowing sense of guilt as a member of an unjustly privileged class: but he did demand of politics more than it could give, just as in war he had over-estimated the effect of the moral gesture upon the leaders of men and men themselves. His temperament and his humanity revolted equally against the drab compromise of the non-reformed society and from the indiscriminate violence and injustice that he feared would attend radical change. Lacking a reforming vision, he could only wander aimlessly in the no-man's land between, letting off stray shots at scattered enemies.

To be successful, the satirist must have total confidence in his own standpoint or, at least, a stable sense of self. For Sassoon in the aftermath of a war that had demanded of him such lacerating action, as for many of his contemporaries, the inner self was still to be explored and known. Gradually, as objective action came to seem increasingly futile, his gentle, introspective nature came back into its own. Following at last the example of his "fellow poet in Peace and War", Edmund Blunden, he withdrew into his past and explored it for the values and coherence the present seemed to deny. Through this withdrawal, his poetic self blossomed in prose—and the prose of the years from 1928 to 1938, the Sherston trilogy and the first 'straight' autobiography, *The Old Century*, is his highest achievement: in both the narrower aspect of finished style and the wider one of human appeal. In the war narratives, this appeal derives from the singularly searching and honest portrayal of one representative man's response to the challenge

2. *World Within World*, 1951, p. 139.

of "an age that has sentenced every second man to ordeal by battle,"[3] and from a celebration, without hysteria or sentimentality, of man's capacity to suffer and endure. The narratives of peace will have an enduring appeal for those who regret the ever-widening separation between man and nature: though in this respect, it has been argued, they are flawed and can feed a false nostalgia. Sassoon himself, unlike his prophet Hardy (whom he had followed more closely in the *Memoirs*), cannot be acquitted on this count: but the reader will understand—and forgive—much if he remembers the background of the cruel years in whose shadow they were written. Then he will be free to relish *Memoirs of a Fox-Hunting Man* and *The Old Century* for their true gifts: the love of nature and country life expressed in an exquisitely modulated prose (worked with an artistry all too rare in the plethora of contemporary reminiscences), the delicate recapturing of enclosed childhood, the sympathetic and humorous portrayal of youth's gropings and triumphs, the warm avowals of friendship and the intuitive insight into the lives of many who crossed the writer's path. When the severest criticisms of the way of life they portray have been allowed, it can still be said that these books celebrate more attractively than most its positive virtues. Finally, they are autobiographies, not social history: when all criticisms are balanced, they will surely rank among the classic autobiographies of the age.

In his prose Sassoon exhibits qualities for which he himself is drawn towards Meredith: "He can make us remember what it felt like to be young ... can make us breathe the air of early morning"; "He is the poet of Nature in action and the joy of earth."[4] Meredithian qualities, but muted—closer in tone to some eighteenth century poets of 'retirement'—for "I am myself an inveterate quietist and self-corrector of inherent excitability."[5] Not the Meredithian 'philosophy': the Meredith he approves, "Freed the fret of thinking ... would

3. Robert Graves, *The Crowning Privilege* (Penguin, 1959, p. 153).
4. *M.*, pp. 115 and 263 respectively.
5. Ibid., p. 197. Compare Matthew Green's 'A Cure for the Spleen' and John Dyer's 'Grongar Hill', from which these lines especially are apt:

> O may I with myself agree,
> And never covet what I see:
> Content me with an humble Shade,
> My Passions tam'd, my Wishes laid;
> For while our Wishes wildly roll,
> We banish Quiet from the Soul:
> 'Tis thus the Busy beat the Air;
> And Misers gather Wealth and Care.

revert to the semi-pagan self of his prime—pagan in the acceptance
of the life-giving and joy-giving power of Nature . . . And it may be
said that this is the best of him which survives."[6] As Sassoon's religious
poetry shows, this "lifegiving power" was not only to sustain him
through desolate years but ultimately to assist him to a belief far
removed from Meredith's pantheism. Whether or not one can walk
with him "the way of Henry Vaughan", less debatable is Sassoon's
honourable place amongst those few serious contemporary poets
(Edward Thomas, D. H. Lawrence, Edmund Blunden, Andrew
Young, Dylan Thomas and Herbert Read are others) who by attesting,
in their different ways, the enduring importance of Nature—not
superficially, or ornamentally, merely as a source of imagery, but as
integral to man's whole awareness—have kept alive a distinctive
quality of the English Romantic tradition.

A further suggestive affinity—chiefly of personality and the development of their attitudes—is one between Sassoon and Tennyson.
They share, above all, a deep self-division, between the active and the
contemplative, the involved and the acceptant, the public and the
private selves. The unevenness of tone and the shifting viewpoints
which result from this inhibit them as social satirists and moralists, as
does their ill-proportioned mingling of thought and emotion. Generous
feeling led them both to sympathise with the radical movement of
their time, but an intense fear of violence caused them to react strongly
against it when it proved extremist. Both felt the need to come to
terms with deeply disruptive personal experience and to rebuild the
self, a process which preoccupied them almost obsessively in their

6. Ibid., p. 262. Sassoon's biography of Meredith is an unusual compound of
sympathy and admiration for the man and his spirit and touchy rejection of the
mind which flaws the inspiration—yet "to be at one's best is to be Meredithian."
It is as if, in the process of writing of Meredith, Sassoon were anxious to preserve
also "unity of life" in himself, whilst seeking at the same time to exorcise what would
distort and mislead. If there had been space here, one would have praised this
book, not as an important contribution to Meredith criticism, but as a model of
what Dr. Johnson demanded of biography: that it should "lead the Thoughts into
domestic Privacies, and display the minute Details of daily Life, where exterior
Appendages are cast aside, and Men excel each other only by Prudence, and by
Virtue" (*The Rambler*, No. 60). Sassoon is most successful in showing Meredith the
Private Man: his warm and lasting friendships, his love for his son, the failure of
his first marriage—all are treated with intuitive sympathy; and he understands
also the two selves of Meredith, the inward, reflective and sensitive self and the
outgoing "outdoor self", each of which must have its proper satisfaction, till at
last, with age, the first must grow stronger. There are many parallels between
subject and biographer in both temperament and private life—as a biographer
of Sassoon would show more clearly than he himself has wished to do.

middle years. In the course of this their writing, reflecting their reaction against the uglier aspects of the present, became deeply imbued
with nostalgia and they moved also toward a religious belief won
slowly but finally attested by "inward evidence"—ultimately sealed
in Sassoon's case by his acceptance of a definite doctrine.

In the quiet cadences of *Vigils* Sassoon celebrated, as Meredith
had done, "the love of earth that is my law," but for him it was a
love that served as a balm to the growing conviction of his own—
and of man's—radical imperfection. It was not in itself an end. The
burden of almost thirty years of poetry from *The Heart's Journey*—
begun, but not ending, in a sadness akin to Hardy's—to its full
realisation in *The Tasking* is the discovery of the spirit. He takes
a path well worn by others before him, in a direction—far removed,
one imagines, from that Owen might have pursued—which "misses
the march of this retreating world" and so, it must be said, misses
that complex synthesis of world and other-worldliness which makes
for greatness, as does Vaughan when we think of him as the contemporary of Milton.

Sassoon's religious poetry is modest and self-effacing. Its deliberately
muted colours and movement express the diffident gropings of the
true contemplative: they suggest analogy with a rule of abstinence.
There is little obscurity of meaning and no spectacular poetic device—
scant appeal to the admirers of contemporaries so various as Eliot,
Muir, or Dylan Thomas—but it would be unjust to write this poetry
off as a survival of the minor Georgian mode, as one critic has done.
On stylistic grounds, this criticism must be granted some force, for
the restraint entails monotony and allows too little surprise. On the
other hand, of the cardinal Georgian vices of faint, or false feeling and
self-indulgence, Sassoon is rarely guilty. There is complexity of feeling,
if not of form. No unprejudiced reader of *Sequences* can doubt that he
is in the presence of a religious sensibility of great integrity. Though
in manner Sassoon has, on the whole, less affinity with his contemporaries than with his spiritual fathers of the seventeenth century, *The
Tasking* deserves to be distinguished as the most poetic of his sequences
and the one most likely to satisfy modern taste: economical in language,
pointed in idea, lucidly and sparely imaged, it fitly celebrates that
stage of spiritual awareness where feeling is crystallized and finds its
own clear form.

The pilgrimage these poems record is centred upon the self as fallen, an intuitive religious sense of the incompleteness and unworthiness of body and mind: "in spirit I am far / From self, the dull control with whom I dwell." His "seeking" is, in no pejorative sense, self-centred: linking him in spirit (as in expression) rather with Herbert and Vaughan than with such contemporaries as T. S. Eliot and Edwin Muir, whose religious poetry shows greater "general awareness."[7] Sassoon builds on a less ambitious scale, using as in his prose the material of a "local, limited world" of self and of setting: the essential harmonies are, for him, the inner harmony of a man at peace with his spirit, and the outer, of man linked, through Nature, with God and a sense of rightness beyond time. By the non-religious, the self-centredness of such poetry—and most English devotional poetry is of this kind—is sometimes held to be its own condemnation. What is the validity of a poetry, they demand, which excludes so much human experience? In fact, what they reject is the conviction that man's spiritual experience is supreme: yet once this conviction *is* felt, the discipline it exacts is surely no less severe than that endured by those whose subject-matter is 'life'. In religious terms, man's first duty is to communicate with his God, then he may speak to man: or, rather, there will be one communication; his spiritual pilgrimage will speak for him.

7. Eliot's phrase (*Selected Essays*, p. 391). Muir provides a more complete contrast, for his qualified 'belief' stops far short of Eliot's dogmatism, and to the last takes agonised account of the injustices suffered and perpetrated by men here and now (e.g. see his 'The Last War'; *Collected Poems*, p. 281).

APPENDIX A

Note: The details of publications given in the following notes owe much to *A Bibliography of Siegfried Sassoon*, by Sir Geoffrey Keynes.

(1) Sassoon began publishing poetry with *Poems* in 1906. This was the first of ten privately printed pamphlets to appear before the outbreak of the Great War. The full list of these, in order of publication, is as follows: *Poems* (1906); *Orpheus in Diloeryium* (1908; never published in revised form, as was intended in 1913); *Sonnets and Verses* (1909); *Sonnets* (1909); *Twelve Sonnets* (1911); *Poems* (1911); *Melodies* (1912); *Hyacinth* (1912); *Ode for Music* (1912); *The Daffodil Murderer* (1913). (Two further pamphlet collections of early lyrical poems are: *Discoveries* (1915) and *Morning Glory*, 1916). The pre-War pamphlets included, altogether, eighty-nine poems, chiefly lyrical, a short dramatic 'episode', *Orpheus in Diloeryium*, an *Ode for Music* and a lengthy narrative poem, *The Daffodil Murderer*, intended as a parody on Masefield's *The Everlasting Mercy*. With the exception of the last-named, all of these pamphlets were printed in numbers between thirty-five and fifty and distributed privately. Two of them were virtually still-born: the story of the mishaps attending the two printings of *Orpheus* is amusingly recounted in *The Weald of Youth* (pp. 149-151), to the effect that no copy of the revised version exists, even in the author's possession; *Sonnets and Verses*, including thirty-four poems, suffered an almost equal fate, since Sassoon was so disgusted with his efforts on receiving them back from the printers that he threw all but four copies on the fire (see *The Weald*, p. 24 and *A Bibliography*, p. 25).

From these pamphlets only eleven poems, dating from 1908 onwards, survive in the *Collected Poems* and one, 'By the Way', appears in *The Weald* (p. 23), to exemplify the poverty of the young poet's imagination in 1908; in addition to these, only *The Daffodil Murderer* is now (though with some difficulty) obtainable. However, two further pamphlets published before his first volume, *The Old Huntsman*, appeared in 1917, yield a much higher survival-rate: from *Discoveries* (1915) eleven out of thirteen poems, and from *Morning Glory* (1916) all seven lyrical poems, have earned re-publication in the *Collected Poems*. These eighteen poems were, many of them, reprinted, with some revisions, in *The Old Huntsman*, but in the collected edition Sassoon has placed them in his Section III, 'Lyrical Poems: 1908-1916', since in style and subject-matter they should be separated from the early War poems.

This chapter is concerned, firstly, with the thirty early lyrical poems that Sassoon has chosen to preserve (and which form a more than fairly

representative selection of his early poetry: he has himself shown an understandable disinclination to assist any further critical grubbing amongst his
juvenilia); secondly, with the narrative poems, *The Daffodil Murderer* and
'The Old Huntsman'. The latter poem, though first published with the War
poems in 1917, belongs with the earlier work in subject-matter and forms
a convenient bridge between the two groups.

(2). It is interesting to compare Sassoon's beginnings with those of his
fellow warpoet Wilfred Owen, who was also as a poet unrealised before
he went to war. Like Sassoon, Owen was aided by his mother in his early
ambition to write, for which she made all allowances; Owen, too, developed
late, confined (more unavoidably than Sassoon) to a provincial life until
his early twenties and, apart from his contact with the French poet Laurent
Tailhade, lacking a critical environment. But Owen's early life was shadow-
ed, unlike Sassoon's, by his family's shortage of money: there was a continual
conflict between his own conviction that he could only realise himself as
a writer and the pressure of family circumstances which necessitated his
working and making his way in the world. It is in this essential difference
between their beginnings that one sees why Owen could meet the challenge
of the Great War with a tougher mind, more able than Sassoon's to ob-
jectify suffering. But the Great War stimulated both poets in much the
same way as did the French Revolution the tame young Wordsworth: it
released their vital being from stifling circumstance.

(3) Sassoon's poems of the Great War have almost all been republished
in *Collected Poems*: 35 from *The Old Huntsman*: 38 from *Counter-Attack* (one
omission: 'The Triumph') and all 10 from the English edition of *Picture-
Show* (if one includes 'Everyone Sang', which perhaps most readers regard
as simply welcoming the Armistice; Sassoon, while including it in *War
Poems*, stresses in *Siegfried's Journey*, p. 141, that it was intended also to
applaud the coming "Social Revolution"). The ten war poems included in
the *Collected Poems* version of *Picture-Show* are: 'Reconciliation', 'Concert
Party', 'Night on the Convoy', 'The Dug-Out', 'Battalion-Relief', 'I stood
with the Dead', 'Memorial Tablet', 'Ancient History', 'Aftermath' and
'Everyone Sang'. Sassoon included all but 'Ancient History' in *War Poems*.
In the American edition of *Picture-Show* (1920), two war poems, 'In an
Underground Dressing-Station' and 'Atrocities', were added: together with
'Return of the Heroes', these were published in England in *War Poems*
(1919), but have not been reprinted. Sassoon has therefore retained altogether 83 of the 87 poems originally published. This is a much larger
number than any of the other principal war poets has left: almost twice as
many as Owen and Blunden, and incomparably more than Read, Graves,
Rosenberg or Richard Aldington.

  The very number puts the critic on his guard. It is notable, as in the
case of his early poems, that Sassoon has reprinted poems such as a poet
like Robert Graves would long ago have omitted from his *Collected Poems;*

Graves retains none of his war poems printed in *Over the Brazier* (1916) and only a few from *Fairies and Fusiliers* (1917). Whereas Graves's criterion has been a fairly rigorous one of poetic excellence, Sassoon seems to have been more concerned to render a true picture of his varied responses to war. That Sassoon could be critical of his work is shown by the fact that in the special edition of *War Poems* which he compiled for publication in 1919 as "A tract against War" he omitted no fewer than 28 of his 89 poems—21 more than he excludes from *Collected Poems*. In compiling *War Poems* he was clearly concerned with quality and force: he omits most of the early romantic poems and many of those that are weakened by sentimentality or extreme subjectivism. The poems omitted from *War Poems* but included in *Collected Poems* are: 'Absolution', 'To My Brother', 'The Dragon and the Undying', 'France', 'To Victory', 'Golgotha', 'A Mystic as Soldier', 'A Subaltern', 'A Whispered Tale', 'To His Dead Body', 'The Choral Union', 'Enemies', 'Stretcher Case', 'Conscripts', 'Secret Music', 'The Last Meeting' (from *The Old Huntsman*); 'The Investiture', 'Thrushes', 'Invocation', 'Dead Musicians', 'In Barracks' (from *Counter-Attack*). Though one would wish to add to this list, only 'Enemies' seems to have been harshly treated. There is no doubt that if these omissions were made from *Collected Poems*, the impact of Sassoon's war poetry would be greatly strengthened. When it is realized how self-critical Sassoon could be, one is grateful to him for preserving almost intact the map of his poetic response to the War and not leaving it to be laboriously unearthed from scarce and faded volumes.

(4) With the publication of *Picture-Show* in June, 1919, Sassoon returned to his pre-war practice of private printing. The original (English limited) edition contained 34 poems, all of which, with the single exception of 'Cinema Hero', are reprinted in *Collected Poems*. An American edition appeared in 1920, with 7 additional poems: 'In An Underground Dressing-Station', 'Atrocities', 'The Portrait', 'Phantom', 'Early Chronology', 'Falling Asleep' and 'Limitations'; of these, only the last three have been reprinted. Thus, of the 41 poems contained in the two editions, 36 are reprinted in *Collected Poems*. Ten of these have already been considered as war poems, and two—'Early Chronology' and 'Sporting Acquaintances'—come under the heading of Satirical Poems and will be considered in Chapter IV.

(5) In poems IV, V and VI in *The Heart's Journey* and 'In Sicily' (*Vigils*, 11), but these are also marred by clichés and poeticalities; only the last-named, a Mediterranean 'Dover Beach' in a muted key, has freshness (and hints, like 'The Imperfect Lover', tantalisingly at unexplored areas of feeling.)

Another kind of love, between father and son, is expressed more strongly in *Rhymed Ruminations*: though three of the four poems, 'Meeting and Parting', 'To My Son' and 'A Blessing', are given a somewhat cramped sincerity by the bareness and formality of expression; the most satisfying is 'The Child at the Window', where the reflections upon the relationship between father and child spring from a natural occasion by which that relationship is warmly evoked:

> Remember this, when childhood's far away;
> The sunlight of a showery first spring day;
> You from your house-top window laughing down,
> And I, returned with whip-cracks from a ride,
> On the great lawn below you, playing the clown.
> Time blots our gladness out. Let this with love
>   abide . . .

The reflections that follow, on the child's unconscious power to lighten the cares of maturity, though their phrasing tends back to the conventional, command the greater indulgence because of the intimacy established by the fresh opening stanza. One wishes Sassoon had allowed himself more such moments in his personal poetry.

(6) *Recreations* and *Lingual Exercises*, the two volumes immediately following *Picture-Show*, contain poems chiefly satirical: these were incorporated in a single volume, *Satirical Poems*, published in 1926, which represents the principal part of Sassoon's post-war output to that date. After 1926, few satirical poems were written; in the Second Edition of *Satirical Poems* (1933) only five new poems were added, and of these the two last-named are not, strictly speaking, satirical: 'The Utopian Times', 'Mammoniac Ode', 'Memorial Service for an Honest Soldier', 'The Traveller to His Soul' and 'Facts'. *The Road to Ruin* (1933) contains seven inter-related poems prophesying war: it is distinct in style and purpose from the contents of *Satirical Poems* and will, together with a few allied poems from later volumes, receive separate consideration.

It seems unnecessary to give any detailed consideration to *Poems by Pinchbeck Lyre*, pseudonymously published in 1931. It is a collection of 14 brief jeux d'esprit, some witty, others scarcely so, but none having the least serious purpose, satirical or otherwise. They are chiefly absurd pieces on the themes of beauty and romantic love, mingling the 'poetic' with the prosaic, or rueful laments for the poet's lot in the modern world; this, entitled 'Requiem', may be taken as a typical sample:

> Swing tripe, swing tosh! You need no longer worry
> About your sales; now Nemesis is drumming;
> No need to sing of Switzerland or Surrey,
> Or ask when immortality is coming.
> Scrawl slowlier, fountain-pen; put by your bosh.
> Prepare to be forgot. Swing tripe, swing tosh!
>
> Swing tosh, swing tripe! The game indeed is up.
> You must imbide your bowl of Lethe Cup.
> The absurd advertisement, the gushed reclâme
> Henceforth can do you neither good nor harm.
> Only in cold irrevocable type
> Your requiem remains. Swing tosh, swing tripe!

(7) Surtees furnishes many models for these bold descriptions; he achieves his effect by an accumulation of epithets and a concentration upon a single aspect of the character's appearance or physique, building it up to absurd proportions. The following example is the introductory description of Mr. Jogglebury Crowdey, who is a *very* poor hunting-man:

... when we say that he went by the name of Woolpack, our readers will be able to imagine the style of man he was: long-headed, short-necked, large-girthed, dumpling-legged little fellow, who, like most fat men, made himself dangerous by compressing an unreasonable stomach into a circumscribed coat, each particular button of which looked as if it was ready to burst off, and knock out the eye of any one who might have the temerity to ride alongside of him. He was a puffy, wheezy, sententious little fellow, who accompanied his parables with a snort into a large finely plaited shirt-frill, reaching nearly up to his nose. His hunting-costume consisted of a black coat and waistcoat, with white moleskin breeches, much cracked and darned about the knees and other parts, as nether garments made of that treacherous stuff often are. His shapeless tops, made regardless of the refinements of 'right and left', dangled at his horse's sides like a couple of stable buckets; and he carried his heavy iron hammer-headed whip over his shoulder like a flail (*Mr. Sponge's Sporting Tour*).

Trollope's description of Mr. Slope also provides an excellent parallel: "His hair is lank and of a dull pale reddish hue. It is always formed into three straight lumpy masses, each brushed with admirable precision, and cemented with much grease; two of them adhere closely to the sides of his face, and the other lies at right angles above them ... His face is nearly of the same colour as his hair, though perhaps a little redder: it is not unlike beef,—beef, however, one would say, of a bad quality ... His nose, however, is his redeeming feature: it is pronounced straight and well-formed; though I myself should have liked it better did it not possess a somewhat spongy, porous appearance, as though it had been cleverly formed out of a red coloured cork" (*Barchester Towers*). Trollope also has the faculty of succinct caricature: "Captain Culpepper was a man with an enormous moustache, and a great capacity for slaughtering game" (*Framley Parsonage*).

(8) Other characteristics of diction occur less frequently than in the poetry: such coinages as "aunthood", "jogglesome", "whiskyfied", and double-epithets—as in the descriptions of Mr. Bellerby's mare ("ewe-necked, weak-middled, dun-coloured,") and Fred Buzzaway ("blue-jowled, dog-faced",) —form a relatively minor part of the comic description. The latter feature seems to be a part of 'horsey' vocabulary; it is very common in Surtees, who has, for example: "a worn-out, three-legged, four-cornered hack" (*Jorrocks's Jaunts*); "the well-known Mr. Thomas Slocdolager, a hard-riding, hard-bitten, hold-harding sort of sportsman" and "long-headed, short-necked, large-girthed, dumpling-legged little fellow" (*Mr. Sponge's Sporting Tour*).

(9) *Memoirs of an Infantry Officer* must be almost as well known as the first volume of the trilogy, though it has probably been much less widely read. (Though extracts were serialized in *The Daily Telegraph*, 6-26 August, 1930; *Sherston's Progress* was also serialized, but in extracts in the American *Nash's Pall Mall Magazine*, June—August, 1936). First published in 1930 as one of the sudden crop of War books which appeared in that and the previous two years, it was issued in eight different editions (including three illustrated) during the next four years. Unfortunately, the figure for the total number of copies published is not available: but 20,000 copies were published in the first edition alone and the number published in the cheap edition, five times reprinted, must have been much greater. An American edition (number of copies undisclosed) was also published in 1930. A German translation appeared as late as 1947, perhaps reflecting a post-Second War interest in such books—no doubt it would have been risky to publish an anti-war book in the Germany of the 1930s. A Swedish translation of 3250 copies was published in 1952. There was no French translation, which is surprising. *Sherston's Progress* also went through a large number of editions —six in England (plus a re-publication in Penguin Books, in 1948) and a Swedish translation (1955). There was no American edition, though (as noted above) extracts were published, and it was included in an American edition of the *Complete Memoirs*. There was no French translation and, as was to be expected at the time, no German.

(10) It is interesting to compare the mature approach of two Socialist-minded near-contemporaries of Sassoon, Leonard Woolf and H.G. Wells, to this question. Both take the middle way. Leonard Woolf defends bourgeois family life of this period in terms which, considering his socialist sympathies, might have been expected of Sassoon:

It is because I condemn its economic basis and its economic effect upon other classes that I have been a socialist for most of my life. But the social standards of value in Lexham Gardens [his London home] were very high, much higher than in any proletarian society today or in the proletarian section of a mixed class society. There is much which can be or has been legitimately said against family life on the grand scale, as developed by the middle classes of the nineteenth century: its snugness and smugness, snobbery, its complacent exploitation of economic, sexual, and racial classes . . . Yet it also had high aesthetic values . . . The actual relations between the human beings living in these large house-holds and between the several households related by blood or friendship were, on the whole, in my remembrance extraordinarily human and humane. How much simpler everything would be if everything were either black or white, good or bad. (*Sowing*, 1960, pp. 36-37).

H. G. Wells, whose autobiography reveals the hardships of a lower class family and the odds against which their children struggled to win some kind of education in the latter part of the 19th Century, nevertheless acknowledges the positive influence of the more leisured and privileged class:

Out of such houses came the Royal Society, the Century of Inventions, the first museums and laboratories and picture galleries, gentle manners, good writing, and nearly all that is worthwhile in our civilization today. Their culture, like the culture of the ancient world, rested on a toiling class. Nobody bothered very much about that, but it has been far more through the curiosity and enterprise and free deliberate thinking of these independent gentlemen than through any other influences, that modern machinery and economic organization have developed so as to abolish at last the harsh necessity for any toiling class whatever . . . (*Experiment in Autobiography*, 1934, pp. 136-137).

(11) This conclusion relates to Sassoon's political position and is an attempt to explain his failure to commit himself to the socialist cause. Nevertheless, despite his disillusionment brought about by the General Strike, he did not lose his sense of social justice, as is shown by his championship of the depressed miners two years later. In the *New Leader* of May 4, 1928, he published a satirical poem 'Doxology de-Luxe' (not reprinted) attacking the gilded frolics of the London 'season' at a time when thousands of miners scarcely knew where to turn for the barest necessities of life. In a footnote to the poem he wrote: "I will recant these words when the Mansion House Fund for Distressed Mining Areas has reached £ 500,000. At the time of writing the Conscience of the British Nation appears to be worth about £ 80,000 (which includes the consciences of several banks and prosperous commercial organisations)."

But this was an humanitarian rescue operation, not a political act. His heart was on the right course, but his head feared to follow where it might lead him.

Sassoon was not alone in his reaction. As the last quotation given from *Laughter in the Next Room* suggests (see p. 167), Sir Osbert Sitwell's sympathies underwent an evolution—or decline—similar to Sassoon's. The angry young satirist of *Before the Bombardment* and the 'vers-libres' broadsides of the 1920s was also to become bitterly disillusioned by the course of events. Looking back after thirty years, he writes: "In 1919 the popular reign of piracy, exalted to a creed, had begun. Whole classes were eradicated so that the world should in time be made safe, on the one hand, for a beer-logged trades-unionism in the victorious countries, and, on the other, for Hitler and Bolshevism" (*Laughter in the Next Room*, p. 5). Antony Clarendon, the hero of a novel by a third war poet surviving into the 'Twenties, Richard Aldington, reflects more soberly on the reason for his disillusionment with Socialism; he concludes "The only effective revolution is a change in people's minds and hearts. And then violence isn't necessary" (*All Men Are Enemies*, 1948 (reprint) p. 313).

(12) *On Poetry* was delivered at the University of Bristol in 1939. The principal secondary source for his poetic ideas is *Meredith*, where his comments upon Meredith's poetry are interesting rather insofar as they reveal Sassoon's views about the nature and purpose of poetry than for anything

very illuminating about Meredith. Elsewhere his views on the subject can
be pieced together from passing comments on his own and others' poetry,
notably in *Siegfried's Journey* and *The Weald of Youth*, and in his articles as
Literary Editor of, or contributor to *The Daily Herald*.

The view that Sassoon said most of what he thought worth saying on the
subject in his lecture is borne out when we consider what he has to say
elsewhere. In his Foreword to *Piers Prodigal* (1960) we find a voice identical
with that of over twenty years previously in the lecture and in the early
autobiographies. He had had little to say publicly about poetry before 1939,
so that by the time he came to write his lecture his views had been forged
and hardened by the practice of some thirty years.

(13) He describes himself in *Meredith* (p. 153) as "no critic, but a tolerable
appreciator," and "appreciator" where others would write critic is a recurrent term in his *Daily Herald* articles. He has an aversion for the scholar's
methods, as is well shown in the brief correspondence in *The Times
Literary Supplement* which followed the publication of *Meredith*. In the December 4th, 1948 issue of this magazine there appears a letter from an
American scholar, Richard B. Hudson, in which some facts concerning the
management of Meredith's estate in his youth are cited as contradicting
"the standard treatment of Meredith's youth" as followed by Sassoon
(after S. M. Ellis).

On December 11th, Sassoon writes acknowledging the new facts "ruefully". He welcomes them, he goes on, because "so little is known of
Meredith's early life that any 'new facts' are valuable." But he adds a tart
piece of advice for those "who pursue such researches among documents
in public record offices." They would "do well to digest one of Meredith's
sayings to his friend Clodd: 'chiefly by that in my poetry which emphasizes
the unity of life, the soul that breathes through the universe, do I wish to be
remembered; for the spiritual is the eternal.'" Sassoon has, of course, no
obvious justification for treating Hudson so roughly: that he should have
offered this gratuitous advice denotes the strength of his animus against
"the journeyman critic."

(14) Had Sassoon written at length on Hardy's poetry instead of Meredith's,
it is likely that, valuable though that would have been biographically,
heart and head language would have become similarly confounded. He did
once think of doing so, but decided against it because, he wrote to Sir
Sydney Cockerell, "Plenty of people can do, and have done it, better than I
could" (*The Best of Friends*, p. 200). Inevitably, his relationship to Hardy
in recent years has become analogous to that of one of Hardy's earliest—
and best—critics, Lionel Johnson. Reviewing Johnson's *The Art of Thomas
Hardy* in 1923, Sassoon commented how "The book has an unusual interest
through the fact that Johnson was an ardent convert to Roman Catholicism.
In writing his essays on Hardy's novels he was confronted by Hardy's
philosophy of determinism, which was the antithesis to his own cloistral
ritualism"; despite this, "his integrity as a critic stood the shock; and no

one has paid a nobler tribute to Hardy's genius" (*The Daily Herald*, 27 June 1923). At that time, of course, Sassoon knew no such divided sympathies as Johnson's. An earlier article on Thomas Hardy in the 'Great Names' series which he ran in the *Herald* is highly eulogistic: Hardy is praised for his "flawless artistic integrity", for realising that "the true satisfaction of life lies in imaginative conflict"; "*The Dynasts* stands among the greatest works of all time"; his "wistful understanding of the human scene" and his "despair" are acknowledged, but as "mitigated by tenderness and pity for his fellows" (27 October, 1920). Nothing in these articles suggests the extent to which Sassoon's personal vision would later diverge from Hardy's, but, regardless of this, there is no doubt (as the portrait in *Siegfried's Journey* and the poem 'At Max Gate' witness) that Sassoon's respect for Hardy's integrity and compassionate attitude has, like Johnson's, prevailed over differences of creed.

(15) It is salutary to note that, although in *Meredith* Sassoon consistently objects to Meredith's uncongenially didactic poetry on artistic grounds, he is prepared much later to relax his attitude in favour of a heavily didactic poem, 'Babylondon', in Ian Davie's *Piers Prodigal* (1961), which he praises as "a deep indictment of the murderous din and desecration which pervade our modern materialism" (Foreword). It is indeed a preaching poem, in which William Blake is imagined orating at Marble Arch; it opens:

> I behold Babylon in the opening streets of London:
> Soul-mongers, vendors of flesh,
> Fouling the secret places of desire,
> Lechers and lank youths in an evil corner,
> Reversing all the order of delight.

These opening lines are a fair sample of the whole. The rhetoric rings hollow: the opening—"I behold"—at once gives an inflated, artificial effect, which is carried on by the too inevitable near-clichés "soul-mongers", "vendors of flesh," the euphemistic third line, the archaic "lechers" and the weak last line, which adds nothing significant to the meaning of the third. These first lines characterise the poem's tone: it is an exercise in artifice, a "sermon" without bite; its rhetorical denunciations, in an awkward archaic mode, could be applied to any time—there is no vital reference to our own. "Modern materialism" is not distinctly under attack. Sassoon's approval of the poem stems, as is not the case in his response to Meredith, from the fact that he can now share the poet's religious convictions: he praises Davie's poem "yet more", he writes, "for its concluding compassionate appeal to redemption and absolution through Divine Authority." It is this poem's very purpose, it seems, that makes it praiseworthy.

(16) For the first publication of the poems to be discussed here Sassoon reverted to his earlier practice of small private printings: *Common Chords* was published in an edition of 107 copies, *Emblems of Experience* in one of 75,

and there were 100 copies of *The Tasking*. Together, these did not receive ordinary publication until 1956, when they were published by Faber and Faber under the title *Sequences* (3000 copies). A small edition of this volume appeared in the United States in 1957, his first poems to be published there since the *Collected Poems* of ten years before. Similarly, 'Lenten Illuminations', a long poem about his adoption of the Roman Catholic faith, also received only limited publication, of 35 copies, in November 1958. It was reprinted, together with 'Sight Sufficient' in a large edition of 2000 copies in 1959: but since this was published by the Catholic *Downside Review* (Downside Abbey, Bath), it is unlikely to have been widely read outside Catholic circles (see Chapter XIII).

(17) "Aftercome" is an uncharacteristic coinage: it is probably an echo of Hopkins' "aftercomers" ('Binsey Poplars'). Sassoon's coinages are, like Hardy's—a stronger influence—almost invariably more straightforward: typical are double-epithets uniting various parts of speech (though chiefly nouns and participles), e.g. death-fearing, gloom-regarding, blind-souled, and nouns coined by simply adding a suffix (usually 'ment' or 'hood') to a noun or verb, e.g. vintagement, consolement, revealment, worldhood, guesthood, soulhood. Their meaning is usually immediately apparent and they lack the intensity of Hopkins' coinages; they seldom violate conventional grammar. Other examples more akin to Hopkins are: "unworlded" ('"We Shall Not All Sleep"'), "disfleshment" ('The Present Writer'), and "unfuturing" ('The Worst of It').

(18) Sassoon had been received into the Church in 1957: he refers in a letter to *The Times*, dated October 1st, 1957, to "my submission" to the Roman Catholic faith. This "submission" was apparently recent, since it had become the occasion of a distasteful piece of journalism involving *The Sunday Express*. This newspaper had sent a reporter to interview the famous convert, who had promptly informed his interviewer that he was unwilling to be 'written up'—a reaction which he believed was understood. Accordingly, he had entertained the journalist to tea and talked freely, on the understanding that nothing he said was to be reported. In the event, a lengthy story appeared in the paper, treating the conversation as an interview. Sassoon protested in the letter to *The Times* (Oct. 1st, 1957) against "my most sacred intimacies being exhibited as newspaper publicity"; he wrote again on October 5th in answer to a defensive letter from the editor of *The Sunday Express*. No apology was made.

(19) *The Path to Peace* comprises poems drawn mainly from the later volumes but going back also to the 1909 *Sonnets* (with 'Before Day'); it was published by the Stanbrook Abbey Press in two private editions severely limited by both number and price: there were 20 copies of the one, at £ 12 12s, and 480 of the other, at £ 5 5s. Of the 30 poems, six were of recent date and previously unpublished. The poems in order of appearance in the volume, with the dates of the new ones given in brackets, are:

Awaitment (November 1960)
The Power and the Glory
A Prayer to Time
As I was Walking
Heart's Journey [*Vigils* '14']
Morning-Glory
The Merciful Knight
Before Day
Befriending Star
It Has Been Told
Alone
Another Spring
Human Bondage
Resurrection
Redemption
The Need
The Contention
Can It Be? . . .
Renewals
Faith Unfaithful
A Chord
Nativity [*H. J.*, XXXII]
Lenten Illuminations II, lines 22-46.
Deliverance (1957)
Lenten Illuminations IV
Arbor Vitae (1959)
Unfoldment (1960)
Sight Sufficient
Rogation (1959)
A Prayer at Pentecost (1960)

(20) 'Marshianism' seems a term preferable, in this context, to 'Georgi-
anism', which is too broad and much debased: it is used here of the insipid
'regulars', as James Reeves calls them, of Marsh's anthologies—not of the
true poets, Sassoon himself, Housman, W. H. Davies, De la Mare, Edmund
Blunden and Andrew Young, who wrote and were to continue to write if
not in modern forms at least out of genuine emotional and sensuous experience, a quality which distinguished them from their fellow contributors
in the *London Mercury*. With these poets in mind, one cannot use the term
'Georgian' in the wholly pejorative sense which has become customary—
as, notably, in C. Day Lewis's witty *A Hope for Poetry*. It is to Marsh's credit
that he included such poets, but his name must carry the blame for his
encouragement of so much that was trivial—though it should be conceded
that his editing was often, if not critical, charitable.

APPENDIX B

The Daffodil Murderer

If anybody likes to hear
A tale of wretchedness and beer,
Though 't isn't much to brag about,
The prison-chaplain's wrote it out.

When round the farmstead I was wanderin',
I always did a deal of ponderin',
But since they've clapped me here in quod
I've tackled all things under God.
And also not being used to settin'
Indoors all daytime without sweatin',   10
Where once my hands and feet was busy,
Now brains keep working till I'm dizzy:
So chaplain says he's sure I'd best
Be brave and get it off my chest.

It's rotten here in Lewes gaol,
Where chaps eat porridge out of a pail
And chew potatoes badly boiled
And chunks of bread that baker's spoiled.

It's rotten here to lie and listen
To lovers in the twilight kissin'   20
Out in the street on Tuesday nights
Before the man goes round and lights
The flaring lamps between the houses:
And in the country where the cows is,
It fair upsets me for to think
That now the lads go up and drink
At village pub where barman serves
Them out a tonic for their nerves.

When I'd done work and had my tea,
And jumped the kiddies on my knee,   30
I used to go like them chaps now
And fuddle at the 'Barley Mow':
I used to go and squander wages

On beer that swills but never 'suages;
For Mugglesby, the publican,
He don't deal fairly with a man;
It's 'nutty flavour', so he tells us
That makes the thirsty shag he sells us
Taste salt and sour; I dunno what 'e
Puts in with it, I'm almost dotty.   40

'Tis autumn now and winter's comin',
And in my head I hear a drummin'
Of 'Lewes 'sizes, Lewes 'sizes;
The Judge has done, the jury rises.'

And there I'm standing in the dock
Before the rail, and taking stock
Of crowds of faces ranged around me;
And listening when they say they've found me
GUILTY! the same as every pup
Know'd when first they shut me up.   50
My name'll be in all the papers,
And lace-figged Sheriff cuts his capers;
Judge puts a black thing on his head
And drones 'you hang till you be dead.'
I know it all; I've seen it often;
The Judge's face will never soften;
The lawyers'll whisper about their fees
And pleecemen go home to their teas.
And one fine morning bright and early
They'll wake me, though I'm sleepin' rarely,   60
And Ketch will slip into my cell
And bind me for his drop to Hell.

I hope I shan't stand looking sickly;
I hope they'll get it done with quickly;
And as they lead me to the gallows
I'll think of peewits on the fallows,
Flapping their wings and sadly calling
Because it's cold and twilight's falling.

If you would hear of gold and glory,
You'd best turn up another story;   70
My days were always drab and sordid;
What gold I earned I never hoarded;
If you've seen shires and country places,
You've met a million such-like faces
As mine, no better and no worse,
With mouths that drink and brawl and curse.

When father took a maid to wive,
I never asked to be alive;
When parson at the altar wed 'em
And through the marriage-service read 'em,   80
And on her finger clapped the ring,
I never asked to live and swing.

Parson soon will preach a homily
In church of how I've shamed my family;
With book and saw he'll curse and pray for me,
Then never another word will say for me.
Village soon will tire of chatter,
And gabble of a newer matter:
And for a month I'll live notorious,
A bye-word to the smug and curious;   90
Another month and I'll grow rotten
Like a dead dog, and sleep forgotten.

God alone, if God there be,
Will have a word to say to me:
He'll ask for no excuse, I'm sure,
When I come up to Heaven's door
With saints and infidels and thieves,
And every mortal thing that grieves,
And dies like I do, glad to go,
And learn whatever is to know.   100

So snug I lie in Lewes gaol;
Chaplain's corking down my tale,
Quick across the page he scrawls it;
'Human document' he calls it—
Chaplain he's both hard and soft,
And has rebuked my folly oft;
Says I've an unrepentant mind;
But he's a homely man and kind.
He knows there's dirtier rogues than me,
Wearing broadcloth, walking free;   110
Knaves as go to church on Sunday,
And cheat their fellow-men on Monday.
I'd sooner starve than live like that,
And wear a shiny Sunday hat:
I've done a crazy deed of shame,
And never thought to 'scape the blame:
But shifty lawyer robs his lord,
Then takes a ship and bolts abroad;
Cheating broker makes his pile,
And then sets up to live in style,   120

I was christened Albert Meddle;
My father used to trudge and peddle
From house to house with tracts and hymnals,
And books that godly folk and criminals
Could read and take a sober lesson from,
And hope to gain God's holy blessin' from.
Dad wasn't sober nor forgiving;
He sold his stuff to make a living;
He didn't bring us kids up cleanly;
Let us run wild and fed us meanly;   130
He never taught us wrong from right,
But squatted by the fire at night
Dipping his nose into a tumbler;
As for his wife, he liked to humble 'er:
His clothes were bad, but hers were tatter'd;
For him the only thing that matter'd
Was earning money, not to bank it,
For every night he sat and drank it.

Dad never loafed in public-housen,
But bought his whisky by the dozen;
Bottles, bottles, how he loved 'em;   140
Along the cupboard-shelf he shoved 'em,
One by one he'd count their number:
His children were like useless lumber.
Nine young children had he got,
Live or die, it matter'd not:
Mother went without her dinner,
And watched us grow, not tall but thinner:
Mother loved when first she mated him;
When she died, cripes, how she hated him!

You that sneer and look askance   150
At gaol-birds, ask if they'd a chance
Of ever being honest men;
And you'll not find there's one in ten
But grew to manhood lesson'd well
In every trick that fills up hell.
I was taught to lie and snivel
And palter to the parson's drivel;
I was taught that folk as lack
Must rob behind another's back:
I grant you I'm an evil person;   160
The wonder is I'm not a worse 'un.

When I'd done school, I went to labour
For Farmer Clay, that was a neighbour;

I used to mind the horses draggin'
To and fro the jolting waggon—
Did easy jobs about the farm;
Mayhap I came to no great harm—
But soon I know'd what little evil
Father'd not learned from the devil:
Reaching twenty years, and choosin'   170
To get wed, I married Susan;
That was seven winters gone,
And we've seven children born;
Two was twins, and all are living,
Dad's ill deeds to be forgiving.

Now Susan mopes at home and stitches
At mending Sydney's Sunday breeches,
And wonders how she'll buy 'em food,
Them kiddies sitting hushed and good:
Syd and Tom and Kate and Sue,   180
Bob and George and baby Loo;
One by one she counts them over,
Loving pledges of her lover;
She was happy to be his'n;
Now he's fast in Lewes prison—
Little good he ever did her,
Yet she'll weep when she's a widder.

Lord of grace and charity,
Make my children better'n me:
I'm a broken man and low;   190
Through my weakness let them know
How to build on fairer hope
Than of hangman and his rope;
Let them make a brighter end
Than to welcome death as friend.

* * * *

Now darkness falls, and weary Sue
Gets up and draws the curtains to,
And stirs what little fire there's burning;
To the victual-cupboard turning,
Gets out the loaf, and spreads the cloth,   200
And wishes there was mutton-broth
And eggs and jam for children's bellies,
To feed them plump and glad, poor sillies.
Then she puts the kettle on,
And knows that all the milk is gone,

And there's scarce wood to make the water
Boil for tea-time as it oughter.

Four and thirty nights ago
Home I trudged and found 'em so;
Kids to table sitting up,   210
Drinking milk from mug and cup;
George and Tom, as bold as brass,
And blue-eyed Kate, the eldest lass;
Baby rolling eyes at ceiling;
And cat a-chawing 'tater peeling;
Kettle squeaked and clock went tick-tack;
Lamplight shined on brass and knick-knack,
Text and coronation picter;
I trod on pussy's tail and kicked 'er;
Chucked me boots down by the dresser,   220
And likely kissed the baby, bless 'er.
'Twasn't many words I spoke;
I finished tea and had a smoke,
Then put on my boots again
To walk the half-mile up the lane,
And have a pint at 'Barley Mow',
Same as I allus used to do.

In the bar I found 'em sittin',
Talking garbage, drinkin', spittin';
Amos Smith'd got half-a-crown   230
For digging out a fox on the down—
Dug 'im out for dogs to eat 'im;
Huntsman know'd as they'd defeat 'im;
He's a turrible one to catch 'em—
Killed a leash last week at Patcham.
Ted Brown come in then, cousin t' Amos;
He'd got a dirty yarn to shame us;
Med us laugh to split our throttles,
While Mrs Mugglesby 'ranged bottles,
And looked as if she'd served out ale   240
Twelve years and never heard sich a tale.
They were all of 'em drink-merry;
Amos' face was red as a berry;
Ted Brown, as usual, 'gan to stick up
His nose and argue 'tween his hiccup;
For he's a chap that when he's drinking,
Must allus differ in his thinking
From what another says, and then 'e
Will back his 'pinion, quid to a penny!

I never utter'd nowt that night   250
But what he starts to set me right;
We wrangled, waxing lousy-hot,
And then he ups my beer, the sot!
'Look out', says I, 'you take and drop it;
'You're swiggin' at my mug, so stop it.'
Says he, 'You hold your gabble, Bert.'
'It's mine, I say, you lump o' dirt.'
'I say it ain't.'
              'It's mine, I tell 'ee.'
'Then, Bert, your beer's gone down my belly.'
'Gimme that jug, you blasted skug,   260
'Or else I'll bash your ugly mug.'
'I won't.'
      'You will.'
             'Leggo my ear.'
'If you must take and booze my beer,
'I'll pour it down your blanky neck.'
'Then pour it, and you'll larn a trick
'My knuckles know, you knock-kneed shrimp!'
'Come on and try, you filthy pimp!'

The lads were watching tense and eager,   270
But publican, so thin and meagre,
Steps in with Bill, the chucker-out;
Says he, 'Now, now, what's 't all about?'
We'd started scuffle, stopped to holler,
When Bill, he grabbed me by the collar,
Down steps and through the door he pitch'd me,
And as I stagger'd out there, fetch'd me
A clout as left me cold and dizzy
Where all my brains had bin so busy.
Soon Ted in 's turn came flying after;   280
Bill grunted; them chaps shook wi' laughter:
I heard 'em plain though door was shut;
My elbows ached, my head was cut,
I'd bumped my shoulder on the scraper:
He'd hoofed me out as light as paper,
And all the guts inside my belly
Were shaking like a Christmas jelly.

'Another pint for me', says Hewitt,
Though he was greasy-drunk and knew it;
I heard 'im plain; the other blokes   290
Were all so jolly making jokes
About the vinegar and plasters
As Ted and me would want, poor blasters.

I heard that mutton-fisted Bill
Drop some pennies in the till,
And Mugglesby was whining mockery
At us, and sweeping up the crockery
We'd smashed; I heard the glasses tinkle,
And Hewitt wheezed, 'Now, lads we'll drink all
'A health to Bill-the-barman's feet,
'Because he kicked 'em out so neat.'
Another up and shouted, 'Fill 'ee
'A mug o' stuff for good ole Billy.'

So all the fools began to toast 'im,
And butter his conceit and boast 'im
The finest chap they'd clapped their eyes on;
Folk loves a lout to waste their lies on—
'Here's health to Bill; if Ireland's troublin',
'They ought to make 'm King o' Dublin.'
And 'Cheer-o, Bill, here's luck to you;   310
'You blanky gave them beans, those two.'
'Here's good ole Bill;' 'Bill, you're a toff.'
Bill grinned and swigged his beer straight off.
I looked at Ted and scratched my chin,
And felt the smear of blood begin
Down my stubbly cheek to trickle;
Then, because brawling makes men fickle,
I said, 'Ole man, belikes we oughter
'Slip home and stick our heads in water.
'Inside the 'Barley Mow' it's snug   320
'Swilling ale from a blue mug,
'But crouching in a stinking gutter
'And harking to the bilch chaps utter,
'That ain't the work for you and me.'
Ted got up and rubbed his knee;
A pretty pair of bucks we showed
As we went slouching down the road.

Ted never spoke but limped on surly:
The hour was neither late nor early;
I heard the bark of parson's setter,   330
And thought meself was feeling better;
Grocer'd gone to bed I knew,
And the village lights was few.
I wondered was the missis sitting
Beside the empty grate and knitting,
Or getting up to let the cat in
When at the door she heard it scrattin'.
We got to parson's gate; Ted stopped

And said, 'I'll catch 'im what I've copped;
'I won't be knocked about by Bill;
'I'll do 'im in, by cripes, I will.'

I wasn't feeling angry then,
But Ted, he roused me up again;
I'd have just gone home to bed,
And missus plastered my sore head;
I'd got no spite for him as struck
And pitched me out into the muck:
Big Bill and me'd bin boys together;
My aunt had wed his cousin's father
That was a carpenter at Ripe   350
And died of eating poisoned tripe:
To Hailsham Fair with him I'd been;
I'd bowled his wicket on the green;
His uncle shaved me once, that's barber
And keeps a shop by Seaford harbour.
But Ted kept on until he'd got
Me fair upset and rankling hot,
And when I'm mad I'll own I'm double
The chap is Ted for making trouble.
Says he, 'Of water Bill's not fond;   360
'We'll take and put 'im in a pond.
'I'm not afeard of scum like that.'
I felt the cut throb where my hat
Had lost the lining; 'Aye, let's chuck 'im,
'We'll give 'im plenty worse than water,
And smash him proper as we oughter.'
'He's stronger 'n me,' says Ted, 'or you;
''Tis cunning as we've got to do;
'Slink up behind and knock 'im silly;   370
'That's how we oughter settle Billy.'

So back we turned, and past the 'Barley'
With windows lit and noise of parley;
The booze was all they cared for heeding;
No scholarship for them nor reading;
But pouring porter down their neck'n
Was what they wanted most I reck'n.

A narrow lane runs up to Bill's;
His cottage stands close to the hills,
A lonely mile from pub and village,   380
Among the turnip fields and tillage.
I wonder'd whether Ted would budge;

Up lane we went through mire and sludge:
O clod-pole feet so blindly going,
O seed that wasn't worth the sowing,
O bumpkin bodies filled with hate,
A-picking squabbles with your fate!
I didn't think of Susan then,
And how the kids 'd grow to men
And curse the murderin', blundering dad   390
Who made their name sound rotten bad;
I only said, 'You wait, by Gosh,
'And see me ketch that swine a cosh.'

Nigh half-way up the lane we set
Under the hedge so dripping wet;
I heard dogs bark a distance off;
Out in the fields a sheep 'ud cough
Like an old man that's got an ague
Or any ill that comes to plague you.
The sky was clear and rain had gone;   400
I watched the blinking stars that shone
And thought, 'Them things 'll see us broke,—
'Me and many another bloke.
'They watch some beggar breaking stone
'For workhouse task, all skin and bone;
'They hear 'im bashing till he sickens
'Of grinding grit for some one's chickens.
'They see the King and Queen at Windsor,
'And hear the story that he spins 'er
'Of how he's been to pheasant-shoots   410
'With Jew-boy lords that lick his boots;
'And they look down on all the wonder
'And sorrow that do make men ponder.'

Ted was afraid; he sat and shook;
I knew he'd like to take his hook;
He weren't so bucksome now, Ted weren't,
And would have said so but he durn't.
I thought how in the summer weather
When Bill and me was boys together,
We'd often come this way when trudgin'   420
Out by brooks to fish for gudgeon.
I thought, 'When me and Bill are deaders,
'There'll still be buttercups in medders,
'And boys with penny floats and hooks
'Catching fish in Laughton brooks.'
I'd often scrapp'd that lubber Bill,
And never bore 'im no bad-will;

I knew it wasn't that I cared
For what Bill had done; but Ted had dared
Me for to give him back a clout   430
Because he'd bin and chuck'd us out.

'He'll see us here,' Ted whisper'd soon.
'No fear,' says I, 'there ain't no moon.'
Clock struck eleven, slow and careful;
Church-bells do often make me prayerful—
Thoughts holy-like, as if you heard 'em
But didn't reckon how to word 'em.
'Twas silent then; Bill's feet approachin'
Sounded like keeper's, when you're poachin'
And close you crouch amid the trees'n,   440
Hold your breath as will come wheez'n,
Till keeper shouts, 'Come out, so please yer,'
And blunders on and never sees yer.

Bill seemed hours and hours a-comin';
'Home, Bill Bailey,' he was hummin';
Kicking flints up with his toes,
Back from his evening's work he goes—
I wonder now what Bill was thinking;
Belike 'twas nowt, for he'd bin drinking,
And blokes that stumble home from boosing,
They haven't got no thoughts worth losing;
He pass'd me by, all strained and ready;
Thump went my heart, but I was steady;
I'd got the pluck as wants no bracing;
I tripp'd him up and kick'd his face in—
Bill blinked his eyes and gave a guggle,
And lay there stiff without a struggle;
'Here, Ted,' says I, 'I've clumped 'im fair'—
Looked round, but Ted, he wasn't there.
Ted never had the guts to do it;   460
I done the job and got to rue it.

Bill huddled there across the road;
I felt his face all wet with blood;
He mid be stunn'd; I went to fetch
A drop of water from the ditch;
I sluiced him well; he never stirred;—
Holler'd his name; he never heard.

*   *   *   *

At 'Barley Mow' Bill's done with drawing;
He'll never hear the chaps there jawing

All evening through, and singing catches,   470
And calling out for beer in batches.
He'll never hear the wind come blowing
Through door in gusts when some one's going
Out to the dark where no one fuddles,
And starlight glints on roadway puddles.

I thought, 'Here's summat can't be hidden;
'They mid suspect me and they midden;
'If they can prove 'twas me, that settles
'My hash', I wiped my boots on nettles;
Took one more gape at Bill there dead,   480
And then went lurching home to bed.
The house was dark and Sue was snorin';
That bed I only slept once more in.
Next day was Sunday; fate had bested me;
'Bout dinner-time the police arrested me.
I held my tongue; gave no denial;
And Squire committed me for trial.

                    *   *   *   *

Dusk falls; in here 'tis lonesome-like;
Some chap goes down the street on a bike,
Ringing his bell; he's gone in a jiffey
Down Brighton road; I wonder if 'e
Has got his lamp lit; then some motors
Goes by; and a hawker selling bloaters.
Perhaps there's folk as know'd me well
Looks up and wonders if I'd sell
My soul alive to get out pardon'd;
They dunno how my heart is harden'd
Agin the thought of living on;
I'll not be sorry to be gone:

There's one I'd like to have a word with,   500
And get a hand-shake to be cheer'd with;
And tell 'im I took no offence
For how he treated me long since.
'Tis certain sure before I die
They'll let Sue in to say good-bye.
She'll have to leave a lot unsaid;
Her face'll be so swelled and red.
Like a good gal she'll make small fuss;
I'll hug her once and gi' 'er a buss;
Because her man she mun be leaving,
Her man as isn't worth the grieving.

She'll have to live with her old mother;
Mayhap in time she'll wed another.

Goodnight to life; good-bye to Sussex
With all its lanes and shaws and tussocks;
When I'm away and out beyond,
Belike of Sussex I'll grow fond:
It ain't a lushy place to live in,
But ther's some worse 'uns under heaven.

Now the stars come out and gleam
Over flood and field, and stream;
Rooks and daws have gone home winging;
Cows are in, and church-bells ringing:
Train goes by and stops at station;
Foxes bark in Firle plantation,
Out there I laboured from a lad,
And lived and found it none so bad.
Here like a rat in a cage I wait
For the hangman and his mate.

O seasons passing by   530
Like clouds across the sky,
There's summat mortal strange
In storm and shine and change;
I see it now so clear,
The waking of the year,
When Easter wind is keen
And woods are growing green;
O dusty summer days
When cattle drink and graze
Till harvest builds the rick,   540
And ground's as hard as brick.
O autumn falling slow,
When maids and children go
For blackberries, and fill
Their baskets on the hill.

O golden autumn weather,
And apples ripe to gather,
And white rime-frost at morn,
When huntsman blows his horn;
O all things I remember,   550
Who've seen my last September.
O all pure things I've known,
Let now my feet be shown

The way that leads aright
My spirit through the night;
And when my breath shall cease,
Grant me to sleep in peace.

(First published, 1913)

APPENDIX C

SOME BOOKS OF THE GREAT WAR COMPARED

This does not pretend to be a comprehensive survey of the English narratives of the Great War: its limited purpose is to put the Sherston Trilogy in the broad context of war writing by comparing it with a few other war books whose angle of vision is near to Sassoon's. The wide range of war books can be divided into two utterly distinct categories: describing war experience either from the viewpoint of the necessarily responsible and necessarily detached officer or from the level of the ranks, where suffering had to be so much more passive than active. The books to be chiefly discussed–with the partial exception of the novelistic *Death of a Hero*, which fits to some extent into both categories and comfortably into neither–belong to what may be called the officer's war. The War as seen from the mass subordinate level was, as Frank Richards puts it in his unique account by a regular private soldier, *Old Soldiers Never Die* (1933), "a different war". Richards, though capable of humane and compassionate feeling, was tough, hardened to war's most atrocious shocks, exceptionally qualified to endure all with resignation. But a more unusual kind of private, Frederic Manning, refined, scholarly, deeply concerned with ultimate questions, who proudly called himself 'Private 19022', and who projected much of his own experience and outlook into the character of Private Bourne, also gives us a different war. Inevitably, in *Her Privates We* (1930), it is his fellow privates whose reflections, fears and imaginings are at the centre: the officers are seen, though plausibly, consistently from without—we never live in their consciousness and feel the weight of their special burden of responsibility and decision (and Bourne realises that his taking a commission will radically alter his outlook). To compare such books as these, excellent though they are within their own field of reference, with Sassoon's work would suggest too many differences for profitable comparison: but later in this essay something more will be said about what seems the most important element that distinguishes narratives of the privates' from those of the officers' war.

   The books which we shall consider chiefly are those by Edmund Blunden, Robert Graves, Richard Aldington and Sir Herbert Read.[1] Sassoon's

1. Edmund Blunden, *Undertones of War* (1928: World's Classics, 1956); Robert Graves, *Goodbye to All That* (1929: Penguin, 1961); Richard Aldington, *Death of a Hero* (1929); Herbert Read, *The Contrary Experience* (1963: including for the first time "A War Diary, 1915-1918," in addition to "In Retreat," which, written as early as 1919, was first published in 1925, and "The Raid", first published in *The Innocent Eye*, 1946.)

narrative, like these others, hinges upon the experiences and reactions of one man who feels bound to bear the burden of others' fate as well as his own under the unique stress of war. It is distinguished from them mainly in that it gives the reader a more complete and profound insight into the *shaping* effects of this test upon the character and sensibility of this man. This distinction derives partly from the structure of the narrative, partly from the nature of the hero.

Throughout the Trilogy we are in the closest touch with the (often contradictory) thoughts and emotions of the hero in all their intensity. This produces a more concentrated effect than is the case with the narratives of Blunden and Graves, which are more objective and reveal minds more resilient under the stress of war. Read's two accounts, the "Diary" and the short narrative of an episode from his experience, do not form an integrated whole; the longer of these, the "Diary", is chiefly an account of the intellectual activity that the writer maintained in spite of the War. *Death of a Hero* most resembles the *Memoirs* in design—and here one would have to include the latter part of the first volume of Sassoon's trilogy— in that the focus of concern is the mind of the hero and its response to a succession of testing experiences.

Winterbourne (Aldington's hero) is, however, a very different kind of character from Sherston. At the outbreak of the War he has already achieved intellectual maturity and, as he thinks, emotional security: he is happily married and lives in an environment that both stimulates and satisfies his mind (more than half the book is devoted to his pre-War life; it corresponds in this respect to the major part of *Memoirs of a Fox-Hunting Man*). The War abruptly terminates this life and causes him, at first, acute mental suffering: "from the shock of the abrupt change from surroundings where the things of the mind chiefly were valued, to surroundings where they were ignorantly despised"[2]. At war, he extends his human experience and develops his sympathies; he learns, too, to value the positive qualities men display in times of adversity. He compares his comrades with his former companions who had failed to volunteer and finds the latter wanting. His experience is the familiar one: as time passes, the Front Line and the men there become the reality, at home there is only ignorance, hysterical patriotism, forgetfulness. Forgetfulness above all: he finds himself estranged from his wife, who no longer recognizes the man she knew; to her, he is dull, his mind has gone dead, he harps only upon the War. The crisis for Winterbourne is her rejection of him and her identification with the civilian world he despises. He becomes increasingly morbid about the War, leaves for France for the last time in an overwrought condition and finally exposes himself deliberately to machine-gun fire and is killed.

If, as in the *Memoirs*, the hero of Aldington's book is the focus of interest, the psychological stresses which he undergoes are more diverse than Sherston's and are not wholly attributable to War experience. In Sherston we see the shaping of a mind under stress of war; in Winterbourne we see

2. *Death of a Hero*, p. 276.

that the War has acted as a disruptive agent upon a mind and a life already, in essential respects, formed. Sherston develops, albeit painfully, enlarging his awareness and capacity for life: Winterbourne decays, the fabric of his life torn to shreds: "Once he had been extremely interested in himself and the things he wanted to do; now he didn't care, he didn't want to do anything in particular . . . If he had been told there and then that he was discharged from the Army and could go, he wouldn't have known what to do except stay there and stare at the poppies or daisies."[3]

Sassoon's hero differs also from Aldington's—and from the portrayals of themselves given by Graves and Read—in that his mind is intellectually a virtual *tabula rasa*. This fact, combined with a high degree of emotional vulnerability, renders him more susceptible to the extreme effects of the immediate experience. Whereas it is clear from their accounts that both Graves and Read possessed a more phlegmatic temperament and a degree of maturity which enabled them better to come to terms with their environment. In Graves's case, as the early chapters of *Goodbye to All That* show, the battle for survival in public school life had already produced in him a considerable hardening to conditions of adversity. Similarly, Read's early struggles to make his way in the world had led him into a wider involvement with people of all kinds and had brought rapid intellectual maturity. In 1915, he tells us, he was already "a regular reader of the *New Age*",[4] and his "Diary" written in the Front Line reflects a greater concern with the new Socialist State that is to be built after the War than with the immediate horrors and discomforts he endures: "as soon as peace is declared," he writes, "the one and only hope is International Socialism."[5] The abstract theorising of the "Diary" is far removed from the emotional socialism toward which Sherston fumbles in his fellow-feeling for the men who serve under him.

In kind Sassoon's hero has most affinity with Blunden's.[6] They share a certain ingenuousness; neither of them is "life-learned" and neither has achieved an intellectual standpoint: "What my book does not include," writes Blunden, "is obvious to a new generation—political and sociological interests, for instance . . ."[7] They have a similar sensibility: an acute aliveness to their natural surroundings, from which they draw a certain resigned and acceptant consolation, and whose beauties they take every opportunity to record. Their reflections are often homely and nostalgic: "it was as though in this part the line could only be a trifling interruption of a happy landscape. I thought, the vicarage must lie among those sheltering boughs."[8] They feel compassion for the men they command and devote themselves to their welfare (a characteristic they share with the other

3. Ibid. p. 394.
4. *The Contrary Experience*, p. 210.
5. Ibid. p. 118.
6. In his contribution to *Edmund Blunden: Sixty-Five* (Hong Kong, 1961), Sassoon writes: "I have known Edmund Blunden for forty-two years; and from our first meeting recognised him as my fellow poet in Peace and War" (p. 166).
7. *Undertones of War*, Preface, p. ix.
8. Ibid. p. 12.

writers). One could extend these affinities much further, but this would
involve transferring attention from the heroes to the narrators. The fundamental difference between the two accounts is that, in Blunden's, the
immediate reactions to experience and the retrospective view of it are
inextricably intermingled; Blunden does not set himself, like Sassoon, to
recapture the complex psychological reactions of an earlier self developing
under the stress of war. Blunden's young officer is not shown as mentally
tortured; he appears from the outset more phlegmatic and is more emotionally balanced: "for once," he recalls his feelings after an especially ruthless
German attack, "a little hate was possible."[9] "For once"—such moments
are rare in Blunden's account.[10] We see him surviving as best he can *within*
the situation, as if (though this is not stated) he were already sadly reconciled
to the knowledge of man's illimitable inhumanity to man. He is not torment-
ed by the wider issues: as in his war poems, Blunden's emphasis is upon
the twin consolations—those of nature and of human comradeship: "The
heartiness of tried companions was the only real refuge."[11] His detachment,
as he points out in the last paragraph of the book, stems from an essential
innocence: "I might have known the war by this time, but I was still too
young to know its depth of ironic cruelty"; he characterises his recollected
self, most aptly, as "a harmless young shepherd in a soldier's coat."[12]

It is, then, in the intensive delineation of the shaping of a man's character
and sensibility under the pressure of war experience that the *Memoirs* are
most distinctive. Also distinctive is their underlying poetic texture, (discussed in Chapter VI), by means of which the doings of men at war are
thrown into tragic relief against the background of the timeless and indestructible processes of nature. There is nothing of this second dimension
in Aldington and Graves, little in Read:[13] Aldington is concerned chiefly
with psychological analysis of his hero, Graves with recording the sheer
reality of life in the trenches, and Read's only studied accounts are brief
and deal with two episodes, giving the flavour of action and some insight
into the problems an infantry-officer had to face; he aspires to nothing
more, the "Diary", as has been said, being primarily a means of intellectual

9. *Ibid.* p. 82.
10. "Here are neither heroics nor loud complainings against fate. Here, if anywhere,
is a gentleman at war" (A. C. Ward, *The Nineteen-Twenties*, 1930, p. 160). Doubtless,
"gentleman" is used here in its purest sense.
11. *Undertones*, p. 240.
12. *Ibid.* p. 314.
13. For Read, as for Sassoon and Blunden, Nature can be a consolation, but it
represents nothing more. There is evidence in the following quotation from the
"Diary" of a desire to avoid going beyond the strictly personal: "The fields are all
misty and the shadowy trees mysterious. In many places we have just reaped a
harvest sown by the Germans in spring. And what scene can compare to a harvest-
field by moonlight? Yellow stooks pitched like the tents of an army: perhaps a
dark wood flanking one side of the picture: and the clumsiest farmstead you could
possibly desire somewhere in the misty perspective. Such joys as these make us
forget entirely the horrors none of us desire to remember. Things even seem 'worthwhile." (*The Contrary Experience*, p. 108.) Had Read employed such material for the
composition of a longer narrative, such passages would probably have acquired
symbolical significance.

self-communing. Again, the narrative that most resembles Sassoon's in this respect is *Undertones of War*.

Blunden's book is also manifestly the work of a poet, of one who "loves the experiment of words."[14] Upon every page, however humdrum the subject-matter, there is a care for the precise word and for imaginative description. This care is never more evident than when he turns to nature, to reflect with autumnal sadness upon her cruel torment at the hands of men: "Still I hear their slouching feet at last on the footbridge over the Ancre by Avelny, where a sad guard of trees dripping with the dankness of autumn had nothing to say but sempiternal syllables, of which we had our own interpretation. The shadows on the water were so profound and unnavigable that one felt them as the environment of a grief of gods, silent and bowed, unvisitable by breeze or star ...";[15] or, "taking the joyful path away from the Line," to find: "Acres of self-sown wheat glistened and sighed as we wound our way between, where rough scattered pits recorded a firing-line of long ago. Life, life abundant sang here and smiled; the lizard ran warless in the warm dust; and the ditches were trembling quick with odd tiny fish, in worlds as remote as Saturn".[16] One could quote many more such passages, each one as finely textured, which stand in silent contrast with man's busy destruction. "Silent" because, unlike Sassoon, Blunden seldom points the contrast by a sharp juxtaposition of the symbols of peace and war or by explicit comment; moreover, he has an eye for the smaller effects (the "rural petty beauties")[17] and thus achieves none of the broader, more portentous contrasts we find in Sassoon. A restrained sadness governs his perceptions: "The worst of the place was that one only had to go to the doorway to see at one view (between the crashes) as brutal a landscape as ever was, and a placid distance of grey-blue hills gently regretting that one more harvest was done."[18] One feels that he sympathizes with Nature in the rôle of a fellow and—because powerless to resist—most undeserving sufferer: "On the blue and lulling mist of evening, proper to the nightingale, the sheep-bell, and falling waters, the strangest phenomena of fire inflicted themselves."[19] Nature lives for him in an almost human sense, the personification of gentleness and tranquillity. At the end of the book, looking upon the freshly ripened fields around the once devastated Albert, he asks wistfully: "The mercy of nature advances. Is it true?"[20] A question Sassoon does not raise, since, like Hardy, he presents Nature as indifferent to man's worst endeavours and certain to outlast them, but he is at one with Blunden in desiring her "advance".

Concomitant with the more refined poetic texture of their books is

14. *Undertones*, Preface, p. x.
15. Ibid. pp. 154-155.
16. Ibid. p. 31.
17. Ibid. p. 181.
18. Ibid. p. 287.
19. Ibid. p. 17.
20. Ibid. p. 313.

Blunden's and Sassoon's abstention from what one might term 'total' realism. This does not mean, as we have seen in Sassoon's case, that they do not paint the horrors of war: it does mean that their realism is selective. Only in *Goodbye to All That*, amongst these English prose accounts of the War, do we find unstinting realism.[21] Graves concentrates less upon his own reactions (i.e. those of the hero) than do the other writers, but acts rather as reporter and commentator, setting down 'the worst'. One recalls that it was Graves, not Sassoon, who initiated the realistic poetry of the War[22]; one is also reminded of Sassoon's comment upon Graves's attitude to the War (in the character of Cromlech): "[He] distrusted sublimation and seemed to want the War to be even uglier than it really was. His mind loathed and yet attached itself to rank smells and squalid details".[23] Graves's method of achieving mastery over the experience is to set it down precisely as it is, forcing oneself to encompass the worst: a form of defence for the sensitive mind.

In this respect the distinctive feature of *Goodbye to All That* is not its greater proportion of horrors, but its franker *human* realism. It reveals, not merely the cowardice or cynicism in man, but also his sadism, ruthlessness and obscenity with a degree of lifelike exactitude that extends even beyond the range covered by Sassoon's poetry of the War. In a passage like this we hear the authentic voice of man speaking in tones that none of the other writers we have discussed endeavours to reproduce:

We had to stand aside to let a stretcher-case pass. "Who 'sthe poor bastard, Dai?" the guide asked the leading stretcher-bearer. "Sergeant Gallagher," Dai answered. "He thought he saw a Fritz in No Man's Land near our wire, so the silly booger takes one of them new issue percussion bombs and shoots it at 'im. Silly booger aims too low, it hits the top of the parapet and bursts back. Deoul! man, it breaks his silly f—ing jaw and blows a great lump from his silly f—ing face, whatever." The wounded man had a sandbag over his face. He died before they got him to the dressing-station.[24]

Many readers would no doubt, find this shocking; they might even reject it as callous and untypical. They would be wrong: here, as Maugham's hero in *Of Human Bondage* discovers in hospital experience, are "facts"—

---

21. Blunden's realism has not been discussed; though certainly it is less marked than Sassoon's or Graves's, the following brief example illustrates that the horror is not wholly absent: ". . . the shell had burst all wrong. Its butting impression was black and stinking in the parados where three minutes ago the lance-corporal's mess-tin was bubbling over a little flame. For him, how could the gobbets of blackening flesh, the eye under the duckboard, the pulpy bone be the only answer?" (*Undertones*, p. 74). Such passages gain force from their rarity. The following note from his "Diary" shows Read's distaste for realism (he refers to a volume of war-poetry): "I'd rather write one pastoral than a book of this realism. My heart is not in it: it is too objective" (*The Contrary Experience*, p. 122).
22. See *Goodbye to All That*, p. 146.
23. *M.I.O.*, p. 152.
24. *Goodbye*, p. 84.

life as it is, men as they are. In a similarly objective manner, Graves records many other 'facts'—more unpalatable than cowardice and desertion: "At all events, most overseas men, and some British troops, made atrocities against prisoners a boast, not a confession."[25] "There were no restraints in France; these boys had money to spend and knew that they stood a good chance of being killed within a few weeks anyhow. They did not want to die virgins. The *Drapeau Blanc* saved the life of scores by incapacitating them for future trench service. Base venereal hospitals were always crowded. The troops took a lewd delight in exaggerating the proportion of army chaplains to combatant officers treated there."[26] Sassoon makes no such assertions as these, from a reluctance, it seems, to report anything he has not observed at first hand. He refers disapprovingly to Cromlech's (Graves's) attitude in this respect: "His information was all secondhand; but to hear him talk—round-eyed but quite the man of experience—one might have imagined that Amiens, Abbeville, Bethune, and Armentieres were mainly illuminated by 'Blue Lamps' and 'Red Lamps', and that for a young man to go through Havre or Rouen was a sort of Puritan's Progress from this world to the next."[27] Whatever the truth of the matter, it is evident that, if Graves has an inclination to pay exaggerated attention to the strongly animal aspects of man's reactions to danger, Sassoon tends to play them down. Blunden virtually excludes them, and it is on this score especially that he is open to the charge he alludes to in his Preface to *Undertones of War*, of "casting a romantic light on such a damnable subject as real war."[28]

25. Ibid. p. 154.
26. Ibid. p. 195.
27. *M.I.O.*, pp. 152-153.
28. The differences in approach between these three writers may best be illustrated by means of three parallel passages—on the theme of bayonet instruction:
(i) Sassoon: "But the lecturer's voice still battered on my brain. 'The bullet and the bayonet are brother and sister.' 'If you don't kill him, he'll kill you.' 'Stick him between the eyes, in the throat, in the chest.' 'Don't waste good steel. Six inches are enough. What's the use of a foot of steel sticking out at the back of a man's neck? Three inches will do for him; when he coughs, go and look for another" (*M.I.O.*, p. 16).
(ii) Blunden: ". . . a Scottish expert, accompanied by well-fed, wool-clad gymnastic demonstrators, preached to us the beauty of the bayonet, though I fear his comic tales of Australians muttering 'In, out,—on guard', and similar invocations of 'cold steel' seemed to most of us more disgusting than inspiring in that peacefully ripening farmland" (*Undertones*, pp. 100-101).
(iii) Graves: "In bayonet-practice, the men had to make horrible grimaces and utter blood-curdling yells as they charged. The instructors' faces were set in a permanently ghastly grin. 'Hurt him, now! In at the belly! Tear his guts out!' they would scream, as the men charged the dummies. 'Now that upper swing at his privates with the butt. Ruin his chances for life! No more little Fritzes! . . . Naaoh! Anyone would think that you *loved* the bloody swine, patting and stroking 'em like that! BITE HIM, I SAY! STICK YOUR TEETH IN HIM AND WORRY HIM! EAT HIS HEART OUT!' Once more I felt glad to be sent up to the trenches" (*Goodbye*, pp. 195-196). Blunden registers his disgust, barely suggesting its cause, and turns away with distaste from an uncongenial subject, better forgotten; Sassoon gives a fair impression of the reality, though he seems to have censored it, perhaps in the interests of 'good taste'; only in Graves's vigorous reportage does the initiated reader recognise total reality.

However they may differ in their presentation of war experience, these writers are all much akin in their attitude to the War and to war in general. Each narrative is clearly anti-war—even Blunden's "sketch of a happy battalion",[29] for he is continually forced to lament its destruction—while from two, Sassoon's and Read's, we learn of minds driven to positive pacifist action.[30] Graves, though he takes no such action, is seen at the beginning of 1917 (shortly before Sassoon's protest) to share Sassoon's convictions: "We no longer saw the war as one between trade-rivals: its continuance seemed merely a sacrifice of the idealistic younger generation to the stupidity and self-protective alarm of the elder."[31]

In each book the development of the pacifist attitude is closely related, not so much to revulsion from the horrors of war as to a passionate valuation of what Sassoon terms "the humanly rewarding aspects of war service";[32] the growth, under the stress of war, of comradeship and cooperation between men. The significance of this is well expressed in these words about Aldington's hero, Winterbourne: "He hated the War . . . hated all the blather about it, profoundly distrusted the motives of the War partisans, and hated the Army. But he liked the soldiers, the War soldiers, not as soldiers but as men. They had saved something from a gigantic wreck, and what they had saved was immensely important—manhood and comradeship, their essential integrity as men, their essential brotherhood as men".[33] The painful question became, How to save these men from further senseless destruction, so that these qualities could be applied to the struggle, not of war, but of peace? Sassoon, as we have seen, sought in time of war to awaken the

29. *Undertones*, Preface, p. viii.
30. Here again there is a contrast between characters and reactions: Sassoon's pacifism, as we have seen, was emotional in both origin and expression, whereas Read's stems from the wedding of his War experience with his theoretical socialism. In the *Memoirs* we find Sherston struggling with a book by 'Thornton Tyrell' in a vain endeavour to complete his education as an "intellectual pacifist" (*M.I.O.* pp. 298-299): we find Read, on the other hand, in a "Diary" entry (dated 10.1.18) writing an article for *New Age* drawing attention to the "immense growth of pacifist opinion" in these terms:
I know my men and the sincerity of their opinions. They know the impossibility of a knock-out blow and don't quite see the use of another long year of agony. We could make terms now that would clear the way for the future. If, after all that Europe has endured, her people can't realize their most vital ideal (Goodwill)—then Humanity should be despaired of—should regard self-extinction as their only salvation. But I for one have faith, and faith born in the experience of war (*The Contrary Experience*, p. 117).
31. *Goodbye*, p. 202. These writers all criticize politicians and senior staff officers for their inhumane conduct of the War. Their attitude cannot be ascribed wholly to a poet's abnormal sensitivity, for, though various generals and politicians have found apologists, there are sober historians enough willing to commit themselves to a similar view: "In truth, the politicians and soldiers of the First World War were gamblers; not however in the sense of risk, but of obsession . . . As with a gambler, the concentration on each current play mentally obscured the total extent of mounting losses, prevented any sober and detached assessment of the mounting cost of further continued losses. So they went on deeper into the blood, the lies and the hatred" (C. Barnett, *The Swordbearers*, 1963).
32. *S.J.*, p. 22.
33. *Death of a Hero*, p. 296.

APPENDIX C

conscience of the ignorant and complacent by means of his public protest.
That he would fail in this was realized at the time by Graves, who believed
that the only way to give effect to one's convictions was to continue to
sustain, as far as one could, the human values one had discovered by
serving at the Front where one belonged: ". . . I took the line that everyone
was mad except ourselves and one or two others, and that no good could
come of offering common sense to the insane. Our only possible course
would be to keep on going out until we got killed."[34] Sassoon represents
Graves's attitude in a similar way: "[only] people who've been in the real
fighting have any right to interfere about the War . . . All they can do is to
remain loyal to one another."[35] Aldington's Winterbourne seeks more
emotionally to identify himself with the men whose qualities he has learnt
to admire; he feels "that he ought to stay in the ranks and in the line, take
the worst and humblest jobs, share the common fate of common men."[36]

   That this admirable unity should have been born of a war in which
ideals were so little at stake is a tragic irony. It is ironical, too, that the
inspiring view of humanity in adversity that each of these writers redeems
should itself be something whose existence we can only imagine: "All that
comradeship," says Read in the Preface to his "Diary", "was to vanish
once the storm was over and the expeditionary forces (as they were significantly called) had returned to the platitudes of life . . ."[37] Wistfully, Blunden
reflects of his "old friend Sergeant Clifford": "This man loved his work,
and wrestled with its problems as nowadays people struggle to prepare huge
strikes."[38] But none of these writers is led, by a nostalgic wish for this ideal
state of human unity which it had been their privilege to know, to glorify
war.[39] Each, within the varying limits prescribed by his own temperament
and the aim he has set himself, has followed Sassoon's vital dictum, that
"All squalid, abject, and inglorious elements in war should be remembered."[40]

* * * * * * *

As was pointed out at the beginning of this essay, all the books so far
considered are about 'the officers' war': they focus, to a greater or lesser
extent, upon the response of the single hero or 'leader'. With regard to
unified narrative structure and a certain kind of moral interest—such as
springs from our feeling of involvement with the concerns of the self-

34. *Goodbye*, p. 215.
35. *M.I.O.*, p. 329.
36. *Death of a Hero*, p. 388.
37. *The Contrary Experience*, pp. 66-67.
38. *Undertones*, p. 221.
39. It is gratifying in this connection to be able to quote a German memoirist of the
Second World War, who says: "There is something comforting in the knowledge
that you can depend on the next man under any circumstances. The phenomenon
of comradeship has a fascination all its own. Even such an all-encompassing catastrophe as war brings virtues in its train—when a handful of decent men are
thrown together, their characters allow them no alternative to comradeship. But
what a fantastic argument it is to defend war on the grounds that some of its minor
by-products are not entirely shameful" (Peter Bamm, *The Invisible Flag*, 1st pub.
1956, Penguin trans. 1962, p. 117).
40. *M.F.H.*, p. 291.

revealing narrator—this single focus is an essential part of their strength. But if we think of war rather as a catastrophe that afflicts vast humanity, a recurrent, not local, tragedy, so that man at war becomes the central theme, then none of these books makes the overwhelming impact such a theme requires.

In English, only two books offer to fulfil this larger demand, Frederic Manning's *Her Privates We* (1930) and David Jones's *In Parenthesis* (1937). Both these writers, as the theme requires, seek to withdraw themselves from the centre of the action and to focus attention upon a representative group of suffering humanity: the action takes place, as it must, at the private soldier's level. Both, purely with regard to this high theme, have written noble failures. Whilst Manning's book is unsurpassed for catching the very accent of the common soldier and whilst it breathes an unsentimental compassion, the narrative does oscillate disturbingly between the complex self-awareness of Bourne, the 'hero', and Bourne's detailed and sensitive rendering of what he hears, sees and feels in his relationship with his less complicated comrades. In *In Parenthesis*, the main focus of interest is also the experiences and reactions of men in or near the front line together during a limited period in 1915-1916, before the Somme holocaust; like Bourne's company, these men are shattered and divided by the War. The fault with this book, the most ambitious and deeply pondered attempt to universalize the War, is its conscious literariness. There is certainly much vivid description, both straightforward and 'symbolic', searching reflection and true dialogue, but the total narrative is weighted with literary allusion, both in itself and in discursive footnotes, and with gratuitously elaborate description. One is never allowed to forget the fact—or rather to accept it without the author's insistence—that he has cut his figures to a pattern celebrating 'Britons at war through the ages': "Every man's speech and habit of mind," Jones writes in the Preface, "were a perpetual showing: now of Napier's expedition, now of the Legions at the Wall, now of 'train-band captain,' now of Jack Cade, of John Ball, of the commons in arms . . ." Not only are immediacy of impact and individuality of characterization sacrificed to the painstaking composition of a literary pageant, but also the refined detachment essential to the achievement of Jones's purpose. The literariness always, contrary to his intention, keeps the author before us. Manning, on the other hand, also a fine scholar, limited this kind of resonance to chapter headings in the form of apt quotations from Shakespeare, relying for the rest upon his own capacity to meet creatively the unprecedented demands of a war in which men, more literally than ever before, died like cattle.

Vision will not come by design, though design may produce a painted visionary mask: the 'myth-making' of *In Parenthesis* certainly has a strong appeal today when, lacking an implicit belief in myths, many writers and readers have nevertheless found them an essential framework for their themes. For an example of an unforced visionary quality one must look outside English writing—to Henri Barbusse's *Le Feu*. This book, completed in 1915 and published in early 1916, was—almost incredibly—the very first full-length prose narrative of the War and was written during a few months' convalescence in a military hospital.[41] It is a remarkable example of a total immediate response to harsh experience, controlled by the writer's firm and unsentimental idealism, and expressed with the heightened imagery and force of tragic poetry. Barbusse, like Manning and Jones, takes a squad ('escouade') of ordinary soldiers for his microcosmic description of this world at war, and it must be admitted that in a sense he is less detached in his treatment than either of the English writers: the book doubtless appealed to Sassoon because of its passionate anti-war feeling and it is also the work of an idealistic socialist. But the passionate feeling is controlled at the level of intense conviction; there is no stridency and no self-indulgence. Barbusse is, though present, present as a voice of true feeling, detached from the suffering self, unconcerned with self; he uses his strength to rise above the disintegrating effects of local tragedy and to take a compassionate view which sets it in the context of man's eternal and incomprehensible struggles against the evil he generates.

It is a tragedy of humanity at war, in which war appears as no local manifestation, but as a vast doom encompassing humanity. Upon "un éternel champ de bataille"[42] we watch a representative fraction of this humanity, each of whom we come to know and feel for profoundly, struggling to maintain this essential truth that Barbusse puts into the mouth of one of them: "Nous ne sommes pas des soldats, nous, nous sommes des hommes", dit le gros Lamuse.[43]

The men we see are both men as we know them, in their everyday selves—but weighed upon by the daily abnormal strains of war—and men seeking, in a succession of searching dialogues, to learn why they suffer (as through the ages men have questioned the dispensation of their God). We see man not only as he is, but as he might be.[44] Barbusse endows man, in these dialogues, with the words he would speak if he could but learn to express his deepest perceptions, in the same way as Shakespeare makes his Bates and Williams articulate in *Henry V*.

Le Feu has a quality of concentrated vision, best exemplified in the closing

41. And it was first read by Sassoon when convalescing after receiving his first wound. He describes its strong impact upon him, with characteristic understatement, in *Sherston's Progress:* "I will not describe the effect it was creating in my mind; I need only say that it was a deeply stimulating one. Someone was really revealing the truth about the Front Line." He was moved to place a quotation from *Le Feu* at the beginning of *Counter-Attack*. The book has received variable treatment from English critics: for an enthusiastic view, see A. C. Ward, *The Nineteen-Twenties;* B. Bergonzi, in *Heroes' Twilight*, prefers *In Parenthesis*.

42. p. 7: all quotations are taken from *Le Feu*, published by Ernest Flammarion, Paris 1916).

43. p. 49.

44. Blunden seems to overlook this point when he says, of the men who served under him: "... what men were they? willing, shy, mostly rather like invalids, thinking of their families. Barbusse would have 'got them wrong', save in this: they were all doomed." (*Undertones*, p. 142.) It seems that Blunden has Barbusse wrong: though full of life, Barbusse's men are intended to be more than literal transcripts from life.

scene of the drowned battle-field (Chapter **XXIV**: L'Aube) upon which
the men of both sides are perforce equal in their misery:

Tous ces hommes à face cadavérique, qui sont devant nous et derriére
nous, au bout de leurs forces, vides de paroles comme de volonté, tous ces
hommes chargés de terre, et qui portent, pourrait-on dire, leur ensevelisse-
ment, se resemblent comme s'ils étaient nus. De cette nuit épouvantable il
sort d'un coté ou d'un autre quelques revenants revêtus exactement du
même uniforme de misère et d'ordure.

C'est la fin de tout. C'est, pendant un moment, l'arrêt immense, la
cessation épique de la guerre.

In their last dialogue they are nameless men, who rise above the ignoble
and demoralising hatreds of today:

"Aujourd'hui, le militarisme s'appelle Allemagne . . . Mais demain, comment qu'il s'appellera?"

* * *

Ils voulaient savoir et voir plus loin que le temps présent . . . 'L'résultat! Etre vainqueurs dans cette guerre', se buta l'homme-borne, 'c'est
pas un résultat?'

* * *

Ils furent deux à la fois répondirent, 'Non!"

"C'est nous la matière de la guerre . . . Oui, c'est nous tous et c'est nous
tout entiers."

This is the awareness Barbusse would have men grasp, to use it beyond
today: "Je leur dis que la fraternité est un rêve, un sentiment nuageux,
inconsistant . . . On ne peut rien baser sur la fraternité. Sur la liberté non
plus . . . Mais l'égalité est toujours pareille." But the final word is given,
appropriately, to "un soldat":

Et un soldat ose ajouter cette phrase, qu'il commence pourtant à voix
presque basse:

"Si la guerre actuelle a fait avancer le progrès d'un pas, ses malheurs et
ses tueries compteront pour peu."

APPENDIX D

On Saturday, 5th June 1965, the Honorary Degree of D. Litt. was conferred upon Siegfried Sassoon in a Convocation held at the University of Oxford. The speech delivered by the Public Orator on that occasion was as follows:

Summa profecto salutamus voluptate e secessu illo amoeno elicitum summum poesis ac solutae orationis artificem. in bello quidem illo priore fortiter militavit, a caede tamen immani atque irrita valde abhorruit. qua de re scripsit sane carmina candida quadam indignatione praeclare, at mentio eorum, quamvis honorifica, fortasse poetae saltem opinione statis saepe iam facta est. idem carmina etiam alia interdum edidit, vel ineptias hominum facetiis politis irridens vel gaudia rusticantium serena sapientia contemplatus. inter prosae autem eloquentia exempla maxime, credo, memorati sunt Commentarii Venatoris Vulpium et Tribuni Peditum, in quibus equini generis virtutes et stolida Martis flagitia pari subtilitate ante oculos nostros repraesentat; sed et Vitam Georgii Meredith conscribendo criticum se perspicacem praestitit. si de indole hominis quaeretis, diversitatem quamdam naturae reperietis. celebritatem famae aversatur, iustam sui aestimationem diligit; multos iam annos in villa seclusa degit, idem ingenua arte curriculum vitae suae, idque non uno volumine, lectoribus prodidit, plurimosque omnis aetatis amicos libentissime excipit. nec tamen cuiquam nostrum dubium est quin generosa simplicitate ac mollitia animi ornatus, velut ipse Georgius Sherston, persona huic scriptori nostro non dissimilis, quicquid acciderit, verum rei saporem sua sponte possit percipere. denique non obliviscimur quanta pietate ambo regem salignum observaverint. praesento vobis rusticum urbanissimum, Siegfried Sassoon, Excellentissimi Ordinis Imperii Britannici Commendatorem, Collegii de Clare honoris causa Socium, ut admittatur honoris causa ad gradum Doctoris in Litteris.

Oxford University Gazette vol. XCV, pp. 1288-9 10th June 1965)

The following is the Public Orator's English translation of his speech:

It gives us great pleasure to welcome from his charming retreat an eminent artist in verse and prose. In the first war he served with outstanding courage, but viewed with horror what he felt to be the useless slaughter. His protest he expressed with frank sincerity in his war poems, but the poet himself may be now feel that, however great our admiration, he has been often enough reminded of them. His other poems wittily satirize the follies of mankind, or with quiet wisdom contemplate the joys of country life. Of his prose works perhaps the most important are *Memoirs of a Fox-Hunting Man* and *Memoirs of an Infantry Officer*, in which he vividly portrays the good qualities of the horse and the senseless barbarities of war. His powers as a literary critic he revealed in his biography of George Meredith. His character shows features that may seem somewhat hard to reconcile; he has always disliked publicity, but liked recognition; a large part of his life has been spent in rustic seclusion, yet he has published several delightful volumes of autobiography, and loves to be visited by crowds of friends young and old. But we all recognise his innate good taste and deep sensitivity; in fact like George Sherston, a character who may bear some resemblance to our author, he has an instinct for getting the full flavour of an experience. And we do not forget that they are both devoted to cricket. I present to you a country-dweller of the utmost urbanity, Siegfried Sassoon, C.B.E., Honorary Fellow of Clare College Cambridge, for admission to the Honorary Degree of Doctor of Letters.[1]

1. Reproduced by courtesy of the Public Orator of the University.

APPENDIX E

ARTICLES ETC ABOUT SASSOON'S WORKS

N.B. There has been, hitherto, neither a critical work nor a biography devoted solely to Sassoon.

The following is a guide to the more comprehensive critical pieces or references, with notes indicating their scope:

Anonymous: *The Times Literary Supplement* reviews of (1) *Memoirs of an Infantry Officer*, September 18, 1930;
(2) *Siegfried's Journey*, January 5, 1946; (3) *Meredith*, September 18, 1948;
(4) *The Path to Peace*, February 24, 1961: of the many *TLS* reviews of Sassoon's work these are, critically, the best (See also Woolf, Virginia).

Bergonzi, Bernard: *Heroes' Twilight* (London, Constable, 1965): A chapter on the war poetry; a brief discussion of the 'Sherston Trilogy' in a general chapter about autobigraphical accounts of the War.

Blunden, Edmund: (i) "Siegfried Sassoon's Poetry" (*Edmund Blunden: A Selection of His Poetry and Prose:* London, Hart-Davis, 1950). First published in *The Mind's Eye*, 1934: from the Early Poems to *The Heart's Journey.*
(ii) *War Poets 1914-18* (London, Longmans, 1958) pp. 25-31. General discussion of the war poetry.

Cohen, Joseph: "The Three Rôles of Siegfried Sassoon" (*Tulane Studies in English*, Vol. VII, Tulane University, New Orleans, 1957): the most comprehensive critical essay, written after the publication of *Sequences* in 1956, distinguishing three aspects of personality in Sassoon's poetry— those of 'country gentleman,' 'angry prophet,' and 'self-effaced hermit.'

Darton, J. H.: *From Surtees to Sassoon: Some English Contrasts* (London, 1931).

Enright, D. J.: "The Literature of the First World War" (*The Modern Age:* London, Penguin, 1961). Comparative critical discussion of the war poetry.

Johnston, J. H.: *English Poetry of the First World War* (Oxford, 1964): a chapter on the War poetry.

Maguire, C. E.: "Harmony Unheard: The Poetry of Siegfried Sassoon" (*Renascence*, Vol. XI, No. 3, Spring 1959). Mainly upon the content of the religious poetry from a Roman Catholic viewpoint.

Murry, Middleton: "Mr. Sassoon's War Verses" (*The Evolution of an Intellectual*, London 1920): originally a review in *The Nation*, July 13, 1918.

Parsons, I. M.: *Men Who March Away:* An Anthology of First World War Poetry: Introduction, *passim* (London, Chatto & Windus, 1965).

Pinto V. de S.: *Crisis in English Poetry* (London, Hutchinson, 1951). Chapter VI: "Trench Poets." Comparative critical discussion of the war poetry.

Swinnerton, F.: *The Georgian Literary Scene* (London, Hutchinson, 1935) and *Figures in the Foreground* (London, Hutchinson, 1963): general biographical and critical comment.

Welland, D. S. R: *Wilfred Owen: A Critical Study* (London, Chatto & Windus, 1960). Frequent critical comment on the war poetry, by comparison with Owen's.

Woolf, Virginia: Two reviews in the *Times Literary Supplement:* (1) *The Old Huntsman,* May 31, 1917; (2) *Counter-Attack,* July 11, 1918.

ACKNOWLEDGEMENTS

The author is grateful to the following for permission to quote from the works listed:

RICHARD ALDINGTON: For extracts from *Death of a Hero* and *All Men Are Enemies* to Madame Catherine Guillaume & Mr. Allister Kershaw & Rosica Colin Ltd.

W. H. AUDEN: For an extract from *Look! Stranger* to the author and Faber & Faber Ltd.

PETER BAMM: For an extract from *The Invisible Flag* to the author and Faber & Faber Ltd.

HENRI BARBUSSE: For extracts from *Le Feu* to Ernest Flammarion & Co (Paris).

CORELLI BARNETT: For an extract from *The Swordbearers*, to the author and Eyre & Spottiswoode, Ltd.

HILAIRE BELLOC: For an extract from *Collected Poems* to the author's estate and A. D. Peters & Co.

ARNOLD BENNETT: For an extract from *The Journals of Arnold Bennett*, to the Owner of the copyright, Penguin Books Ltd and A. P. Watt & Son, also to Doubleday & Co., Inc., for quotation from *The Journals of Arnold Bennett*, compiled by Newman Flower (Copyright 1932, 1933, by the Viking Press, Inc.)

BERNARD BERGONZI: For extracts from *Heroes' Twilight* to the author and Constable & Co., Ltd.

EDMUND BLUNDEN: For extracts from *Undertones of War* and *War Poets 1914-1918* to the author and A. D. Peters & Co. For extracts from *Edmund Blunden: A Selection*, to the author and Rupert Hart-Davis Ltd.

GUY CHAPMAN: For an extract from an esssay in *The Victorians and After* ed. B. Dobree, to the author and The Cresset Press.

JOSEPH COHEN: For extracts from 'The Three Roles of Siegfried Sassoon' to the author and the editor of *Tulane Studies in English*.

DAVID DAICHES: For extracts from *The Present Age* to the author and the Cresset Press.

IAN DAVIE: For an extract from *Piers Prodigal*, to the author and the Harvill Press, Ltd.

W. H. DAVIES: For an extract from *Collected Poems* to Mrs. H. M. Davies and Jonathan Cape Ltd.

WALTER DE LA MARE: For an extract from *Collected Poems* to the author's estate and Faber & Faber Ltd.

T. S. ELIOT: For extracts from *Selected Essays, Collected Poems* and *The Four Quartets* to the author's estate and Faber & Faber Ltd.

WILLIAM EMPSON: For extracts from *Seven Types of Ambiguity*, to the author and Chatto & Windus Ltd.

D. J. ENRIGHT: For extracts from 'The Literature of the First World War' (*The Pelican Guide to English Literature, Vol 7: The Modern Age*) to the author and Penguin Books Ltd.

ROY FULLER: For extracts from *Collected Poems* to the author and André Deutsch Ltd.

DAVID GASCOYNE: For an extract from *Collective Poems* to the author and Oxford University Press.

SIR EDMUND GOSSE: For an extract from *Father and Son*, to the author's estate and Wm. Heinemann, Ltd.

ROBERT GRAVES: For extracts from *The Crowning Privilege* and *Goodbye to All That* to the author, Cassell & Co, Ltd., A. P. Watt & Son, and Collins-Knowlton-Wing, Inc.

THOMAS HARDY: For extracts from *The Life of Thomas Hardy*, by Florence Emily Hardy, to the author and Macmillan & Co., Ltd.; For an extract from *Friends of a Lifetime*, edited by V. Meynell, to Jonathan Cape Limited.

C. HASSALL: For extracts from *Edward Marsh* to the author's estate Longmans, Green & Co, Ltd., and David Higham Assoc. Ltd.

G. M. HOPKINS: For an extract from *Collected Poems* to the author's estate and Oxford University Press.

G. HOUGH: For an extract from *The Last Romantics* to the author and G. Duckworth & Co., Ltd.

HUMPHRY HOUSE: For an extract from *Coleridge*, to the author's estate and Rupert Hart-Davis Ltd.

DAVID JONES: For an extract from *In Parenthesis* to the author and Faber & Faber Ltd.

SIR L. E. JONES: For an extract from *Georgian Afternoon*, to the author's estate and Rupert Hart-Davis Ltd.

NORMAN KELVIN: For an extract from *A Troubled Eden* to the author and Oliver & Boyd Ltd.

SIR GEOFFREY KEYNES: For extracts from *A Bibliography of Siegfried Sassoon* to the author and R. Hart-Davis Ltd.

C. DAY LEWIS: For extracts from *Collected Poems 1954* to the author, Jonathan Cape Ltd. and The Hogarth Press, and A. D. Peters & Co. For an extract from *The Poetic Image* to the author and Jonathan Cape Ltd.

JACK LINDSAY: For extracts from *After the Thirties* to the author and Lawrence & Wishart Ltd.

CHARLES MORGAN: For an extract from *Reflections in a Mirror* (2nd Series) to the author's estate and Macmillan & Co. Ltd.

EDWIN MUIR: For an extract from *An Autobiography* to the author's estate and the Hogarth Press, Ltd. For an extract from *Collected Poems* to the author's estate and Faber & Faber Ltd.

Oxford University Gazette: For an extract from the Gazette, to the Public Orator of the University and the Delegates of the Press in the University of Oxford.

WILFRED OWEN: For an extract from *Collected Poems* to Mr. Harold Owen and Chatto & Windus Ltd.

V. DE SOLA PINTO: For extracts from *Crisis in English Poetry*, to the author and Hutchinson Publishing Group Ltd.

SIR HERBERT READ: For extracts from *Collected Poems* and *The Contrary Experience* to the author and Faber & Faber Ltd.

FRANK RICHARDS: For an extract from *Old Soldiers Never Die* to the author's estate and Faber & Faber Ltd.

SIEGFRIED SASSOON: For extracts from *Collected Poems* (1908-1956), *Memoirs of a Fox-Hunting Man*, *Memoirs of an Infantry Officer*, *Sherston's Progress*, *The Old Century*, *The Weald of Youth*, and *Siegfried's Journey* to the author and Faber & Faber Ltd; also to Viking Press, Inc.
For extracts from *Meredith* to the author and Constable & Co., Ltd.; also to Viking Press, Inc.
For extracts from the Foreword to *Piers Prodigal* to the author and the Harvill Press, Ltd.
For extracts from the Foreword to the *Collected Works of Isaac Rosenberg* to the author and Chatto & Windus Ltd.
For an extract from *Poems by Pinchbeck Lyre* to the author and G. Duckworth & Co. Ltd.
For extracts from *The Best of Friends* (Ed. Sir. S. Cockerell) to the author and R. Hart-Davis Ltd.
For extracts from *The Daily Herald* to the author and Odhams Press Ltd.
For extracts from *On Poetry* to the author.

R. SCOTT-JAMES: For an extract from *Fifty Years of English Literature* to the author, Longmans, Green & Co., Ltd., and David Higham Assoc. Ltd.

SIR OSBERT SITWELL: For extracts from *Before the Bombardment* and *Argonaut and Juggernaut* to the author and G. Duckworth & Co., Ltd. For extracts from *The Scarlet Tree, Laughter in the Next Room, Left Hand, Right Hand*, and *Noble Essences* to the author, David Higham Ass., Ltd., and Little, Brown & Co (Boston, Mass.).

STEPHEN SPENDER: For an extract from *World Within World* to the author and A. D. Peters & Co.

F. SWINNERTON: For extracts from *Georgian Literary Scene* and *Figures in the Foreground*, to the author and Hutchinson Publishing Group, Ltd.

DYLAN THOMAS: For an extract from *Letters to Vernon Watkins* to the author's estate and Faber & Faber Ltd.

Times Literary Supplement, The: For extracts from various reviews.

H. G. WELLS: For an extract from *Experiment in Autobiography* to the Executors and Victor Gollancz Ltd.

HUMBERT WOLFE: For an extract from *Notes on English Verse Satire* to the author's estate and the Hogarth Press Ltd.

LEONARD WOOLF: For extracts from *Sowing* and *Growing* to the author and the Hogarth Press, Ltd.

Note: The author apologises for omissions from the above list: in a few cases no reply arrived in time for acknowledgement to be made; if there are other omissions, they are inadvertent.

PAGE REFERENCES

(Chapters V-IX)

The numerals at the left refer to pages in this book. The two italicized words which follow the numerals are the end of the sentence or phrase which is being annotated. The abbreviations used are as given on p. viii.

CHAPTER V: THE SHERSTON TRILOGY (I)

(All references are to *Memoirs of a Fox-Hunting Man*, 'Faber Library' edition)

71 *calling distance.'* " 7
socially impossible.' " 9
73 *the Packlestone.*" 244
to defend." ibid.
goodness meant." 209
her up." 179
(their) faces." 68
74 *his chronicle.*" 185
to it." 262-3
young thruster." 39
modest narrative." 233
75 *or write.*" 130
one field." 17
of myself. 50
in future." 52
76 *unconfessed sympathy.*" 239
and incoherent." 81
looming landscape . . ." 96
of it." 128
been doing?" 150
77 *to happen . . .*" 267
of youth" 270
kill someone." 335
the Churches" ibid.
obscure private?" 313

be done." 341
for 'stand-to'." 344
79 *than vegetative*"), 97
any older"). 98
Morning Post." 75
80 *of characters*" 188
brick-red coats." 32-3
ever encountered" 33-4
absolutely undefeatable . . . 202
81 *patent leather* 218
plum-coloured" 132
niggardly subscriber" 135
automatic style." 90-1
momentous happenings," 82
82 *keen gardener.* 279
to speak." 253
aggressively competitive." 257
83 *green country*") 86
the world . . . 24
and immaturity . . ." 195
84 *contented-looking place.*" 62
without fail . . ." 63
a bridge." 64
the afternoon." 72
85 *kindly scene*" 216

CHAPTER VI: THE SHERSTON TRILOGY (II)

(All references to *Memoirs of an Infantry Officer* are from the first English edition, Faber and Faber, 1930; those to *Sherston's Progress* are taken from the 'Faber Library' edition, 1940.)

CHAPTER VII: THE MAKING OF A POET (I)

(References to *The Old Century and Seven More Years*, Faber & Faber First Edition, Fifth Impression, 1946.)

CHAPTER VIII: THE MAKING OF A POET (II)

(References to *The Weald of Youth*, Faber and Faber First Edition, Third Impression, 1944.)

CHAPTER IX: SIEGFRIED'S JOURNEY

(References to the Faber and Faber First Edition, December 1945)

INDEX